Perspectives on Financing Innovation

Although much has been written about innovation in the past several years, not all parts of the innovation lifecycle have been given the same treatment. This volume focuses on the important first step of arranging financing for innovation before it is made, and explores the feedback effect that innovation can have on finance itself.

The book brings together a diverse group of leading scholars in order to address the financing of innovation. The chapters address three key areas: intellectual property; venture capital; and financial engineering in the capital markets, in order to provide fresh and insightful analyses of current and future economic developments in financing innovation. Chapters on intellectual property cover topics including innovation in lawmaking, orphan business models, the use of intellectual property to protect financial engineering innovations and developing intellectual property regimes in Brazil, Russia, India, and China. The book also covers the tax treatment of venture capital founders, the treatment of preferred stock by the Delaware Courts, and corporate governance for small businesses after the Dodd-Frank financial reform bill.

The book will be of interest to scholars, practitioners, and students in law, innovation, finance, and business.

James E. Daily is a Post-doctoral Research Associate and Administrative Director at the Stanford University Hoover Institution Project on Commercializing Innovation.

F. Scott Kieff is Fred C. Stevenson Research Professor of Law at George Washington University Law School, and was the Director of Planning and Publications for George Washington University's C-LEAF and Ray and Louise Knowles Senior Fellow at the Stanford University Hoover Institution, where he was a co-director of the Project on Commercializing Innovation. He is on leave from his post as Fred C. Stevenson Research Professor at the George Washington University Law School in Washington, DC, having been nominated by President Barack H. Obama, and confirmed by the Senate, to serve as a Commissioner at the U.S. International Trade Commission, commencing on October 18, 2013. He worked on this book while in his academic positions before being sworn in and taking up his government post.

Arthur E. Wilmarth, Jr. is Professor of Law at George Washington University Law School and the Executive Director for George Washington University's C-LEAF.

Routledge/C-LEAF Studies in Economic and Financial Law

Available titles in this series include:

Perspectives on Financing Innovation
James E. Daily, F. Scott Kieff and Arthur E. Wilmarth

Perspectives on Financing Innovation

Edited by
James E. Daily, F. Scott Kieff and Arthur E. Wilmarth, Jr.

LONDON AND NEW YORK

First published 2014
by Routledge
2 Park Square, Milton Park, Abingdon, Oxon, OX14 4RN

and by Routledge
711 Third Avenue, New York, NY 10017

Routledge is an imprint of the Taylor & Francis Group, an informa business

First issued in paperback 2016

British Library Cataloguing in Publication Data
A catalogue record for this book is available from the British Library

Library of Congress Cataloging-in-Publication Data
Perspectives on financing innovation / James E. Daily, F Scott Kieff, Arthur E. Wilmarth.
pages cm.—(Routledge/C-LEAF studies in economic and financial law)
Papers presented at a conference on "Financing Innovation : Toward Our Economic Future" hosted by the George Washington University Law School's Center for Law, Economics and Finance (C-LEAF)" on March 25-26, 2011.
ISBN 978-1-138-01795-5 (hardback)—ISBN 978-1-315-77730-6 (ebk)
1. Venture capital—Law and legislation—United States—Congresses.
2. Technological innovations—Finance—Law and legislation—United States—Congresses. 3. Intellectual property—Economic aspects—United States—Congresses. I. Daily, James, editor of compilation.
II. Kieff, F Scott, editor of compilation. III. Wilmarth, Arthur E., 1951- editor of compilation. IV. George Washington University. Center for Law, Economics and Finance, sponsoring body.
KF1428.P47 2014
658.5'14—dc23 2013046460

ISBN13: 978-1-138-01795-5 (hbk)
ISBN13: 978-1-138-68510-9 (pbk)

Typeset in Baskerville
by Keystroke, Station Road, Codsall, Wolverhampton

Dedication

This book is dedicated to the memory of Larry E. Ribstein, who passed away on December 24, 2011. Professor Ribstein was the Mildred Van Voorhis Jones Chair, Associate Dean for Research, and Co-Director of the Illinois Business Law and Policy Program at the University of Illinois College of Law. A prolific scholar, author, and commentator, he wrote over 170 articles, books, treatises, and casebooks. His contributions to the study of formal and informal business organizations and corporate law were invaluable, and we are honored to include one of his works in this volume.

Contents

Notes on contributors

Michael B. Abramowicz Professor of Law, The George Washington University

Tamir Agmon Professor of Financial Economics, University of Gothenburg

Senem Alkan PhD candidate, Bocconi University, Milan, Italy

Stefano Bonini Assistant Professor, Department of Finance, Bocconi University

Peter Conti-Brown Academic Fellow at the Rock Center for Corporate Governance, Stanford University

James D. Cox Brainerd Currie Professor of Law, Duke University

Victor Fleischer Professor of Law, University of San Diego

Shubhashis Gangopadhyay Research Director, India Development Foundation

Bruce H. Kobayashi Professor of Law, George Mason University

Michael Peneder Deputy Director, Austrian Institute of Economic Research

Larry E. Ribstein Mildred Van Voorhis Jones Chair, Associate Dean for Research, and Co-Director of the Illinois Business Law and Policy Program, University of Illinois

Dr. Yochanan Shachmurove Professor, City College of New York

Stefan Sjogren Senior Lecturer, University of Gothenburg

Joseph Straus Professor of Law, Universities of Munich and Llubljana

Acknowledgments

This book consists of articles authored by the participants of the "Financing Innovation: Toward Our Economic Future" conference held at the George Washington University Law School's Center for Law, Economics and Finance (C-LEAF) on March 26, 2011. The conference was supported by a generous grant from the Ewing Marion Kauffman Foundation. We would like to thank Mark Sapwell, our editor at Routledge, for his efforts and patience. We are particularly grateful to the individuals whose work makes up this book.

This book is part of broader work through the Project on Commercializing Innovation at Stanford University's Hoover Institution, which studies the law, economics, and politics of the whole range of legal and business relationships that can be used to bring ideas to market. We would like to thank the Hoover Institution for its support of the project, particularly Richard Sousa, senior associate director of the Hoover Institution. More about the project is available on the Internet at www.innovation.hoover.org.

Finally, we must note again that F. Scott Kieff worked on this book while serving as Fred C. Stevenson Research Professor, George Washington University Law School and Ray & Louise Knowles Senior Fellow, Stanford University Hoover Institution on War, Revolution, and Peace, before taking up his government post as a Commissioner at the U.S. International Trade Commission (USITC). He took a leave of absence from George Washington University Law School and resigned from Stanford University Hoover Institution before becoming a Commissioner. The views expressed in this book are those of the chapter authors and do not necessarily reflect those of the other chapter authors or co-editors. Nor are the views expressed in this book properly attributable to the USITC.

James E. Daily, F. Scott Kieff, and Arthur E. Wilmarth, Jr.

Introduction

James E. Daily, F. Scott Kieff, and Arthur E. Wilmarth, Jr.*

Although much has been written about innovation in the past several years, not all parts of the innovation life cycle have been given the same treatment. The *Perspectives* series, for example, has previously focused on commercializing innovation on the back end, after it has been made. This volume focuses on the equally important and precursor step of arranging financing for innovation before it is made, as well as on the feedback effect that innovation can have on finance itself. Financing can help ensure that innovation occurs, and the success or failure of each particular venture provides valuable feedback to technologists and capitalists alike. Indeed, some innovations are in the art and science of financing itself, a topic that is particularly germane to contemporary debates about so-called business method patents. The many interactions between finance and innovation are a key part of the overall economy and their study is of help to scholars, practitioners, and students in law, innovation, finance, and business, including market analysts, policymakers, executives, and investors.

The nineteen chapters in this volume were first presented together at a conference on "Financing Innovation: Toward Our Economic Future" hosted by the George Washington University Law School's Center for Law, Economics and Finance (C-LEAF). The conference was made possible by a generous grant from the Ewing Marion Kauffman Foundation. C-LEAF gratefully acknowledges the Kauffman Foundation's financial support for the conference.

The chapters in this volume have been circulated through rounds of peer review for further comment and revision to incorporate appropriate feedback from C-LEAF and other audiences. This diverse group of leading scholars addresses three general areas relevant to the financing of innovation: intellectual property, venture capital, and financial engineering in the capital markets. The

* Kieff worked on this book while serving as Fred C. Stevenson Research Professor, George Washington University Law School and Ray and Louise Knowles Senior Fellow, Stanford University Hoover Institution on War, Revolution, and Peace, before taking up his government post as a Commissioner at the U.S. International Trade Commission (USITC). He took a leave of absence from George Washington University Law School and resigned from Stanford University Hoover Institution to take up his government post. The views expressed in this chapter are those of the chapter authors and do not necessarily reflect those of the other chapter authors. Nor are the views expressed in this book properly attributable to the USITC.

chapters constitute a blend of new ideas and perspectives, empirical research, analysis, and practical guides that cover both international and domestic issues.

Intellectual property protection is generally considered necessary to the financing and commercialization of complex innovations. Such concrete property rights allow the many stakeholders involved to negotiate complex deals enforceable with relative certainty. Without these rights, many other conversations surrounding financing innovation would be moot, and so that is where we begin in Part I: Intellectual Property and Innovation with chapters by Michael Abramowicz, Bruce Kobayashi, Larry Ribstein, and Joseph Straus. Part II moves on to venture capital, with chapters by Yochanan Shachmurove, Stefano Bonini, Senem Alkan, Michael Peneder, Tamir Agmon, Subhashis Gangopadhyay, Stefan Sjogren, and Victor Fleischer. Part III rounds off the book with a discussion of financial engineering in capital markets with a chapter by James Cox. The book concludes with an afterword by Peter Conti-Brown, written from the perspective of his role as the student assistant to the faculty organizer of the conference at which these chapters were first presented together, to pass along some of the practical payoffs that initially emerged from the ground fertilized by the bringing together of these diverse ideas and authors.

The opening chapter, by Michael Abramowicz, explores "Orphan business models: toward a new form of intellectual property." Abramowicz discusses the hotly debated question of patented business models through the comparative context of "orphan drugs." He describes a scenario in which there may well be increasing enthusiasm for intellectual property—although of a different variety than patents—for useful business models, but for which there are few incentives for development and marketing. Abramowicz imagines a legal framework that would allow these kinds of ideas to exist, with intellectual property protection, even before their marketability is clear.

Bruce Kobayashi and Larry Ribstein analyze the process of innovation through public and private lawmaking in "Law as product and byproduct", a context not often included in the standard conversation on innovation. After explaining why innovation is undeniably important and welfare enhancing in the lawmaking context, Kobayashi and Ribstein argue that there are few strong incentives to engage in innovative lawmaking, in either the public or private sector.

Joseph Straus addresses intellectual property issues at the intersection of international politics and economic development in "The impact of the new world order on economic development: the role of intellectual property rights system." Straus describes how many countries are parties to the Trade Related Aspects of Intellectual Property Rights (TRIPs) agreement not because intellectual property was high on their priority list, but because they liked the entire General Agreement on Tariffs and Trade package of liberalized markets for their exports. Using Brazil, Russia, India, and China as examples, Straus shows that TRIPs was negotiated as a political concession for open access to markets, and it may not necessarily be what developing countries want or need as they move from being intellectual property importers to intellectual property exporters. According to Straus, a principal focus for the continuing debate over access to developing markets is pharmaceutical intellectual property—an area to watch, both for scholars and policymakers.

Beginning Part II on venture capital, Yochanan Shachmurove discusses the disruptive impact of the recent financial crisis on first-round venture capital financing. His empirical research is based on a comparative analysis that employs a long-term data set covering 15 years of first-round financing.

Stefano Bonini and Senem Alkan describe new empirical research showing that social and political structures and institutions matter for the success of venture capital-backed firms in "The political and legal determinants of venture capital investments around the world." Using data from 16 countries from 1995 to 2002, they confirm previous results showing that active initial public offering markets, interest rates, corporate income tax rates, and most importantly, research and development spending, are meaningful factors in explaining the cross-country variation in levels of venture capital investment. They also demonstrate new results showing that there is a strong and positive correlation between a favorable socioeconomic and investment environment and venture capital investment activity, as well as a strong correlation between legal system rigidity and venture capital investment activity. In particular, countries with less rigid legal systems, such as those derived from the UK common law system or the French system, had more venture capital investment.

Michael Peneder continues the empirical research theme in "The impact of venture capital on innovation behavior and firm growth" using data from about 250,000 Austrian firms. He concludes that venture capital-backed firms are more innovative and grow faster in terms of employment and sales revenue than other firms. However, he also concludes that this is the result of selection effects: venture capital investors select firms with above-average levels of innovation rather than making the firms more innovative. Venture capital thus provides a useful signaling function to the economy at large.

Tamir Agmon, Subhashis Gangopadhyay, and Stefan Sjogren analyzed macro indicators of fund allocation in "Savings and innovation in the United States capital market: defined benefit plans and venture capital funds." They bring their analysis home to the experience of household savers, focusing on the financial management of both venture capital funds and private equity funds.

Victor Fleischer provides a different perspective on venture capital financing in "Capital gains and entrepreneurial entry." Fleischer looked not at the empirical consequences of venture capital financing but rather at the assumptions that many analysts have made about the utility and desirability of the reduced tax load that founders of venture capital funds receive in the form of tax-preferred equity stock in their companies. Fleischer's chapter challenges long-held assumptions and makes a compelling case that what many scholars have long viewed as a logical and intuitive rationale for current tax treatment of venture capital founders may be neither logical nor intuitive.

James Cox begins Part III on financial engineering in the capital markets by discussing the Dodd-Frank financial reform bill and its effect on small-cap companies in "Tweaking governance for small companies after Dodd-Frank." In contrast to the attention given by many scholars to Dodd-Frank's re-regulation of financial markets, Cox focuses on firms that were at least partially deregulated – namely, the smaller, publicly traded companies that Dodd-Frank exempts from Section 404 of the Sarbanes-Oxley Act (SOX). The exemption was based on Congress's assumption that smaller issuers are disproportionately harmed by the cost of obtaining independent auditor attestations of internal management controls. Cox challenges the assumption underlying this exemption. He points out that smaller public issuers operate in a less information-rich environment, with fewer institutional investors and analysts who can effectively monitor the firms' accounting practices. In Cox's view, Dodd-Frank's invitation to the Securities and Exchange Commission to exempt additional companies from Section 404 of SOX is questionable. Cox helpfully provides some alternatives to Section 404 audits that smaller issuers might adopt to ensure that their financial statements are accurate.

The book concludes with an afterword by Peter Conti-Brown, discussing the legacy of Harvard Law School professor William J. Stuntz's approach to legal scholarship that celebrates deep challenges to conventional wisdom, the defiance of traditional ideological labels, and scholarly humility. Conti-Brown suggests ways in which perspectives such as those offered in this book can be profitably used through a Stuntzian approach when applied to the study of business law and innovation.

Financing innovation is a dynamic field. Many of the approaches that we may take for granted today, such as equity financing and venture capital, were once novel and untested. As time goes on, new business models are evolving to meet the challenges of developing increasingly sophisticated solutions to increasingly complex problems. Financing these innovations will also be a challenge, and we believe that the scholarship presented in this book is an important piece of the response to that challenge. In part this consists of learning from the past and refining existing models, often informed by empirical research. And in part it consists of proposing and exploring entirely new models. We hope that this book provides a useful guide to this continually developing field.

Part I

Intellectual property and innovation

1 Orphan business models: toward a new form of intellectual property

*Michael B. Abramowicz**

Harold Demsetz famously observed that property rights will tend to emerge when the value from recognizing them is sufficiently great to make their transaction costs bearable.[1] Demsetz's theory is descriptive,[2] but when the trade-offs inherent in particular property rights are nearly in balance, normative debate about the desirability of those rights is likely to be lively.[3] The business method patents controversy underlying the Supreme Court's decision in *Bilski v. Kappos*[4] might thus be seen as an epiphenomenon of the broader sweep of Demsetzian institutional evolution. The immediate policy question is whether the costs inherent in a regime of patents on business methods (including patents on business models)[5] outweigh the benefits.[6] Over the long

* Professor of Law, George Washington University. I am grateful to Kenneth Rodriguez for exceptional research assistance and to the Kauffman Foundation for financial support. For helpful comments and discussion, I am grateful to Thomas Colby, John Duffy, and anonymous reviewers, as well as participants in workshops at Georgetown University Law Center, George Washington University Law School, and the University of Pennsylvania Law School. A version of this chapter was previously published in the Harvard Law Review. Michael Abramowicz, *Orphan Business Models: Toward a New Form of Intellectual Property*, 124 HARVARD L. REV. 1363 (2011).

1 Harold Demsetz, *Toward a Theory of Property Rights*, 57 AM. ECON. REV. 347, 350 (1967) ("[P] roperty rights develop to internalize externalities when the gains of internalization become larger than the cost of internalization.").

2 Brett Frischmann, *Spillovers Theory and Its Conceptual Boundaries*, 51 WM. & MARY L. REV. 801, 814 & n.54 (2009) (noting, however, that the theory is sometimes used as a defense of creating a particular property right).

3 Demsetz notes that property rights could "be the result of a conscious endeavor to cope with new externality problems," but that they usually arise "as a result of gradual changes in social mores and in common law precedents." Demsetz, *supra* note 1, at 350. James Krier notes that parts of Demsetz's theory "can be reasonably taken to suggest that he was thinking about an evolutionary account based on intentional design," but that "[o]ther bits and pieces of Demsetz's argument point in the direction of an unintended-consequences (invisible-hand) type of account." James E *Evolutionary Theory and the Origin of Property Rights*, 95 CORNELL L. REV. 139, 147 (2009). This chapter serves both to describe gradual changes that have led to protection of orphan business methods and to consider consciously the possibility of redefining such protection.

4 130 S. Ct. 3218 (2010).

5 A usage note: a "business method" may be either a method of operation useful in some set of businesses (*e.g.*, a new accounting system) or a type of business (*e.g.*, an accounting firm that would be the first to use such a system). This chapter uses the phrase "business model" to refer to the latter—informally, an idea that a prospective entrepreneur might pitch in a business plan. The focus here is on business models, though the line is often thin, and much of the analysis applies to business methods as well.

6 *See, e.g.*, *Bilski*, 130 S. Ct. at 3255–57 (Stevens, J., concurring in the judgment).

run,[7] however, if Demsetz's core insight is correct, we should expect evolving legal institutions to find some means of protecting business methods at least in those cases where such protection is most critical and can be accomplished most cheaply.

The form of protection that ultimately emerges, however, might be quite different from patent protection for business methods as understood today. Perhaps the patent office and courts will develop more effective doctrines for avoiding issuing unnecessary patents, for example by toughening the nonobviousness test.[8] At least as importantly, the subject matter of business method protection—not necessarily business method *patent* protection—could change. Business method patents protect ideas for new business methods,[9] because of longstanding rules that inventions need not be reduced to practice[10] or commercialized[11] to be entitled to patent protection. Yet there is a strong argument, reflected in a recent literature[12] and an older one,[13] that what may be especially important for

7 *See* Stuart Banner, *Transitions Between Property Regimes*, 31 J. LEGAL STUD. S359, S360 (2002) (noting that "[t]he Demsetz story is a happy one, because it implies that over the long run, property rights will be reallocated in the direction of efficiency," although the story "fails to specify the mechanism by which the transition actually occurs").

8 For a recent proposal, see Michael Abramowicz & John F. Duffy, *The Inducement Standard of Patentability*, 120 YALE L.J. 1590 (2011), *available at* http://papers.ssrn.com/sol3/papers.cfm?abstract_id=1694883.

9 The word "idea" is not meant here to be equivalent to an "abstract idea." In *Bilski*, the Court unanimously held that the particular business method patent at issue was ineligible patentable subject matter because it constituted an abstract idea. *See Bilski*, 130 S. Ct. at 3229–31.

10 *See* Jeanne C. Fromer, *The Layers of Obviousness in Patent Law*, 22 HARV. J.L. & TECH. 75, 78 (2008) ("Many areas of patent law elevate the inventive role of conception over that of actual reduction to practice, be it with regard to what must be accomplished to secure a patent, what must be contributed to an invention to be recognized as a joint inventor, or the on-sale bar." (footnotes omitted)).

11 *See, e.g.*, Amy L. Landers, *Liquid Patents*, 84 DENV. U. L. REV. 199, 234 & n.246 (2006) ("[C]ourts have made clear that the strength and existence of the patent right is unaffected where the owner decides not to commercialize or license the invention." *Id.* at 234.).

12 *See generally* Michael Abramowicz & John F. Duffy, *Intellectual Property for Market Experimentation*, 83 N.Y.U. L. REV. 337 (2008) (arguing that intellectual property law should and to some extent does encourage commercial experimentation even absent technological innovation); Oren Bar-Gill & Gideon Parchomovsky, *A Marketplace for Ideas?*, 84 TEX. L. REV. 395 (2005) (suggesting separating property rights for ideas from rights in downstream invention and commercialization); Benjamin N. Roin, *Unpatentable Drugs and the Standards of Patentability*, 87 TEX. L. REV. 503 (2009) (focusing on the problem specifically in the context of drugs); Ted Sichelman, *Commercializing Patents*, 62 STAN. L. REV. 341 (2010) (proposing "commercialization patents"). Sichelman is the only recent commentator to propose creating property rights for commercialization. Sichelman recognizes: "Just as the Orphan Drug Act supplements the patent laws to stimulate commercialization of drugs for rare diseases, there are arguably a number of other areas for which this sort of stimulus is justified, including environmental technologies, mobility technologies for the disabled, medical devices to diagnose rare diseases, reading aids for the blind, and so forth." *Id.* at 387. As this description suggests, however, Sichelman does not view orphan drugs as a subcategory of business methods. The proposal that he ultimately develops is for a form of protection that is far narrower than patent protection. *See id.* at 400 (excluding processes and thus all business methods from his proposal); *id.* at 401 ("[T]he claims *should be limited exactly to the product described in the specification.*"); *id.* at 405 (explaining that the primary benefits of the commercialization patent would be defensive, providing "complete immunity from injunctive relief from suits for invention patent infringement" and limitations on damages); *id.* at 408 (providing a term of only "five to eight years"). This chapter, in contrast, explores the possibility of relatively broad protection, even if only for narrow classes of inventions (such as orphan drugs).

13 *See* DIRECT PROTECTION OF INNOVATION, 2–3 (William Kingston ed., 1987); William Kingston, *Innovation Patents and Warrants*, *in* PATENTS IN PERSPECTIVE 68–69 (Jeremy Phillips

intellectual property to protect is not so much investments in developing ideas for new business methods but investments in commercializing and experimenting with untested business models.[14] However society ultimately incentivizes new ideas for business models, property rights may emerge to protect at least particularly important *orphan* business models, that is, business models previously conceived and disclosed that no one has had sufficient incentives to implement. Although patents could perhaps provide such property rights, it is also possible to imagine new forms of intellectual property targeting the orphan business model problem more directly.

As this chapter will show, the process of Demsetzian emergence of property rights in orphan business models has already begun, and it has begun precisely where Demsetz would expect, for a technology whose financial and welfare stakes are so high that the benefits of internalizing property rights have been recognized as exceeding the costs: pharmaceuticals. One area where this is true is in protection of what are known as "orphan drugs," that is existing drugs that in the absence of protection would not be tested or marketed by pharmaceutical companies. Because the challenge for orphan drugs is not creating the compounds but bringing them to market, the business of shepherding an orphan drug through clinical testing and to market can be considered an orphan business model when no one has sufficient incentives to undertake it. There are at least two other areas of our drug laws that also can be seen as providing property rights in orphan business models.[15] Together, these three areas of drug law provide a window into the broader question of when and how orphan business models might best be protected.

Although property rights in orphan business models are beginning to emerge, legal scholarship has failed to explore how such property rights should be designed. One reason for this is that the development of a new *sui generis* regime of intellectual property that could apply across all categories of business models seems likely to occur, if at all, only in the distant future, once the benefits of internalizing property rights clearly exceed the costs. But systematic thinking about the design and administration of such property may be useful in determining whether it is possible to reduce the costs and increase the benefits of such rights. In the short term, this can be helpful in generating proposals for tweaking and reforming the areas in which such property rights already exist; in the medium term, in identifying other areas where such property rights might be useful; and in

ed., 1985); Hermann Kronz, *Patent Protection for Innovations: A Model*, 5 EUR. INTELL. PROP. REV. 178 (1983).

14 The topic of commercialization of intellectual property has received extended attention. *See generally* F. Scott Kieff, *Property Rights and Property Rules for Commercializing Inventions*, 85 MINN. L. REV. 697 (2001) (arguing that "the treatment of patents as property rights is necessary to facilitate investment in the complex, costly, and risky commercialization activities required to turn nascent inventions into new goods and services," *id.* at 703); Edmund W. Kitch, *The Nature and Function of the Patent System*, 20 J.L. & ECON. 265 (1977) (developing a "prospect theory" of the patent system that "reintegrates the patent institution with the general theory of property rights," *id.* at 265). What differentiates the works in notes 12 and 13 from this treatment is that they focus on intellectual property for commercialization rather than on how intellectual property for new technologies may encourage commercialization.

15 *See infra* Section 1.2.1.

the long term, in sketching what a *sui generis* intellectual property regime for orphan business models might look like and how such a regime can avoid the disincentives to new business creation that business method patents can create.

Sometimes, the lack of implementation of an orphan business model is efficient—for example because the social costs of bringing a drug to market exceed the benefits—but in other cases the orphaning of a business model may be inefficient—for example where others may free-ride on clinical testing and other expenses of drug introduction. Any legal regime that seeks to combat the problem of orphan business models must seek to encourage commercialization only in the latter case, yet government officials are unlikely to be well positioned to distinguish the former from the latter. Thus, a simple subsidy mechanism, such as where the government pays private companies to bring drugs to market, will not work well if it is dependent on the discretion of individual decisionmakers. This chapter will suggest mechanisms that harness private incentives so that those mechanisms should work effectively even if government information is poor.

Of course, this chapter cannot itself confidently distinguish efficiently and inefficiently orphaned business models, and so we cannot project precisely what business models a new governmental protection regime would encourage. We can, however, identify business models where free-riding on commercialization is especially pernicious and thus where the establishment of orphan business model rights might help. For example, private attempts to build networks of electrical car battery charging stations would be quite risky, and if successful would attract second-movers, and so, absent protection, such networks will take longer to emerge.[16] We can also compare the problem of orphan business models to the related problem that states and localities have insufficient incentives for legal experimentation;[17] as a result, this chapter will consider how approaches used to protect business models might also be used to encourage legal experimentation by preventing free-riding on tests of legal models.[18]

A second reason for the failure of legal scholarship to address rights in orphan business models may be the great attention that has been focused on business method patents.[19] This focus has led to a debate on whether property rights are needed to encourage the creation of ideas for new business methods, rather than a debate on whether and how to encourage entrepreneurs to bring to market the large subset of business methods that consist of new business models. To the

16 *See infra* Section 1.3.1.

17 *See* Susan Rose-Ackerman, *Risk Taking and Reelection: Does Federalism Promote Innovation?*, 9 J. LEGAL STUD. 593, 610–11 (1980) (noting that state legal innovation may be suboptimal because states will free-ride on the experimentation of others).

18 *See infra* Section 1.3.2.3.2.

19 *See, e.g.*, John R. Allison & Emerson H. Tiller, *The Business Method Patent Myth*, 18 BERKELEY TECH. L.J. 987 (2003); Jeffrey R. Kuester & Lawrence E. Thompson, *Risks Associated with Restricting Business Method and E-Commerce Patents*, 17 GA. ST. U. L. REV. 657 (2001); Kevin Michael Lemley, *Just Turn North on State Street and Then Follow the Signs Given by the Federal Circuit: A Sophisticated Approach to the Patentability of Computerized Business Methods*, 8 J. TECH. L. & POL'Y 1 (2003); Michael J. Meurer, *Business Method Patents and Patent Floods*, 8 WASH. U. J.L. & POL'Y 309 (2002); Sam Stake, In re Comiskey *and E-Commerce Patentability*, 90 J. PAT. & TRADEMARK OFF. SOC'Y 148 (2008).

extent that intellectual property scholars have considered whether it is worthwhile to encourage commercialization of business models, it has generally been as part of the assessment of whether business method patents should exist.[20] A possible benefit of business method patents is that the holder of a business method patent need not worry that others will free-ride on information that only the commercialization of the business model can produce—information, for example, about consumer demand for a novel good or service or the feasibility of providing it. But business method patents will not always encourage commercialization, and business method patents can discourage commercialization when the patents are held by nonpracticing entities.[21]

This chapter's task is not to establish that the amount of commercialization of business models will generally be less than socially optimal. The argument against the intuition that market competition will produce enough business innovation has already been made elsewhere,[22] and this chapter assumes that absent intellectual property protection or other intervention, there will be socially suboptimal commercialization of new business models. This chapter asks, if law is to protect orphan business models through the traditional strategy of intellectual property—that is by granting limited exclusivity—what form should such property rights take?[23] This question has at least three components.

First, even though patent law currently provides only indirect protection for orphan business models, should the existence of such orphan business models affect patent law doctrine on the margins? Second, in areas of drug law where property rights for orphan business models already exist, how might regulation be improved? And third, over the long term, what new forms of protection for orphan business models are possible and how should these be regulated to ensure that the Demsetzian emergence of property rights comes at the lowest possible costs?

The three questions correspond, respectively, to Sections 1.1, 1.2, and 1.3 of the chapter. A theme developed in each Section is that a principal difficulty with using conventional strategies of intellectual property regulation for orphan

20 *See, e.g.*, Rochelle Cooper Dreyfuss, *Are Business Method Patents Bad for Business?*, 16 SANTA CLARA COMPUTER & HIGH TECH. L.J. 263, 270 (2000) (arguing that "business method patents protect businesses from competition" and "[t]hus . . . can function in a way that preserves inefficiencies in the marketplace").

21 This assumes, however, that the ideas for business methods would have emerged quickly without the patent and that the nonpracticing entity does not seek a partner to commercialize it exclusively. For an empirical defense of nonpracticing entities, see generally Sannu K. Shrestha, *Trolls or Market-Makers? An Empirical Analysis of Nonpracticing Entities*, 110 COLUM. L. REV. 114 (2010).

22 For previous work developing a model of the market experimentation problem, see Abramowicz & Duffy, *supra* note 12, at 353–63.

23 This chapter does not address issues of whether protection for orphan business methods outside the patent statute would be constitutional. For an argument that the Orphan Drug Act is unconstitutional, see John J. Flynn, *The Orphan Drug Act: An Unconstitutional Exercise of the Patent Power*, 1992 UTAH L. REV. 389. *But see* Thomas B. Nachbar, *Intellectual Property and Constitutional Norms*, 104 COLUM. L. REV. 272 (2004) (arguing that Congress can take advantage of its Commerce Clause powers to provide intellectual property protection not justified by the Constitution's Patent and Copyright Clause).

business models is that governments may be ill-suited to identify when orphan business models should receive property protection. Patent examiners, challenged enough in determining whether business methods are novel and nonobvious,[24] do not have the institutional capability to determine which business models will need legal exclusivity in order to be commercialized. History provides a lesson in the form of exclusive royal grants, which reflected government determinations that exclusivity would benefit commerce.[25] Unsurprisingly, royal prerogatives were sometimes abused, as when an exclusive charter for printing books allowed the Crown to exercise censorship.[26] Even well intentioned government officials might be ill-equipped to forecast whether exclusivity is necessary, and they seem especially unlikely to make good decisions in ex parte hearings in which the only arguments they hear are from companies seeking exclusivity.

The specter of governments arbitrarily granting monopolies is sufficient to counsel that protection for orphan business models should not be extended absent decisionmaking mechanisms that will prevent such abuse. Perhaps the most significant reform that could prevent this is to give both orphan business model applicants and third parties, including competitors, the ability and incentive to block orphan business model applications when a long term of exclusivity is unnecessary to induce commercialization. It is easy enough for an applicant for government protection to argue that exclusivity is essential to creation of a new business model, or for a competitor to argue that it is not, but the government is unlikely to be able to evaluate such claims with high accuracy. A better approach is to create financial incentives for those with the best information to make accurate assessments and act on them.

There are different varieties of this approach, but a simple one would allow competitors of those seeking orphan business model applications to adopt the orphan business models themselves for a shorter period of time than the original applicant would receive. Suppose, for example, that *X* Corp. seeks a 10-year period of exclusivity on a drug that would not otherwise be entitled to patent protection, for example because it was discovered long ago but never tested for its effectiveness against a particular disease. *X* Corp. argues, as it might today in an application under the Orphan Drug Act,[27] that no one would have adequate incentive to take the drug through the expensive FDA approval process without a guarantee of exclusivity. If a competitor, *Y* Corp., agrees to a significantly shorter period of exclusivity (say, seven years), and also commits to conducting at least as much research and development as *X* Corp.'s commitment, then it would receive

24 *See, e.g.*, Gregory Mandel, *The Non-Obvious Problem: How the Indeterminate Nonobviousness Standard Produces Excessive Patent Grants*, 42 U.C. DAVIS L. REV. 57, 78 (2008) (identifying various challenges facing examiners).

25 For the history, see Edward C. Walterscheid, *The Early Evolution of the United States Patent Law: Antecedents (Part I)*, 76 J. PAT. & TRADEMARK OFF. SOC'Y 697, 706–08 (1994).

26 *See, e.g.*, Malla Pollack, *Purveyance and Power, or Over-Priced Free Lunch: The Intellectual Property Clause as an Ally of the Takings Clause in the Public's Control of Government*, 30 SW. U. L. REV. 1, 93–95 (2000).

27 *See infra* section 1.1.1.1.

the property right instead. Of course, if *Z* Corp. will do the same with just one year of exclusivity, then it would receive the property right, so such competition can drive the period of exclusivity close to zero.

An alternative approach would rely on information from competitors and third parties about whether an orphan business model would likely be created if an application for an exclusive business model adoption right were denied. For example, the applicant might be required to put up a sum of money as a bond to back up the applicant's claim that the business model will *not* be attempted in the application period requested if the application is refused. Others would then have the option of putting up a sum of money as a bond to back up the opposite claim. If anyone took this option, the application would be denied, and the bonds would ultimately be paid to the party who turned out to be correct. If no one did so, that would validate the original applicant's claim.

This mechanism is elaborated below,[28] but ultimately both this mechanism and the term competition mechanism have two significant advantages over existing systems of intellectual property: they are much simpler to administer, and they bear a much lower risk of providing unnecessary exclusivity. And so, while an absence of a perceived need for orphan business model protection helps to explain the absence of prior scholarship and the limited ambit of existing protections, the cost of providing protection is sufficiently low that it might be efficient even where the stakes are much lower than they are in pharmaceuticals. The chief obstacle to implementation may be congressional hesitance to experiment with unfamiliar goals of and approaches to intellectual property protection. This chapter is but a first step toward demonstrating that such protection is both desirable and plausible.[29]

1.1 Responses within patent law: business methods and related doctrines

Outside of drug law, the area of law that seems most likely to respond to concerns about orphan business models is, for better or worse, patent law. After *Bilski*, it appears that at least some business method patents survive. When such patents are granted, concerns about orphan business models will generally be alleviated, because at least one party will have an exclusive opportunity to enter a market without worrying about other parties' free-riding on information from such entry. To what extent should patent law directly take into account concerns about orphan business models? This Section suggests that a desire to foster market experimentation could play a more explicit role on the margins of patent law

28 *See infra* section 1.3.2.

29 The ambition of this project is thus similar to the ambition of the economic literature on mechanism design: to create alternative ways of structuring markets and decisionmaking institutions. The path from theoretical construct to implementation, however, is a long one that demands many inputs beyond the initial theoretical framework. *See generally* Alvin E. Roth, *The Economist as Engineer: Game Theory, Experimentation, and Computation as Tools for Design Economics*, 70 ECONOMETRICA 1341 (2002) (describing the challenge for the mechanism design literature).

doctrine, but that patent law is ill-suited to making orphan business models a central concern.

The relationship of orphan business models to the debate on business method patents can be spotted in *Bilski* itself. The majority opinion[30] focused primarily on legal arguments[31] rather than policy considerations in holding that business methods could not categorically be excluded from patenting,[32] but that some business methods, including the business models that were at issue, were "abstract ideas" unentitled to patent protection.[33] Justice Stevens's concurring opinion,[34] arguing in favor of a categorical bar, addressed the policy question more directly. "Business innovation . . . generally does not entail the same kinds of risk as does more traditional, technological innovation," Justice Stevens argued.[35] The words "same kinds of risk" reflect a recognition that the risks involved in business innovation are not the types patent law seeks to mitigate.

Typically, entrepreneurs face little risk that others will copy their *undeveloped* ideas. Even absent intellectual property protection, would-be entrepreneurs commonly hawk their ideas to angel investors or venture capitalists without any protection from nondisclosure agreements.[36] Although informal norms may help explain why stealing of prospective business models is rare, another explanation is that often the relevant scarcity in the business world is not a scarcity of ideas but of funds for implementing them. Providers of financing generally would not expect to benefit by stealing an idea and potentially competing against the team of entrepreneurs who developed that idea and likely have a comparative advantage in its implementation.

Both entrepreneurs and financiers must worry, however, about the prospect of competition should their ideas prove successful in the market. Anticipation of "second-mover advantages,"[37] including the ability to withhold investment until it is proven that there is a market for a good or service and the ability to gain

30 Five Justices supported the critical parts of the decision, though Justice Scalia declined to concur in part of the reasoning. *See Bilski*, 130 S. Ct. at 3223 (identifying the sections that are not part of the opinion of the Court).

31 Central to the Court's decision not to bar business method patents categorically was its view that the existence of atextual exceptions to the patent statute, for example for abstract ideas, does not give "the Judiciary *carte blanche* to impose other limitations that are inconsistent with the text and the statute's purpose and design." *Id.* at 3226.

32 This conclusion may be dicta, because the Court ultimately found the invention unpatentable. *See* Michael Abramowicz & Maxwell Stearns, *Defining Dicta*, 57 STAN. L. REV. 953, 1029–32 (2005) (explaining why "nonsupportive propositions" should generally count as dicta, but noting that the Supreme Court has more latitude than other courts to define its holdings broadly).

33 *Bilski*, 130 S. Ct. at 3229–31.

34 *Id.* at 3231 (Stevens, J., concurring in the judgment).

35 *Id.* at 3254 & n.52 (Stevens, J., concurring in the judgment) (citing Dan L. Burk & Mark A. Lemley, *Policy Levers in Patent Law*, 89 VA. L. REV. 1575, 1618 (2003); *see also* Michael A. Carrier, *Unraveling the Patent-Antitrust Paradox*, 150 U. PA. L. REV. 761, 826 (2002); David S. Olson, *Taking the Utilitarian Basis for Patent Law Seriously: The Case for Restricting Patentable Subject Matter*, 82 TEMP. L. REV. 181, 231 (2009)).

36 *See* Arthur R. Miller, *Common Law Protection for Products of the Mind: An "Idea" Whose Time Has Come*, 119 HARV. L. REV. 705, 714–15 (2006) (suggesting that, except during brief booms, angel investors generally refuse to sign nondisclosure agreements).

37 *See, e.g.*, Kieff, *supra* note 14, at 708–09 (identifying second-mover advantages).

information about how to avoid mistakes made by the first mover, will sometimes mean that the anticipated profits from first moving in the event of success will not compensate for the risks of initial failure and subsequent defeat by the second entrant. Thus, free-rider problems may cause as much or more inefficiency from socially suboptimal new business model commercialization as from socially suboptimal new business model idea development. But business method patents focus entirely on the latter.

Justice Stevens's opposition to business method patents on policy grounds does not appear to stem from a view that competition will magically produce an optimal amount of business innovation. "[F]irms that innovate," Justice Stevens noted, "often capture long-term benefits from doing so, thanks to various first mover advantages, including lockins, branding, and networking effects."[38] But he admitted, "Concededly, there may [be] some methods of doing business that do not confer sufficient first-mover advantages,"[39] acknowledging a recent article arguing that intellectual property can and should protect market experimentation.[40] Just as technological experimentation produces information about whether a particular set of scientific steps will produce a useful result that can bring market rewards,[41] market experimentation produces information about whether a particular type of business or business model is likely to be effective and embraced by consumers. There may be insufficient incentives to invest in either technological or market experimentation when future competitors will dissipate profits if experimentation proves successful.

This does not mean, however, that the same type of intellectual property protections should be used to incentivize both the creation of business methods and their commercialization. Business method patents are a crude mechanism for encouraging commercialization, because the criteria for granting such patents reflect the risk inherent in developing business model ideas rather than the risk inherent in bringing business models to market. Some business models that receive patent protection might well be implemented by entrepreneurs even absent patent protection; in that case, patent protection is unnecessary and will lead to high prices and deadweight loss.[42] Much of the debate about whether the *Bilski* Court should have found business methods to be unpatentable subject matter has focused

38 *Bilski*, 130 S. Ct. at 3254.

39 *Id.* at 3254 n.51.

40 *Id.* (citing Abramowicz & Duffy, *supra* note 12, at 340–42).

41 Although the utility doctrine is often viewed as not demanding, the courts seem to use the nonobviousness doctrine to protect only inventions that are in some sense useful. *See, e.g.*, *In re Dow Chem. Co.*, 837 F.2d 469, 473 (Fed. Cir. 1988). The *Dow* approach is sensible where what is scarce is the willingness of scientists to test chemicals that may require minimal creativity to synthesize.

42 It is plausible that the nonobviousness doctrine can combat this, if the Supreme Court takes seriously its admonition that the purpose of the doctrine is to identify inventions that need the patent incentive. *See Graham v. John Deere Co.*, 383 U.S. 1, 11 (1966); Abramowicz & Duffy, *supra* note 8 (arguing that courts should consider whether inventions are patent-induced). In that case, the only business methods to receive patents would be those that would not have ended up in the public domain absent patent protection.

on this concern.[43] Meanwhile, other business methods may not qualify for patent protection, because the ideas underlying them are abstract or do not meet patent law's requirements, such as that an invention be novel[44] and nonobvious.[45] These include our eponymous "orphan business models."

1.1.1 Market experimentation after **Bilski**

Neither Justice Stevens nor the majority opinion in *Bilski* considered whether courts can or should directly assess market experimentation considerations. Nonetheless, the approach of the *Bilski* majority opinion as a whole does provide some basis for incorporating market experimentation in patent doctrine, and other aspects of the statute also allow some role for such considerations.

1.1.1.1 Abstractness and suitability for experimentation

The *Bilski* Court found Bilski's invention unpatentable on the ground that it was an "abstract idea." Yet the Court did little to make clear just what constitutes an abstract idea, and indeed it explicitly rejected the possibility of "adopting categorical rules that might have wide-ranging and unforeseen impacts."[46] Instead, the Court summarized its line of cases distinguishing abstract from concrete ideas,[47] without engaging either scholars who insist that the Court had distinguished the indistinguishable[48] or Justice Stevens's arguments that the patent claims at issue arguably are closer to the concrete than to the abstract side of the line.[49] What does appear clear from Justice Kennedy's opinion is that the test for abstractness is fact-specific and that it embraces considerations that patent lawyers ordinarily might consider only under other sections of the patent statute. Justice Kennedy noted, for example, that the basic concept of hedging is old in the art,[50] even though under orthodox patent law that fact might be more relevant to novelty or nonobviousness than to patentable subject matter.[51]

Lower courts thus must either assess abstractness in a fact-specific but unsystematic way or develop tests for determining abstractness in the business

43 *See, e.g.*, Alan Devlin & Neel Sukhatme, *Self-Realizing Inventions and the Utilitarian Foundation of Patent Law*, 51 WM. & MARY L. REV. 897, 902, 945–50 (2009) (recommending a new approach before the Court issued *Bilski*).

44 35 U.S.C. § 102 (2006).

45 *Id.* § 103.

46 *Bilski v. Kappos*, 130 S. Ct. 3218, 3229 (2010).

47 *See id.* at 3229–30 (discussing *Diamond v. Diehr*, 450 U.S. 175 (1981); *Parker v. Flook*, 437 U.S. 584 (1978); and *Gottschalk v. Benson*, 409 U.S. 63 (1972)).

48 *See* Gerard N. Magliocca, *Patenting the Curve Ball: Business Methods and Industry Norms*, 2009 BYU L. REV. 875, 882 n.29 ("*Diehr*'s effort to distinguish the Court's precedents rejecting software patents, especially *Parker v. Flook*, was unpersuasive and is widely criticized."); *id.* (citing other critical scholarly commentary).

49 *See Bilski*, 130 S. Ct. at 3235–36 (Stevens, J., concurring in the judgment).

50 *Id.* at 3231 (majority opinion).

51 *See* 35 U.S.C. § 101 (2006) (patentable subject matter); *id.* § 102 (novelty); *id.* § 103 (nonobviousness).

method context.[52] Evaluating abstractness may appear challenging in part because the Court rejects the proposition that a business method must be embodied in a machine or transform matter.[53] What does it mean for an idea to be concrete? A starting point is the recognition that intellectual property is designed to encourage the production of useful information. The particular type of information relevant here is information derived from experimentation, whether technological or market, with ideas. When an idea is sufficiently abstract, experimentation is unlikely to produce valuable information about the potential usefulness of the idea. Concrete ideas, in contrast, can be tested, and experimentation with them will generally produce useful information. This distinction links the abstractness inquiry to the traditional scientific insistence on falsifiability,[54] although what matters is not whether an idea is falsifiably correct (as with a mathematical theorem), but whether it is falsifiably useful.

The usefulness of a business method idea can be falsifiably tested. When a business method patent has many potential embodiments, market experimentation with any one embodiment will provide relatively little information about whether the various embodiments described in and claimed by the patent will be effective. In this case, there is a strong argument that the business method is abstract. A business method could be viewed as concrete where experimentation with any particular business method falling within the patent's scope seems likely to produce valuable information about the market feasibility of the specific techniques invented. Claims that narrow a business method idea to arbitrary contexts will not help make the idea more concrete, however, unless testing in these contexts will provide especially useful information about the idea as a whole. Meanwhile, if an idea is already well established, a new application of that idea often will not benefit from testing, because it will be clear in advance what the effect of the application will be.

The argument is perhaps best understood through an example. In an earlier patentable subject matter case,[55] the Supreme Court reasoned that the Pythagorean Theorem was an unpatentable abstract idea and "would not have been patentable, or partially patentable, because a patent application contained a final step indicating that the formula, when solved, could be usefully applied to existing surveying techniques."[56] The analysis here calls the Court's conclusion into

52 In proposed regulations, the Patent and Trademark Office (PTO) has taken the approach of suggesting that examiners may consider a wide range of factors. *See* Interim Guidance for Determining Subject Matter Eligibility for Process Claims in View of *Bilski v. Kappos*, 75 Fed. Reg. 43922, 43925–26 (July 27, 2010).

53 *See Bilski*, 130 S. Ct. at 3226.

54 The Supreme Court embraced the relevance of falsifiability in the scientific evidence context in *Daubert v. Merrell Dow Pharmaceuticals*, 509 U.S. 579 (1993). *See id.* at 593 ("[T]he criterion of the scientific status of a theory is its falsifiability, or refutability, or testability." (alterations in original) (quoting KARL POPPER, CONJECTURES AND REFUTATIONS: THE GROWTH OF SCIENTIFIC KNOWLEDGE 37 (5th ed. 1989)) (internal quotation marks omitted).

55 *Parker v. Flook*, 437 U.S. 584 (1978).

56 *Id.* at 590.

question.[57] The Theorem by itself would have been abstract. There are so many contexts in which it might be applied that information that someone was able to use it profitably in one context (say, to improve origami designs) would not be very relevant to an assessment of whether it would be profitable in some other context (say, to improve architectural rendering). But narrowing the patent to surveying makes the idea much more concrete. If the formula turns out to be useful for some type of surveying businesses, it is likely to be useful for others as well. Meanwhile, once the Theorem has long been known, a patent for some new application of the Theorem (say, use of the Theorem to survey grassy lands) seems unlikely to be within patentable subject matter, since experimentation does not seem likely to provide any additional information about whether the Theorem is useful.[58]

Justice Kennedy did not explain abstractness in this way, but this approach helps make sense of some of his logic. Justice Kennedy began by noting that "[h]edging is a fundamental economic practice long prevalent in our system of commerce and taught in any introductory finance class."[59] It is possible to view this statement as simply importing novelty and nonobviousness concerns into the patentable subject matter inquiry, but an alternative interpretation is that because some claims of the patent[60] seem similar to broad swaths of economic activity, the exercise of the patented method would not provide much information about the feasibility of accomplishing business ends with the techniques described in the patent. In the next paragraph, Justice Kennedy characterized some other claims in the patent as "broad examples of how hedging can be used in commodities and energy markets," noting that the examples "instruct the use of well-known random analysis techniques."[61] These claims are certainly narrower, but Justice Kennedy did not view them as more concrete. A justification for this conclusion is that implementation of these business methods seems

57 I borrow the Court's implicit assumption that the patent system existed at the time of Pythagoras's invention and that Pythagoras sought the patent. *See id.*

58 The test for concreteness also could be applied to the facts of *Flook* itself. *Flook* involved a method for updating alarm limits during catalytic conversion processes. *See id.* at 585. The patent included a formula for calculating: "[A]n updated alarm limit once [an operator] knows the original alarm base, the appropriate margin of safety, the time interval that should elapse between each updating, the current temperature (or other process variable), and the appropriate weighting factor to be used to average the original alarm base and the current temperature." *Id.* at 586. Whether such a formula is likely to be useful, relative to alternatives such as determining when the process is complete by using expert judgment, seems eminently testable, and the idea is likely to be concrete. A caveat, however, is that the patent covers use of the formula in "numerous processes . . . in the petrochemical and oil refining industries." *Id.* If these processes are so varied that the fact that the formula was useful in one context would tell little about whether it was useful in another, then the idea might be too abstract. Considering whether an idea is abstract or concrete in this way is not mechanical, but it does highlight the type of testimony that might be relevant. Of course, even if an idea is concrete, that does not mean that it is patentable; it still must meet the other criteria of patentability, including nonobviousness.

59 *Bilski v. Kappos*, 130 S. Ct. 3218, 3231 (2010) (quoting *In re Bilski*, 545 F.3d 943, 1013 (Fed. Cir. 2008) (Rader, J., dissenting)) (internal quotation marks omitted).

60 Specifically, Claims 1 and 4, which "explain the basic concept of hedging, or protecting against risk." *Id.* at 3222.

61 *Id.*

unlikely to produce valuable information about the allegedly innovative idea in the patent.

In *Bilski*, it seems likely that, had the questions been before the Court, it would have also found the patent invalid on other grounds, at least based on § 103 of the patent statute.[62] But the Court's approach to understanding abstractness suggests the possibility of a business method patent that is clearly nonobvious, a stroke of genius even,[63] while still being too abstract. Imagine, for example, that in the early years of the Internet, someone sought a patent on Internet-based e-commerce, and included both broad claims and narrow claims targeted to particular areas of e-commerce (books, flowers, and so on). Even if novel, the patent as a whole might be too abstract. Patent-induced experimentation with any single e-commerce embodiment would provide little information that would help entrepreneurs improve their evaluations about the feasibility of e-commerce as a whole. Admittedly, assessing abstractness in this context requires some subjective judgment, for experimentation with any one implementation of e-commerce likely would provide some information, but all approaches to defining abstractness will require some degree of line-drawing.

For an example of this kind of e-commerce, consider experimentation with selling books. Such experimentation might give information about the feasibility of selling books online, but if the patent's innovations do not relate directly to book sales, that will not suffice. A concrete idea is one where experimentation will provide useful information about the feasibility of that specific idea, and an actual online bookstore does not provide much information about the feasibility of the idea of e-commerce. The narrowing does not help make the idea any more concrete than would narrowing to e-commerce sites beginning with the letter "E." A patent or patent claims targeted toward specific techniques for selling books online might be more concrete.

Abstract patents in the sense identified here are the patents that seem least likely to promote market experimentation and reduce the problem of orphan business models. In sum, the *Bilski* Court has divided business methods into two groups: abstract ones, which are unpatentable, and concrete ones, which are potentially patentable. The question whether any given experiment on a business method described in a patent seems likely to produce useful information would determine whether that business method counts as concrete or abstract. Because of the additional requirements of patentability, some business methods that could benefit greatly from market experimentation might still be excluded from patentability, just as many orphan drugs are not entitled to patents even though they clearly fall within patentable subject matter. This approach would, however, roughly limit patentability to cases in which patent law may have been needed

62 35 U.S.C. § 103 (2006).

63 The patent statute's legislative history rejects the notion that a flash of genius is required. *See* 35 U.S.C. § 103 note (2006) ("The second sentence states that patentability as to this requirement is not to be negatived by the manner in which the invention was made, that is, it is immaterial whether it resulted from long toil and experimentation or from a flash of genius."). But it will still generally be sufficient to meet the nonobviousness requirement.

both to induce the idea of a business method *and* to provide incentives to conduct useful experiments on it. This chapter will consider reasons that this might be counterproductive,[64] though it may well make as much policy sense as other approaches to distinguishing abstract from concrete business methods.

1.1.1.2 Other patent doctrines

A desire to encourage market experimentation and reduce the danger of orphan business models may be relevant to other areas of patent law, as well. One statutory section of the patent laws directly reflects concerns about market experimentation. This section grants prior use rights for business methods in certain situations, providing a defense for someone who commercially used a business method at least one year before someone else filed a patent.[65] Concerns about orphan business models seem relatively more important for business methods than for many other types of technologies. Ordinarily, patent rights *reduce* the danger of orphan business models, but where business models are already being practiced, patents may serve as a tax on the continuation of such experiments. Congress might have done even more to reduce the risk that patents could discourage business innovation; a further step might have been to prohibit nonpracticing entities from receiving business method patents. Nonetheless, the congressional recognition of the importance of encouraging the practice of business methods highlights the potential relevance of this policy consideration to patent law more broadly.

The goal of encouraging market experimentation may already be relevant in the Supreme Court's decision regarding whether an injunction should issue after a court determines that patent infringement has occurred. In *eBay Inc. v. MercExchange, LLC*,[66] the Court held that injunctions should not automatically issue and that the Court's traditional four-factor test for injunctive relief applies in the patent context.[67] Since *eBay*, a number of district courts have taken the status of a patentee as a nonpracticing entity into account in refusing to issue injunctions.[68] Concerns about orphan business models provide some support for such considerations. An injunction by a nonpracticing entity against a practicing entity, along with the threat of such injunctions, makes market experimentation less desirable and increases the risk of orphan business models. Although there may be countervailing considerations, this should be a particularly powerful consideration where the underlying technology is a business model, because market experimentation is particularly critical to establishing the usefulness of business technologies.

64 *See* Section 1.2.2, TAN 141–150.
65 *See* 35 U.S.C. § 273(b)(1) (2006).
66 547 U.S. 388 (2006).
67 *Id.* at 391, 394.
68 *See* Shrestha, *supra* note 21, at 134–35 & n.112 (2010) (citing sources).

A final area in which the goal of encouraging market experimentation may be relevant is in nonobviousness analysis, and in particular in the courts' analysis of the "secondary considerations" of patentability.[69] Under Federal Circuit doctrine, the most important factor in patentability is whether the invention has produced commercial success.[70] Commentators have generally been skeptical of the relevance of commercial success,[71] but with a qualification, it makes some sense as a partial antidote to orphan business models. For an invention to be commercially successful, it must be marketed, and this need creates a danger that imitators will free-ride not only on the patent disclosure, but also on information developed in marketing. So, in a close obviousness case, successful marketing by the patentee should tilt the inquiry in the direction of nonobviousness. On the other hand, when a nonpracticing entity seeks to use a patent offensively against an alleged infringer, commercial success by the alleged infringer should not count in the patentee's favor and arguably should count against the patentee.

1.1.2 Problems with incorporating market experimentation concerns

In short, there exist doctrinal means through which the courts could seek to encourage market experimentation and discourage orphan business models, and consideration of such goals could help rationalize some areas of patent doctrine that have little foundation in theory. This should not be taken to suggest, however, that encouraging market experimentation should emerge as a coequal goal of the patent statute, as important as encouraging technological experimentation,[72] with the patent office awarding patents wherever needed to avoid the problem of an orphan business model. There are several reasons that this is not a desirable course, and to a lesser extent, these reasons may even counsel against considering market experimentation goals on the margins of patent law.

The most obvious problem is that the patent statute focuses on the goal of encouraging technological experimentation rather than the goal of encouraging market experimentation. Sometimes, these goals align, but at other times they do not. From the perspective of rewarding only new ideas for business methods, it may make sense, as Justice Kennedy suggested, to have a vigorous nonobviousness doctrine.[73] But that may tend to discourage market experimentation. If market experimentation becomes a factor in such analysis, it could complicate the

69 *Graham v. John Deere Co.*, 383 U.S. 1, 17–18 (1966) (introducing the secondary considerations).

70 *See* Andrew Blair-Stanek, *Profits as Commercial Success*, 117 YALE L.J. 642, 647–49 (2008); *see also In re Sernaker*, 702 F.2d 989, 996 (Fed. Cir. 1983).

71 *See, e.g.*, Edmund W. Kitch, Graham v. John Deere Co.*: New Standards for Patents*, 1966 SUP. CT. REV. 293, 332–34.

72 *See* Abramowicz & Duffy, *supra* note 12, at 405–08 (considering whether the patent system can embrace pure "commercialization patents").

73 *See Bilski v. Kappos*, 130 S. Ct. 3218, 3229 (2010) (plurality opinion) (noting that "business method patents raise special problems in terms of vagueness and suspect validity" and that the nonobviousness requirement is one tool to avoid "granting patents when not justified by the statutory design").

nonobviousness inquiry, especially because there is no straightforward way of balancing the concerns about encouraging technological and market experimentation. Similarly, if abstractness of an idea is defined with reference to its falsifiability, then there might be insufficient incentives to develop novel and nonobvious business models that are abstract in this sense. The goals of the patent system are different from those of statutes encouraging adoption of orphan business models (such as the Orphan Drug Act), and seeking to serve both of these goals in a single intellectual property regime would produce inevitable tensions.

An additional problem is the question of institutional competence. There have been challenges enough to the effectiveness of the Patent and Trademark Office (PTO) in making determinations such as the nonobviousness of inventions,[74] but at least examiners currently focus on retrospective inquiries. It would be far more difficult for a patent office to assess how a decision to grant a property right will affect a business's potential development. That is a determination that cannot easily be made just on the basis of papers, but requires familiarity with a particular industry. It also requires a willingness to make decisions that ultimately are subjective and probabilistic, and the PTO has generally veered toward more objective standards even where it is impossible for bright-line rules to capture needed nuance adequately.[75] In administering the Orphan Drug Act, the Food and Drug Administration at least is specialized in a particular industry, though even in this instance we have seen that the agency has preferred bright-line thresholds to more open-ended inquiries into whether protection is necessary.[76]

A final problem is that the patent term is fixed. Even if a patent office could identify business models that will not be commercialized in the near future absent some form of exclusivity protection, the full patent term in many cases may not be needed to encourage market entry. In a very small number of situations, it is possible that a full patent term might be insufficient to encourage entry, yet one should hesitate to empower an agency with discretion to grant protection longer than 20 years. The patent office likely does not have the competence to customize patent terms on the basis of all possible relevant factors, including those relating to both technological and market experimentation.[77] The proposal described in Section 1.3 for competition to provide the shortest protection term provides an antidote, but it would not fit well within the patent system, because patents must be awarded after inventions are produced.

The patent system, of course, is not the only form of existing intellectual property protection that may encourage market experimentation. Trade secret law may help by making it easier to protect financial and scientific data about the success of market and technological experiments, thus making it more difficult for

74 *See, e.g.*, Mandel, *supra* note 24, at 78.

75 Michael Abramowicz & John F. Duffy, *Ending the Patenting Monopoly*, 157 U. PA. L. REV. 1541, 1560 (2009).

76 *See infra* p. 29

77 For examples of such factors in proposals for tailored patent terms, see sources cited *infra* note 164.

competitors to free-ride.[78] But sometimes, even casual analysis by consumers suffices to reveal the success of a new business model. In addition, if copyright law were expanded to entail data exclusivity,[79] that might help as well, but only incompletely. In principle, protecting orphan business models requires only protection of the information resulting from market experiments, but in practice this is often impossible, and so a targeted, effective protection scheme must protect the right to perform the business model. An expansion of copyright law to include data exclusivity would not be able to accomplish this.

1.2 Subject-specific responses: the case of pharmaceuticals

Among most intellectual property scholars, the case for patent law is generally considered to be stronger for pharmaceuticals than for other areas of technology.[80] It seems plausible that other technologies could advance relatively rapidly even without patent protection, but in pharmaceuticals, removal of the patent incentive would virtually eliminate private sector drug research. Private sector research depends on the patent reward because of the extraordinary costs associated with research into new drugs and the relative ease with which generic drug manufacturers can copy drugs. But scholars' embrace of patent protection for pharmaceuticals does not imply that the general patent framework is optimally tuned for pharmaceuticals. Indeed, the existence of many exclusivity provisions that are specific to drugs reveals that, because of the importance of drug development, Congress has sought to address inefficiencies and imperfections of the patent system in that context.[81] This Section describes some of the patent-specific exclusivity provisions and explains how they partly allay concerns about orphan business models. It also describes remaining weaknesses in these approaches and how they might be fixed.

The existing system, even with these drug-specific fixes, is suboptimal. In an important recent article, Professor Benjamin Roin explains in detail how the patent system fails to give sufficient incentives to develop many potentially useful

78 For an explanation of how trade secret doctrine helps promote market experimentation, see Abramowicz & Duffy, *supra* note 12, at 389–91.

79 *See, e.g.*, Amol Pachnanda, *Scientific Databases Should Be Protected Under a* Sui Generis *Regime*, 51 BUFF. L. REV. 219, 241 (2003).

80 *See, e.g.*, JAMES BESSEN & MICHAEL J. MEURER, PATENT FAILURE: HOW JUDGES, BUREAUCRATS, AND LAWYERS PUT INNOVATORS AT RISK 120–21, 138–41 (2008) (finding net benefits of patent protection only for the pharmaceutical and chemical industries). In the general public, the opposite may be true because of concerns that legal regulation will prevent individuals from obtaining affordable drugs. For a proposal for a system of tradable patent terms that would seek to improve access to medicines, see Michael Ilg, *Market Competition in Aid of Humanitarian Concern: Reconsidering Pharmaceutical Drug Patents*, 9 CHI.-KENT J. INTELL. PROP. 149, 169–73 (2010).

81 Judicial doctrine may also tailor patent law to particular technological contexts. *See* Dan L. Burk & Mark A. Lemley, *Is Patent Law Technology-Specific?*, 17 BERKELEY TECH. L.J. 1155, 1160 (2002). But technology-sensitive orphan business method protection has not emerged from such customization.

drugs.[82] Pharmaceutical firms, Roin explains, weed out of their drug pipelines drugs that they do not expect to be able to patent,[83] even though these drugs are generally not available on the market. The requirements of patentability, particularly the requirements of novelty and nonobviousness,[84] make sense to the extent that the goal of patent law is viewed as the *conception* of drugs that might turn out to be clinically beneficial after a long testing process. But if a goal is actually to encourage drug manufacturers to undertake that testing process, patent law will work only so long as the firm that conceives of a drug proceeds to seek a patent and then undertake the clinical testing process. Ironically, Roin notes, if a third party observes in a scientific publication that a particular compound seems like a very promising drug candidate it is less likely that an unrelated pharmaceutical company will research that compound, because the company will be concerned that if the research turns out to be successful, the drug will be unpatentable.[85]

In such a case, the business model of researching a compound, shepherding it through the FDA approval process, and bringing it to market is an orphan business model. As with other orphan business models, the problem is that second movers can take advantage of information produced by the first mover and dissipate the profits that the first mover could expect to receive. Being first to market and being able to offer the brand-name drug may, as a result of trademark law,[86] furnish some first-mover advantages,[87] but at least in many cases these will be insufficient to make the research path appear profitable, even if it would be socially beneficial. The type of information on which the second mover is free-riding is different from the relevant information in a typical orphan business model case, where the second mover might wait to see whether there is consumer demand rather than regulatory approval. As with all orphan business models, though, there is a private risk that it will not be feasible to earn a profit providing a good or service, and first movers may not be willing to make expensive investments that have a high chance of producing no profits if second movers can enter the market in the unlikely case success is achieved.

Section 1.2.1 describes ways in which the drug laws already respond to concerns about orphan business models, and it notes the danger that these approaches sometimes may provide too little protection and other times may provide too much. Section 1.2.2 explores various possible improvements to the existing

82 Roin, *supra* note 12, at 515–45.

83 *Id.* at 545–56.

84 35 U.S.C. §§ 102, 103 (2006).

85 Roin, *supra* note 12, at 537 ("The most troubling aspect of the nonobviousness requirement is that it denies patent protection to inventions *because* they seem likely to work while ignoring the question of whether a patent is needed to motivate that invention's development.").

86 For a discussion of the extent to which trademark law encourages market experimentation, see Abramowicz & Duffy, *supra* note 12, at 381–89.

87 Trademark law also can accent existing first-mover advantages by allowing brand-name drug manufacturers to earn rents even after the patent term. *See* Gideon Parchomovsky & Peter Siegelman, *Towards an Integrated Theory of Intellectual Property*, 88 VA. L. REV. 1455, 1473–81 (2002).

regimes, concluding that existing proposals and other familiar solutions will not likely be adequate. The best solution, to be considered later,[88] may be to have potential adopters of an orphan business model compete with one another based on length of proposed exclusivity period.

1.2.1 Statutory regimes

Drug laws reflect concerns about orphan business models in at least three ways. First, the Orphan Drug Act provides protection for a class of drugs where pharmaceutical companies might not have sufficient incentives to undertake the process of clinical testing and regulatory approval. Second, an unrelated part of the drug laws with a similar effect generally assures some period of exclusivity to the first company that obtains approval for a drug by delaying approval of generic versions. Finally, the Hatch-Waxman Act,[89] which provides incentives for generic drug manufacturers to challenge drug patents, reflects a concern about a different type of free-riding: free-riding by additional generic manufacturers on the litigation endured by a first generic challenger.

1.2.1.1 Orphan Drug Act

The Orphan Drug Act seeks to protect "orphan" drugs, that is, drugs that need to be adopted by a pharmaceutical company if they are to be brought to market.[90] The title of the statute might at first appear to be a misnomer because it applies to any drug that is for a "rare disease or condition,"[91] but the definition of "rare disease or condition" is expansive. It includes not only any disease that "affects less than 200,000 persons in the United States,"[92] but also any disease that "affects more than 200,000 in the United States and for which there is no reasonable expectation that the cost of developing and making available in the United States a drug for such disease or condition will be recovered from sales in the United States of such drug."[93] In other words, the statute presumes that a drug for a disease affecting a relatively small number of people needs protection[94] because

88 *See infra* Section 1.3.1.

89 Drug Price Competition and Patent Term Restoration Act of 1984, Pub. L. No. 98–417, 98 Stat. 1585 (codified at 21 U.S.C. § 355), *amended by* Patient Protection and Affordable Care Act, Pub. L. No. 111–148, 124 Stat. 119 (2010) (codified in scattered sections of the U.S. Code).

90 Representative Henry A. Waxman explains the name, saying that these drugs "are like children who have no parents, . . . and they require special effort." Thomas Maeder, *The Orphan Drug Backlash*, SCI. AM., May 2003, at 82 (quotation marks omitted).

91 21 U.S.C. § 360bb(a)(1) (2006).

92 *Id.* § 360bb(a)(2)(A). For an analysis of whether the Orphan Drug Act's subsidy provisions are justified on distributive justice grounds, see Arti K. Rai, *Pharmacogenetic Interventions, Orphan Drugs, and Distributive Justice: The Role of Cost-Benefit Analysis*, SOC. PHIL. & POL'Y, Aug. 2002, at 246, 253–69.

93 21 U.S.C. § 360bb(a)(2)(B) (2006).

94 The initial version of the statute passed in 1983 did not include this provision because Congress "considered such definitions too rigid and impractical." Stephan E. Lawton, *Controversy Under the Orphan Drug Act: Is Resolution on the Way?*, 46 FOOD DRUG COSM. L.J. 327, 328 (1991). Concerns

there will generally be reduced incentives to develop drugs for smaller patient populations.[95] The statute, however, in theory also allows drug manufacturers to demonstrate that a drug affecting a larger number of people needs protection. For any drug designated as being for a rare disease or condition, the statute provides for seven years of marketing exclusivity.[96] However, exclusivity can be cancelled if the holder "cannot assure the availability of sufficient quantities of the drug."[97] Outside the United States, a number of countries, plus the European Union, have adopted statutes similar to the Orphan Drug Act.[98]

Most studies of the Orphan Drug Act indicate that it has helped promote further research into drugs for rare diseases. Professor Wesley Yin, for example, finds that the Orphan Drug Act promotes drug development, and the effect is greater for relatively prevalent rare diseases.[99] Even skeptics of the Orphan Drug Act generally conclude that it has done more good than harm.[100] There is dispute, however, whether the Orphan Drug Act itself provides the primary incentives that induce the development of drugs that have been brought to market. Robert Rogoyski, for example, argues that even for orphan drugs, patent incentives dwarf the incentives provided by the Orphan Drug Act, though he concedes that the Orphan Drug Act may have some effect in encouraging the introduction of drugs to market.[101] At the least, it serves "as a form of insurance" in the event that "patents are weak or invalidated through litigation."[102]

Many critics, meanwhile, argue that the Orphan Drug Act has in some instances provided protection that was unnecessary to induce drug development. These critics note that some orphan drugs have earned more than US$1 billion per year, suggesting that they could have been developed even without an orphan

emerged, however, that too few drugs were being approved under the statute. *See Orphan Drug Act Oversight Hearings Before the Subcomm. on Health and the Env't of the H. Comm. on Energy and Commerce*, 98th Cong., 2d Sess. 719–20 (1984), *discussed in* Lawton, *supra*, at 328–30.

95 For economic evidence that patients benefit from increased research when many others have the same conditions they do, see Frank R. Lichtenberg & Joel Waldfogel, *Does Misery Love Company? Evidence from Pharmaceutical Markets Before and After the Orphan Drug Act*, 15 MICH. TELECOMM. & TECH. L. REV. 335, 348 (2009).

96 21 U.S.C. § 360cc(a) (2006) ("[T]he Secretary may not approve another application . . . for such drug for such disease or condition . . . until the expiration of seven years from the date of the approval of the approved application. . . .").

97 *Id.* § 360cc(b)(1).

98 Maeder, *supra* note 90, at 87. *See generally* Mae Thamer and others, *A Cross-National Comparison of Orphan Drug Policies: Implications for the U.S. Orphan Drug Act*, 23 J. HEALTH POL. POL'Y & L. 265 (1998) (comparing different countries' approaches).

99 *See* Wesley Yin, *Market Incentives and Pharmaceutical Innovation*, 27 J. HEALTH ECON. 1060, 1073 (2008); *see also* Daron Acemoglu & Joshua Linn, *Market Size in Innovation: Theory and Evidence from the Pharmaceutical Industry*, 119 Q.J. ECON. 1049, 1049 (2004) (finding that increased market size increases research and development).

100 *See, e.g.*, Alan M. Garber, *Benefits Versus Profits: Has the Orphan Drug Act Gone Too Far?*, 5 PHARMACOECONOMICS 88, 91 (1994) (concluding that despite a tendency of the Orphan Drug Act to contribute to health care inflation, the Act still should not be overhauled).

101 Robert Rogoyski, *The Orphan Drug Act and the Myth of the Exclusivity Incentive*, 7 COLUM. SCI. & TECH. L. REV. 1, 22 (2006).

102 *Id.* at 22.

designation.[103] Based on concerns about blockbuster orphan drugs, both houses of Congress approved the Orphan Drug Amendments of 1990,[104] which would have allowed shared exclusivity in certain circumstances, for example when subsequent applicants rapidly initiated their own clinical trials.[105] The Amendments would have also allowed FDA revocation of exclusivity were the population of potential consumers to grow beyond the 200,000 threshold.[106] President Bush, however, vetoed the bill, worried that permitting multiple winners of a race to develop orphan drugs would decrease development incentives.[107]

One strategy that pharmaceutical companies have used to obtain potentially unnecessary Orphan Drug Act protection s to design studies so that drugs will be indicated only for a small segment of the population. Later, the companies may seek through additional testing to have the drugs, already guaranteed exclusivity, approved for other groups.[108] Commentators often refer to this strategy as "salami slicing," and as Patricia Kenney explains, "companies can use the exclusivity provision . . . to create an unintended windfall and a barrier to innovation."[109] Empirical studies suggest that at least some research and development after "salami slicing" would have been conducted even absent the Orphan Drug Act.[110]

To try to prevent drug makers from receiving Orphan Drug Act protection by arbitrarily specifying a small subset of the real patient population, the FDA requires an explanation for why the drug seems likely to work better for that subset.[111] But it is not uncommon for a drug to be particularly beneficial for one group, and the FDA will not generally reject an orphan drug application merely

103 *See, e.g.*, Maeder, *supra* note 90, at 82 ("Several orphan drugs—notably epoetin alfa [Epogen], which builds up red blood cells—have now become blockbusters, leading critics to question whether drug companies are abusing the Orphan Drug Act."). The FDA refused to revoke the market exclusivity for Epogen, concluding that in 1989 it had correctly determined that the patient population was under 200,000, because fewer than 200,000 patients had been diagnosed, even though subsequent diagnoses led to a great increase in the patient population. *See* Lawton, *supra* note 94, at 337–38 (citing Letter from Ronald G. Chesemore, Assoc. Comm'r for Regulatory Affairs, Food and Drug Admin., to Joseph T. Sobota, M.D., Chugai-Upjohn, and Bruce M. Eisen, Genetics Inst. (Jan. 11, 1991)).

104 Orphan Drug Amendments, H.R. 4638, 101st Cong. (1990).

105 *See id.* § 3(a).

106 *See id.* § 2(b).

107 Lawton, *supra* note 94, at 343 (discussing this and other reasons for the veto).

108 In addition, "once a drug has obtained marketing approval for a particular indication, it subsequently may be prescribed for any number of diseases or conditions." David B. Clissold, *Prescription for the Orphan Drug Act: The Impact of the FDA's 1992 Regulations and the Latest Congressional Proposals for Reform*, 50 FOOD & DRUG L.J. 125, 134 (1995).

109 Patricia J. Kenney, *The Orphan Drug Act—Is it a Barrier to Innovation? Does it Create Unintended Windfalls?*, 43 FOOD DRUG COSM. L.J. 667, 678 (1988).

110 *See* Wesley Yin, *R&D Policy, Agency Costs and Innovation in Personalized Medicine*, 28 J. HEALTH ECON. 950, 959–60 (2009).

111 21 C.F.R. § 316.20(b)(6) (2010) (requiring "[w]here a drug is under development for only a subset of persons with a particular disease or condition, a demonstration that the subset is medically plausible"). "This requirement exists to prevent an applicant from unduly restricting the cited orphan disease prevalence or unnecessarily subdividing its characteristics into artificial and medically implausible subsets, thus creating unreasonable market niches that allow the applicant to reach the prevalence threshold." Paul V. Buday, *Hints on Preparing Successful Orphan Drug Designation Requests*, 51 FOOD & DRUG L.J. 75, 80–81 (1996).

because a drug might also be helpful to some other segment of the population that would push the class of potential consumers above the Act's population threshold. The phenomenon of indicating a drug for a small segment of the population is likely to become more serious with development of pharmacogenomic technology that targets particular patients based on their genes, because that technology will likely make it easier to identify discrete subsets of the potential patient population that might especially benefit from drugs.[112] One commentator anticipates the possibility that pharmacogenomic orphan drug applications will flood the FDA and "slow down the application process for all drugs,"[113] and therefore argues that Congress should create a separate regulatory structure to incentivize pharmacogenomic drugs.[114]

In short, as one critic observed, "[T]he Act is overinclusive. The Act extends the benefits of orphan status to drugs that would be profitable without the incentives."[115] Salami slicing, meanwhile, is not the only problem. For example, because the Act refers only to the number of patients in the United States, it also may grant unnecessary protection when there are large numbers of patients outside the United States, as is the case for some drugs that treat parasitic diseases.[116] The result of unnecessary protection is unnecessarily high prices for consumers.[117]

What the literature does not address is that the Act is also underinclusive. Some drug candidates will not be developed because neither the patent statute nor the Orphan Drug Act provides enough of an incentive for companies to do so. Roin makes this point about the patent laws,[118] and in a footnote he notes that the Orphan Drug Act provides an occasional means of encouraging drug development,[119] but he does not explore the possibility of expanding the Orphan Drug Act to address concerns about insufficient incentives to develop unpatentable drugs.

A simple illustration of the underinclusiveness of the Orphan Drug Act can be seen in a current crisis over the impending absence of antivenom for coral snake bites, which affect about 100 people per year.[120] Wyeth, the manufacturer of the

112 "Pharmacogenomics might allow drug sponsors to nudge salami slicing from the arena of medical judgment towards the arena of scientific fact." David Loughnot, *Potential Interactions of the Orphan Drug Act and Pharmacogenomics: A Flood of Orphan Drugs and Abuses?*, 31 AM. J. L. & MED. 365, 374 (2005).

113 Dov Greenbaum, *Incentivizing Pharmacogenomic Drug Development: How the FDA Can Overcome Early Missteps in Regulating Personalized Medicine*, 40 RUTGERS L.J. 97, 126 (2008).

114 *See id.* at 126–27.

115 Cynthia A. Thomas, *Re-Assessing the Orphan Drug Act*, 23 COLUM. J.L. & SOC. PROBS. 413, 414 (1990).

116 *Id.* at 429.

117 High prices have generated some controversy even for drugs that appear to have been induced by the Act's protections. Industry advocates insist that drug companies charge much less than they could. *See* Maeder, *supra* note 90, at 86. Nonetheless, public concern about orphan drug pricing has risen with more general concern about pharmaceutical prices. *See, e.g.*, Carolyn H. Asbury, *The Orphan Drug Act: The First 7 Years*, 265 JAMA 893, 896–97 (1991).

118 Roin, *supra* note 12, at 515–56.

119 *Id.* at 552 n.259.

120 *See* Glenn Derene, *The Venom Crisis*, POPULAR MECHANICS, June 1, 2010, at 26, *available at* http://www.popularmechanics.com/science/health/snakebites-about-to-get-more-deadly.

current antivenom treatment, stopped production several years ago because it was unprofitable. Supplies are currently running low, so future victims may need to be intubated on ventilators for weeks, potentially at a cost of hundreds of thousands of dollars.[121] An alternative candidate treatment, Coralmyn, exists, but the snake bites are sufficiently rare that it appears the manufacturer does not want to pay the several million dollars that it would likely cost to test the treatment. It is possible that for some hypothetical long term of exclusivity, the manufacturer would be willing to bear these costs, but the Orphan Drug Act does not allow extra long terms of exclusivity for especially rare diseases.

The absence of proposals to extend Orphan Drug Act protection may seem sensible given both political and practical constraints. Congress's recent concern that the Orphan Drug Act has extended too much protection renders unlikely congressional action to allow even more overinclusivity. Thus, extending the term or simply changing the threshold patient population size to a number greater than 200,000 seems undesirable. Meanwhile, the FDA already has the authority to approve orphan drug status for drugs targeting more than 200,000 patients, and so no additional legislation is needed to allow the FDA to ignore this threshold. Apparently, the FDA, already under criticism for approving drugs unnecessarily, is hesitant to invoke that power.[122]

Ideally, the FDA should be more willing to grant an orphan drug designation the *less* likely clinical testing is to be successful, because the lower the *ex ante* probability of success, the greater the expected return companies will require when testing *is* successful. This places in an awkward position both the FDA and orphan drug status applicants, who will need to maintain that their plans are promising enough to justify testing on human subjects.[123] Even when the FDA correctly concludes that orphan drug status is necessary because success is unlikely, it would be criticized in the few cases in which clinical testing proved successful for having made a poor forecast.

1.2.1.2 Protection from generic competition

Although Roin does not address the possibility that Congress might modify the Orphan Drug Act to increase the incentives of pharmaceutical companies to develop unpatentable drugs, he does identify another feature of drug law that lawmakers might easily modify to increase such incentives. After it approves a drug, the FDA cannot approve the same drug from another manufacturer for five

121 Part of the problem may be that Wyeth charged less than US$5000 for a basic course of treatment. *See* Keith Morelli, *Red Touches Yellow—Kills a Fellow*, TAMPA TRIBUNE, May 24, 2010, at 1, *available at* http://www2.tbo.com/content/2010/may/24/na-red-red-touches-yellow—kills-a-fellow-touches/. Perhaps Wyeth believed that to be the most it could charge without suffering adverse public relations.

122 *See supra* p. 22 (noting that the FDA is similar to other agencies in preferring bright-line tests).

123 *See* 21 C.F.R. § 50.25(a)(3) (2010) (noting that to obtain informed consent, each human subject must receive a description of the expected benefits of the treatment).

to seven and a half years.[124] Roin notes that the legislative history suggests that one justification for these regulatory delays may specifically have been to encourage development of unpatentable drugs.[125] This protection from generic competition is more inclusive than the Orphan Drug Act in that it applies to every drug, not just those intended for diseases with fewer than 200,000 patients or where the expenses of research and development cannot be recouped. The concerns about the Orphan Drug Act's overinclusiveness thus have an even more powerful analogue here; some firms may have been willing to go through the clinical trial process even without these built-in regulatory delays.

At the same time, however, this form of protection is considerably weaker than that provided by the Orphan Drug Act in one respect: generic manufacturers can still enter the market if they furnish their own clinical testing data,[126] whereas the Orphan Drug Act has no such exception. Thus, the built-in regulatory delays still leave a significant danger that bringing drugs to market will be an orphan business model. If the problem is not merely the *expense* of trials, but also the *risk* that trials may fail, a second mover may free-ride on the information from successful clinical tests by beginning its own. In sum, regulatory delays can potentially ameliorate the problem of orphan business models for drugs other than the select few targeted by the Orphan Drug Act, but in other respects the mechanism suffers more from both overinclusion and underinclusion than the Orphan Drug Act.

1.2.1.3 Encouragement of generic competition

Ironically, the final area of drug law that reflects concerns about orphan business models has the opposite goal of delaying generic competition. Under the Hatch-Waxman Act,[127] a generic drug company that challenges the patent protecting a pioneer drug receives a 180-day exclusivity period,[128] meaning that no other generic drug manufacturer can enter the market during that time. The goal is thus to accelerate generic competition. The authorized generic manufacturer can charge considerably above marginal cost, allowing it to earn a profit and providing an incentive to challenge pioneer patents. In the absence of

124 *See* 21 U.S.C. § 355(c)(3)(E) (2006). Roin details the calculation of the waiting period. *See* Roin, *supra* note 12, at 565 n.332.

125 Roin, *supra* note 12, at 566 n.333 (citing H.R. REP. NO. 98–857, pt. 1, at 29 (1984)). Roin further adds that "scholars and policymakers have (until now) been unable to identify categories of unpatentable drugs that would justify the delays." *Id.* The Orphan Drug Act has long been understood to be justified by the desire to encourage development of unpatentable (as well as patentable) drugs, but Roin is correct that scholars have not generally noted that regulatory delays serve a similar purpose.

126 As Roin notes, "generic companies can bypass the FDA-enforced exclusivity periods by submitting their own clinical-trial data." Roin, *supra* note 12, at 566 n.332.

127 Drug Price Competition and Patent Term Restoration Act of 1984, Pub. L. No. 98–417, 98 Stat. 1585 (codified at 21 U.S.C. § 355 (2010)).

128 The 180-day exclusivity period applies only when the generic manufacturer justifies filing an Abbreviated New Drug Application on the ground "that such patent is invalid or will not be infringed by the manufacture, use, or sale of the new drug." 21 U.S.C. § 355(j)(2)(A)(vii)(IV) (2010).

this protection, Congress worried, generic drug manufacturers might have insufficient incentives to undertake the risk of filing an Abbreviated New Drug Application and weathering patent litigation against a party that will have much more at stake than it does. Each generic manufacturer would want to free-ride on the litigation efforts of others, and often, none would have sufficient incentive to challenge the patentee.

That the drug laws serve opposing goals in providing incentives for orphan business models does not mean that they are necessarily in tension. Congress is willing to afford the relatively long term associated with a patent only to a relatively small class of drugs, relegating those that do not meet the requirements of patentability to rely on the Orphan Drug Act or regulatory approval delays. Patent litigation is a component of the regulatory system that helps ensure that drugs that are not entitled to it do not receive patent protection, and Congress was concerned that incentives to engage in patent litigation might be inadequate. Thus, just as the Orphan Drug Act reflects concern that few would be interested in launching a business if the first step were expensive regulatory approval and success would allow everyone to enter, so too does the Hatch-Waxman Act reflect concerns where the first step is expensive litigation. The existence of laws reflecting orphan business model concerns to both discourage and encourage generic entry reinforces that where property rights are sufficiently valuable, and where entry into a market is particularly expensive and prone to free-riding, some form of exclusivity protection is likely to emerge. The problem of free-riding on litigation is, of course, a much more general one,[129] and some scholars have proposed general incentives to challenge invalid patents,[130] but Congress has focused on the problem only in one area where the social costs of not providing protection are especially apparent.

The example of the Hatch-Waxman Act, however, also illustrates that poorly designed orphan business model protections may fail to advance the goals of those who create them. The stakes are sufficiently high for pioneer drug manufacturers to identify and exploit loopholes. And loopholes they have found. The most infamous involves "reverse payments"—settlements where the generic manufacturer delays market entry in exchange for cash.[131] Though it is possible to defend such settlements,[132] they clearly seem inconsistent with the legislative

129 *See* Steven Shavell, *The Level of Litigation: Private Versus Social Optimality of Suit and of Settlement*, 19 INT'L REV. L. & ECON. 99, 99–100 (1999) (noting that incentives to sue may be socially suboptimal because others benefit from the deterrence provided by lawsuits).

130 *See, e.g.*, John R. Thomas, *Collusion and Collective Action in the Patent System: A Proposal for Patent Bounties*, 2001 U. ILL. L. REV. 305, 340–42 (2001).

131 *See, e.g.*, Jeremy Bulow, *The Gaming of Pharmaceutical Patents*, 4 INNOVATION POL'Y & ECON. 145, 165–68 (2004); C. Scott Hemphill, *An Aggregate Approach to Antitrust: Using New Data and Rulemaking to Preserve Drug Competition*, 109 COLUM. L. REV. 629, 634–41 (2009) [hereinafter Hemphill, *An Aggregate Approach*]; C. Scott Hemphill, *Paying for Delay: Pharmaceutical Patent Settlement as a Regulatory Design Problem*, 81 N.Y.U. L. REV. 1553, 1557 (2006).

132 "The most fundamental [defense] is that permitting settlement increases the brand-name firm's profit, and hence its expected reward for developing innovative drugs. . . ." Hemphill, *An Aggregate Approach*, *supra* note 131, at 637.

intent of encouraging generic entry. Another loophole, under which pioneer drug manufacturers took advantage of a provision allowing a 30-month stay of generic entry during patent litigation by using multiple patents to obtain repeated 30-month stays, was closed by later legislation.[133] Another bug in the original legislation started the 180-day clock running as soon as a court decision was issued, even though generic entry would often be stayed pending appeal.[134] Finally, pioneer drug manufacturers have licensed authorized generics to compete with the generics entitled to the 180-day period of exclusivity, cutting the profits from exclusivity by about 80 percent and deterring future patent challenges.[135]

Although these statutory design bugs involve technical issues specific to drug law, they highlight some general points about the design of orphan business model protections. First, statutes should anticipate side deals by parties whose interests the statutes would harm. For example, in order to regulate such side deals, the Hatch-Waxman Act might have tolerated settlements between generic challengers and pioneer drug manufacturers, but required that any such settlements affect only the date of generic entry and not involve exchanges of money or other consideration. Second, statutes should identify any actions that would result in termination of exclusivity and the possibility of another party's receiving exclusivity. A decision to stop pursuing invalidation of a patent should presumably qualify, allowing others to pursue litigation. A pioneer drug manufacturer may be willing to pay "greenmail"[136] only so many times.

Third, the statutes should carefully delineate the scope of the exclusivity. Hatch-Waxman, for example, likely should have specified that authorized generics were prohibited, but in the absence of a specific statement to that effect, the courts concluded otherwise, recognizing the general power of a patent holder to license and market inventions.[137] Fourth, the term of exclusivity, including the identification of which events can toll the statute of limitations, should be clear.

That does not necessarily mean, however, that the term should be of fixed length. Indeed, the history of the Hatch-Waxman Act shows that the fixed 180-day term is likely longer than necessary in some cases to induce litigation.

133 Medicare Prescription Drug, Improvement, and Modernization Act of 2003, Pub. L. No. 108–173, 117 Stat. 2066 (codified in 21 and 42 U.S.C.). *See generally* Stephanie Greene, *A Prescription for Change: How the Medicare Act Revises Hatch-Waxman to Speed Market Entry of Generic Drugs*, 30 J. CORP. L. 309 (2005).

134 For a discussion of amendments that eliminated this bug, see John R. McNair, *If Hatch Wins, Make Waxman Pay: One-Way Fee Shifting as a Substitute Incentive to Resolve Abuse of the Hatch-Waxman Act*, 2007 U. ILL. J.L. TECH. & POL'Y 119, 126–27 & n.69 (2007).

135 *See* NARINDER S. BANAIT, AUTHORIZED GENERICS: ANTITRUST ISSUES AND THE HATCH-WAXMAN ACT 4 (2005), *available at* http://www.fenwick.com/docstore/publications/IP/Authorized_Generics.pdf; *see also* Beth Understahl, Note, *Authorized Generics: Careful Balance Undone*, 16 FORDHAM INTELL. PROP. MEDIA & ENT. L.J. 355, 374–77 (2005).

136 In the corporate context, "greenmail" consists of payments by a target of an acquisition attempt to the potential acquirer in exchange for ceasing the attempted takeover. For a discussion of greenmail, see generally Jonathan R. Macey & Fred S. McChesney, *A Theoretical Analysis of Corporate Greenmail*, 95 YALE L.J. 13 (1985).

137 *See, e.g.*, *Teva Pharm., Indus., Ltd. v. FDA*, 355 F. Supp. 2d 111, 117 (D.D.C. 2004).

One problem that the FDA faces is that sometimes, two or more generic manufacturers file Abbreviated New Drug Applications on the same day. These cases are no coincidence, but occur when there is a clear first day on which such challenges could be filed.[138] In those cases, 180 days is an unnecessarily large incentive. The FDA and later congressional response—to allow shared exclusivity—may address this problem in part by effectively reducing the size of the reward in such cases, but it is a crude solution. And, of course, 180 days may be too short a period of exclusivity in other cases to justify the burdens of filing the first Abbreviated New Drug Application and undertaking litigation risk. Section 1.3.1 will consider the possibility of a term not fixed by statute.[139] First, however, we will consider other possible reforms to the various protections of orphan business models in the drug laws.

1.2.2 Potential reform paths

1.2.2.1 Longer protection term

Perhaps the simplest reform to reduce problems of orphan business models in the drug context would be to lengthen the relevant periods of exclusivity. There has been renewed media attention given to the relatively limited incentives that drug companies have to develop their products through the FDA approval process,[140] and extending the term of the Orphan Drug Act might improve incentives. Roin, meanwhile, proposes that the regulatory delay term be lengthened "to somewhere between ten and fourteen years," noting that this change would "at least provide a rough substitute for patent protection" and "eliminate the distortions arising from the novelty and nonobviousness requirements."[141] Similarly, once the problems in the Hatch-Waxman Act are ironed out, if there is still inadequate incentive to seek invalidation of patents, Congress could extend the 180-day exclusivity period afforded to the first generic. These solutions might well be justified, compared to the alternative of doing nothing. But a significant drawback of

138 *See* CTR. FOR DRUG EVALUATION & RESEARCH, U.S. DEP'T OF HEALTH & HUMAN SERVS., GUIDANCE FOR INDUSTRY: 180-DAY EXCLUSIVITY WHEN MULTIPLE ANDAS ARE SUBMITTED ON THE SAME DAY 4 (July 2003), *available at* http://www.fda.gov/downloads/Drugs/GuidanceComplianceRegulatoryInformation/Guidances/ucm072851.pdf ("Same day patent challenges generally occur when the expiration of 4 years of a 5-year exclusivity period under section 505(j)(5)(D)(ii) permits submission of ANDAs containing a paragraph IV certification as of a specific date, and multiple applicants vie to be first to make such a submission."); *id.* (identifying a separate scenario in which applicants also submit applications on the same date).

139 *See infra* Section 1.3.1.

140 *See, e.g.*, Sharon Begley & Mary Carmichael, *Desperately Seeking Cures; How the Road from Promising Scientific Breakthrough to Real-World Remedy Has Become All but a Dead End*, NEWSWEEK, May 31, 2010, at 38, 39 (arguing that "potential cures, or at least treatments, are stuck in the chasm between a scientific discovery and the doctor's office: what's been called the valley of death"). Begley and Carmichael tell the story of a researcher who has been unable to develop what he believes is a possible cure for osteoporosis because he is unable to obtain a patent. *See id.* at 40.

141 Roin, *supra* note 12, at 567.

each proposed solution is that it would lead to more protection in cases in which that protection is not needed, just as extending the patent term would induce more discoveries but also lead to protection in some cases where it would not be necessary. In addition, the terms might still be too short for some orphan business models.

1.2.2.2 Ceilings on exclusivity based on inputs or success

The problem of unnecessary protection could be combated by placing ceilings on profits earned by drug manufacturers. This strategy has been debated and proposed in the context of the Orphan Drug Act,[142] and it could be adopted in conjunction with a strategy to increase the available protection term. A statistical justification for this approach is that the distribution of sales of approved orphan drugs is highly skewed, with a small number of orphan drugs accounting for a high percentage of overall revenues.[143] A ceiling could thus be set at a relatively high level and would likely affect only a relatively small number of orphan drugs. A similar approach could be used for generic exclusivity under the Hatch-Waxman Act, with the period of generic exclusivity ending after some revenue (or, harder to measure, profit) threshold is reached.

This approach, however, works poorly if the goal is to encourage clinical testing on a drug that has only a small chance of being successful but a large impact if successful. The Orphan Drug Act, after all, is designed to give incentives where there is some probability of failure; if it were certain that a drug would be successful and approved, there would be little need for an expensive approval process. High revenues may indicate that there was more than enough incentive to develop the treatment even absent the Orphan Drug Act, though that conclusion raises the question why no one developed the drug earlier.[144] It may be that the treatment was simply thought to have only a small probability of success, in which case the large revenues in the event of success may be a necessary inducement.

An additional problem is that a revenue limitation amounts to a price control, and the usual drawbacks of price controls apply.[145] Facing an artificially limited profit potential, a manufacturer might not market the drug even if many doctors and patients do not know of its existence, or a manufacturer might decide to cut

142 *See* 136 CONG. REC. H6194 (daily ed. July 31, 1990) (statement of Rep. Stark); *see also* Gary A. Pulsinelli, *The Orphan Drug Act: What's Right with It*, 15 SANTA CLARA COMPUTER & HIGH TECH. L.J. 299, 336 (1999).

143 Sheila R. Shulman and others, *Implementation of the Orphan Drug Act: 1983–1991*, 47 FOOD & DRUG L.J. 363, 379–80 (1992) (noting skewed distribution of sales).

144 There may be an answer: for example, a recent scientific discovery that made a treatment seem more likely to be successful than before. *Cf.* WILLIAM M. LANDES & RICHARD A. POSNER, THE ECONOMIC STRUCTURE OF INTELLECTUAL PROPERTY LAW 304 (2003) (noting that when an exogenous shock occurs, simultaneous invention is common).

145 For a discussion of a past legislative attempt to enact a windfall profit tax on oil, see Eric Kades, *Windfalls*, 108 YALE L.J. 1489, 1546–52 (1999).

back on quality controls to save money.[146] More relevantly from this chapter's perspective, a manufacturer of an orphan drug will only have incentives to seek approval to market the drug to additional groups of the patient population when expected revenues are below the threshold at which exclusivity will be lost. Once the manufacturer is sure to make the maximum amount of money permitted before exclusivity is lost, the problem of orphan business models arises again, as the manufacturer will have no incentive to seek FDA approval for additional patient subpopulations. There are potential solutions: perhaps other manufacturers could be given a chance to seek approval. This, however, would tend to undercut the scope of the Orphan Drug Act's protection more generally, so that the protection would no longer extend to a drug, but only to a particular use of a drug.

Similar critiques apply to proposals that seek to tailor the protection to the amount spent on research and development (or, in the case of Hatch-Waxman, the amount spent on prosecuting an Abbreviated New Drug Application and patent litigation). This expenditure-based limitation is in effect equivalent to setting higher maximum revenue thresholds when a drug manufacturer has invested more in the clinical trial process, and this may be an improvement on a plan to set a fixed threshold. But in focusing on one variable—the expense of the process—this proposal ignores another equally important, but much harder to measure, variable: the probability that efforts will be successful. Meanwhile, if the system is not administered well, it may lead to inefficient expenditures. If, for example, firms are allowed some multiple of what they invest in the clinical trial process, and a pharmaceutical company is confident that it will succeed in clinical trials, it may spend unnecessarily high amounts of money on clinical trials to get a longer exclusivity term.

1.2.2.3 Administrative discretion

An alternative remedy would be for the government to exercise greater discretion, perhaps by offering longer terms when research and development is more expensive or when it seems less likely to succeed. Roin, for example, notes that protection terms "could be tailored in accordance with the varying R&D costs and risks of different drugs."[147] The extent to which this is an improvement depends, of course, on the performance of the agency charged with making these assessments. It is possible, for example, that the agency might systematically err in

146 One commentator sees an analogous effect as potentially beneficial: "A ceiling on the length of exclusivity would induce companies to keep costs down, knowing that at some level the marginal benefit of additional research expenditures will not be reflected in the length of exclusivity." Greenbaum, *supra* note113, at 136.

147 Roin, *supra* note 12, at 568; *see also id.* ("Longer and more expensive clinical trials likely require more protection, whereas shorter and cheaper trials could be motivated by a briefer period of exclusivity."). Roin notes that the FDA is likely to be institutionally more capable than the PTO of making judgments about extending term, and that it is better positioned to prevent unnecessary races to run clinical trials, because it must authorize such trials. *See id.*

one direction, for example by granting longer terms than are necessary. This seems especially plausible if such decisions, like current ones, are made ex parte.[148] Or the agency might err in particular cases, for example by overestimating or underestimating the chance that a particular set of clinical trials would be successful. One potential contributor to misestimation is that the applicant is placed in an odd position: it must argue that its plans have a sufficient chance of success to justify the launching of human trials, but a relatively low chance of success to garner a long protection term.

Another problem is that the FDA may lack institutional competence to make such assessments. Such assessments depend on many empirical considerations, including the cost of testing, the probability of a successful outcome, the level of consumer demand and the potential existence of competing products. A commentator on the Orphan Drug Act notes: "Predicting which drugs will be profitable during the developmental stages is difficult. Using the size of the patient population does not always work."[149] Presumably, the FDA's general reliance on the 200,000 patient threshold reflects its greater comfort in administering tests that require it to make medical determinations rather than economic forecasts. Ideally, the term of orphan drug protection would be variable, but the length of the term would not depend on the caprice of a governmental decisionmaker.

1.3 New approaches to intellectual property protection for orphan business models

The goal of achieving variable terms without government intervention motivates two different potential approaches to providing intellectual property protection for orphan business models. The first approach involves an auction design, with the exclusive right being granted to the company offering the shortest term, but with the initial proponent of protection receiving some advantage as a reward for developing the initial proposal. This approach addresses several structural challenges with the proposals considered above: their tendency to be over- or under-inclusive, the strategic behavior of drug manufacturers, and the limits of government officials in exercising discretion. The second approach involves a bonding mechanism encouraging third parties to assess the probability that a business model would be tested even without protection. The applicant can choose a term without an auction, but has an incentive to choose a relatively short term lest third parties conclude that the business model would be developed anyway within a longer proposed period.

148 Thomas, *supra* note 115, at 437 ("The application for orphan designation is a confidential, ex parte procedure. The FDA gives neither other researchers nor groups interested in the disease notice of pending applications, nor does the FDA grant them an opportunity to present their views on whether the proposed drug deserves orphan status."). Thomas argues that the FDA should make decisions through notice-and-comment procedures. *See id.* at 438–40.

149 Patricia J. Kenney, *supra* note 109, at 675.

1.3.1 Term competition

1.3.1.1 The general mechanism

Providing orphan business model protection to the company willing to accept such protection for the shortest term, as summarized in the introduction,[150] would be straightforward in the pharmaceutical context. The first party willing to adopt an orphan business model in exchange for an exclusive right files an application. Depending on the context, this could be an Orphan Drug Act application or an Abbreviated New Drug Application. The purpose of these applications need not be to give regulators all the information that they would need to allow a new drug onto market. Rather, the applicant would need to establish that the relevant orphan business model is indeed an orphan business model. In the Orphan Drug Act context, this would require a showing that no other manufacturer is marketing the drug or taking it through clinical trials; in the Hatch-Waxman context, the applicant would need to show that no one else has yet challenged the validity of the pioneer drug patent.

The applicant also would specify the protection term that it is requesting. The goal is to eliminate the arbitrary seven-year or 180-day terms specified in the respective acts, so the applicant might be able to request a longer term, though there might still be some statutory maxima (such as 20 years for the Orphan Drug Act and two years for Hatch-Waxman). The applicant also would need to provide some information about itself to demonstrate its preparedness to undertake steps to adopt the business model, for example by demonstrating its financial ability to carry out clinical trials or to undertake the patent litigation. Competitors would then be given some period during which to submit their own proposals to adopt the orphan business model, indicating both the term that they seek and the investments they will make if they receive the right. The original applicant and various competitors might then be allowed to revise their investment proposals based on those of others. The term proposals could be sealed, or applicants might be allowed to view the terms proposed by others and lower their own proposals if they deem it necessary.[151]

The agency's task would then be to choose the best proposal, but to give some incentive to be the first applicant, who must alone bear the cost of filing the original application.[152] One possible implementation, involving relatively little administrative discretion, would be for the agency to consider the proposal for

150 *See supra* p. 12.

151 If sealed bids are used and the government chooses the shortest exclusive right meeting some minimum investment criteria, then the exclusive right granted should be equal to the shortest exclusive term offered among the unsuccessful bidders. The resulting dynamic is akin to a Vickrey auction and ensures that each bidder will bid the shortest exclusive term it can afford. *Cf.* William Vickrey, *Counterspeculation, Auctions, and Competitive Sealed Tenders*, 16 J. FIN. 8, 24 (1961).

152 Preparing an Orphan Drug Act application can be expensive. *See* Buday, *supra* note 111, at 83 ("For sponsors to succeed in gaining designation awards, considerable library and in-house research and documentation, as well as clear, expositive, and enthusiastic replies and answers to the information sought by the FDA are needed.").

the shortest term first, but apply some statutorily specified discount to the first applicant's requested term. So, if the discount were 30 percent and the first applicant requested 10 years and the second applicant requested eight years, the first applicant's application would be considered first. If that applicant demonstrated a sufficient commitment to pursuing the orphan business model—for example, by promising to spend at least a certain amount of money on trials or in the Hatch-Waxman context to hire a qualified law firm—then its application would be accepted. Otherwise, the agency would look to the next application. In an alternative regime, requiring more discretion, the agency would simply consider all applications and choose the best one, allowing the first applicant a substantial, but not mathematically determined, advantage.

If the advantage to the first applicant is measured as a specific percentage or in some other quantifiable way, it would still be possible to design a system that would eliminate the need for the legislature to determine the precise amount measured. The core insight of the auction can be applied recursively. So, for a particular drug, there could first be an auction for the duty to write the proposal, and the winner of that auction would be the party that agrees to write the proposal for drug testing in exchange for the smallest advantage in the second auction. For example, a first-auction bidder who offers to write the proposal if a 10 percent discount would be applied to its bid for an exclusivity term in the second auction would defeat a first-auction bidder who insists on a 20 percent discount, because the 10 percent discount would be less of an advantage than a 20 percent discount. Of course, either the government would then need to initiate the first auction or some smaller advantage would be needed as an incentive for a private party to initiate the auction, but because specifying the drug is likely less work than explaining what testing of that drug is required, less of an inducement, if any, will be necessary. This recursive approach may be more complicated than is necessary, but it helps illustrate the logic underlying the auction proposal.

Nonetheless, the agency will still need to exercise some discretion. (Later, we will consider a decentralized approach that would eliminate the need for governmental discretion.[153]) Specifically, it must determine whether a bid is a serious one. One would not want a bidder to be able to submit a bid for a very short term and hold onto the right as an option to proceed with further development. This is, however, not a new burden; the agency must already ensure that proposals are serious today. Moreover, this is a far simpler task than the task of figuring out the minimum term length needed to induce development.

The agency need merely monitor to assure itself that the bidder is proceeding with implementation. Monitoring need not be complicated. An Orphan Drug Act rights holder would be expected to document that it was proceeding with trials, and a Hatch-Waxman applicant, that it was proceeding with litigation. In any event, the agency need not perform this monitoring itself. Rather, the statute could provide that a new application may be filed by any party when a previous

153 *See infra* Section 1.3.2.

recipient of an exclusive term failed to meet the obligations to which it committed.[154] At that point, the agency could adjudicate in an adversarial proceeding whether the award process should begin anew. Challenging an awardee is an expensive process on which others might free-ride, but the successful challenger would receive the advantage of being a first applicant in the new bidding process if the right were taken away from the initial awardee.

One slight complication for term competition may occur when the scope of the right is potentially ambiguous. In an Orphan Drug Act application, for example, an applicant might seek to adopt only a particular compound or a set of closely related compounds. Allowing relatively broad scope may be justified when clinical testing on one compound produces information about whether a closely related compound will likely also be effective, and it may be important to protect the adopter of the orphan drug from another party's free-riding on the result of clinical trials. But the FDA already faces this problem, when it determines whether a new drug is the "same drug" as one already approved for exclusivity.[155] In theory, the FDA might apply its current definition of sameness to solve this problem and also continue its policy that "if the subsequent drug can be shown to be clinically superior to the first drug, it will not be considered to be the same drug."[156] Often, however, it may be useful to resolve such issues *ex ante*, and the original applicant might be expected to identify any situation in which there might be a case for more expansive scope than is ordinarily permitted, allowing the agency to make an early determination.[157]

An additional complication is the question of what occurs if the agency receives only one (or perhaps even only two) bids. A concern is that there might be insufficient competition for the agency to be confident that it has given away the right at the lowest possible term. An absence of competition is particularly likely if the first applicant is viewed by others as likely to be unbeatable given the statutory advantage that it receives. A rule providing for publication of bids and preventing the first applicant from lowering its bid later in the process would increase agency confidence in competition in the single-bid context. Under this approach, other applicants would presumably enter bids if they thought it possible to undercut the first applicant's bid by a sufficient amount. This structure presents

154 This would require public release of both the initial application and information needed to show compliance.

155 The courts have generally been willing to defer to the FDA on this issue. *See, e.g., Genentech, Inc. v. Bowen*, 676 F. Supp. 301, 313 (D.D.C. 1987) (resolving a dispute, but indicating a willingness to defer to FDA determinations).

156 21 CFR § 316.3(b)(13)(i) (2010).

157 Some commentators have argued that the FDA has not done a good job of adjusting its inquiry to different categories of drugs. Professor Robert Bohrer suggests that the FDA's approach should depend on the type of drug, with that classification driving the breadth of a presumption that other substances will offer no significant clinical advantage and thus cannot be sold until after the orphan drug's exclusivity period is over. *E.g.*, Robert A. Bohrer, *It's the Antigen Stupid: A Risk/Reward Approach to the Problem of Orphan Drug Act Exclusivity for Monoclonal Antibody Therapeutics*, 5 COLUM. SCI. & TECH. L. REV. 1, 4, 20–21 (2003); *see also* Robert A. Bohrer & John T. Prince, *A Tale of Two Proteins: The FDA's Uncertain Interpretation of the Orphan Drug Act*, 12 HARV. J.L. & TECH. 365, 416 (1999).

a disadvantage for the first applicant, but the built-in advantage for the first applicant could still sufficiently incentivize applying first. If this approach is viewed as potentially insufficient to address the concern of uncompetitive auctions, an agency might be given discretion to negotiate with the applicant deemed the best bidder when there are a small number of applications.

1.3.1.2 The unconventionality of the mechanism

The term competition auction is admittedly an unconventional mechanism from the perspective of patent law in at least three ways. But each of these unconventional aspects highlights a significant difference between patents and exclusive rights to adopt orphan business models and thus helps justify the exercise of conceiving of intellectual property rights tailored to those business models. First, assessments are made *before* the occurrence of what the intellectual property system seeks to induce. The patent law system seeks to induce inventions, yet assessments of the requirements of patentability are made *after* the conception of an invention.[158] *Ex ante* forecasts of the effects of granting patent rights are generally infeasible, because it will often be impossible before a process of technological experimentation to conceive of what might be invented. A resulting significant challenge in the patent context is evaluating incentives in hindsight.[159] By contrast, a system of intellectual property protection for orphan business models seeks to induce commercialization, and it is feasible to grant rights well before commercialization will occur. Currently, the Orphan Drug Act permits designations of orphan drug status to be made before completion of clinical investigations,[160] but the ultimate prize of exclusivity is not granted until the completion of clinical trials.[161]

Second, with exclusivity term competition, the party that applies for intellectual property protection is not necessarily the party that ultimately will receive such protection. This unconventional aspect follows directly from the previous one; because the party that files for orphan business model protection need not yet have expended the resources to commercialize the business model, that party need not receive the exclusivity protection. The social benefit is that the system gives competitors incentives to credibly reveal to the government that a long period of protection is not necessary. The original applicant should still receive some advantage in the process, lest there be insufficient incentives to go through the work of applying, as each potential applicant would hope to free-ride on the orphan business model applications of others. The logic underlying this point

158 *See* 35 U.S.C. § 112 (2006) (allowing filing of a patent after conception of the invention to serve as a constructive reduction to practice).

159 *See* Mandel, *supra* note 24, at 76–79 (discussing the hindsight problem in the context of the nonobviousness requirement).

160 21 U.S.C. § 360bb(a)(1) (2006) ("A request for designation of a drug shall be made before the submission of an application. . . .").

161 For a discussion of the effects of orphan drug races, see Patricia J. Kenney, *supra* note 109, at 675–77.

should be familiar: it is the general logic to justify intellectual property protection for orphan business models, with the business model now defined narrowly as the application for protection of another orphan business model.

Third, the term of protection is not fixed, but depends on the competition. This distinctive aspect also is possible as a result of the previous one. The competition among potential owners of the intellectual property right can be expected to create a kind of auction in which the winner is the company that agrees to undertake the relevant expenses for the shortest period of exclusivity.[162] Some patent scholars have proposed a variable term, with duration depending on any of a number of factors.[163] Objections to such proposals are that the decisionmaking process would become intractable and that the government would have too much discretion. Competition for exclusivity terms saves the government from the necessity of making optimal term calculations.

1.3.1.3 Extensions

Could orphan business model protection rights be offered beyond the drug context? There are two possibilities: First, Congress might authorize additional regimes similar to the Orphan Drug Act for specific instances of what otherwise would be orphan business models. Second, Congress might create a full-fledged intellectual property system to offer exclusive rights for adoption of any orphan business models either within a specific domain (such as software) or across domains. The second is not likely to occur, if at all, until more targeted protections can be reformed to establish palpable social benefit and decrease currently extant controversy over false positives. A badly designed system of protection could do far more harm than good. This section seeks to explore how orphan business model rights might be offered in a limited way, potentially not covering some situations in which they might be useful but almost certainly not providing counterproductive protection.

Drug law addresses orphan business models because the stakes are sufficiently high that Congress believed it worthwhile to create a customized property rights protection regime. If Congress is to extend orphan business model protections over the coming decades, it is likely to be only in areas where the stakes seem similarly high. This section identifies some possibilities, though the specific contexts identified are of less significance than the general problems they are meant to illustrate.

162 For a discussion of whether patents might be auctioned in a similar way, see Michael Abramowicz, *The Uneasy Case for Patent Races over Auctions*, 60 STAN. L. REV. 803, 847–49 (2007).

163 *See, e.g.*, Eric E. Johnson, *Calibrating Patent Lifetimes*, 22 SANTA CLARA COMPUTER & HIGH TECH. L.J. 269, 292–93 (2006); Amir H. Khoury, *Differential Patent Terms and the Commercial Capacity of Innovation*, 18 TEX. INTELL. PROP. L.J. 373, 405–12 (2010); Frank Partnoy, *Finance and Patent Length* 27–38 (Univ. San Diego Sch. of Law, Law & Econ. Research Paper No. 19, 2001), *available at* http://papers.ssrn.com/abstract=285144 (2001).

1.3.1.3.1 NONAPPROPRIABLE NETWORK EFFECTS

In the past two decades, the law and economics literature has considered the policy implication of "network effects," specifically where the fact that some people use a particular good or service makes that good or service more valuable to others.[164] For example, computer users may be more likely to choose an operating system that others also choose because of interoperability concerns. Much of the literature addresses the policy challenge of ensuring that such networks do not lead to abuse of monopoly power,[165] though the literature also recognizes that sometimes the existence of network effects means that centralized institutions could promote the development of such networks.[166] Promoting network effects will be most challenging when no private party can appropriate a portion of the benefits of the networks. If Company *A* builds a network with which Company *B* can interoperate, then the orphan business model problem arises. *A* may have insufficient incentives to make risky investments to build a network when competition from *B* will erode profits *A* otherwise would earn.

Consider the following example: the development of battery charging or switching stations for electric cars.[167] A principal challenge facing developers of all-electric cars is the absence of battery stations at which drivers can charge batteries or swap out near-empty batteries for full ones. Customers may have little incentive to buy electric cars in the absence of battery stations, and there may be little incentive to create battery stations until there are a sufficient number of customers. If a company invests in building large numbers of battery stations, it may jumpstart the electric car market, but then other companies may take advantage and open their own battery stations. If creating the network is sufficiently risky—for example, because electric cars may fail to catch on for reasons other than an absence of battery stations—incentives may be too low even though it would be socially beneficial to try.

Theory cannot tell us, however, whether exclusivity is genuinely necessary or even whether it would be helpful. Similar problems have been overcome previously; we do, after all, have gas stations. Perhaps there will be a tipping point at which the development of electric cars becomes inevitable and entrepreneurs begin opening battery stations. Or, battery station owners may find other means

164 *See generally, e.g.*, Amitai Aviram, *Regulation by Networks*, 2003 BYU L. REV. 1179 (2003); David A. Balto, *Networks and Exclusivity: Antitrust Analysis to Promote Network Competition*, 7 GEO. MASON L. REV. 523 (1999); Mark A. Lemley & David McGowan, *Legal Implications of Network Economic Effects*, 86 CAL. L. REV. 479 (1998); S.J. Liebowitz & Stephen E. Margolis, *Network Externality: An Uncommon Tragedy*, J. ECON. PERSP., Spring 1994, at 133.

165 *See, e.g.*, Lemley & McGowan, *supra* note 164, at 496.

166 *See* Bruce H. Kobayashi & Larry E. Ribstein, *Uniformity, Choice of Law and Software Sales*, 8 GEO. MASON L. REV. 261, 287–88 (1999) (noting this possibility but also noting that centralized institutions may not choose the optimal network). A counterargument is that inefficient standards may win a standards race, and collective action problems will prevent a better standard from emerging. *See id.*; Lemley & McGowan, *supra* note 164, at 497–98.

167 *See, e.g.*, Nelson D. Schwartz, *In Denmark, Ambitious Plan for Electric Cars*, N.Y. TIMES, Dec. 2, 2009, at A1 (discussing difficulties in creating a sufficient number of charging stations for electric cars in Denmark).

of ensuring that their investments are appropriable, for example by patenting machines that can change a particular type of battery. Patent law is a crude mechanism for achieving this goal, however. A patent will issue so long as such machines are nonobvious and meet the other requirements of patentability, but the most important investments might be opening battery stations rather than designing the machines. Moreover, if battery station owners are successful in using patent law to make the network effects appropriable, they may enjoy a term that is longer than necessary to induce building the network, and consumers may pay higher prices as a result.

Congress could solve the problem with a system similar to that suggested for the Orphan Drug Act above, but with the goal of creating a single exclusive right.[168] A statute (or regulation) might specify a minimum number of battery stations, which must be opened within a specified period of time, and would identify any characteristics such stations must meet, such as an ability to serve at least a specified number of motorists per day. Private firms would then offer to meet these requirements in exchange for an additional exclusivity period after the specified period of time. This description is, of course, a simplified description of such a regime, which would need to include means of assessing the bidders' ability to meet the promised goals and of assessing progress. But it is similar to familiar regimes of bidding for government contracts, with the exception that the winning bidder receives an exclusivity period instead of government money.

The approach described above suggests that government subsidies will often be an alternative approach to encouraging development of orphan business models, but an advantage of the approach described here is that there is a smaller cost associated with the risk that the government will overestimate the benefits of the network. In a standard government subsidy arrangement, the government might spend US$100 billion to build battery stations, which will be wasted if other impediments prevent the development of the electric car. With the orphan business model approach, private sector judgments can serve as an additional check on the government's positive view of the business model because if private actors expect the battery stations to be a waste, no one will bid. Meanwhile, the framework might allow the winning bidder to back out, for example, after paying some penalty, should the market appear not to be as promising as previously thought. At that point, the government might hold a new auction to find a new company willing to adopt the orphan business model, if such a company exists.

1.3.1.3.2 LONG TIME HORIZONS

An exclusive right of just a few years might someday sufficiently incentivize the building of a network of battery stations, but in other situations even the current

168 Ideally, such a decision might be made at an international level, but it seems unlikely that existing intellectual property coordination systems could easily be harnessed to create a property right quite different from existing ones, at least until such rights become commonplace in individual countries.

20-year length of the patent term may be insufficient to spur needed research and commercialization. Consider, for example, proposals to build machines that would remove carbon dioxide from the air to offset global warming.[169] It is not clear whether such machines could ever be made sufficiently cost-effective to have a significant impact on global warming, making any private research risky. Suppose, however, that against all odds, a company succeeded in developing such a machine. This development would considerably lessen concern about global warming, and governments might retrench on efforts to tax or cap carbon emissions. Unless catastrophe is imminent, they might wait to purchase the carbon removal technology until it enters the public domain. The time between the present and when global warming is expected to cause major problems is likely greater than the length of the patent term,[170] so patent incentives to reverse global warming may be absent.

An orphan business model exclusive adoption right again could be helpful. The government might set a minimum amount of research and development that the recipient of such a right would need to commit to invest as a condition of retaining the right. It would then award the exclusive right to the company willing to engage in this amount of research for the shortest term of exclusivity, even if that term were 50 or 60 years. A risk of this approach, though, is that the government might set the required investment at too low a number, making real progress unlikely, or too high a number, resulting in longer terms than necessary to accomplish the desired result. An alternative is for the government to set the term and grant the right to the company willing to invest the most in research and development. The government should do this, however, only if it is relatively confident that sufficient research and development activity would not occur in the absence of the exclusive rights incentive.

1.3.1.3.3 DEREGULATION AND REREGULATION INCENTIVES

Orphan business models may also merit property rights protection where the principal obstacle to development is that government regulation may impede progress. Take, for example, supersonic jet travel. An obstacle to the development of new supersonic jets is the existence of regulations that prevent supersonic travel over land.[171] To succeed both technologically and legally, the prospective developer of a jet design that would reduce sonic booms[172] must persuade

169 *See, e.g.*, Klaus S. Lackner, *Washing Carbon Out of the Air*, SCI. AM., June 2010, at 66–67.

170 Many of the serious anticipated effects of climate change noted by the Intergovernmental Panel on Climate Change are expected to begin by mid-century. *See, e.g.*, Intergovernmental Panel on Climate Change, *Summary for Policymakers*, in: CLIMATE CHANGE 2007: IMPACTS, ADAPTION AND VULNERABILITY 7, 11–18 (Martin Parry and others eds., 2007), *available at* http://www.ipcc.ch/publications_and_data/publications_ipcc_fourth_assessment_report_wg2_report_impacts_adaptation_and_vulnerability.htm.

171 For a discussion of the origin of such regulation, see John R. Thomas, *The Question Concerning Patent Law and Pioneer Inventions*, 10 HIGH TECH. L.J. 35, 93–94 (1995).

172 *See generally Fixing What Yeager Broke: Reducing Sonic Booms*, NASA (Jan. 28, 2004), http://www.nasa.gov/missions/research/sonic_booms.html (discussing development of sonic boom reduction technology).

Congress or the Federal Aviation Administration to permit certain types of supersonic jet aircraft. The problem is that given such success, other jet designers may invent other forms of sonic boom reduction technology and free-ride on the lobbying efforts of the first manufacturer.

An orphan business model protection scheme might involve an auction of an exclusive right to sell supersonic aircraft, either to the firm that promises to commit at least a specified amount of money to research in exchange for the shortest exclusive right or to the firm that promises to commit to conducting the most research in exchange for a fixed exclusivity period. Congress might create such a scheme as a less drastic step than immediately removing regulatory impediments to supersonic travel. This might make sense if the policy question depends in part on the quality of technology developed, and if there is no easy way *ex ante* to specify minimal technical standards that must be achieved. In creating such a scheme, Congress does not promise deregulation, but it gives some firm an incentive to create a technology that can persuade Congress to ease the regulation.

The example, meanwhile, illustrates a potential hazard of orphan business model protection. It could produce lobbying that is undesirable. The creation of the property right in supersonic travel yields a new special interest. This property right may be desirable as a means of encouraging technology research and avoiding the orphan business model problem that may arise where some firms would like to free-ride on the lobbying of others, for much the same reason that the Orphan Drug Act is effectively an inducement to lobby the FDA to approve a particular drug. But it also can increase the danger of a bad regulatory decision, if lobbyists can persuade the decisionmakers to make such a choice. This is more broadly a danger of any broad property right over orphan business models. Granting broad rights will likely increase incentives for lobbying, and that may or may not be a positive development.[173]

Use of orphan business models protection need not be a one-way ratchet toward deregulation. The same approach could be used to encourage regulation or reregulation. Suppose, for example, that there is insufficient support in Congress for a carbon tax. There might yet be enough support to try to balance lobbying spending on the issue, if anti-tax forces were seen as having a lobbying advantage. Congress might then auction an orphan business model to a firm that promises to spend the most over some period to lobby for the carbon tax. In exchange, the firm would receive a small percentage of the tax, for a period of time determined by the auction, if the effort were successful.

1.3.1.3.4 INDUSTRY-SPECIFIC STATUTORY COMPROMISES

Admittedly, some of the previous examples seem fanciful, and they are intended to be illustrations of the range of potential applications of protections for orphan

173 Lobbying costs arising from rent-seeking opportunities may be inefficient regardless of the success of such lobbying. *See* Gordon Tullock, *The Welfare Costs of Tariffs, Monopolies, and Theft*, 5 W. ECON. J. 224, 228, 231–32 (1967).

business models rather than proposals. Congress would not consider adopting such approaches until the basic framework for giving orphan business model rights became commonplace. The most likely trajectory by which such rights would become commonplace would be for them to emerge in specific industries in response to perceived problems, in much the same way as the Orphan Drug Act emerged. It is possible that greater awareness of the existence of mechanisms for protecting orphan business models could spur regulatory compromises in areas in which intellectual property protection is particularly controversial.

One such area is software. Many observers have complained about software patents, contending that they are an impediment to innovation.[174] But there are enough competing interests that benefit from accumulating software patents that lobbying on the issue may be at a stalemate. It is possible that some software companies' sympathy for software patents may stem more from concerns about protecting market experimentation than from concern about protecting technological experimentation. Microsoft, for example, took a substantial business risk in replacing menu bars with a "ribbon" in its Office software.[175] Patent protection for this user interface may seem a bit silly, because the idea of the ribbon probably would have emerged even absent patent incentives.[176] But Microsoft might not have been willing to introduce the ribbon if it thought that there were a substantial chance of failure and a substantial chance that, in the event of success, competitors would rip off the user interface.[177] The ribbon is really an orphan business model, but it is understandable that Microsoft would protect it with whatever tools are available. Similarly, patent protection likely was not needed for Google's founders to conceive of the core algorithm underlying that company's success, but it may well have been needed to protect Google's investments in building server farms to implement the idea.[178]

Once the possibility of orphan business model protection emerges, there is an alternative to software patents. A possible statutory compromise would be for some weakening of the software patent regime—at least a statutory strengthening of the nonobviousness requirement, and perhaps a decrease in patent term, if not

174 For a summary of one strain of such a criticism, see Ronald J. Mann, *Do Patents Facilitate Financing in the Software Industry?*, 83 TEX. L. REV. 961, 999 (2005).

175 *See, e.g.*, Jack Schofield, *Don't Get Lost on Your Way to the Office: Prepare for the Most Dramatic Changes Ever Made to a Major Suite of Applications, as Microsoft Opts for a New User Interface*, GUARDIAN (London), July 6, 2006, Guardian Technology Pages, at 3. (A disclosure: Microsoft has supported the intellectual property program at the author's law school, including supporting a conference at which this chapter was originally presented as a paper.)

176 For arguments that the patented technology is similar to prior art, see *KDE to sue MS over Ribbon GUI?*, KDE DEVELOPER'S JOURNALS, http://kdedevelopers.org/node/1617 (last visited Feb. 14, 2011).

177 Indeed, Microsoft's strategy has been to license many software developers to use the ribbon, but to refuse such licensing to competitors. *See* Jordan Running, *Microsoft Sets Office's Ribbon UI Not-Quite-Free*, DOWNLOAD SQUAD (Nov. 22, 2006, 2:00 PM), http://www.downloadsquad.com/2006/11/22/microsoft-sets-offices-ribbon-ui-not-quite-free/.

178 For a discussion of how the validity of Google's PageRank patent may be in doubt following recent court decisions, see John F. Duffy, *The Death of Google's Patents?*, PATENTLY-O, http://www.patentlyo.com/patent/law/googlepatents101.pdf (last visited Nov. 12, 2010).

an outright block on new software patents—in exchange for the creation of a system of protection to avoid the problem of orphan business models in software. One reason this compromise may make particular sense in the software context is that the patent term seems absurdly long in an industry where progress is rapid.[179] With competition determining orphan business model terms, the resulting periods of exclusivity would likely be relatively short (perhaps just a couple of years for a significant software innovation), but that might be enough to justify greater risk-taking in software development and thus accelerate improvements in software design without the full costs of software patents.

1.3.2 A bonding mechanism

A regime of orphan business model protection for software would require careful design. One challenge is in determining when any protection is necessary: competition can make protection terms short, but the transaction cost of the system is likely not worthwhile for very short terms. Another challenge is in defining the requirements on the holder of an exclusive right and the scope of protection for such an exclusive right. These details appear relatively straightforward in the context of the Orphan Drug Act. The recipient of protection must take the drug through clinical trials, and then no one else can market the same drug. Even in the context of the Orphan Drug Act, however, there may be ambiguity about the scope of a "drug,"[180] and there may be greater ambiguities of this type if orphan business model protection is applied to a field such as software. Another danger is that a holder of an exclusive right may perform inadequately (crafting software that does not work well), and use its right primarily to extract revenues from anyone else using the right. It may be too much to expect an administrative agency to make sufficiently good decisions on a case-by-case basis to avoid this problem.

It is possible, however, to imagine a decentralized approach to defining the scope of orphan business model protection, enforcing the business model rights, and even determining when such rights should be granted. Such a system could greatly simplify the challenge of creating orphan business model rights in a particular field, such as software, or even across all fields of business. The possibility of such a system highlights that novel forms of intellectual property need novel systems for protection.

One means of implementing a decentralized approach for determining whether an exclusive right should be offered is through a bonding mechanism. For example, a party seeking exclusivity would offer to bet that the proposed business concept will *not* be developed in the time period of the requested exclusive right if no right is given. If no third party accepts the bet, that absence of action

179 *See* Daniel R. Cahoy, *An Incrementalist Approach to Patent Reform Policy*, 9 N.Y.U. J. LEGIS. & PUB. POL'Y 587, 648 & n.254 (2006); Allen Clark Zoracki, *When Is an Algorithm Invented? The Need for a New Paradigm for Evaluating an Algorithm for Intellectual Property Protection*, 15 ALB. L.J. SCI. & TECH. 579, 594–95 (2005).

180 *See supra* note 158.

establishes a presumption that the right should be granted to the applicant. If a third party does accept the bet, then there ordinarily would be no exclusive right, and the resolution of the bet would depend on whether a firm—either the firm originally requesting exclusivity or another—implements the specified business concept. This system provides incentives for the prospective rights-holders to specify the scope and terms of the intellectual property protection, preventing a prospective rights-holder from including within the scope of the business model a business that likely would have been created anyway.

In a minimalist "first step scenario," the odds for such a mechanism could be set to make false positives (unnecessary protection) extremely unlikely.[181] Thus, if Congress were to consider extending protection for orphan business models, either in the software industry or in other areas, it could ensure that the only rights initially granted would be those for which the case for protection is especially strong. Over time, the mechanism could evolve in ways that would tolerate some false positives in exchange for additional market experimentation. In addition, a possible extension of the mechanism would limit rights to situations in which bonding transactions reveal that the right is likely to lead to a sufficiently large increase in the probability that the business will in fact be developed. Under this proposal, an initial system with only very modest, but almost certainly positive, effects within a given area could be gradually changed into a more economically significant new intellectual property regime. Section 1.3.2.1 elaborates the mechanism that can serve as the first step scenario, and Section 1.3.2.2 explains how protection might be expanded if the initial experiment proves successful.

1.3.2.1 First step scenario: a bonding mechanism

To apply for intellectual property protection for market experimentation, an entrepreneur would first delineate the property right, describing the market experiment to be performed and selecting a term of years over which the right would run. The description would specify the nature of the market experiment, and the application might limit the proposed protection, for example, by specifying a minimum scale for the proposed business or other aspects of how the business would operate. The entrepreneur would then deposit the application with a government agency, paying a deposit (say, US$10,000, although the required deposit might usefully vary depending on the proposed scale of the market experiment). The agency in turn would make the application publicly available on the Internet. Any private third party would be allowed to reject the market

181 The mechanism would also have the socially beneficial effect of generating rigorous information about the degree to which free competition discourages entrepreneurial entry. Such empirical information is currently nonexistent because it is impossible to point to the businesses that would have been launched but that never were. The system described here would reveal this information in cases in which a right seeker was thwarted from obtaining an exclusive right because some third party bet that the marketplace would produce the relevant market experimentation. If the third party ultimately loses that bet, then society would have good evidence that an exclusive rights system would have been superior in encouraging entrepreneurial entry.

experiment by placing a separate deposit with the government agency.[182] At least in the initial experiment, this deposit should be considerably lower (say, US$1000) than that paid by the entrepreneur.

If no third party rejects the property right, then the property right would be granted to the applicant, and it would be published on the Internet as an accepted application. The recipient of the right would then be able to enforce it against third-party infringers. While the precise contours of this enforcement regime could be debated, at least the right-holder would be able to receive damages for any infringement.[183] As with any intellectual property regime, the enforcement mechanism will be somewhat costly. If the property right is poorly drafted, or if it is well drafted but nonetheless includes some vague or ambiguous provisions, expensive litigation to determine the scope of the property right may result. But the original applicant will at least have an incentive to draft the property right sufficiently clearly to avoid expensive litigation.[184] To reduce the danger that this intellectual property regime might impose costs on innocent third parties, it might be appropriate in the initial experiment to impose a one-way fee-shifting rule, requiring the rights-holder to pay the attorneys' fees of the challenging party if that party prevails.

If, on the other hand, a third party rejects the property right by tendering a deposit, then no property right would be granted. The fate of the deposits would then depend on whether the market experiment occurs nonetheless in a way that matches the parameters of the rejected property right in the specified time frame.

182 The advantage of a higher deposit is that it provides additional incentives for third parties to investigate carefully the possibility of placing deposits to cancel the property right. There is at least a strong case for allowing the party placing a deposit to offer more than the minimum, with the required deposits of third parties rising proportionately. If a proposed market experiment would be conducted in any event, a larger deposit increases the probability that a third party will be willing to challenge the proposed property right. But if the entrepreneur is correct in its confidence that the property right is necessary to justify the experiment, a larger deposit should improve the analysis of potential challengers and thus decrease the probability of a challenge.

183 A significant question would be whether the holder of the intellectual property right would also be able to obtain injunctive relief. A tentative conclusion is that injunctive relief should generally be appropriate in such cases. In patent cases, an argument against injunctive relief is that a patented technology may be bundled with many other technologies in an infringing product, and the patentee therefore may be able to extract value beyond that of the patented technology with the threat of an injunction. *See eBay Inc. v. MercExchange*, L.L.C., 547 U.S. 388, 396–97 (2006) (Kennedy, J., concurring) ("When the patented invention is but a small component of the product the companies seek to produce and the threat of an injunction is employed simply for undue leverage in negotiations, legal damages may well be sufficient to compensate for the infringement and an injunction may not serve the public interest."). Whatever the validity of this argument, it seems less likely to be applicable in the case of market experimentation. Allowing injunctive relief can ensure that infringers cannot take advantage of situations in which courts might be expected to undervalue damages.

184 A counterargument is that the original applicant will draft a vague property right in the hope that this will discourage suit by increasing the threat of litigation costs. The possibility of settlement, however, weakens this counterargument. The phenomenon of "strike suits," in which plaintiffs file weak cases in the hope of extracting settlements, suggests that defendants will have incentives to demarcate property boundaries relatively clearly. *See generally* Robert G. Bone, *Modeling Frivolous Suits*, 145 U. PA. L. REV. 519 (1997) (discussing plaintiff incentives to engage in frivolous litigation).

If the market experiment occurs despite the absence of the property right, then the deposits (plus any interest accrued) would be awarded to the third party; if it does not, then the deposits would be awarded to the original applicant. As with patent claims, there may be difficult questions of interpretation, though as noted above, the original applicant will have an incentive to draft a clear application to reduce the possibility of litigation. A drawback is that any litigation may necessarily involve third parties, who could be required to answer subpoenas about the extent of their business practices. This spillover cost too could be reduced, for example, by requiring compensation of third parties for their time, and placing any trade secrets produced during the litigation under seal.[185]

The intuition behind the system is simple. If there is even a small probability (given the deposits suggested above, at least a 1 in 11 chance) that the market experimentation described will occur over the time frame, then a third party will have an incentive to tender a deposit and reject an application, in effect entering into a bet with the property rights applicant.[186] Anticipating this bet, the prospective entrepreneur will not apply in the first place. There is a danger that third parties sometimes might reject applications without adequate warrant. That is by design, however, because we are more concerned in the initial implementation of this system with avoiding false positives (inefficient grants of rights) than false negatives (inefficient rejections of rights). If no third party is willing to tender a deposit on such attractive terms, that provides a strong indication that no market experiment is likely to take place in the absence of an intellectual property right. Given the stakes, some private parties would presumably go into the business of evaluating applications, so there should be no shortage of potential challengers. When a right is granted, there is thus little risk that it will merely enhance the profits of an entrepreneur who would have entered the market in any event.

After a third party rejects an application by tendering a deposit, both the original entrepreneur and the third-party challenger remain free themselves to initiate the market experiment. These rules will make seeking an application somewhat less attractive, further reducing the costs of false positives. When the original entrepreneur engages in the market experimentation despite a rejection, the bonding system has worked effectively. In this case, the entrepreneur does not really need the intellectual property incentive to create the market experimentation; the entrepreneur will enter the market even without a right, and even though the entry entails forfeiture of the deposit to the third party. Meanwhile, the prospective entrepreneur's deposit serves as a subsidy to anyone else who might be considering entering the market. A third party that places a bet that the

185 Trade secrets are not absolutely privileged in the course of litigation, but a party can seek a protective order from discovery pursuant to FED. R. CIV. P. 26(c)(1)(G). A protective order may require "that a trade secret or other confidential research, development, or commercial information not be revealed or be revealed only in a specified way." FED. R. CIV. P. 26(c)(1)(G); *see also E. I. Du Pont De Nemours Powder Co. v. Masland*, 244 U.S. 100, 103 (1917) (recognizing the trial judge's discretion to determine to whom trade secrets should be revealed).

186 Note that 1/11 * US$10,000 = 10/11 * US$1000, so at that probability, total expected winnings equal total expected losses. Of course, this analysis ignores transaction costs for simplicity.

market experimentation will occur can be sure of winning that bet by entering. The regime thus has the potential to encourage market experimentation even in cases where an application is rejected.[187]

Not every entrepreneur is likely to seek a business model adoption protection right. In addition to the cost associated with the danger of losing the bond, there are two other costs: first, the legal expenses of filing the application and, second, any loss of trade secrecy from filing the application. With respect to the first, potential litigation costs will likely be lower than those associated with patents, because there is no need to meet legal hurdles such as nonobviousness. Still, entrepreneurs would presumably benefit from experienced counsel in determining how broadly to define a right and from business consultants in anticipating whether third parties are likely to challenge the application. The loss of trade secrecy, meanwhile, will mean that some will forego the opportunity to receive a business model adoption right because of the possibility that others will be able to bring the idea to market even earlier. This situation is most likely to occur if the business model is rejected, though publication also might give competitors a head start even when a short period of exclusivity is granted. Entrepreneurs, of course, are put to a similar choice between trade secrecy and patent protection. In any event, the potential loss of trade secrecy is likely to be a minor consideration in the cases where business model protection is most necessary: those where the business model is easily reverse-engineered and there will be inadequate incentives to try the business model without exclusivity.

In some instances, an entrepreneur might first try to obtain a broad property right, and failing that, apply again with narrower claims and a new deposit. An entrepreneur also might reapply with the same application if the entrepreneur believes that the third party's rejection was erroneous; the third party would then have to decide whether to reject the application again and bet that the market experiment will occur in any event. One advantage of the possibility of such repeated filing is that it decreases the chance that a third party will repeatedly reject an application for reasons other than seeking to obtain the entrepreneur's deposit. For example, the third party might worry that the entrepreneur's business model will challenge the third party's own business model. It may be feasible to reject an application for reasons such as this once or twice, but a competitor is unlikely to be willing to take on repeated bets unless the competitor is confident that business model protection is unnecessary. A social advantage of the system of repeated filing is that it allows an entrepreneur to take advantage of market feedback to refine a proposal for exclusivity.

In this system, then, a prospective entrepreneur has the incentive to draft the proposed property right as broadly as possible, but not so broadly that a third

187 In a limited subset of cases, this regime could discourage market experimentation. An entrepreneur who would have engaged in a market experiment in the absence of the system might decide, once the property right is rejected, not to engage in the experiment in the hope of winning the bet instead. In the few cases in which the deposits would be as large as the expected profits, the market experiment is unlikely to be worthwhile in any event.

party will reject the application. For example, imagine that this regime had existed some years ago and Netflix had sought protection for its software-based DVD rental business.[188] Had it sought a right on all DVD-by-mail sales, someone surely would have taken up the challenge, because there was a high *ex ante* probability that at least one small business would rent DVDs by mail somewhere in the United States. So Netflix might instead have limited its proposal by carefully elaborating a set of features that any software would need to have, including queues and the availability of different plans under which customers could rent different numbers of movies, for example. At least as importantly, Netflix might have narrowed its right by focusing on large businesses, such as those renting at least a million DVDs a year or those spending at least US$10 million a year on marketing. Such limitations should be permissible. An orphan business model protection scheme should seek not only to encourage someone to try a business model in a particular way, but also to encourage a firm to try a particular business model on a large scale. An experiment on a small scale, after all, might tell us little about the feasibility of operating the business on a large scale. Such a limitation would entail a concession that smaller entities could compete against it, but could have protected Netflix from major competitors such as Blockbuster and Wal-Mart.

A principal difference between this proposal and others requiring competition is that in this proposal, the initial applicant receives the right; there need not be an auction of the right to the party who agrees to the shortest possible enforcement term. What makes it possible to dispense with the auction is that there is an alternative incentive system that should ensure appropriate length terms. An applicant will not want to seek a term so long that someone else will be able to adopt the orphan business model in the interim, leading a challenger to reject the right. Thus, third parties continue to constrain the length of exclusivity terms, but in a different way. To be sure, it would be possible to have some type of auction of the right, but this new mechanism has a significant advantage over an auction: it reduces the informational demands on an administrative agency overseeing the process. Under this regime, the agency is required neither to make its own assessment regarding the need for or scope of protection, nor to determine what constitutes sufficient exercise of the exclusive right. With the simple term auction, the agency must guard against the possibility that bidders will bid very short protection terms and then not vigorously adopt the orphan business model. Lowball bidding and neglect of adopted orphan business models will be of much less concern under the bonding mechanism proposal, because the initial applicant will seek the longest term that it thinks it will be able to obtain.

It is still possible, though, that some recipients of orphan business model rights will not engage in market experimentation. Suppose that it is highly unlikely that it will make sense for anyone to enter a market in the next 10 years, but that there is a small chance (say, one in 20) that demand conditions will change in a way that will make entry obviously advisable. If the market is sufficiently large, then it

188 For an explanation of why Netflix would have been a strong candidate for orphan business method protection, see Abramowicz & Duffy, *supra* note 12, at 366–71.

might be worthwhile to secure the intellectual property right just in case demand conditions evolve in this way. Warehousing of market experimentation intellectual property rights could mean that some rights will protect entry that might have occurred even in the absence of the issuance of the right. This outcome is not necessarily inefficient—perhaps entry will occur somewhat earlier as a result of the property right, and even in such cases the probability of entry may rise—but this situation is undesirable if the principal goal of an initial regime is to avoid false positives.

There is, however, a simple solution to this problem. The regime can be flipped so that a third party is also allowed to challenge a claim that entry will occur if the intellectual property right is granted. If no one rejects the application on the ground that entry would occur anyway, then a third party would be permitted to tender a deposit (once again, perhaps just US$1000) on the prediction that entry will not occur despite the grant of the right. This action produces a choice for the applicant: the applicant can withdraw the application, in which case the deposits are awarded to the third party, or the applicant can tender another deposit (say, US$1000 again) to keep the intellectual property right. When this step occurs, the process can repeat recursively, with further third-party challenges and further deposits. If, however, this process ends with an unchallenged deposit by the applicant, then the intellectual property right is auctioned. All challenges are then resolved based on whether the recipient of the right in fact carries out the proposed market experiment.

Under this system, the probability that the applicant will follow through and perform the market experiment must be very high (at least about a nine in 10 chance) if the applicant hopes to receive the intellectual property right. If the recipient of the right does not seem very likely to follow through, there should be no shortage of third parties willing to challenge the applicant, especially with such favorable odds on the challenger's side. An applicant hoping simply to warehouse intellectual property rights in the unlikely event that they should become useful will be unable to withstand these challenges. At some point, the total amount deposited will begin to approach the expected benefits of the intellectual property right, and the amount deposited will be lost if the market conditions do not change in ways that would make entry worthwhile. The challenges themselves provide additional incentive for the third party to engage in the market experiment, thus further promoting the goal of market experimentation. If those who are unwilling to take on risk end up subsidizing those who genuinely wish to embark on risky experiments, so much the better.

1.3.2.2 Potential improvements to the bonding mechanism

This proposal entails little risk. It covers only orphan business models that are highly unlikely to be adopted in the absence of protection and that are highly likely to be adopted with protection. More traditional approaches to intellectual property reform cannot make such promises, because no matter what legal standard applies, there are empirical uncertainties about how administrative officials will interpret the established standard. If this proposal is to be criticized, it should be criticized for providing too little reward. With the specifications provided here, perhaps too few market experiments will be covered, in which case the apparatus devoted to the system might not be worthwhile.

One answer to this criticism is that the proposal could easily be adapted to cover the next best set of proposed market experiments. If the applicant need deposit only a smaller amount of money, or if third-party challengers must deposit a larger amount, then a greater number of proposals will be accepted. One useful aspect of this decentralized system is that transitions can easily be controlled. A legislature[189] need only change the applicable numbers; it need not merely choose among vague verbal formulations. Depending on the experience with the initial proposal, it should be straightforward to change the approach so that some applications are accepted even when there is a nontrivial probability that intellectual property protection is not necessary or that intellectual property protection will be insufficient to prompt any actual experimentation. Empirical analysis to determine the optimal numbers will not be easy, and there will be some danger that the legislature will grant excessive protection. This risk provides perhaps the strongest argument against this mechanism and the best reason for waiting to adopt the mechanism until the benefits from doing so in a particular field seem especially high.

Experience might also lead to development of structurally different approaches to decentralized assessment of the need for intellectual property protection. One possibility is that conditional prediction markets might be used to assess the probabilities that entry will occur with and without the grant of intellectual property protection.[190] A burgeoning literature shows that prediction markets can serve as useful tools for making probabilistic assessments,[191] and that such markets may not be easily manipulated by private parties.[192] Other market mechanisms, such as Professor Michael Kremer's proposed auctions to facilitate government buyouts of intellectual property rights,[193] could also be combined with this system, so that the government generally would be subsidizing market experimentation with dollars instead of with exclusive rights. Assessments of prediction markets and Kremer's proposal are beyond the scope of this discussion, but the proposal

189 The system could be implemented by a state legislature for local experiments as well as by a national legislature.

190 For a discussion of conditional prediction markets, see Michael Abramowicz & M. Todd Henderson, *Prediction Markets for Corporate Governance*, 82 NOTRE DAME L. REV. 1343, 1353–54 (2007).

191 *See, e.g.*, MICHAEL ABRAMOWICZ, PREDICTOCRACY: MARKET MECHANISMS FOR PUBLIC AND PRIVATE DECISION MAKING (2007); INFORMATION MARKETS: A NEW WAY OF MAKING DECISIONS (Robert W. Hahn & Paul C. Tetlock eds., 2006).

192 *See, e.g.*, Robin Hanson and others, *Information Aggregation and Manipulation in an Experimental Market*, 60 J. ECON. BEHAV. & ORG. 449 (2006); Paul W. Rhode & Koleman S. Strumpf, Manipulating Political Stock Markets: A Field Experiment and a Century of Observational Data (June 2008) (unpublished manuscript) (on file with the Harvard Law School Library), *available at* http://www.unc.edu/~cigar/papers/ManipIHT_June 2008(KS).pdf.

193 See Michael Kremer, *Patent Buyouts: A Mechanism for Encouraging Innovation*, 113 Q.J. ECON. 1137, 1146–48 (1998).

here is not intended as an insistence on a particular means of effecting a decentralized approach to the issuance of intellectual property rights for market experimentation. The goal here is to illustrate the feasibility of such a system, not to conclusively identify the optimal system.

1.3.2.3 Further applications: beyond conventional business models

If a general *sui generis* regime for orphan business model protection or a number of targeted regimes ever developed, questions would arise about contexts that ordinarily might not be conceived as involving orphan business models, yet where similar dynamics are present and where exclusive rights in theory could advance efficiency. This section offers preliminary consideration of two such contexts: scientific research and legal experimentation. Although in both cases it is possible to imagine relying on a version of term competition, this choice would necessitate a fair degree of governmental discretion in determining the scope of the applicable rights,[194] and these proposals would be more feasible if a general system for protecting orphan business models developed.

1.3.2.3.1 SCIENTIFIC RESEARCH

It may seem odd to apply the orphan problem to research, because patent law already provides incentives to conduct scientific research. Indeed, the premise of this chapter is that intellectual property law should focus not only on encouraging technological experimentation, but also on encouraging market experimentation. Yet conducting scientific research in a given area is itself a business model, and some free-riding is inevitable even given the existence of patent protection. Suppose, for example, that a drug company is considering research into a particular metabolic pathway specific to a disease. Assume that it seems unlikely but possible that such research ultimately could lead to the development of effective treatments. There are two dangers. First, a drug company may worry that if it makes some preliminary unexpectedly positive research findings, it will be unable to keep those secret, and other drug companies will begin exploring the same pathway. Second, the company may worry that even if it finds a successful drug, further research into the molecule that the drug targets will produce many other drugs, thus reducing the company's market share. As a result, the company—and indeed, all drug companies—may decide that research on that pathway is not yet cost-justified. Perhaps it will be someday, once society is rich enough to pay more for the drug or once new tools reduce the cost of research. Yet such research may be socially worthwhile right away, and it might be privately worthwhile as well if it were possible to prevent free-riding on research successes.

194 Indeed, concerns about governmental discretion help explain why the patent system is likely to be superior to a system of governmentally decreed auctions of intellectual property rights. See Abramowicz, *supra* note 162.

Patent law scholars might ask whether the patent term should be made longer or the patent scope made broader. These suggestions, however, are crude solutions with costs potentially larger than the benefit of accelerated research. The proposals developed above provide alternative antidotes with potentially smaller costs. In a decentralized regime like that described here, an exclusive right might be awarded only if third parties are confident both that no drug targeting the pathway would otherwise be developed during the exclusive right and that granting the exclusive right considerably increases the probability that such a drug will be developed. A firm that receives the exclusive right to conduct research ultimately would seek patents on any drugs developed. The orphan right is to the business model of conducting research in the area, and this right can complement patent rights in drugs that are developed.

Orphan business model adoption rights are thus responsive to a problem addressed in the patent literature: that patent races can be needlessly duplicative and that research competition can thus create inefficient rent dissipation.[195] Professor John Duffy has shown that the prospect of such rent dissipation will generally delay innovation.[196] Duffy argues that when a long, drawn-out patent race is expected, the patent race will begin *later* than it otherwise would. Early grants of exclusive rights are thus justified as a means of assuring patent racers that their losses will be relatively limited, thereby stimulating early patent racing at the cost of less ex post competition. Thus, Duffy's article is a defense of the patent prospect theory claim that patents should be rewarded relatively early.[197] But early grants of exclusive rights are not a complete solution, particularly if the patent system will issue patents only to those inventors who have made substantial contributions. There will often still remain a period of time in which no one will bother racing, even though research would be socially beneficial. A number of companies may each recognize that if it were worthwhile for it to race, it will also be worthwhile to several other companies. Thus, the patent race will not begin until each potential racer recognizes that the anticipated rewards of a patent are sufficiently great that the risk of wasted research-and-development expenses from a lost patent race is worth bearing.

Before this point, research might be worthwhile only if a company could be assured it would be the only racer. The grant of exclusive research rights even for short periods of time, such as two or three years, might then accelerate research. If the only way to generate research during a time period is to grant exclusivity, there is little loss from granting such exclusivity. An interesting aspect of this application of orphan business model protection is that it does not rely on the prospect of free-riding on information. Concerns about rent-dissipating simultaneous development of information can also generate a case for orphan business model

195 *See, e.g.*, Michael Abramowicz, *Perfecting Patent Prizes*, 56 VAND. L. REV. 115, 181–93 (2003) (discussing how the patent system may entail a common pool problem).

196 See John F. Duffy, *Rethinking the Prospect Theory of Patents*, 71 U. CHI. L. REV. 439, 469–475 (2004).

197 *Id.* at 443; *see also* Kitch, *supra* note 14 (introducing the patent prospect theory).

protection. CVS and Walgreen's, for example, may each delay entry into any given market for some period because of a concern that the other may enter the market simultaneously. Entry becomes justified only once the anticipated returns are sufficiently great to compensate for the possible redundancy. Orphan business model protection could thus in theory lead to earlier entry of stores. The most relevant questions in assessing whether such protection is justified are empirical ones about whether an agency or a decentralized bonding regime can make sufficiently accurate assessments about the prospects of research in particular areas and about the size of transaction costs from administration of such a system.

1.3.2.3.2 LEGAL INNOVATION

Ordinarily, orphan business models are potential businesses that might be created by private sector firms, but in principle legal regimes that provide exclusivity to encourage adoption of orphaned ideas and inventions also could be used to foster public sector innovation. This is obvious where public entities compete with private entities. A public university, for example, in principle should be able to receive exclusivity if it conducts the clinical testing demanded by the Orphan Drug Act. Exclusivity should also be available where legal goods are provided entirely by multiple public entities. Indeed, many governmental programs can be analogized to business models, with the caveat that the government is a nonprofit entity rather than a for-profit entity. Just because an entity is nonprofit does not mean that it maximizes social welfare,[198] so free-riding on information from legal experiments can pose much the same problem as free-riding on information from market experiments.[199] The concept of free-riding may seem alien in the legal experimentation context, but legal experimentation, like market experimentation, can generate useful information that others may seek to appropriate, and the possibility of licensing revenues could improve incentives to be the first innovator.

For example, suppose that health care were provided entirely by states, and that it appears that there is a 10 percent chance that paying nurses to telephone chronic care patients regularly with reminders would decrease overall medical costs, but a 90 percent chance that such a program would increase costs with no attendant health benefits.[200] This experiment might be socially worthwhile, because if it were successful, many states could benefit from that information. But any given state might have little incentive to take the risk. A state might be more willing to do so if for some period of time it had an exclusive right, under federal law, to license the program to other states. A federal agency committed to health care

198 State officials, for example, may care more about that state's citizens than about citizens of other states.

199 See Rose-Ackerman, *supra* note 17, at 594.

200 This example is chosen because it was recently the subject of a federal Medicare experiment. See Nancy McCall and others, Centers for Medicare & Medicaid Services, Evaluation of Phase 1 of Medicare Health Support (Formerly Voluntary Chronic Care Improvement) Pilot Program Under Traditional Fee-for-Service Medicare 12 (2007).

innovation might auction the exclusive licensing right to the state that agrees to undertake the experiment in exchange for the shortest period of exclusivity.

This example involves experimentation in an area in which governments are acting as market participants, performing services that private sector actors could perform. But it is also possible to imagine exclusive rights for innovations in areas in which the government is not acting as a market participant, at least as market participation is conventionally conceived. For example, we might imagine exclusivity rights being granted to a state that experiments with a new form of policing, that replaces jail terms for drug possession with treatment programs, that tries a new approach to education, that implements a set of civil procedure reforms, that implements a new set of corporate governance rules, and so on. Innovation exists in all these areas, but the overall level is likely to be inefficiently low and states are unlikely to experiment with dramatic reforms, in part because they do not internalize the benefits of such experimentation. The result is that we do not have as much empirical data about the effects of legal innovations as we otherwise would. Exclusivity could increase both incentives for experimentation and incentives for conducting such experimentation in a way that would maximize its informational value.[201]

That possibility does not mean that the case for rewarding legal experimentation with exclusive rights is the same as the case for rewarding market experimentation. Using orphan business model protection to increase legal experimentation raises a number of questions specific to legal innovation. For example, could the federal government insist that a state copying another state's innovation pay a licensing fee?[202] Will state actors be as motivated by financial incentives as private actors to undertake experiments and to copy successful ones? Can the success of legal experiments be judged as easily as the success of market experiments? Is it better for the federal government to encourage experimentation by paying states that agree to undertake pilot programs? Should exclusive rights be given to private firms instead of states, with the private firms then having incentives to enter into contracts with governments willing to engage in experimentation?

Answers to these questions are beyond this chapter's scope, and the existence of these questions suggests that careful design would be needed to import a scheme of orphan business model protection to a legal context. The failure of legal scholarship to consider the possibility of granting exclusive rights to legal innovators, however, highlights that the orphan business model problem in general is undertheorized—assumed to be present only in specific exceptional contexts, such as orphan drugs, rather than pervasive in the legal system. A literature does exist on the permissibility of patents for *private* innovations in legal contexts,

201 For example, states might wish to conduct randomized experiments to better isolate the effects of a legal change. *See generally* Michael Abramowicz and others, *Randomizing Law*, 159–4 U. PA. L. REV. 929–1005 (Jan. 1, 2011).

202 *Cf. Fla. Prepaid Postsecondary Educ. Expense Bd. v. Coll. Sav. Bank*, 527 U.S. 634, 646–47 (1999) (finding a state patent defendant protected by sovereign immunity).

such as novel tax strategies, litigation positions, or poison pills.[203] But the legal literature does not appear to consider protection of innovations in law itself. Perhaps this is because the normative case for incentivizing new ideas for legal innovation is weak, given the surfeit of ideas in law reviews and elsewhere. It is experimentation itself that is lacking, and intellectual property theorists have generally assumed that promoting nontechnological experiments is outside the concerns of intellectual property.

1.4 Conclusion

The absence of robust intellectual property frameworks for protecting orphan business models suggests, under the Demsetz framework, that either the benefits of providing such protection are smaller than the benefits of providing existing forms of intellectual property protection such as patent and copyright, or that the costs of providing the protection are larger. Even so, some level of social inefficiency likely occurs as a result of orphan business models, and yet the absence of past scholarly attention to this potential category of intellectual property has prevented policymakers from viewing seemingly unrelated problems in a unified policy framework. The goal of this chapter is to provide such a framework, not to advocate a rush to create a new form of intellectual property prematurely. This framework shows that existing systems of orphan business model protection in the pharmaceutical context could be made more efficient. Perhaps someday such improvements might evolve into additional or broader protections for orphan business models. With careful design, the risks of this new form of protection can be reduced, and at least some drawbacks of existing property rights protection schemes, such as patent law, can be avoided.

203 *See, e.g.*, Andrew A. Schwartz, *The Patent Office Meets the Poison Pill: Why Legal Methods Cannot Be Patented*, 20 HARV. J.L. & TECH. 333 (2007).

2 Law as product and byproduct

*Bruce H. Kobayashi and Larry E. Ribstein**

2.1 Introduction

Lawmaking generally has been considered the province of government agents subject to political control. At the same time, policymakers and scholars long have recognized the potential shortcomings of government-enacted laws. Powerful interest groups may successfully promote laws opposed by—or block laws favored by—society in general. Also, public lawmakers have weak incentives to produce socially valuable legal innovations, in part because they share little of the public benefits of producing laws.[1] Thus, public lawmaking can simultaneously underproduce desirable laws and overproduce undesirable ones. This chapter considers whether, and under what conditions, private lawmaking can usefully fill gaps in and substitute for publicly produced laws—particularly those laws that enhance private ordering.

Laws that assist private ordering might seem less important than public regulatory and criminal law because of the ubiquitous role played by private contracts in filling gaps in the former, but not the latter, setting. However, innovative statutory standard forms that provide expanded sets of default rules for contracts can add significant social value by reducing errors in formulating contracts that cause ambiguity and reduce predictability.[2] This is particularly

* Professor of Law, George Mason University School of Law and Mildred van Voorhis Jones Chair in Law, University of Illinois College of Law. The authors acknowledge very helpful comments from Robert Ahdieh, Omri Ben-Shahar, Bob Bone, Robert Cooter, Mark Grady, Gillian Hadfield, Erin O'Hara O'Connor, Mark Patterson, Eric Talley, Andrew Verstein, as well as from participants at the George Washington University School of Law program, "Financing Innovation: Our Economic Future"; a Berkeley Law and Economics Workshop; the International Society of New Institutional Economics 2011 Annual Conference; Midwest Law & Economics Association 2011 Annual Meeting; Conference on Regulatory Competition in Contract Law and Dispute Resolution, Munich, Germany; Washington University School of Law Advanced Corporate Law Colloquium; Fordham University School of Law, and Yale Law School's Wasserman Workshop in Law and Finance.

1 Gillian Hadfield & Eric Talley, *On Public vs. Private Provision of Corporate Law*, 22 J. L. ECON & ORG. 414, 439 (2006).

2 See Charles J. Goetz & Robert E. Scott, "The Limits of Expanded Choice: An Analysis of the Interactions Between Express and Implied Contract Terms," 73 CAL. L. REV. 261, 263 (1985); Bruce H. Kobayashi & Larry E. Ribstein, 'Private Lawdrafting, Intellectual Property, and Public Laws,' in REGULATORY COMPETITION IN CONTRACT LAW AND DISPUTE RESOLUTION,

important in long-term, open-ended relationships like business associations, which call for complex governance structures that can enable the parties to adjust to future unknowable circumstances.[3] Standard forms are also useful in clarifying the effect of contracts on parties whose express agreement is costly to obtain, informing the world at large of contract terms, and providing the basis for interpretive case law and privately provided forms.[4]

Since innovative statutory standard forms can reduce costs and add value to private transactions, it is critical to have an adequate and appropriate supply of such forms. Yet, if public lawdrafters have weak and misaligned incentives to innovate, they may miss opportunities to provide useful clarity and certainty for firms by failing to produce the right number and types of statutory standard forms for business relationships. For example, if left to public lawmakers, standard forms may lag behind new technologies and business methods, and therefore become misaligned with prevailing contracting practices. This may, in turn, stall the development of private contracting, as parties must balance the benefits of innovation against the costs of misalignment with prevailing law.

Given the problems of lawmaking by government and the need for such laws to support private ordering, it is worth exploring the potential for private alternatives to government-drafted laws. Private lawmakers could have stronger and better aligned incentives to produce efficient laws than do public legislators.[5] Thus, private lawmaking can be a potential solution to both the under-production and the malproduction of law. Enhancing private lawmaking, therefore, could be the type of systemic change that stimulates growth by encouraging welfare-enhancing laws.[6]

Indeed, private parties such as lawyers already draft and promote laws for adoption by legislatures. However, such private lawmaking can exaggerate the public choice problems of public lawmaking by directly promoting laws that do not reflect the preferences of society.[7] Moreover, even in the absence of direct

Horst Eidenmüller ed., Hart Publishing (2013), working paper version *available at* http://ssrn.com/abstract=1986455.

3 Larry E. Ribstein, *Statutory Forms for Closely Held Firms: Theories and Evidence from LLCs*, 73 WASH. U. L. Q. 369, 375–76 (1995) (noting particularly the value of standard forms in filling in end-period terms).

4 *Id.*

5 *See* Hadfield & Talley, *supra* note 1, at 417–19.

6 *See* Henry N. Butler & Larry E. Ribstein, *Legal Process and the Discovery of Better Policies for Fostering Innovation and Growth*, in RULES FOR GROWTH: PROMOTING INNOVATION AND GROWTH THROUGH LEGAL REFORM, The Kauffman Task Force for Law, Innovation and Growth 463 (2011) (discussing the importance of such systemic changes); *see also* Gillian K. Hadfield, *Producing Law for Innovation*, in RULES FOR GROWTH: PROMOTING INNOVATION AND GROWTH THROUGH LEGAL REFORM, The Kauffman Task Force for Law, Innovation and Growth 23, 26 (2011); Gillian K. Hadfield, *Legal Infrastructure and the New Economy*, 8 I/S: J. L. & POL'Y INFO. SOC'Y 1, 57–58 (2012).

7 *See* Brendon Greeley & Alison Fitzgerald, "Pssst ... Wanna Buy a Law?", *Business Week*, December 1, 2011, http://www.businessweek.com/magazine/pssst-wanna-buy-a-law-12012011.html (discussing the activities of the American Legislative Exchange Council in drafting and promoting privately produced statutes for adoption by state legislatures).

incentives, parties often engage in these lawdrafting efforts as a byproduct of other activities. These byproduct incentives also are often associated with political rent-seeking rather than solely, or even primarily, intended to produce an attractive product for the market for laws. For example, litigants produce precedents, but only as a byproduct of dispute resolution; trade groups produce and lobby for laws that serve the group's, rather than society's, interests; lawyers help write laws that enhance their ability to earn legal fees; and the National Conference of Commissioners on Uniform State Laws (NCCUSL) cartelizes state laws. Thus, both direct and byproduct private lawdrafting often share with public lawdrafting some of the problems of the political process. The result may also be the same: weak and misaligned incentives for producing efficient laws.[8]

The drawbacks of byproduct lawmaking raise the question of the potential for private lawmaking that is not dependent upon byproduct incentives and could bypass political rent-seeking. We posit the existence of a private firm, which we dub "Hammurabi, Inc.," that makes money by drafting and selling laws.[9] In such a market, the lawmaker's incentives come from capturing a share of the reduction in transaction costs and other social gains generated by the use of the firm's legal innovation.

This chapter's main contribution is showing how the promise of private parties' supplementing public lawdrafting is compromised by two main problems. First, private laws may lack a critical attribute of public laws: the certainty of enforcement that can be provided mainly by government. Second, where government adopts privately produced rules and gives them the force of law, this may limit the private lawdrafters' intellectual property rights in their creations. This follows from the law acquiring its power from the government's authority to enforce its provisions against unwilling parties. Once a provision acquires this power of law, those who are subject to it must be assured of being able to prosecute or defend actions charging violations. Combining these two points, private parties may lack incentives to produce precisely those most necessary rules—the rules that are deemed worthy of public enforcement as law.

Private lawmaking might be encouraged by clarifying the existence of private property rights in materials that are adopted as law. In other words, we consider how to move private creation of law from *byproduct* to *product*. The beginning point is for Congress to allow private lawdrafters to maintain effective intellectual property right protection after they sell their works to the government. To mitigate due process concerns, these rights can be subject to a fair use defense or limited license that would allow the royalty-free use by those bound by the law. This would effectively unbundle the lawmaking process and have government outsource

8 See Gabriel V. Rauterberg & Andrew Verstein, *Index Theory: The Law, Promise and Failure of Financial Index Theory*, 30 YALE J. REG. 1 (2013) (examining direct and byproduct incentives to produce and maintain financial indexes).

9 Although the use of Inc. implies a corporate, for-profit firm; as discussed below, we are agnostic on the particular structure of the law-drafting firm, including whether it is organized as a corporation, partnership or limited liability company (LLC), or as a for- or nonprofit.

some of its lawmaking function to private parties while retaining its exclusive power to enforce the law.

Several problems with this approach to private lawmaking could limit its usefulness. First, how would a system of private lawmaking and government enforcement be implemented? This involves questions concerning the property rights private lawmakers would retain and the government's role as a potential intermediary in selling the laws to individuals and firms.

Second, it is important to consider whether this system would improve the law as compared with the current system of public and byproduct lawmaking. In particular, as long as the government retains a key role in determining which private law proposals are enacted and enforced—that is, as long as the demand side of the equation is fixed—what is the chance that the adopted laws will improve? Giving private parties intellectual property rights in law and enabling them to sell their products to potential users might improve lawmakers' incentives over those of public and byproduct lawmakers. Problems of political rent-seeking by governments in purchasing laws might be addressed to some extent by jurisdictions' incentives to compete with other jurisdictions for residents and business.[10] However, this conclusion must remain somewhat speculative until private lawmakers' property rights are clarified and a market in private law has a chance to develop.

Finally, given the potential problems with a hybrid system of private lawdrafting and government enforcement, it is worth considering the feasibility of relying exclusively on private enforcement and not having privately drafted provisions adopted as law. As noted above, this approach would cost lawmakers the law's critical feature of likely enforcement, which in many situations can make the law cheaper and more effective than other enforcement mechanisms, such as reputational incentives or spontaneous coordination. However, private parties may be able in some situations to achieve a level of coordination comparable to the certainty of enforcement we attribute to the law.[11] Thus, in some circumstances, it may be feasible for the parties to avoid choosing between property rights and certainty of enforcement by pursuing purely private enforcement mechanisms. The availability of alternatives to laws increases the importance of examining the costs of formal lawdrafting, including the certainty/property rights dilemma discussed in this chapter.

This chapter proceeds as follows. Section 2.2 discusses the problems of public lawdrafting, particularly including the weak incentives of public lawdrafters. Section 2.3 discusses the alternative of private lawmaking, focusing on the problems resulting from the weak property rights of lawdrafters whose proposals are adopted as law. Section 2.4 compares the idealized approach to private lawdrafting with the current approach—private lawmaking as a byproduct of

10 *See* Erin A. O'Hara & Larry E. Ribstein, THE LAW MARKET (2009). Of course, such competitive forces also serve to improve the current public and byproduct lawmaking system.

11 *See* Gillian K. Hadfield & Barry Weingast, *What is Law? A Coordination Model of the Characteristics of Legal Order* 4 J. LEG. ANALYSIS 471 (2012).

political rent-seeking. Section 2.5 discusses how a private lawmaking market might be developed, focusing on a number of potential questions and problems with this market.

2.2 Problems with public lawmaking

As discussed in the Introduction to this chapter, statutory standard forms can reduce firms' transaction costs as compared with private contracts for which there are no standard forms. Ideally, legislatures would produce statutes suited to diverse business types in order to minimize the total of these transaction costs and the costs of promulgating and enforcing the statutes. The optimal number and content of statutes may depend on factors such as firms' demand for statutory default provisions and the need to avoid confusion from a proliferation of forms.

The actual number and quality of statutes produced depends, however, on legislators' incentives. Public lawmaking entails a political competition among interest groups.[12] Politicians have an incentive to produce new laws in order to attract or avoid losing interest group support. Interest groups, in turn, are motivated to some extent by the benefits they earn when these new laws attract revenues and residents from other states in interstate competition.[13]

Interest group pressure may, however, give legislators only weak incentives to produce efficient and innovative new laws that meet firms' needs. First, the state may be unable to capture the benefits of a new statute. Even a high quality and innovative new standard business form may face insuperable competition from a dominant existing law, such as Delaware's corporate law. Also, because governments generally lack property rights in their laws,[14] they may not be able to gain enough from making the law competitive to justify investing in innovation.

Second, even if governments have incentives to enact efficient and innovative statutes, individual legislators may have weak incentives to draft these statutes. Public legislators gain from legislative innovations only up to the point that these innovations enable them to gain reelection.[15] At the same time, legislators risk reputational harm from failed experiments and backlash from interest groups injured by the innovation.[16]

12 Gary S. Becker, "A Theory of Competition Among Pressure Groups for Political Influence," 98 Q. J. ECON. 371, 372 (1983).

13 *See* O'Hara & Ribstein, *supra* note 10.

14 There are exceptions. The United Kingdom protects government works through Crown Copyrights. *See* Bruce H. Kobayashi & Larry E. Ribstein, *Law's Information Revolution*, 53 ARIZ. L. REV. 1169, 1177 (2011) (discussing some implications of protecting government works with intellectual property rights).

15 *See* Hadfield & Talley, *supra* note 1, at 417 ("But the rewards [legislators] face—satisfying voters and campaign contributors and hence achieving reelection—do not create the kind of marginal incentives that lead to efficient offerings.").

16 Douglas J. Cumming & Jeffrey G. MacIntosh, "The Role of Interjurisdictional Competition in Shaping Canadian Corporate Law," 20 INT'L REV. L. & ECON. 141, 145–46 (2000); see also Susan Rose-Ackerman, "Risk Taking and Reelection: Does Federalism Promote Innovation?," 9 J. LEG. STUD. 593 (1980).

Although this analysis indicates that states cannot gain an edge through innovation, significant statutory variation nevertheless exists in some contexts. For example, we document the existence of significant variation in LLC statutes.[17] These differences may be attributed to the legislators' incentives to engage in social wealth-reducing innovation at the behest of powerful interest groups. Lawyers in particular have political power resulting from their control of the judiciary and the organizational advantages that have likely tilted many aspects of the law in lawyers' favor.[18] Lawyers could instigate innovations that complicate the law and thereby create business for lawyers while simultaneously imposing costs on the rest of society.[19] In other words, legal innovation may exist under the current regime but may not be welfare-enhancing. We explore the incentives underlying the production of such lawmaking below in Section 2.3.

2.3 Private lawmaking

Given the problems of public lawmaking, we consider whether there is a potential for a purely private market in lawdrafting by our private lawdrafting firm, Hammurabi, Inc. Hammurabi ideally would have the same robust profit-making incentives of actors in any other private market. Depending on the "buy" side of the market for law, and particularly the amount and type of jurisdictional competition,[20] Hammurabi could have more of an incentive than public or byproduct lawmakers to draft laws that serve the interests of potential users or that transfer wealth from one group to another.

This Part presents a theoretical analysis of private lawdrafting. We focus on business association standard form contracts, but our model can be generalized to include statutes for other types of contracts, market structures, or private relationships. For example, marriage and other domestic relationships are amenable to statutory standard forms analogous to those for business associations.[21] Section 2.3.1 presents a basic theory of socially optimal legal innovation based on the objective of reducing parties' mismatch costs.[22] This analysis indicates the potential advantage of private laws that supplement the inadequacies of public lawmaking discussed in Section 2.1. Sections 2.3.2 and 2.3.3 discuss problems associated with private lawmaking—greater uncertainty of enforcement, which gives rise to higher expected reorganization costs, and the lack of effective intellectual pro-perty rights in privately produced works that may be adopted as

17 See Bruce H. Kobayashi & Larry E. Ribstein, "Delaware for Small Fry: Jurisdictional Competition for Limited Liability Companies," 2011 U. ILL. L. REV. 91, 102–03 (2011).

18 Benjamin H. Barton, "The Lawyer-Judge Bias in the American Legal System," 1–3 (2011).

19 See Gillian Hadfield, "The Price of Law: How the Market for Lawyers Distorts the Justice System," 98 MICH. L. REV. 953 (2000).

20 *See infra* Section 2.5.3.

21 *See* Larry E. Ribstein, *A Standard Form Approach to Same-Sex Marriage*, 38 CREIGHTON L. REV. 309, 316–18 (2005); Larry E. Ribstein, *Incorporating the Hendricksons*, 35 WASH. U. J. L. & POL'Y 273, 275 (2011) [*hereinafter* RIBSTEIN, *Hendricksons*].

22 *See* Kobayashi & Ribstein, *supra* note 2 (presenting an explicit model of private and public lawmaking).

law. These problems create a fundamental tension between creating products that may have little or no market value because of enforcement uncertainty, and creating more valuable products that, when adopted as law, result in the creators having weak or no property rights.

2.3.1 Mismatch costs

As discussed in the Introduction, statutory standard forms can assist in various ways in private ordering. By the same token, contracting parties that have no close-fitting standard form may choose the next best option of using an ill-fitting one that forces them to incur greater costs.[23] A key objective of providing additional public and private standard forms is to reduce these costs, which we refer to as "mismatch costs."

The following example will assist in visualizing mismatch costs. Assume the situation that existed at the middle of the twentieth century in the U.S., where there were only two types of statutes suited for closely held firms: the Uniform Partnership Act (UPA) as adopted by all states and the corporate statute. The corporate statute provides for limited liability but has the wrong tax consequences and significantly constrains small firms' flexibility. The general partnership statute gives parties broad freedom to structure their relationship but forces the firm's owners to assume vicarious liability for the firm's debts. Although the parties could form a limited partnership in which passive investors have limited liability, one who exercises the power of a general partner in such a firm necessarily takes on vicarious liability. At that time, most states did not provide for a flexible form of business that limits the personal liability of managing owners of small firms for the firm's debts.

Also assume that each individual firm has a preferred structure. Given that general partnership and close corporation statutes were the only existing statutes, a firm faced a choice of incurring high mismatch costs because the existing statutes did not provide its preferred structure or trying to draft for its desired provisions. The firm would likely be unable to avoid the high mismatch costs, however, because drafting for a desired structure is problematic for two key reasons. First, a court is unlikely to enforce the parties' contractual expectation of limited liability against a third party who neither expressly nor impliedly agreed to the liability limitation if the firm organizes under the existing general partnership statute. Second, the tax consequences of the parties' contract ultimately depend on tax law rather than the parties' agreement. Thus, a firm opting for limited liability under the existing corporation statute will face entity level taxation.

A firm's mismatch costs of organizing under an ill-fitting statute increase rapidly with the differences between the statute and provisions ideally suited to the

23 *See* Goetz & Scott, *supra* note 2, at 272 ("[P]arties may adapt to a risky environment by using safe but inexact formulations. When this occurs, the potential gains from trade are not fully exploited.") (footnote omitted).

firm's needs. For example, the mismatch costs of using the existing partnership statute are large because of the significance of owners' limited or personal liability for the firm's debts. Other factors equal, all firms that want the liability and tax terms listed above will prefer to organize and operate under the new limited liability company (LLC) statute, compared to forming under the existing UPA. The new statute accordingly may increase social wealth by reducing firms' transaction costs.

2.3.2 Reorganization costs

An alternative to the choice between statute and customized contract presented in Section 2.3.1 is for private lawmakers to promulgate a standard form for a relationship that—like an LLC—provides the desired characteristics of limited liability, partnership taxation, and members' direct participation in management. The private form critically lacks the characteristics of "law," by which we mean a rule that reliably determines how a court or administrative agency will act when confronted with the provision. Snyder cites Justice Holmes' statement that "a legal duty so called is nothing but a prediction that if a man does or omits certain things he will be made to suffer in this or that way by judgment of the court; and so of a legal right."[24] Consistent with this definition, we assume statutes adopted as law by a legislature are enforced with a greater certainty than privately produced provisions not adopted as law.

Continuing our example from Section 2.3.1, assume our private lawmaker Hammurabi, Inc. promulgates sets of provisions that are similar to LLC statutes and therefore include the relevant characteristics of management flexibility, limited liability, and partnership taxation. Assume further that the private form is *not* adopted as law. Hammurabi, Inc.'s privately produced provisions would then impose not only mismatch costs on some firms but also "reorganization" costs that adopting firms will incur if the provisions are ultimately not enforced.

Reorganization costs are likely higher than mismatch costs under the existing statute because they include not only the costs of having to reorganize under an existing mismatched law or statute, but also include additional costs associated with the disruption of business plans, as well as legal fees, penalties, and liabilities. For example, relying on limited liability, the firm might fail to enter into non-recourse arrangements with its creditors, with the result that its members face personal liability when courts refuse to enforce contractual limited liability. Further, relying on the partnership tax, the members may fail to minimize corporate taxes by characterizing distributions as wages rather than dividends.[25] Firms' expected costs of organizing under the private form thus equal the sum of its expected reorganization and mismatch costs. It follows that the additional

24 David V. Snyder, *Private Lawmaking*, 64 OHIO ST. L.J. 371, 373 n.1 (2003) (citing Oliver Wendell Holmes, Jr., *The Path of the Law*, 10 HARV. L. REV. 457, 458 (1896)).

25 *See* Ribstein, *supra* note 3, at 376–80 (noting that statutory forms differ from nonstatutory private forms in part in clarifying the enforcement of mandatory rules).

value of a statute over an identical set of private provisions is the savings of expected reorganization costs resulting from the higher probability of enforcement of a government-promulgated form.

Because reorganization costs exceed mismatch costs, even firms that would rather organize under a new *statute* that more closely fits their needs than the existing statute may not prefer an equivalent new *private* provision because of the risk of nonenforcement and consequent reorganization costs. There is a critical probability of enforcement of private terms below which firms will prefer organizing as a mismatched firm under the existing statute over the new better-fitting private provision. Table 2.1 summarizes this tradeoff.

A similar tradeoff applies to a firm organized under the current statute and facing high mismatch costs that attempts to contract for provisions that better match its preferred contract. The firm's preferred contract presents a variety of problems related to enforcement given the limited availability of a suitable standard form. Non-standard contract terms may not be clear because neither

Table 2.1 Cost of Organization
Firms that prefer LLC-type provisions to existing UPA provisions operating under:

	Expected Mismatch Costs	*Expected Reorganization Costs*	*Expected Total Costs*
1a. Existing statute (UPA) and firm forgoes its preferred provisions.	*High.*	*None.*	*High mismatch costs, no reorganization costs.*
1b. Existing statute (UPA) and firm attempts to contract for preferred provisions.	*Lower than 1a (when enforced). Provisions enforced with probability < 1.*	*High, incurred when contracted for nonstandard provisions are not enforced.*	*Lower mismatch costs if enforced, high reorganization costs if not.*
2. Nonlaw LLC provisions.	*Lower than existing statute (when enforced). Provisions enforced with probability < 1.*	*High, incurred when private provisions are not enforced.*	*Lower mismatch costs if enforced, high reorganization costs if not.*
3. New public LLC statute.	*Lower than existing statute.*	*Low, given greater certainty of enforcement compared to nonlaw provisions.*	*Lower mismatch costs than organizing under existing statute, lower reorganization costs than nonlaw provision.*

statutes nor judicial decisions instruct courts how to fill the inevitable gaps that arise because of the unpredictability of future events over a long-term relationship. For example, a party may attempt to seize benefits from the relationship that the contract neither expressly forbids nor clearly permits. Although the situation might be appropriate for application of partnership-type fiduciary duties, it may not be clear whether or how a court will apply such duties to a relationship whose default rules differ from a general partnership. The firm therefore also will face significant reorganization costs if it tries to contract for its preferred nonstandard provisions.

To see the distinction between mismatch and reorganization costs, consider a firm that can organize under provisions perfectly matched to its needs so that mismatch costs are zero. If these provisions are enacted as law, we assume there is a low probability that the firm will incur reorganization costs. This firm has no mismatch costs and low reorganization costs when it adopts the statute. A firm that adopts identical private provisions that are not embodied in law has no mismatch costs if the private provisions are enforced, but it has higher expected reorganization costs because of the lower probability these provisions will be enforced.

As discussed above, holding mismatch costs constant, firms prefer a provision that is enforced as law (*i.e.*, a statute) to one that is not because the greater certainty of enforcement lowers their expected reorganization costs. Put another way, firms lose from adopting a new provision instead of organizing as a mismatched firm under the existing statute when their expected reorganization costs exceed the expected reduction in mismatch costs. It follows that the value of a privately produced set of nonlaw provisions becomes negative when the probability of enforcement is below a critical value.

Our analysis recognizes that a government-adopted statute may not always have certainty of enforcement because it may not be clear how courts will interpret the statute or apply it to particular situations. However, it is enough for present purposes that the adoption of a statute increases the probability of enforcement compared to a privately produced provision that is not embodied in the statute. We also recognize that parties may achieve a degree of coordination in some situations that is comparable to that produced by "law."[26] Again it is only necessary for present purposes that adoption as law increases the probability of enforcement compared to an equivalent private law. As discussed below, these differences between law and nonlaw are factored into the calculation of expected reorganization costs, which in turn determine parties' demand for law.

Against this background consider a firm that wants the features of an LLC—including limited liability, partnership taxation, and flexible management—prior to the promulgation of state LLC statues. The firm's preferred set of provisions includes features that differ from existing general partnership provisions. If the firm operates under the general partnership law it will incur high mismatch costs

26 *See* Hadfield & Weingast, *supra* note 11, at 7.

because it must forgo either limited liability or partnership taxation, but it will not face reorganization costs because of certainty of enforcement. However, if the firm decides to adopt Hammurabi, Inc.'s privately produced provisions that have the above characteristics of an LLC, the firm will bear lower mismatch costs than if it organizes under the general partnership statute. However, it will face significant expected reorganization costs if enforcement of these provisions is uncertain.[27]

2.3.3 Private law and intellectual property rights

Section 2.3.2 shows that the adoption of a private lawmaker's work as law may significantly increase the value of the proposal. This Section shows that, simultaneously with its increase in value, adoption as law may cause the loss of the drafter's rights in its intellectual property.

The property rights issue can be illustrated by examining the leading case of *Veeck v. Southern Building Code Congress International.*[28] Veeck posted the building codes of two small North Texas towns, Anna and Savoy, on his website, RegionalWeb, which provided information about North Texas. However, Veeck could not reproduce the actual town codes at low cost. He instead posted the source of these codes, the Standard Building Code written by Southern Building Code Congress International, Inc. (SBCCI), which the towns had copied verbatim. Veeck had obtained this code on a computer disk from SBCCI for a fee under a software licensing agreement and copyright notice which prohibited copying and distribution. Veeck's website identified the codes as those of Anna and Savoy but did not mention that the posted codes were written by SBCCI and copied from an SBCCI disk.

The code author in *Veeck* exemplifies the sort of private lawdrafter that is the focus of this chapter. The court described SBBCI as a nonprofit organization with 14,500 members, including government bodies, construction contractors, business and trade associations, students, and educational institutions.[29] Its main activity was developing and promoting standard building codes. Since SBCCI sought to promote use of these codes, it allowed governments to enact them into law by reference at no charge and without a licensing agreement and freely granted permission to make a limited number of copies of the codes. SBCCI's revenues from sales of the codes to both nonmembers and, at discount, to members, helped fund its $9 million annual budget.[30]

27 If the firm operates in a different jurisdiction, the statute may not be enforced as law in that jurisdiction. This would be comparable to the firm's adopting a private non-law agreement. Thus, the choice of law rule must be factored into whether a given provision is "law."

28 *Veeck v. S. Bldg. Code Cong. Int'l*, 293 F.3d 791 (5th Cir. 2002) (en banc); *see also Bldg. Officials & Code Admin. v. Code Tech., Inc.*, 628 F.2d 730 (1st Cir. 1980); *see also infra* Section 2.5.3 (the precise scope of the public's guaranteed access and commensurately of the authors' property rights in law are discussed).

29 *Veeck*, 293 F.3d at 793.

30 *Id.* at 794.

The central issue in *Veeck* is whether SBCCI retained property rights in its code once it had been adopted as law. The case arose when SBBCI demanded that Veeck stop infringing its copyrights, and Veeck sought a declaratory judgment that he did not violate the Copyright Act.[31] The Fifth Circuit held that Veeck did not infringe SBCCI's copyright by printing the law of Anna and Savoy.[32] The court reasoned that although SBCCI had a valid copyright in its *model codes*, the identical words adopted as *laws* entered the public domain.[33]

Veeck has important implications for any copyrighted work that is adopted as law. Parties may write contracts for themselves, or hire lawyers to do so, whose language copyright law protects.[34] Copyright law similarly protects standard form contracts that contracting parties can adopt for their specific purposes and thereby save some of the costs of drafting customized contracts from scratch.[35] But *Veeck* holds that when the language of the private contract becomes "law"—that is, as part of a judicial ruling or when the standard form is adopted as a statute—the authors are at risk of losing a significant portion of the copyright protection they might have had.[36]

In the absence of effective intellectual property rights, private producers of "law" face free riding by potential users of their work and will be unable to set prices. More precisely, any demand for a copy of a privately produced statute would be based solely on potential users' costs of accessing the statute, which likely would be the same for all firms and statutes. Thus, under *Veeck*, SBCCI will not be able to profitably sell its model codes once they are adopted as law because

31 *Id.* at 791.

32 *Id.* at 817.

33 *Id.* at 793.

34 *See* Melville B. Nimmer & David Nimmer, NIMMER ON COPYRIGHT § 2.18[E] (1978) (noting that "there appear to be no valid grounds why legal forms such as contracts, insurance policies, pleadings and other legal documents should not be protected under the law of copyright."); Kenneth A. Adams, *Copyright and the Contract Drafter*, N.Y. L.J., Aug. 2006, at 2, 4.

35 *See, e.g.*, Adams, *supra* note 34 at 2; *Am. Family Life Ins. Co. of Columbus v. Assurant, Inc.*, 2006 WL 4017651, *6 (N.D. Ga., Jan. 11, 2006) (holding that plaintiff's "narrative" style insurance policy may be protectable under copyright law).

36 Even if *Veeck* were reversed, both the federal government and the states could assert sovereign immunity from the enforcement of federal intellectual property rights, and Congress's ability to abrogate states' sovereign immunity is limited. *See Coll. Sav. Bank v. Fla. Prepaid Postsecondary Educ. Expense Bd.*, 527 U.S. 666, 670 (1999). However, states and the federal government cannot infringe intellectual property rights without consequence. Intellectual property owners could, among other things, require that jurisdictions agree to waive sovereign immunity as a condition of having access to their products in the first place, and licensing jurisdictions could be sued for contract damages if they violate the terms of this license. Patent and copyright holders could seek compensation from non-licensing states through inverse condemnation suits. In addition, intellectual property holders could seek injunctive relief under the *Ex Parte Young Doctrine*. *See Ex Parte Young*, 209 U.S. 123 (1908); *see also* Peter S. Menell, *Economic Implications of State Sovereign Immunity from Infringement of Federal Intellectual Property Rights*, 33 LOY. L.A. L. REV. 1400 (2000); Eugene Volokh, *Sovereign Immunity and Intellectual Property*, 73 S. CAL. L. REV. 1161 (2000). *But see* John C. O'Quinn, *Protecting Private Intellectual Property from Government Intrusion: Revisiting SmithKline and the Case for Just Compensation*, 29 PEPP. L. REV. 435 (2002) (discussing *SmithKline Beecham Consumer Healthcare, L.P. v. Watson Pharmaceuticals, Inc.*, 211 F.3d 21 (2d Cir. 2000) and potential limits of regulatory takings); Alicia Ryan, *Contract, Copyright, and the Future of Digital Preservation*, 10 B.U. J. SCI. & TECH. L. 152, 176 (2004).

users and competing distributors such as Veeck and other jurisdictions can freely copy them. This leaves little incentive for firms like SBCCI to produce and update such codes in the first place. Even if the lawdrafter who cannot set prices did have sufficient incentives to produce statutes because of her cost advantages in distributing the work, she would lack incentives to innovate by differentiating products.[37]

Formal intellectual property rights are not, however, the only possible way to provide adequate incentives to private lawdrafters. Lawdrafters may have informal contractual mechanisms for protecting intellectual property rights to certain types of legal information products. For example, private forms may be protected as trade secrets secured by noncompetition and confidentiality agreements. However, enforcement of these rights may be limited by policy concerns about lawyer independence and public access to law.[38] Moreover, trade secret protection ends upon disclosure, which generally is necessary to generate interpretations of the form. A more potent informal protection of private forms is through first-mover advantages from proposing private standard forms that firms adopt even before the forms are embodied in a statute. Numerous cases and other legal analyses interpreting the form may create network effects that give the form some of the advantages of law.[39] For present purposes, it is unnecessary to evaluate the precise effect of these informal protections, so long as formal intellectual property rights can provide additional protection in some situations and therefore encourage the production of some forms that would not be produced in the absence of this protection.

The obvious problem raised by the discussion so far is the fundamental tension inherent in property rights in private law. On the one hand, the risk that courts will not enforce the private model law's terms raises the expected cost of using the model law and thus lowers the price firms are willing to pay for the term. On the other hand, actual or potential court enforcement or interpretation of the contract terms both increases the form's value and jeopardizes the author's property rights in it because forms adopted as law enter the public domain under *Veeck*. Lawdrafters facing the risk of losing their property rights may have little incentive to produce private provisions for profit, particularly including those provisions which might be most valuable because they are likely to be adopted as laws.

To illustrate the fundamental tension facing private lawdrafters created by the need for certainty and the loss of property rights when a private law proposal is adopted as law, suppose that a legislature adopts privately produced provisions as

37 *See* Kobayashi & Ribstein, *supra* note 14, at 1182.

38 *Id.*

39 *See, e.g.*, Marcel Kahan & Michael Klausner, "Standardization and Innovation in Corporate Contracting (or 'The Economics of Boilerplate')," 83 VA. L. REV. 713 (1997); see also Michael Klausner, "Corporations, Corporate Law, and Networks of Contracts," 81 VA. L. REV. 757 (1995). But see Bruce H. Kobayashi & Larry E. Ribstein, "Choice of Form and Network Externalities," 43 WM. & MARY L. REV. 79 (2001) (showing the weakness in lock-in effects for LLCs).

law and thereby increases the certainty of enforcement. If the lawdrafter can continue to enforce its intellectual property rights, adoption of the private form as law will increase the demand for this set of provisions even as adoption effectively costs the lawdrafter its copyright protection. As a result of the loss of copyright, other jurisdictions and providers could adopt or sell the set of provisions contained in the new statute without having to pay the drafter a licensing fee. This would reduce or eliminate the lawdrafter's incentive to produce statutes except to the limited extent that it can profit by efficiently distributing the statute. In short, the rewards from private authorship of a set of provisions in the absence of effective property rights protection are negatively correlated with the degree to which the products have the valuable feature of certain enforcement attributed to law. Given these limitations on property rights, lawdrafters would have weak incentives to create private forms that are likely to be adopted as law.

This analysis assumes that lawdrafters, like other intellectual property creators, seek to maximize profits from the sale of their inventions. As discussed next, private lawdrafters may, however, act as agents for interest groups who are trying to use the political process to engineer wealth transfers. We have shown that these affect the types of laws produced by the "byproduct" lawdrafters. It follows that byproduct lawdrafters may or may not have better incentives than government legislators.

2.4 Law as a byproduct

Sections 2.2 and 2.3 show why both public lawmakers and private lawdrafters may lack incentives to produce optimal legislative innovation. This Section shows how a type of private lawdrafting—by nonpoliticians as a byproduct of other activities—can help fill this gap. Byproduct lawdrafters derive their gains from political or other activities rather than from selling their model laws on the open market. Accordingly, they have an incentive to engage in lawdrafting even if they cannot share in the political entity's revenues or lack intellectual property rights in their products. Byproduct lawdrafting thus helps explain why investments in lawdrafting occur despite the incentive issues discussed in Section 2.2. But byproduct lawdrafters' incentives can skew their laws away from social welfare compared to laws produced by purely private lawdrafters with property rights in their laws. Section 2.4.1 examines byproduct lawdrafters' incentives and discusses some types of byproduct lawdrafters. Sections 2.4.2 and 2.4.3 discuss specific examples of byproduct laws in connection with corporations and limited liability companies.

2.4.1 Byproduct law drafters

Byproduct lawdrafting enables public lawdrafters to outsource drafting costs to private interest groups, who, for their part, have a political incentive to offer readymade laws to public legislators. Byproduct lawdrafters do not offer statutes directly for sale to the market for standard forms, as in the standard model of private lawdrafting, but instead engage in drafting as a way to enhance their lobbying or other business activities.[40]

The differences between byproduct laws and laws produced for sale in a market for private law derive from the lawdrafters' incentives. Sellers of standard forms sold in a conventional market would seek to share in the combined producer and buyer surplus from commercial exchange. Bargaining over this surplus in an efficient market for forms increases social wealth. In contrast, the benefits to byproduct lawdrafters do not depend solely on what users of the forms would pay for the laws. Rather, byproduct lawdrafters have an incentive to forego profits in a commercial market for law in favor of causing a redistribution of social wealth to their group. This incentive will likely skew byproduct laws away from the mix of forms that would exist in an efficient market for private forms.[41] Thus, although byproduct lawdrafters can add value to public lawdrafting, byproduct laws are only a second-best solution to public lawdrafters' weak incentives compared to private lawdrafters who sell their forms in a market for law.

This difference between byproduct and purely private lawmaking was clearly recognized by one of the dissenting opinions in *Veeck*. Judge Wiener answered the majority's argument that code preparers could and would continue their work without copyright protection:

> Continued maintenance of a revenue source from sales of codes to individual owners, architects, engineers, materials suppliers, builders and contractors as well as libraries and other more attenuated purchasers, all of whom buy copies of the codes directly from SBCCI, serves another public interest. I refer to the continuation of SBCCI's independence from the self interest of its dues-paying members, who otherwise might be in a position to command more influence were SBCCI forced to obtain too great a share of its revenue from such supporters. Clearly, SBCCI's receipts from sales of the codes substantially reduce the potential for greater dependence on its membership, presumably allowing SBCCI to operate without becoming entirely beholden for its existence to self-interested entities.[42]

This argument recognizes that laws drafted by private parties incentivized by property rights would be more likely to reflect firms' actual needs than byproduct

40 Hadfield & Talley also briefly consider the role of interest groups such as the legal profession in generating incentives for states to produce corporate law, noting that this does not detract from their fundamental point that public providers do not face profit-maximization incentives. Hadfield & Talley, *supra* note 1, at 417. We expand on this insight by directly comparing the incentives of these byproduct law drafters, with a pure private model of law drafting.

41 The presence and amount of skewing depends on the circumstances. For example, in contrast to the pure private model of drafting involved in *Veeck*, a key supplier of municipal building codes is the International Code Council supported by the insurance industry, fire marshals, construction industry, and others with high stakes in public safety and therefore strong incentives to act in the public interest. *See* INTERNATIONAL CODE COUNCIL, http://www.iccsafe.org (last visited Mar. 7, 2013). We are indebted to Omri Ben-Shahar for this example.

42 *Veeck v. S. Bldg. Code Cong. Int'l*, 293 F.3d 791, 817 (5th Cir. 2002) (en banc).

laws, which are aimed at redistributing social wealth to the interest groups who drafted the laws.[43] The following sections discuss some of the groups who participate in the political process by drafting laws as a byproduct of their other activities. Section 2.4.2 discusses examples of particular byproduct laws.

2.4.1.1 Lawyers as lawdrafters

Lawyers play an important role in state lawdrafting apart from their role in litigation.[44] There is significant evidence of lawyers' participation in law-drafting activities.[45] Indeed, professional rules establish lawyers' "participation in activities for improving the law, the legal system or the legal profession" as a professional norm.[46]

Lawyers' work as lawdrafters is a byproduct of their other professional activity. Lawyers have special advantages as lawdrafters, including their legal expertise and membership in bar associations that help coordinate political activity. Lawyers also earn reputational benefits from using their law reform work to advertise their expertise and can influence the application and interpretation of law by doing remunerative or reputation-building work writing forms, manuals, and treatises.[47]

Two aspects of the legal infrastructure of the U.S. favor lawyers' participation in lawdrafting. First, lawyer licensing by each state helps motivate lawyers to engage in legal innovation. Licensing gives lawyers a kind of quasi-property right in their licensing state's law by conferring an exclusive right to represent clients in the licensing state and to practice in that state's courts.[48] These rights enable lawyers licensed in a particular state to share in legal innovations' benefits of attracting people to locate in the state and litigate in the state's courts. Second, state choice of law rules enhance licensing's effect by linking the application of a state's law to whether the client resides in or litigates in the courts of the licensing

43 Byproduct law drafters' incentives, like those of all groups, depend to some extent on the group's governance structure. Thus, a nonprofit lawdrafting entity may embrace social welfare objectives to a greater extent than a for-profit entity. *See* Kevin E. Davis, *The Role of Nonprofits in the Production of Boilerplate*, 104 MICH. L. REV. 1075 (2006). However, this is far from clear. Moreover, there may be important incentive differences within the nonprofit and for-profit categories. For purposes of this chapter, we assume only that the entity is designed to maximize certain benefits for the group which may differentiate the social welfare effects of selling the group's products in a market for laws from those of producing laws as a byproduct of some other activity.

44 Lawyers also engage in law drafting directly through their compensated work on behalf of clients. When they are acting only as agents whose interests are aligned with those of clients, lawyers are part of the interest group efforts. *See infra* Section 2.4.3.

45 See Carol R. Goforth, "The Rise of the Limited Liability Company: Evidence of a Race Between the States, but Heading Where?," 45 SYRACUSE L. REV. 1193 (1995); Jonathan R. Macey & Geoffrey P. Miller, "Toward an Interest-Group Theory of Delaware Corporate Law," 65 TEX. L. REV. 469 (1987).

46 Model Rules of Prof'l Conduct R. 6.1(b)(3).

47 *See* Larry E. Ribstein, *Lawyers as Lawmakers: A Theory of Lawyer Licensing*, 69 MO. L. REV. 299, 329 (2004).

48 *Id.*

state.[49] The combination of lawyer licensing and choice of law rules gives lawyers monopoly rights in law and so enables them to internalize the benefit of improving the law. Licensing complements the reputational and other benefits discussed above by encouraging lawyers to seek these benefits through lawdrafting efforts rather than in other ways.

Lawyers have an incentive to shape laws to favor lawyers' interests. Unlike sellers who profit from sales of their products and therefore seek to tailor their laws to buyers' demands, lawyer lawdrafters have a particular interest in laws favoring lawyers. For example, it has been argued that Delaware lawyers seek to make Delaware law excessively lawyer-friendly.[50] More generally, lawyers may seek excessively complex laws that increase the need for and cost of lawyers[51] or laws that directly enhance the value of a law license by excluding nonlawyers from various types of legal work.[52]

Jurisdictional competition can mitigate the negative effects of lawyers' byproduct role. Lawyers cannot make their states' laws too lawyer-friendly without driving potential clients to states with less lawyer-friendly laws. Alignment of lawyers' incentives with social welfare varies depending on a variety of circumstances and conditions. If, for example, the choice of law rule is based on plaintiff's choice of forum, as with most product liability cases, lawyers might maximize their own and the state's interest by maximizing plaintiffs' interests rather than the parties' mutual interests. Lawyers' incentives also may depend on the nature of their practice. Laws promoting litigation may help tort lawyers, who can draw out-of-state defendants into pro-litigation courts, while hurting transactional lawyers, whose clients can choose where to reside depending on the applicable law.[53] And lawyers' incentives may vary with their state's power in the market for state law. Where a state like Delaware has significant market power, the pressure from state competition eases and lawyers are freer to indulge their incentive to seize a larger portion of a fairly stable pie.

2.4.1.2 Uniform laws

NCCUSL, the official promulgator of uniform law proposals in the U.S., is a particularly influential lawdrafting group. Law drafting is a byproduct of NCCUSL's main objective: lobbying by its politically-connected members for state law uniformity. NCCUSL was organized during the nineteenth century codification boom, when legislators sought to reduce legal disorder as well as to protect their authority from competition by other states and growth of the "federal

49 *See* O'HARA & RIBSTEIN, *supra* note 10, at ch 4.
50 *See* Macey & Miller, *supra* note 45, at 38–39.
51 *See* Barton, *supra* note 18; Hadfield, *supra* note 19, at 962.
52 *See* Barton, *supra* note 18.
53 *See* O'HARA & RIBSTEIN, *supra* note 10.

common law."[54] NCCUSL's motto, "Diversity of thought, uniformity of law,"[55] reflects its objective.

The fact that NCCUSL's lawdrafting is a byproduct of its uniformity objective skews its products in two important ways from what would be produced in an ideal private market for law. First, NCCUSL not only does not seek to produce legal innovation, but actively tries to squash it by achieving and maintaining uniformity. Even if individual NCCUSL proposals are innovative, their likely long-run effect will be to reduce innovation.

Second, NCCUSL's structure, which has been designed to further its uniformity objective, may actually encourage inefficient byproduct lawdrafting and so reduce the amount of efficient uniformity that would emerge without NCCUSL.[56] NCCUSL is organized as a private legislature with representatives from every state, enabling it to reflect all states' views (*i.e.*, "diversity of thought") in its uniform law proposals and to present at least the appearance of political legitimacy. But it also forces NCCUSL to delegate responsibility for drafting its laws to drafting committees that are small enough to be able to agree on specific language. The drafting committees, in turn, provide a venue conducive to interest group negotiations. NCCUSL committee members undertake time-consuming drafting work at least partly because they represent interest groups that are seeking to gain from having NCCUSL lobby for their specific interests or positions. Negotiations between the drafting committees and NCCUSL's legislative body further compromise the group's objectives.[57]

In addition to the unique lawdrafting problems added by the uniform lawdrafting process, NCCUSL enhances lawyers' lawdrafting powers discussed above. NCCUSL was founded by the American Bar Association as part of lawyers' move to gain respect and power for the legal profession.[58] Lawyers exercise power in NCCUSL as both part of the general legislative body and as advisers to the drafting committee. This may help explain the complexity, vagueness, and mandatory nature of many uniform laws, which maximize the need for legal advice, drafting, and planning.[59]

As with other private and byproduct lawdrafting, jurisdictional competition disciplines state adoption of uniform law proposals. States will be unwilling to adopt uniform law proposals to the extent that these laws might drive people and firms to other states or inhibit the states' efforts to attract business from other states. Thus, we have shown that states make generally reasonable choices as to which NCCUSL proposals to adopt.[60] But uniform law proposals also might

54 Larry E. Ribstein & Bruce H. Kobayashi, *Economic Analysis of Uniform State Laws*, 25 J. LEG. STUD. 131, 135–36 (1996).

55 UNIFORM LAW COMMISSION, http://www.uniformlaws.org (last visited Mar. 6, 2013).

56 Bruce H. Kobayashi & Larry E. Ribstein, *The Non-Uniformity of Uniform Laws*, 35 J. CORP. L. 327, 329 (2009).

57 *See* Ribstein & Kobayashi, *supra* note 54, at 142–43; *see also* Alan Schwartz & Robert E. Scott, *The Political Economy of Private Legislatures*, 143 U. PA. L. REV. 595, 602 (1995).

58 LAWRENCE M. FRIEDMAN, A HISTORY OF AMERICAN LAW, 652–54 (2d ed. 1985).

59 *See* Ribstein & Kobayashi, *supra* note 54, at 143–44.

60 *Id.* at 132.

resist jurisdictional competition because of NCCUSL's potent lobbying and because these proposals facilitate the formation of state lawdrafting cartels.[61]

2.4.1.3 Lawdrafting by interest groups

Interest groups can write laws themselves rather than supporting legislators who engage in this activity. Interest groups' lawmaking activity can be coordinated by third-party organizations such as the American Legislative Exchange Council.[62] In this situation, the law can be considered a byproduct of the interest group's lobbying effort. Indeed, this can be a very effective form of lobbying because it puts finished legislation into the hands of state legislators who typically lack lawmaking expertise and resources.[63] The fact that interest groups sometimes bear drafting costs may increase the amount of innovation in the public lawdrafting process. The tradeoff, as with other byproduct laws, is that any innovation added by a lawdrafting group reflects the interests of that group, and therefore may enhance, rather than reduce, political rent-seeking.

2.4.1.4 Industry groups

Industry groups write many model law proposals and codes designed to deal with problems specific to themselves.[64] Indeed, commercial law began with rules written by merchant guilds and continues to be developed by trade groups.[65] The Bernstein study of the diamond industry provides a modern example.[66] Securities exchanges write laws regarding trading and listing of shares. U.S. exchanges have a special self-regulatory role under the securities laws, while in the UK, exchange rules are themselves the main regulation of securities. Several organizations write codes and standards that are used by the groups and referenced by lawdrafting bodies.[67] These laws, as well as customs developed by

61 *Id.* at 146–48.

62 *See* Greeley & Fitzgerald, *supra* note 7.

63 *Id.*

64 *See* Davis, *supra* note 43, at 1078–83. These efforts are part of a broader category of the production of standardized contract provisions. *Id.* These provisions are not intended to be laws and therefore are outside the focus of this chapter.

65 Scott E. Masten & Jens Prüfer, *On the Evolution of Collective Enforcement Institutions: Communities and Courts*, 7–9 (Univ. of Michigan Law & Econ., Empirical Legal Studies Center Paper No. 11–013, 2011), *available at* http://ssrn.com/abstract=1773486.

66 *See* Lisa Bernstein, *Opting out of the Legal System: Extralegal Contractual Relations in the Diamond Industry*, 21 J. LEG. STUD. 115 (1992) (exploring the reasons that the diamond industry's system of private governance has developed and endured within the diamond trade).

67 *Veeck v. S. Bldg. Code Cong. Int'l, Inc.*, 293 F.3d 791, 796, n.6 (5th Cir. 2002). Several of these groups were listed as *amici* in *Veeck*: Building Officials and Code Administrators International (BOCA), International Code Council, International Conference of Building Officials, American Medical Association, American National Standards Institute (ANSI), American Society of Association Executives (ASAE), American Society of Heating, Refrigerating and Air-Conditioning Engineers (ASHRAE), American Society of Mechanical Engineers (ASME), National Fire Protection Association (NFPA), Texas Municipal League, and Underwriters Laboratories, Inc. (UL).

particular industries, are designed to fit the group's norms and business practices and may be enforced via reputational sanctions.

Industry groups can internalize their rules' costs and benefits vis-à-vis group members. A relatively small or monolithic industry's rules may fully reflect the interests of all of the firms in the industry. However, even in this situation the rules may not reflect the interests of the industry's customers or others affected by the rules. For example, consider an industry code that reduces market competition that would have resulted in more consumer-friendly practices.[68] Thus, like other byproduct laws, industry group laws and codes may be mechanisms for political redistribution of wealth. Moreover, while industry groups create law proposals, these proposals do not obtain the critical property of laws until the government enacts or enforces them as such. Embodiment in law engages government agents who may distort the industry group's objectives. For example, judicial decisions may reflect lawyers' interests in complicating the law and promoting litigation rather than the industry's interests in clarification and simplification.[69]

Industry groups may be active in standard-setting organizations, such as those that set accounting standards.[70] Although these organizations are not themselves industry groups, they may function in this way because they are populated exclusively by people with the specific expertise necessary to formulate the standards.

2.4.1.5 Litigants as lawdrafters

Parties to private litigation, in effect, contribute to legal innovation as a byproduct of their disputes when they have judges resolve their disputes. Litigants may have to incur extra court and attorney fees to support the production of formal legal opinions. Yet, since judicial decisions are law, the litigants do not receive property rights in return for their investments in litigation. Moreover, courts[71] and state legislatures[72] have resisted litigants' efforts to restrict public access to legal proceedings through confidentiality agreements and protective orders. Some litigants may be willing to bear the extra costs of lawdrafting as the price of better law and decisionmaking. The resulting process, accordingly, may produce efficient

68 *See, e.g.*, American Society of Sanitary Engineering, 106 F.T.C. 324 (1985) (refusal to issue a new standard or to modify the existing standard to cover a production was restraint of trade).

69 *See* Lisa Bernstein, "Merchant Law in a Merchant Court: Rethinking the Code's Search for Immanent Business Norms," 144 U. PA. L. REV. 1765, 1806–07 (1996).

70 See Lawrence A. Cunningham, "Private Standards in Public Law: Copyright, Lawmaking and the Case of Accounting," 104 MICH. L. REV. 291, 297–99 (2005).

71 *See* Arthur R. Miller, *Confidentiality, Protective Orders, and Public Access to the Courts*, 105 HARV. L. REV. 427, 501–02 (1991); *see, e.g., Brown v. Advantage Eng'g, Inc.*, 960 F.2d 1013, 1014 (11th Cir. 1992), *Wilson v. Am. Motors Corp.*, 759 F.2d 1568, 1571 (11th Cir. 1985) (cases refusing to seal court records).

72 *See* FLA. STAT. ANN. § 69.081 (West 1996) (prohibiting orders that conceal information relating to "public hazards"); *see also* TEX. R. CIV. P. ANN. 76(a) (West 1990) (creating a presumption that court records, including unfiled discovery materials and settlement agreements, are open to the public); *see also* Lloyd Doggett & Michael J. Mucchetti, *Public Access to Public Courts: Discouraging Secrecy in the Public Interest*, 69 TEX. L. REV. 643, 684–86 (1991); Miller, *supra* note 71, at 443 (listing enacted and proposed state statutes and rules).

law even if it is a byproduct of the separate activity of dispute resolution.[73] However, the inability to capture the spillover benefits of precedent, coupled with the extra costs of producing judicial decisions and the potential loss of confidentiality, often induces the parties to settle[74] or to resolve disputes through private arbitration.

Given private parties' limited incentives to create common law, our theory predicts that private lawdrafting with respect to common law would have the features we attribute to byproduct laws. The common law may be directly the byproduct of interest groups actively seeking to make law.[75] For example, class action plaintiffs are a special type of litigants involved in creating law. Given class members' presumed inability to coordinate, the key interested party is the lawyer who instigates a suit on behalf of the class. Indeed, a prominent former class action lawyer, William Lerach, famously bragged that he had no clients.[76] Class action lawyers can be viewed as entrepreneurs who use litigation to create an asset in the form of a recovery or settlement.[77] The legal resolutions entailed in class actions are, in effect, sold to lawdrafters (*i.e.*, courts) rather than in broad commercial market for legal forms. This produces innovations skewed toward the lawyer-entrepreneurs' interests in maximizing their fees rather than reflecting the mix of rules that would maximize social efficiency. Class action awards or settlements accordingly resemble byproduct laws.

2.4.2 Corporate law

Corporate law is a leading example of byproduct lawdrafting. In this case the concentrated interest group that derives the most benefits from corporate law—lawyers—has been most active in drafting it. Lawyers operate through state bar associations in each state. Also, on a national level, a subcommittee of the American Bar Association's Business Law Section drafts the Model Business Corporation Act (MBCA), many of whose provisions have been adopted in a substantial number of states. Even with the participation of lawyers, corporate law has exhibited relatively little differentiation over time and across states.[78] There is only one dominant competitor—Delaware—for the "national" market

73 Paul H. Rubin, *Why is the Common Law Efficient?*, 6 J. LEG. STUD. 51, 61 (1977).

74 *See* Owen M. Fiss, *Against Settlement*, 93 YALE L. J. 1073, 1073–75 (1984); *see also* Ezra Friedman & Abraham L. Wickelgen, *Chilling, Settlement, and the Accuracy of the Legal Process*, 26 J. L. ECON. & ORG. 144, 144 (2010); Bruce H. Kobayashi, *An Economic Analysis of Relitigation Rules in Intellectual Property Litigation* (Searle Ctr. on Law, Regulation, and Econ. Growth, Working Paper, 2010); Leandra Lederman, *Precedent Lost: Why Encourage Settlement, and Why Permit Non-party Involvement in Settlements?*, 75 N. D. L. REV. 221, 221–22 (1999).

75 *See* Paul H. Rubin & Martin J. Bailey, *The Role of Lawyers in Changing the Law*, 23 J. LEG. STUD. 807, 825 (1994).

76 William P. Barrett, *I Have No Clients*, FORBES, Oct. 11, 1993, at 52 (quoting Lerach as saying "I have the greatest practice of law in the world, I have no clients.").

77 *See* Bruce H. Kobayashi & Larry E. Ribstein, *Class Action Lawyers as Lawmakers*, 46 ARIZ. L. REV. 733, 780 (2004).

78 *See* Hadfield & Talley, *supra* note 1.

of firms incorporating outside their home state,[79] and this state competes on the basis of the quality of its courts and lawyers rather than primarily on the basis of legal innovation.[80]

Given this history of uniformity and stability it is notable that there is evidence that Nevada has sought to compete with Delaware over the last decade or so.[81] Nevada's strategy has been to compete primarily by providing for relatively lax duties for officers and directors and charging a franchise tax that is significantly lower than in Delaware, although much higher than in most states.

Nevada's emergence as a competitor in the national market for incorporations raises two questions: why Nevada, and why only Nevada? Delaware's prominence and entrenchment can be explained by its legal infrastructure, which other states would find difficult and costly to replicate, and by Delaware's dependence on a corporate franchise tax, which in effect "bonds" its promise to maintain the quality of its law. Nevada, on the other hand, offers neither an infrastructure nor dependence on its corporate tax comparable to Delaware.[82] Barzuza suggests that Delaware cannot compete with Nevada to provide lax law because this could dilute its brand. But even if that is true, it does not explain why some other state could not easily compete with both Delaware and Nevada. A state might offer the same law at a lower price or a different law that is more relaxed than Delaware but stricter than Nevada.

One potential explanation for Nevada's ability to compete with Delaware is Nevada's relatively small population, and therefore the impact that a franchise tax could make on Nevada's tax revenues. An analysis of the legislative history of Nevada's corporate law changes shows that they were intended as a deliberate strategy to compete with Delaware and thereby raise significant incorporation revenues.[83] The law passed over complaints that it would attract "sleaze balls and rip off artists" because of the argument that the additional revenues would help Nevada increase teacher pay.[84]

This history does not, however, explain why some other relatively small revenue-starved state would not try a similar strategy. The answer may lie in Nevada's unique reputation as a "sin" state, based on reliance on its gambling industry. Although relatively lax corporate law may be efficient for some types of firms, it also makes the state a potential refuge for shady firms. Other states may be reluctant to risk damaging their business reputations. Moreover, even legitimate

79 Marcel Kahan & Ehud Kamar, *The Myth of State Competition in Corporate Law*, 55 STAN. L. REV. 679, 685 (2002).

80 Roberta Romano, *Law as a Product: Some Pieces of the Incorporation Puzzle*, 1 J. L. ECON. & ORG. 225, 226–27 (1985).

81 See Michal Barzuza, "Market Segmentation: The Rise of Nevada as a Liability-Free Jurisdiction," 98 VA. L. REV. 935, 953 (2012).

82 *See* Bruce H. Kobayashi & Larry E. Ribstein, "Nevada and the Market for Corporate Law," 35 SEATTLE U. L. REV. 1165, 1170–71 (2012).

83 *See* Barzuza, *supra* note 81, at 949.

84 *Id.* at 954 (citing Nev. Senate Debate, One Hundred and Eleventh Day (May 6, 2011) (statement of Sen. Dina Titus), *available at* http://www.leg.state.nv.us/Session/71st2001/Journal/Senate/Final/SJ111.html).

firms seeking less stringent rules may be reluctant to trust states other than Nevada not to change their laws after they have incurred the costs of incorporating there.

Another possible explanation for the lack of state experimentation in corporate law is the MBCA, prepared by the American Bar Association, Committee on Corporate Laws of the Section of Business Law. The MBCA provides a competent model prepared by expert corporate lawyers. Because it is not designed to create uniformity, it does not share the particular byproduct characteristics of NCCUSL. Unlike Delaware corporation law, the MBCA is not tailored to the particular legal infrastructure of Delaware. The MBCA therefore enables many states with thin legal infrastructures to adopt a corporate law that is reasonably tailored to their corporations' needs and that is probably better than their own lawyers or legislators could draft on their own. At the same time, the existence of the MBCA may reduce the level of variation in corporate law that would otherwise exist.

The point of this story is that it is difficult for states to enter the national market for corporate law. Given their generally weak incentives, states must meet extraordinary conditions to give their lawdrafters sufficient incentives to innovate. Even lawyers' incentives to earn fees from increased corporate business have not been enough to motivate competition except in unusual situations involving high investment in infrastructure (Delaware) and willingness to attract low-quality business (Nevada). This suggests that there might be more legal innovation if private parties had stronger incentives to create laws.

2.4.3 Limited liability companies

The development of LLCs the central paradox of byproduct legislation. On the one hand, the incentives that motivate this lawdrafting can spur more innovation than either public lawdrafting or private lawdrafting under the current weak property rights regime. These new laws accordingly can increase social welfare by providing default rules that reduce firms' transaction costs compared to the situation without the byproduct laws. On the other hand, byproduct lawdrafters' incentives can divert these rules from first-best laws designed to maximize social welfare.

2.4.3.1 The development of LLCs

The LLC ultimately filled the need for a small business form that combined the general partnership's flexibility with corporate-type limited liability. Legislative experiments with such a business form had failed in the nineteenth century.[85] Guinnane and others attribute the failure to the conservatism of common law

85 *See* Wayne M. Gazur & Neil M. Goff, *Assessing the Limited Liability Company*, 41 CASE W. RES. L. REV. 387, 393–94 (1991); *see also* Timothy W. Guinnane, Ron Harris, Naomi R. Lamoreaux & Jean-Laurent Rosenthal, *Ownership and Control in the Entrepreneurial Firm: An International History of*

courts and to states' refusal to enforce sister states' statutes.[86] This does not explain why state legislatures and courts embraced the corporate form. A more complete explanation focuses on states' unwillingness to extend owners' limited liability beyond the controlled corporate setting and the federal government's insistence on taxing such firms as corporations.[87]

Private lawdrafting efforts ultimately broke the impasse. An oil company's lawyer promoted the enactment of a statute in Wyoming authorizing a form of business it had experience with in Latin America.[88] Another company then applied for an Internal Revenue Service (IRS) ruling that a Wyoming LLC would be taxed as a partnership.[89] At the same time, Georgia lawyers drafted and successfully pressed for adoption of a new limited partnership act that gave all members of a limited partnership limited liability. These private lawdrafting efforts ultimately prompted a federal tax ruling classifying an LLC as a partnership for tax purposes.[90] The ruling eventually spurred all states to adopt LLC statutes. Broad state acceptance, in turn, persuaded the IRS to eliminate most tax impediments on limited liability business forms.[91]

The creation and evolution of the LLC illustrates the relationship between byproduct lawdrafting, public lawdrafting, and jurisdictional competition in producing legal innovation. Public lawmakers had little incentive to invest effort and political capital in developing a new limited liability vehicle for which there would be little demand because of the political impediments to extending limited liability and the corporate tax. Private parties, meanwhile, lacked sufficient property rights to have incentives to craft a socially-efficient mix of standard forms that might have helped promote change. The work was done by byproduct lawdrafters, including business lawyers seeking clients and firms in industries like oil and gas seeking particular tax benefits.

The development of the LLC indicates that significant legal innovation can occur. The byproduct theory helps explain evidence of variation in LLC statutes.[92] This contrasts with evidence of corporate nondifferentiation that Hadfield & Talley cite in support of their model.[93] The fact that state LLC innovations were not correlated with state revenues from LLC formations[94] suggests that lawdrafters had byproduct incentives to engage in innovations.

Private Limited Companies, 4 n.1 (Yale Univ. Econ. Growth Ctr., Discussion Paper No. 959, 2007), *available at* http://www.econ.yale.edu/growth_pdf/cdp959.pdf.

86 *Id.*

87 *See* Larry E. Ribstein, RISE OF THE UNCORPORATION, chs 4–5 (2010).

88 *See* William J. Carney, *Limited Liability Companies: Origins and Antecedents*, 66 U. COLO. L. REV. 855, 857 (1995).

89 *Id.*

90 Partnership Classification, 1988–2 C.B. 360 (1988).

91 See Treas. Reg. § 301.7701-1-3 (2004).

92 Bruce H. Kobayashi & Larry E. Ribstein, *Evolution and Spontaneous Uniformity: Evidence from the Evolution of the Limited Liability Company*, 34 ECON. INQ. 464, 468 (1996); Kobayashi & Ribstein, *supra* note 17, at 103.

93 Hadfield & Talley, *supra* note 1.

94 *See* Kobayashi & Ribstein, *supra* note 14.

2.4.3.2 Estate freeze provisions

Although the advent of LLC statutes likely improved public welfare by reducing firms' transaction costs, those who crafted the new statutes, particularly lawyers, were motivated by side benefits from the new business form that may have reduced its utility compared to a first-best design. In particular, lawyers gained benefits from statutes that facilitated tax breaks and debtor protection. Lawyers' pursuit of these benefits, in turn, helped skew the statutes from first-best terms.

An example is estate freeze provisions in state unincorporated business statutes. Business owners often seek to pass their firms onto their heirs. A business owner might ensure continuity of the business after the founder's death or retirement by forming a limited partnership or LLC and making the owner's potential heirs limited partners or nonmanaging LLC members. The surviving members would take control of the firm after the founder's death. However, estate and gift taxes on the transfer of shares could force the children to liquidate the business and thereby defeat the business owner's objective. One way to avoid this result would be to reduce the value of the heirs' interests by contracting around the statutory default rules in LLC statutes that let members dissolve the firm and thereby cash out on a member's death. Under state law the members could contract around the statutory defaults to "freeze" the heirs into the firm, which would reduce the market value of their interests. However, tax law provides that a restriction on transfer does not count for tax valuation purposes unless it is imposed by state statute and not just private agreement.[95] The default provisions of LLC law thus impeded family firms from achieving an important tax objective.

Private lawdrafting efforts intervened to fill a gap in state business forms. A bar drafting committee in Georgia made that state's limited partnership statute the country's first to eliminate limited partners' default buyout rights. Lawyers alert to the tax rule discussed above spearheaded the adoption of similar estate freeze provisions in other limited partnership statutes.[96] The lawyers, in turn, may have hoped to benefit from these statutes through the increased estate planning fees these provisions would encourage. Most LLC statutes also now provide either that LLC members have no default right to dissociate or no right to be paid for their interests when they dissociate.[97]

The estate freeze provisions thus were arguably a byproduct of lawyers' efforts to maximize their own benefits from increased use of limited partnership and LLC statutes as estate tax avoidance devices. These provisions illustrate both the benefits and costs of byproduct laws. On the one hand, estate freeze provisions helpfully accommodated some firms' needs in light of the prevailing tax rule. On

95 *See* I.R.C. § 2704 (2006); *see also* 26 C.F.R. § 25.2704–2.

96 *See* Alan R. Bromberg & Larry E. Ribstein, BROMBERG & RIBSTEIN ON PARTNERSHIPS §17.13(a)–(c) (2004).

97 *See* Bruce H Kobayashi & Larry E. Ribstein, *The Non-Uniformity of Uniform Laws*, 35 J. CORP. L. 327, 335 (2010) (Table 1 §47, showing most adopted form provides no member default right to dissociate); Larry E. Ribstein & Robert Keatinge, RIBSTEIN & KEATINGE ON LIMITED LIABILITY COMPANIES, App. 11–2 (2d ed. 2004).

the other hand, lawyers' motivations might have skewed the statutes away from more efficient approaches. Members of closely held firms often prefer liberal buyout or dissolution as in the traditional partnership standard form to being locked in as in corporations. The estate freeze thus effectively brings back a problem of the close corporation that the availability of limited liability partnership-type forms had solved.[98] Informal firms, which particularly want an exit right, may neglect to craft around the default rule.[99] Others do not need the default rule because they will in any event engage in costly planning.

The effect of byproduct laws in skewing rules from those the market demands becomes evident when considering what a private market might have provided: multiple standard forms that accommodate both firms that want the traditional partnership default rules and those that want the estate freeze. However, lawyers would gain little from offering this variation in terms of attracting new firms to the state because the firms that were aware of the problem and did not care about the tax rule could simply draft around the statutory default rules. Indeed, lawyers may gain from the extra drafting and litigation costs required by the state's failure to offer the alternative form. By contrast, the alternative provisions might be produced by idealized private lawdrafters seeking to sell their laws rather than to use the laws to pursue tax revenues, increased business, or other objectives.

2.4.3.3 Expansion of LLC owners' liability protection

LLC statutes evolved beyond owners' limited liability for their firms' business debts to a mechanism for insulating members from liability for their own debts. Specifically, legislatures modified LLC statutes to permit formation of firms with nonbusiness objectives such as holding the owner's personal residence. These firms then could take advantage of partnership "charging order" provisions that enable members' creditors to reach their income from the firm but not their interest in the firm's assets. These provisions were designed to protect nondebtor members' from destruction of going concern value by debtor members' creditors. However, where the firm has only one owner and holds nonbusiness assets, the provisions effectively allow individuals to use LLCs to hide personal assets from unsuspecting creditors.[100] This development may explain the large number of very small LLCs in the leading asset protection jurisdictions of Nevada and Florida.[101]

Opening up LLCs to single-member, nonbusiness entities may have been an efficient addition to the set of standard forms. However, this modified LLC form

98 *See* Larry E. Ribstein, *The Closely Held Firm: A View from the U.S.*, 19 MELB. U. L. REV. 950 (1995).

99 See Ian Ayres, "Judging Close Corporations in the Age of Statutes," 70 WASH. U. L. Q. 365 (1992).

100 See Larry E. Ribstein, "Reverse Limited Liability and the Design of Business Associations," 30 DEL. J. CORP. L. 199 (2005).

101 *See* Kobayashi & Ribstein, *supra* note 14.

should not have retained partnership provisions designed for businesses that provided an end run around owners' personal liability. One possible explanation for these provisions is that they were added by lawyers, the primary interest group in drafting LLC provisions, as a byproduct of their interest in increasing legal business in their states by attracting clients to the state interested in debtor protection. Private providers of standard forms in an ideal market for such forms may have produced a variety of statutes that would accommodate both property owners' interest in new devices for holding assets and creditors' reasonable expectations regarding debt collection. For example, the statutes might have permitted the use of nonbusiness LLCs for holding property, or the use of single-member LLCs for such purpose that did not provide for charging orders. Such statutes would have better served creditors' interests and would have provided for clearer legal consequences for debtors. These statutes, however, might have reduced lawyers' ability to promote the modified LLC form as an asset protection vehicle.

2.4.3.4 L3Cs

Statutes providing for the "low profit limited liability company" (L3C)[102] provide another illustration of byproduct lawdrafting in the evolution of LLCs. These statutes are intended to facilitate investments by private foundations that seek exemptions as nonprofits under § 501(c)(3) of the Internal Revenue Code. The foundations may be assessed excise taxes if they make investments that jeopardize their charitable purposes. Congress enacted provisions in the Tax Reform Act of 1969 for "program related investments" (PRIs) that would exempt these foundations from the excise taxes.[103] However, 40 years after the birth of the concept few foundations were using PRIs[104]—perhaps because of ambiguity of the definition of PRIs. L3C statutes are intended to solve this problem by creating a form of entity that is clearly limited to charitable-type purposes. As with the estate freeze provisions, the L3C attempted to mesh the state law standard form with firms' tax needs.

Significantly, the L3C germinated not in a legislature but in a presentation by foundation head Robert Lang at the Aspen Institute's 2006 meeting and follow-up by participants.[105] The foundations were looking to clarify the PRI tax break and thereby make it more valuable. Although amendment of the tax law or a tax rule would have been the surest way to provide this clarification, that may not have been politically feasible. The L3C's proponents may have hoped that state statutes would provoke federal action.

102 *Id.*
103 See J. William Callison & Allan Vestal, "The L3C Illusion: Why Low-Profit Limited Liability Companies Will Not Stimulate Socially Optimal Private Foundation Investment in Entrepreneurial Ventures," 35 VT. L. REV. 273, 276–79 (2010).
104 *Id.* at 273 n. 4.
105 See Elizabeth Schmidt, "Vermont's Social Hybrid Pioneers: Early Observation and Questions to Ponder," 35 VT. L. REV. 163, 165 n. 10 (2010).

This new business form arguably illustrates the social value of private lawdrafting in promoting legal innovation. The PRI is inherently a difficult concept to apply since it attempts to graft nonprofit-type restrictions onto for-profit businesses. Many firms do not fit squarely into either the for-profit or nonprofit categories. Entrepreneurs may want profits plus something other than financial gain. For example, they may want to invest in projects that are socially valuable but too risky to be considered positive net present value. These firms may need standard form provisions that differ from those that match the needs of standard for-profit firms.

The L3C arguably facilitates this type of innovation in two ways. First, it mitigates the uncertainty that has hobbled the PRI by providing a state statutory safe harbor that enables the federal tax exemption. Second, the L3C provides default rules that, even apart from the PRI rules, address the difficulty of contracting for hybrid profit/nonprofit entities. This particularly includes defining the fiduciary duties of managers who must serve both society and markets.[106] Although existing business associations let managers of essentially for-profit firms mingle profit-making with social responsibility and permit contracting to alter the mix of these objectives,[107] the L3C adds clear structural rules for defining the duties in such hybrid firms. These rules not only provide guidance for managers, but also help signal the firm's objectives to investors and customers.[108] L3C statutes accordingly fill a gap in available standard forms.

L3Cs also can be seen as a way to avoid the effects of lawyer domination of both public and byproduct private lawdrafting. PRIs arguably illustrate lawyer-driven complexity that attempts to achieve precise accuracy in characterizing firms at the expense of cost-effective simplicity.[109] The L3C enables firms to start up quickly, without going through the costly process of IRS approval that normally accompanies the formation of a 501(c)(3) firm. A survey of the first group of entrepreneurs using the L3C showed that costs and simplicity were critical to their choice of form.[110]

The L3C, however, ultimately failed in important ways to achieve its main objective of simplifying use of PRIs when neither Congress nor the IRS endorsed use of this device. A state law could not protect foundations from having to clear their PRIs with the IRS. In other words, the tax objective of the L3C failed to become "law" in the sense of providing certainty of enforcement. Therefore, the L3C arguably misleads its investors with the false hope of simplicity and certainty

106 *See generally* John Tyler, "Negating the Legal Problem of Having 'Two Masters': A Framework for L3C Fiduciary Duties and Accountability," 35 VT. L. REV. 117 (2010) (proposing a framework for L3C fiduciary duties and their enforcement).

107 *See* Larry E. Ribstein, *Accountability and Responsibility in Corporate Governance*, 81 NOTRE DAME L. REV. 1431, 1433 (2006) ("[T]here is no question whether the parties to the firm may contract to take society's interests into account.").

108 *See* Schmidt, *supra* note 105, at 177 (describing the "branding value" that the L3C label provides entrepreneurs).

109 *See* Hadfield, *supra* note 19, at 965 (describing how the legal profession does not have strong incentives to simplify the law).

110 Schmidt, *supra* note 105, at 176–77.

because the statute's definition of "low profit" LLCs may have little to do with the tax meaning of program related investments.[111]

It is not clear whether the nonPRI-driven benefits of L3Cs outweigh the risk that the law will mislead firms as to the tax consequences of their choice of this form. To be sure, L3Cs provide a mechanism for clarifying the tax rule: a readymade business association that the PRI definition can refer to. However, this mechanism is unlikely to lead to legislation that authorizes states to decide on the scope of a federal tax exemption given the inherent conflict between states' interests in attracting business and the federal government's interest in preserving tax revenues.

The L3C illustrates the compromise nature of byproduct laws. A lawdrafter whose main incentive was to market her intellectual property rather than to lobby for a tax break might have designed a more suitable model for hybrid for-profit/nonprofit firms. Designing the L3C primarily as a mechanism to spur Congress into clarifying the law on PRIs has produced a standard form that actually increases transaction costs by both skewing the terms of the standard form and potentially misleading its users. An efficient set of standard forms for hybrid firms might include statutes designed for low-profit businesses as well as statutes designed for businesses that want to limit themselves to particular types of "program-related" investments. However, the developers of the L3C were focused on their political objective of promoting the tax exemption.

The L3C provides a lesson for other attempted byproduct uses of the LLC's flexibility to achieve political and social objectives. For example, commentators have proposed using business associations, such as partnerships and LLCs, to provide a mechanism for legal approval of same-sex domestic relationships.[112] These laws are designed at least in part to spur recognition of, and overcome legal barriers to, these relationships. However, these proposed actions could result in laws that are ill-suited to domestic relationships and thus both increase transaction costs and reduce certainty.[113]

2.5 Mechanics of private lawmaking

So far we have discussed significant problems with existing public, private, and byproduct approaches to lawdrafting. This Section shows how these problems

111 *See* Daniel Kleinberger, *A Myth Deconstructed: The "Emperor's New Clothes" on the Low Profit Limited Liability Company*, 32 (William Mitchell Coll. of Law Legal Studies Research Paper Series, Working Paper No. 2010–03, 2010), *available at* http://papers.ssrn.com/sol3/papers.cfm?abstract_id=1554045; *see also* Daniel S. Kleinberger & J. William Callison, *When the Law is Understood: L3C No* 3 (William Mitchell Coll. of Law Legal Studies Research Paper Series, Working Paper No. 2010–07, 2010), *available at* http://papers.ssrn.com/sol3/papers.cfm?abstract_id=1568373.

112 *See, e.g.*, Mary Anne Case, *Marriage Licenses*, 89 MINN. L. REV. 1758, 1779 (2005); Adrienne D. Davis, *Regulating Polygamy: Intimacy, Default Rules, and Bargaining for Equality*, 110 COLUM. L. REV. 1955, 1960 (2010); Jennifer A. Drobac & Antony Page, *A Uniform Domestic Partnership Act: Marrying Business Partnership and Family Law*, 41 GA. L. REV. 349, 353 (2007); Martha M. Ertman, *Marriage as a Trade: Bridging the Private/Private Distinction*, 36 HARV. C.R.-C.L. L. REV. 79, 84 (2001).

113 RIBSTEIN, *Hendricksons*, *supra* note 21, at 278–79.

might be reduced by mechanisms that encourage more direct private investment in lawcreation. An important component of this system is enabling private lawmakers to retain property rights in their creations even after they are adopted as law. This would entail at least modifying copyright protection from current law to better balance the public's access rights to privately drafted forms adopted as law against the lawdrafter's right to exclusive ownership. Such protection would address the problem discussed in Section 2.3—the inability under current law to combine the certainty of law with property rights in law. Section 2.5.1 describes the property rights that are necessary to create the appropriate incentives for private lawmakers.

Merely creating property rights in government-adopted law is not enough, however, to sustain private lawmaking. Section 2.5.1 shows that, in order to administer a manageable scheme of private property rights in law, the government must play an active role. This includes not only enacting the laws, which as we discuss above is critical to minimize expected reorganization costs, but also administering the property rights. The question then, discussed in Section 2.5.2, is how to ensure the government will have the right incentives in deciding which privately drafted laws to enact and administer. In other words, an efficient private market for law requires not only properly motivated private lawmakers on the sell side, but also properly motivated government actors on the buy side. Jurisdictional competition, as under the current regime, may or may not provide the necessary discipline. If government is not properly motivated, the private law regime may be no better than the current public/byproduct regime. Section 2.5.3 discusses the alternative of removing government altogether and moving to a fully privatized system of lawmaking.

2.5.1 Creating property rights in law

This Section discusses the basic property rights that could create a foundation for a private market in law. This involves three questions: first, the intellectual property protection based on copyright law; second, the nature of the property rights copyright would entail; and, finally, the types of incentive issues that would remain even given the application of copyright.

2.5.1.1 Application of copyright

Copyright is the primary mechanism for protecting authors' rights in specific laws. As already discussed, current law restricts the availability of copyright for privately produced materials that a government entity adopts as law. Specifically, § 105 of the Copyright Act precludes protection for any work "prepared by an officer or employee of the United States Government as part of that person's official duties."[114] This definition extends to court opinions written by federal judges,

114 *See* 17 U.S.C. §§ 101, 105 (2006).

congressional bills and statutes, and federal regulations. State laws are subject to similar rules. *Veeck* shows that definition has been extended to privately produced works such as model laws that were produced to be adopted as law and have been adopted as law.[115] *Veeck* also has potential application beyond state law. Courts have held that litigation documents in public courts cannot be secured from public access by a confidentiality agreement and protective order without a compelling justification for privacy.[116] Language cited in a judicial opinion might cause the loss of its author's copyright.[117]

The potential social welfare benefits of private lawdrafting and the importance of property rights in achieving those benefits suggest that Congress should explicitly extend a form of copyright protection to private materials that are given the effect of law by enactment, administrative promulgation, or inclusion in a judicial opinion. Permitting copyright of privately produced materials adopted as law would not be a radical legal change. Instead, it would resolve a contentious debate about current law between the majority and dissenting judges in *Veeck*, where the majority broadly held that:

> . . . [P]ublic ownership of the law means precisely that "the law" is in the "public domain" for whatever use the citizens choose to make of it. Citizens may reproduce copies of the law for many purposes, not only to guide their actions but to influence future legislation, educate their neighborhood association, or simply to amuse.[118]

The majority reasoned as a policy matter that the author of the material had survived without copyright protection and likely would continue to promulgate codes for her own purposes even without such protection. However, even the majority opinion recognized exceptions. For example, the majority suggested that the code author would be protected from publication of material in the model code that was not part of the law[119] and from publication of the model code itself as distinguished from statutes based on it,[120] and it suggested a distinction between publication of a law based on the code and the law's reference to the privately prepared standards or other materials. Two dissenting opinions questioned the breadth of the majority's rule and its application to a case involving publication of copyrighted codes on a website where there was no evidence that anyone was actually denied access to the laws. Both dissenting opinions noted the need,

115 *See Veeck*, 293 F.3d at 793.

116 *See Brown*, 960 F.2d at 1014 (vacating district court's order sealing court record, including pleadings and motions); *see also Wilson*, 759 F.2d at 1571; TEX. R. CIV. P. § 76a (1990) (creating a presumption that court records, including unfiled discovery materials and settlement agreements, are open to the public).

117 *See* Cunningham, *supra* note 70, at 304–05.

118 *See Veeck*, 293 F.3d at 799.

119 *Id.* at 799 n.14.

120 *Id.* at 804.

particularly of smaller government entities, to outsource lawdrafting services to code preparers.[121]

2.5.1.2 *The scope of property rights in laws*

Even if Congress clarifies that private parties have property rights in the laws they draft, several questions remain concerning the scope of these rights. The first question concerns the appropriate balance between the scope of property rights necessary to create adequate incentives for drafters and the need to provide reasonable public access to privately drafted legislative proposals adopted as law. The law author should be able to sell or license the law to governments that adopt it or private firms that use it as a standard form. As long as the system results in a public benefit of encouraging legal innovations, the public should be willing to pay the cost.

Thus, in the *Veeck* situation, the model building code author could post the code on a website with a licensing agreement and retain its property rights even after a municipality adopts the code. However, due process demands that the law's content should not be subject to intellectual property protection as against those who simply want to read or write about it. Thus, competing distributors should be able to copy the law's content and distribute it at a lower price. This would encourage efficiencies in distribution while the lawdrafter's ability to license to governments and firms preserves the author's incentives to create original laws.[122]

Second, the copyright on law protects only the precise form of original expression and not the underlying ideas. Thus, even if a particular LLC statute was protected by copyright, a competing producer could sell a similar statute that expressed the underlying ideas in a different way. Moreover, otherwise copyrightable original expression may become merged with the underlying idea and therefore unprotected under copyright law.[123]

Patent-type rights in a legal idea may provide broader protection for ideas. However, such rights face hurdles under rules defining patentable subject matter and requiring nonobviousness.[124] Even if these hurdles could be overcome, the rights conferred in a particular idea still may not cover similar ideas. For example,

121 *See id.* at 807 (Higginbotham, dissenting); *see also id.* at 817 (Wiener, dissenting).

122 These due process concerns could be alleviated though fair use privileges or through jurisdictions requiring licensors to explicitly allow such uses by those bound by the law. Courts could also require similar licenses to be granted by those wishing to file briefs, complaints, and other potentially copyrightable litigation documents. *See* Kobayashi & Ribstein, *supra* note 14, at 1179. For a current example of these issues, *see* Chad Bray, *Keep Your Hands off My Briefs: Lawyers Sue Westlaw, Lexis*, WALL ST. J. L. Blog (Feb. 22, 2012, 6:21 pm), http://blogs.wsj.com/law/2012/02/22/keep-your-hands-off-my-briefs-lawyers-sue-westlaw-lexis/ (discussing the Class Action Complaint in *White, et al. v. West Publishing, S.D.N.Y* (alleging copyright violations by WESTLAW and LEXIS/NEXIS resulting from the unauthorized electronic publication of briefs and other litigation documents); *see also* Kobayashi & Ribstein, *supra* note 77 (discussing the copyrightability of class action complaints and other litigation documents).

123 Goetz & Scott, *supra* note 2, at 292 n.78; Kobayashi & Ribstein, *supra* note 14.

124 Goetz & Scott, *supra* note 2, at 292 n.78; Kobayashi & Ribstein, *supra* note 14.

a patent for a "poison pill" takeover defense might cover takeover defenses that use anti-dilution mechanisms but not all takeover defenses or even all director-approved takeover defenses. Similarly, a patent for an LLC would not necessarily cover other limited liability standard forms for closely held firms such as limited liability partnerships or limited partnerships. Indeed, in view of these considerations, it is not even clear patent rights would materially assist private lawdrafters.

Government addresses the problem of the scope of property rights in law by adopting a specific law governing a type of situation, rather than others covering the same situation. The adoption of the law effectively grants a franchise to the private lawdrafter covering similar types of laws. The tradeoff is that competition among lawdrafters is constrained while the government's power is commensurately enhanced. Section 2.5.3 discusses jurisdictional competition as a mechanism for disciplining this power. But this competition restores the problem of the lawdrafter's scope of property rights. Although a private lawmaker may have property rights in a particular law enacted by a particular government, these rights do not cover similar laws other governments may enact. This affects private lawmakers' incentives, as discussed at Section 2.5.1.4.

2.5.1.3 Enforcement of property rights

Special problems arise in enforcing property rights in law, particularly including how to apply remedies for infringement. As discussed above, law is potentially useful in reducing transaction costs by filling gaps in specific contracts. Although parties can adapt nonstatutory standard forms for their particular relationships, these forms cannot fully provide law's unique gap-filling and enforcement function. Yet statutes' gap-filling role raises a question concerning how to enforce drafters' intellectual property rights. The answer to this question may depend on how the private lawmaker sells her law.

One type of sale of private laws involves business-association-type statutes that firms adopt as their governing law by filing with the state. Suppose, for example, a private party writes a law for a new type of business entity that a government adopts—a "series" LLC. The new law provides, among other things, for the effect of certain types of provisions in private agreements, such as provisions separating management, property, and liabilities of sub-entities that are being operated together. Suppose further the government buys exclusive rights to the law and pays a fee to the drafter, which the government recoups as part of the franchise fee it charges firms for organizing under the law. This resembles the current system except that purely private lawmakers substitute for byproduct lawmakers such as the Delaware Bar, and cash payments to the lawdrafters substitute for political advantages.

The private lawdrafter alternatively could sell the statute directly to firms that form under the law. The state could charge fees and taxes, all of which go to the state treasury. Meanwhile, the private lawdrafter would charge adopting firms a license fee. The lawdrafter would then have to collect fees from the adopting firms and enforce its rights against the adopting firms in court. As long as the government must establish a system for accepting filings and collecting fees, licensing through the government would seem to be more efficient than direct sales to adopting firms. Thus, the government plays a necessary role in providing a collection mechanism.[125]

Remedies for infringement would depend on whether the infringer is a state or a private party. If a private lawdrafter or state seeks to collect fees for a copyrighted statute in violation of the drafter's copyright, the drafter could sue the infringing state for inverse condemnation and the private usurper for infringement.[126] As discussed above, the drafters would have intellectual property rights only in the content of the law—as distinguished from the mechanism of distribution—and only as against firms or states that adopt the law as the controlling statute, not against members of the public who seek to access the law.

Enforcing property rights in law is further complicated where the law provides background rights even for firms that do not formally adopt the law by making a filing. Examples would include sales laws, such as the Uniform Commercial Code, and informal business association laws, such as the law of agency and general partnership. In this situation there is no metering device such as a franchise fee and no mechanism such as a formal filing that identifies potential violators. The law's basic function of operating in the background to clarify or fill gaps in provisions included in parties' agreements creates special problems for applying intellectual property law. Firms might be sued for including specific language in their agreements, provided the law's author could track down these private contracts. However, this seems no different from the statutory language filling gaps in agreements that fit the statutory definition. In short, the special gap-filling feature of law may make intellectual property rights in law impossible to enforce effectively outside the special situation of laws adopted through formal filings.

A possible solution to this problem is to effectuate enforcement of private property rights in law by extending filing requirements and franchise fees to contracts other than business associations. In other words, firms would lose the advantage of these statutory forms unless they affirmatively opted in. However,

125 In effect, the government franchise fee acts like a metering device that includes an upcharge used to compensate the lawdrafter. *See ProCD, Inc. v. Zeidenberg*, 86 F.3d 1447 (enforcing terms of shrinkwrap license that limited use of information contained in database). But *see* Mark A. Lemley, *Beyond Preemption: The Law and Policy of Intellectual Property Licensing*, 87 CAL. L. REV. 111 (1999) (criticizing the holding in ProCD). *See generally* Michelle M. Burtis & Bruce H. Kobayashi, *Intellectual Property and Antitrust Limitations on Contract*, in DYNAMIC COMPETITION AND PUB. POL'Y (2001) (discussing interaction between contract, antitrust and intellectual property); Ronald H. Coase, *The Lighthouse in Economics*, 17 J. L. & ECON. 357 (1974) (discussing an analogous situation of using port fees to pay for lighthouse services); Bruce H. Kobayashi, *Spilled Ink or Economic Progress? The Supreme Court's Decision in* Illinois Tool Works v. Independent Ink, 53 ANTITRUST BULL. 5 (2008) (discussing the economic efficiency of using an implied license and metering instead of direct licensing); Bruce H. Kobayashi & Larry E. Ribstein, *Uniformity, Choice of Law, and Software Sales*, 8 GEO. MASON L. REV. 261 (1999) (discussing the use of restrictive licenses to complement intellectual property rights).

126 *See supra* discussion in note 36.

this would raise the potentially serious problem of leaving in limbo the rights of parties who fail to adopt background laws simply because they are unaware of them. This would make statutory forms useless or even counterproductive for the very parties who most need them to reduce contracting costs.

The complications multiply for privately drafted forms that have not been adopted as laws. Drafters can sell these forms to private parties and sue copycat competitors for infringement.[127] They may also be able to sue parties who use copyrighted language in their agreements, subject to fair use limitations.[128] As with statutory forms that do not involve public filings, private forms lack a government-provided metering or compliance device. Indeed, even apart from the absence of a filing, firms have no clear way to adopt these forms' language by reference as their governing law.[129]

Private producers might promulgate statutes and offer them for licensing, effectively enabling firms to organize under, for example, "Hammurabi law," just as they now form under Delaware law. Whatever the private drafter calls her product, it does not acquire the increased certainty of enforcement "law" unless a state adopts it as such. Accordingly, the state could ignore the form language when its courts interpret and enforce the parties' contract. This could expose adopting firms to potential reorganization costs. As discussed above, firms would have to balance their savings in matching costs from a better fitting statute against the risk of reorganization costs. Despite potential reorganization costs, firms might find it worthwhile to use the purely private law, particularly if it is a widely used form that courts are unlikely to reject out of a concern for frustrating expectations. Indeed, a court might give the form some quasi-legal force. For example, a Delaware court refused to imply an opt-out from fiduciary duties despite the inclusion of a standard provision giving the general partner sole discretion to manage the business. The agreement used language from a popular form but omitted language explicitly preempting default duties.[130]

Even if private producers of nonfiled law or nonlaw forms could enforce intellectual property rights against infringers, copyright law will not protect the creator against competing sellers of similar but not identical ideas or expressions, and effective patent protection may not be available for many legal innovations.[131] The application of copyright law may be critical where the exact expression is important, as with a fiduciary opt-out. If the user must borrow the exact language from a privately promulgated form in order to get the desired effect, it may matter whether the form has retained copyright despite its adoption as law or use in a

127 *See supra* text accompanying note 34.

128 NIMMER, *supra* note 34, § 2.18(e).

129 One possible solution to this set of problems is to link enforcement of contracts to payment for property rights by also privatizing enforcement. *See* Bernstein, *supra* note 66, at 143–44; Hadfield & Weingast, *supra* note 11, at 7.

130 *Miller v. Am. Real Estate Partners*, No. Civ. A. 16788, 2001 WL 1045643, at *9 (Del. Ch. Sept. 6, 2001) (citing Martin I. Lubaroff & Paul M. Altman, LUBAROFF & ALTMAN ON DELAWARE LIMITED PARTNERSHIPS, at F-38 (2000 Supp.)); Larry E. Ribstein, *The Uncorporation and Corporate Indeterminacy*, 2009 ILL. L. REV. 131, 149–50 (discussing *Miller*, 2001 WL 1045643, at *9).

131 *See* Goetz & Scott, *supra* note 2, at 295 and accompanying text.

case, and, if so, whether borrowing the language is fair use. In other cases, as with the series LLC, the idea may be critical and unprotected under intellectual property law. Moreover, a statute may contain several ideas, raising the question whether the organization or selection of ideas in the statute is original enough to qualify for copyright protection. However, the protection afforded such compilations under copyright law is "thin."[132]

In short, even if intellectual property rights in private laws are theoretically attractive and potentially available, enforcing these rights outside a narrow category of contracts requiring state filings may be impractical.

2.5.1.4 Incentives to produce efficient laws

Even assuming the law suitably clarifies drafters' property rights in law, there may be a number of potential problems in the market for private law that require a legal solution. First, even with property rights, private lawmakers may not have an incentive to produce any laws. Conversely, they may have an incentive to produce too many laws. For example, as with orphaned drugs, lawdrafters may lack incentives to create laws for limited niches of users. Also, firms' costs of using a particular form may depend on the extent and quality of the "network" of legal materials available for interpreting and applying the form.[133]

Indeed, this is an important advantage of statutory law. This network may determine both firms' mismatch costs and the degree of legal certainty regarding a particular term.[134] It follows that private incentives to produce statutes may depend on the order in which these statutes are produced over time—not just on firms' intrinsic characteristics and demands apart from network effects. In other words, network effects may prevent entry of private standard forms that would reduce total mismatch and drafting costs in the absence of such effects. Although network effects do not necessarily prevent the emergence of a more efficient form,[135] this might occur.

Second, private lawmakers may over-create laws, so that total drafting and other costs exceed social benefits. Presumably the market can, to some extent, constrain producers from investing in law-production such that expected costs exceed expected benefits. However, market constraints may not be adequate where the expected costs are imposed on parties other than law buyers and sellers. For example, the *numerus clausus* principle limits the menu of property ownership forms from which parties can choose in order to minimize the information and other costs imposed by having too many forms.[136] In the context of business

132 *Feist Publ'ns, Inc. v. Rural Tel. Serv. Co.*, 499 U.S. 340, 349 (1991).

133 Klausner, supra note 39, at 783.

134 In other words, the "law," which we associate with certainty, includes not only statutory provisions but also common law rules interpreting the statutes. The value of all these legal rules, in turn, depends on associated materials assisting in understanding these legal rules.

135 Kobayashi & Ribstein, *supra* note 39, at 115–16.

136 Thomas W. Merrill & Henry E. Smith, "Optimal Standardization in the Law of Property: The 'Numerus Clausus' Principle," 110 YALE L.J. 1, 7 (2000).

association and other contractual standard forms, parties' ability to choose the applicable form and state law likely minimizes this problem. Parties will choose the state law that minimizes users' costs by restricting the number of forms. However, this may be a problem for privately produced property and other rules that may apply without the parties making an explicit *ex ante* choice.

Third, private owners may not produce the right mix of laws. For example, they might maximize their profits by producing statutes that are as different as possible from each other, even if this is not the best fit for the firms that would use the statutes. Even if more firms have use for statutes that are similar to existing statutes, and total welfare would be increased by producing such statutes, the firms that need the dissimilar statutes might pay more for them because their drafting costs increase rapidly with the difference between their preferred rules and other available statutes.[137] This assumption reflects the intuition that shifts in individual contract provisions—such as liability for the firm's debts, management, control, and profit-sharing in a firm's governance structure—change relationships between the characteristics and therefore necessitate redrafting of these other characteristics.[138]

To be sure, these incentive factors do not alone negate the benefits of private lawmaking. Despite these complications, providing property rights in law might improve the mix of available laws over what is available without property rights. However, when added to the other problems discussed in this Section concerning the scope and enforcement of these property rights, private lawmakers' incentives provide a further reason for skepticism about the potential benefits of private lawmaking.

2.5.2 Government's role in private lawmaking

We propose that private parties participate in lawdrafting only as drafters. This proposal responds to public legislators' weak incentives to innovate complex standard forms. Thus, government would be the exclusive enforcer of privately drafted laws. Moreover, as discussed in Section 2.5.1, it may be efficient for government to be the exclusive purchaser or licensor.[139] In any event, it would be left to government to enforce private lawdrafters' property rights in their laws. This reliance on government may seem an odd way to promote optimal private law production because it raises the problems of inadequate government incentives to innovate that private lawdrafting is intended to solve.

Perhaps increased private lawdrafting would improve upon the present system despite government's continued involvement as enforcer because it would at least increase incentives for drafting innovative laws. Governments in effect would be

137 Hadfield & Talley, *supra* note 1, at 418.

138 Hadfield & Talley, *supra* note 1, at 419–20.

139 We focus on government purchase of discrete statutes. Another approach might be for government to contract with third party suppliers to produce laws. One concern with this approach is that the third party might be bound to a particular government and therefore would not avoid the political incentives that plague the "byproduct" market.

outsourcing law drafting to private providers—comparable to the municipal adopters of the building codes involved in *Veeck*.[140] Outsourcing could help overcome public lawmakers' unwillingness to invest in drafting new laws beyond the very limited extent to which the new laws could contribute to their reelection.[141] This could motivate private lawmakers to create laws that reduce users' mismatch costs, rather than mainly for political gain as with byproduct lawmakers. Although byproduct lawmakers would continue to produce laws, they would have to compete with private lawmakers. Even if governments are not perfectly motivated to buy private laws, the stock of privately drafted laws offered for sale would at least inform the public as to potential alternatives to government-adopted statutes.

The development of a significant market for private laws is at least plausible. Small jurisdictions whose lawdrafters lack significant resources for researching and drafting legislation, such as the municipalities that bought the housing codes involved in *Veeck*, would have an incentive to outsource lawdrafting to private drafters, as suggested by the *Veeck* dissenters. A private law supplier could acquire a reputation for high quality drafting and updating, which makes its laws attractive.[142] Such an organization would provide an alternative to the currently limited number of branded lawdrafters like NCCUSL. Even NCCUSL, despite its byproduct incentives, has been able to use its reputation to "sell" its laws to many states.[143] This would enable states and municipalities to offer high quality and diverse laws without being in the relatively limited category of jurisdictions like Delaware that draw on local expertise to reap large gains from competing in the national market for laws. The lawmaking organization's reputation for quality could help bond the adopting jurisdiction's implicit promise not to manipulate the law to appeal to local interest groups.

140 This unbundling of lawdrafting and enforcement is analogous to a proposal for European corporate lawdrafting. *See* Christian Kirchner, Richard W. Painter & Wulf Kaal, *Regulatory Competition in EU Corporate Law After Inspire Art: Unbundling Delaware's Product for Europe*, 34–35 (Univ. Ill. Law & Econ. Research Paper No. LE04–001, 2004), *available at* http://ssrn.com/abstract=617681.

141 This problem explains why it is not enough to simply give public lawmakers property rights in their laws as one author suggests. Stephen Clowney, *Property in Law: Government Rights in Legal Innovations*, 72 OHIO ST. L. J. 1, 3–4 (2011). This would not solve the incentive problem unless governments could pay their lawdrafters a share of any profits or other gains from selling laws. Yet profit sharing would be inconsistent with the inherently public nature of what governments do. Enabling government to outsource lawdrafting to private lawdrafters avoids this problem. *See* Gregory Kroger, *Position Taking and Cosponsorship in the U.S. House*, 28 LEGIS. STUD. Q. 225, 225 (2003) (discussing the evolution of Congress's use of cosponsorship of bills as a way to claim quasi-property rights to legislation); Gregory Koger, *Property Rights of Legislation? When Did That Happen?*, MISCHIEFS OF FACTION (Aug. 3, 2012), http://mischiefsoffaction.blogspot.com/2012/08/this-week-politico-had-story-joe-walsh.html?m=1.

142 The private firm with property rights to their products might also intervene or otherwise participate in litigation to ensure the enforcement of the terms set out in the private statute and to insure adopters against reorganization costs if the terms contained in the private statute are not enforced.

143 Ribstein & Kobayashi, *supra* note 54, at 147.

States could encourage a market for private laws not only by adopting specific laws but by providing a platform for private lawmaking. States might offer open-ended statutes that enforce agreements of specified types, such as a "contractual entity."[144] Hammurabi, Inc. could then sell standard forms that parties might use under this type of statute. The open-ended statute would in effect create the opportunity for an "aftermarket" for standard forms, equivalent to the "app" market for mobile devices. The open-ended statute would give these privately created standard forms some of the effect of law. Interpretation problems might remain which would need to be addressed by additional law in the form of specific statutes or court decisions.

The important question raised by government's involvement on the buy side of the private market for law is whether this would reintroduce all of the problems of rent-seeking that exist under the current public/byproduct regime. Government agents may have political incentives to buy too many or too few laws compared to profit-maximizing private purchasers. Indeed, these incentives produce the skewing from social welfare that we noted above with byproduct laws such as L3Cs.

Although in theory government could continue to choose laws created by byproduct or public lawmakers, or might buy the wrong private laws, jurisdictional competition could be an important mechanism for aligning the government producers of laws with social welfare. Governments can compete with each other not only regarding the outputs of their legislative agents, but also regarding decisions by their government agents as to which private laws to purchase. Firms would choose the laws of jurisdictions that best address these problems, and choice-of-law rules could enforce these choices. This would be analogous to the situation that currently exists with byproduct lawdrafting, where a state legislature like Delaware relies almost completely on local lawyers to write business association laws. The difference is that a market for private laws would enable legislatures to rely on lawyers generally and nonlawyer drafters rather than being limited to help from the local bar.

A potential downside of jurisdictional competition for private lawmaking is that competition can erode private lawmakers' incentives. As discussed in Section 2.5.1, a government's power to adopt law also empowers it to create law franchises that protect private lawmakers' property rights to types of laws. However, other states can invade this space with competing laws. Over time, jurisdictional competition can eventually weed out the excess laws, just as it does in the current system.[145] But until then, private lawmakers must contend with competitors selling laws to all of the states.

In sum, although there are reasons to believe that an "outsourcing" approach to lawdrafting would function better than the current system of law drafting by government and byproduct drafters, there are also reasons to be skeptical. There

144 Larry E. Ribstein, *Limited Liability Unlimited*, 24 DEL. J. CORP. L. 407, 410 (1999).

145 Larry E. Ribstein, *Making Sense of Entity Rationalization*, 58 BUS. LAW. 1023, 1040–41 (2003).

are a number of possible outcomes under a private law system. Governments might not buy outsourced laws from private parties due to concern that the public would not accept this approach. There may be only a small number of buyers and laws would be sold in a captive market, much like the one in which rent-seeking, byproduct lawdrafters operate. Or perhaps bad private laws would proliferate, and state legislators would not be able to distinguish them from good laws. We cannot prove that Hammurabi, Inc. would improve on the existing equilibrium. On the other hand, the possibility of improvement is sufficiently plausible that it is worth analyzing the conditions under which it might occur, particularly including the creation of stronger property rights in privately drafted laws. Moreover, it is not obvious how adding an additional group of private lawdrafting organizations could result in worse laws than the existing mix of government and byproduct lawdrafters.

2.5.3 Private enforcement

The main alternative to a government market for laws would be to find some way for private enforcers to provide government-like legal certainty. Such a regime has worked, for example, in a closed system like the world of the diamond merchants in Bernstein's study.[146] In that study, notice is no problem, and the parties are subject to strong reputational constraints.[147] Effective coordination can occur other than as a result of promulgation of laws in the sense defined in this chapter.[148]

Large-scale private common law systems can emerge, as demonstrated by the development of the Law Merchant.[149] The main impediment to such a system is that a full-fledged private judicial system requires a mechanism not only for deciding cases, as in arbitrations, but also for producing judicial-type opinions that are respected as precedent. The basic problem is that any benefit from the opinion in terms of increased predictability of results would accrue to litigants in subsequent cases, while the fees to judges and indirect costs in terms of lost confidentiality accrue to the parties of an individual case. Parties accordingly would participate in a private common law system only if they benefit over time from having their transactions subject to clear legal rules. The state usually will be in the best position under modern conditions of open trade to provide and guard the integrity of such a durable system.[150] As long as the state provides the law, it arguably must ensure that the public has general access to the proceedings just as for statutory law. This returns to the basic problem of protecting property rights in private lawdrafting and the dilemma inherent in private lawdrafting.

146 Bernstein, *supra* note 66, at 115.
147 *Id.* at 116.
148 Hadfield & Weingast, *supra* note 11, at 7.
149 Masten & Prüfer, *supra* note 65, at 28–29.
150 *See id.* (discussing the conditions that support private and public courts).

Although the state would seem to be the most likely source of a full-fledged common law system, there is some chance a fully private legal system could emerge. One possible path to such a system is through arbitration. Arbitration associations already compete for users through rules and reputations. An association (perhaps a subsidiary of Hammurabi, Inc.) could compete with both public courts and other arbitration associations by offering careful public written opinions by former judges hired as arbitrators. The association could internalize the cost of the system through the fees it charges to users. Parties, especially repeat players in certain types of cases, might be willing to pay the higher cost if they thought the arbitrators had more expertise than government judges or that the association's procedures could save them overall litigation costs compared to a government-run system. Although such a system could not offer enforcement comparable to a government system, in some kinds of cases private sanctions such as reputational bonding might suffice.[151]

2.6 Concluding remarks

Legal innovation is important, but it may be under-produced because of public lawdrafters' weak incentives. Private lawdrafting is a potential solution to this problem. However, under current law this lawdrafting is on the horns of a dilemma: it requires government enforcement and recognition, yet such enforcement and recognition reduces the property rights that are essential to motivate private lawdrafters. The result is that much private lawdrafting today occurs as a byproduct of political and other activities, with results that are often less efficient than would be produced by a purely commercial market for law.

We outline a plausible approach to productive legal innovation by establishing a better balance between public access and private rights than the one that exists under current law. The specific path to our approach would be legislative reversal

151 Indeed, an advantage of a fully private system is the ability to link use of a private statute as background rules with adjudication in private court. This could provide a metering system where no public filings are necessary. *But see* Erin A. O'Hara O'Connor, Kenneth J. Martin, and Randall S. Thomas, *Customizing Employment Arbitration*, 98 IOWA L. REV. 133, 137–42 (2012) (analyzing issues in private arbitration contracts that are reserved for adjudication in court). It can also allow the parties to choose their own procedural rules. *See* Robert G. Bone, *Party Rulemaking: Making Procedural Rules Through Party Choice*, 90 TX. L. REV. 1329 (2012); Kevin E. Davis & Helen Hershkoff, *Contracting for Procedure*, 53 WM. & MARY L. REV. 507 (2011); David A. Hoffman, *Whither Bespoke Procedure?* U. ILL. L. REV. (forthcoming, 2014), TEMPLE U. LEG. STUD. RESEARCH PAPER No. 2013–10. (2013), *available at* SSRN:http://ssrn.com/abstract=2216902. Alternatively, the parties could use the Delaware hybrid system of state judges privately adjudicating cases and charging a direct fee for adjudication services. *See* 10 Del. C. § 349(a) (2012), (giving the Delaware Court of Chancery "the power to arbitrate business disputes when the parties request a member of the Court of Chancery, or such other person as may be authorized under rules of the Court, to arbitrate a dispute."); Larry E. Ribstein, *Practicing Theory: Legal Education for the Twenty-First Century*, 96 IOWA L. REV. 1649, 1668 (2011) (discussing arbitration under the Delaware statute); But see *Del. Coal. for Open Gov't v. Strine, No. 1:11–1015*, 2012 WL 3744718 at *2 (D. Del Aug. 30, 2012) (holding that arbitrations conducted under the Delaware hybrid system could not be closed to the public).

of the *Veeck* rule to clarify that private lawdrafters retain property rights in privately drafted law proposals, even if they are adopted as law. This type of systemic reform might create the conditions necessary for Hammurabi, Inc. to thrive and to supply a richer variety of law than can be expected from a purely public lawdrafting system. To be sure, it is not clear whether the suggested reform would, in fact, improve the current market for law. On the other hand, it is also not clear that the reform could do harm, particularly if the private property rights are carefully limited to preserve public access, as the *Veeck* dissenters suggested.

3 The impact of the new world order on economic development: the role of the intellectual property rights system

*Joseph Straus**

3.1 Introduction

Those who have spent decades studying the field of intellectual property protection will not be particularly surprised by the criticism of the international system of intellectual property rights protection and of the broad view of these rights, which has been increasingly vehement. Even though a widely surprising breakthrough in support of higher, internationally binding standards of intellectual property protection could have been achieved with the acceptance of the International Agreement on Trade-related Aspects of Intellectual Property Rights ("TRIPs") in 1994, TRIPs was at the center of multifaceted criticism, for both developing and developed countries.[1]

Indeed, the criticism of the developing nations soon found support, in part, from internationally recognized economists and lawyers. It did not go unrecognized, even by the critics, that TRIPs, together with the General Agreement on Tariffs and Trade ("GATT 1994"), the Agreement on Trade-related Investment Measures ("TRIMs"), the General Agreement on Trade in Services ("GATS"), together and with all their appendices, represents only one of the pillars of support of the international legal system of the World Trade Organization ("WTO").

It also did not go unrecognized that developing countries would only accept TRIPs in this context in order to secure access to the markets of industrialized countries. However, it was asserted that 90 percent of all patents are granted in

* Joseph Straus is Professor of Law at the Universities of Munich and Ljubljana and the Marshall B. Coyne Visiting Professor of International Law at the George Washington University Law School, Washington D.C. He is also the Chairman of the Managing Board of the Munich Intellectual Property Law Center and Director at the Max Planck Institute for Intellectual Property, Competition and Tax Law in Munich, Germany. This chapter was previously published as Joseph Straus, *The Impact of the New World Order on Economic Development: The Role of the Intellectual Property Rights System*, 6 J. MARSHALL REV. INTELL. PROP. L. 1 (2006).

1 *See generally* THE SECRETARIAT OF THE WORLD INTELLECTUAL PROPERTY ORGANIZATION, PROPOSAL BY ARGENTINA AND BRAZIL FOR THE ESTABLISHMENT OF A DEVELOPMENT AGENDA FOR WIPO, WO/GA/31/11, August 27, 2004, *available at* http://www.wipo.org/documents/en/document/govbody/wo_gb_ga/pdf/wo_ga_31_11.pdf [hereinafter SECRETARIAT].

industrialized states, that TRIPs negotiations are brought to an end without a broad cost benefit analysis of, for example, welfare-related aspects of intellectual property rights for less developed countries, and that developing countries and other net importers of protected knowledge accept TRIPs only on political and not economic grounds.[2]

It was further claimed that TRIPs was the result of a strong and coordinated political lobby of U.S. and European industry, an "aggressive unilateralism" on the behalf of the United States and the European Communities, and lacked a necessary legitimacy because it was not based on the concept of human rights.[3] Even Secretary-General of the United Nations, Kofi Annan, admonished that the progression of free trade and the legal system cannot be taken for granted: "[w]e must resolve to underpin the free global market with genuinely global values and secure it with effective institutions. We must show the same firm leadership in defense of human rights, labor standards, and the environment as we already do in defense of intellectual property."[4]

3.2 The new wave of TRIPs criticism

It would doubtless go too far to attempt even a brief reference to all recent publications that have critically dealt with the current international concept of intellectual property rights. However, in the articles of Maskus and Reichman,[5] Musungu and Dutfield,[6] or those of Boyle,[7] for instance, it is clear that each of them in some way questions the current system and calls for a moratorium on international development of intellectual property rights. These articles suggest that developing nations be given the possibility either to thoroughly evaluate their realm of interests on the basis of the newly gained knowledge,[8] or to impede a

2 Ernst-Ulrich Petersmann, *From Negative to Positive Integration in the WTO: The TRIPs Agreement and the WTO Constitution*, in: INTELLECTUAL PROPERTY: TRADE, COMPETITION, AND SUSTAINABLE DEVELOPMENT 21, 23 (Thomas Cottier & Petros C. Mavroidis eds., The University of Michigan Press 2000).

3 *Id.* at 23, 42. Trade liberalization in the WTO should not only be based on utilitarian objectives of 'welfare maximization' but also on human rights concepts, such as individual freedom, . . . non-discrimination . . ., and rule of law subject to judicial review by national courts and international adjudication. . . . The time has come for recognizing that human rights law offers WTO rules moral, constitutional and democratic legitimacy that may be more important for the parliamentary ratification of future WTO Agreements than the traditional economic and utilitarian justifications. *Id.* at 44.

4 Kofi Annan, *Laying the Foundations of a Fair and Free World Trade System*, in: THE ROLE OF THE WORLD TRADE ORGANIZATION IN GLOBAL GOVERNANCE 26, 27 (Gary P. Sampson ed., 2001).

5 *See generally* Keith E. Maskus & Jerome H. Reichman, *The Globalization of Private Knowledge Goods and the Privatization of Global Public Goods*, 7 J. INT'L ECON. L. 279 (2004).

6 *See generally* SISULE F. MUSUNGU & GRAHAM DUTFIELD, MULTILATERAL AGREEMENTS AND A TRIPS-PLUS WORLD: THE WORLD INTELLECTUAL PROPERTY ORGANIZATION ("WIPO"), *available at* http://www.geneva.quno.info/pdf/WIPO(A4)final0304.pdf.

7 *See generally* James Boyle, *A Manifesto on WIPO and the Future of Intellectual Property*, 2004 DUKE L. & TECH. REV. 0009 (2004), *available at* http://www.law.duke.edu/journals/dltr/articles/PDF/2004DLTR0009.pdf [hereinafter *Manifesto on WIPO*]. *See generally* James Boyle, *The Second Enclosure Movement and the Construction of the Public Domain*, 66 LAW & CONTEMP. PROBS. 33 (2003).

8 Maskus & Reichman, *supra* note 5, at 319.

possible cessation of WIPO activities in TRIPs-plus standards,[9] or finally, as seen in Boyle,[10] to call the entire concept of the system into question. These authors neither entertain the existing circumstances of developing nations and industrialized nations before TRIPs,[11] nor, even more surprisingly, do they base their theoretical deliberations on any empirical insights that they could have accumulated in this matter since the implementation of TRIPs.[12]

Indeed, no single attempt has been made in this direction. Even the moderately worded paper of the British Commission on Intellectual Property Rights ("CIPR")[13] contained explicit allusions that "developing countries accepted TRIPs not because at the time the adoption of intellectual property protection was high on their list of priorities, but partly because they thought the overall package offered, including the reduction of trade protectionism in developed countries, would be beneficial."[14]

There were complaints that these expectations had not been rewarded, but the complaints lacked a reciprocal offering of empirical data. The statistics retrieved from the databanks of the World Bank, which refer to the alleged benefit of patent licenses, according to which the active trade balance of the United States rose from US$14 billion to over US$22 billion between 1991 and 2001,[15] prove nothing about the macroeconomic results of the WTO "package deal" on developing nations.

The comment made by Nobel Prize winner Joseph Stiglitz, that the structure of intellectual property rights has become so extreme that it is harmful to society and especially harmful to developing countries, points in the same direction.[16] Institutional mechanisms should be established "so that we can go back and recognize the need for developing countries, for instance, to have some technology transfer."[17] Similar, but even more explicit, is the Geneva Declaration on the Future of the World Intellectual Property Organization ("WIPO") of October 2004, signed by Stiglitz, among others, which accuses WIPO of "embrac[ing] a culture of creating and expanding monopoly privileges, often without regard to consequence."[18]

9 MUSUNGU & DUTFIELD, *supra* note 6 at 24.

10 *Manifesto on WIPO*, *supra* note 7.

11 *See generally* Joseph Straus, *Implications of the TRIPS Agreement in the Field of Patent Law*, in: FROM GATT TO TRIPS: THE AGREEMENT ON TRADE-RELATED ASPECTS OF INTELLECTUAL PROPERTY RIGHTS, 160 (Friedrich-Karl Beier & Gerhard Schricker eds., 1996).

12 *See, e.g.*, Petersmann, *supra* note 2, at 32–35.

13 *See generally* COMMISSION ON INTELLECTUAL PROPERTY RIGHTS, INTEGRATING INTELLECTUAL PROPERTY RIGHTS AND DEVELOPMENT POLICY (2002).

14 *Id.* at 8.

15 *Id.* at 21. The greatest loser in this regard was Korea with US$15 billion. *Id.*

16 Joseph E. Stiglitz, *Globalism Discontents*, 13 THE AMERICAN PROSPECT 1 (2002), *available at* http://www.prospect.org/print/V13/1/stiglitz-j.html.

17 *See also* interview by Mamudi with Joseph Stiglitz, *How to Fix the IP Imbalance*, in: 143 MANAGING INTELLECTUAL PROP. 28 (2004) ("We need to develop the institutional mechanisms so that we can go back and recognize the need for developing countries, for instance, to have some technology transfer.").

18 GENEVA DECLARATION ON THE FUTURE OF THE WORLD INTELLECTUAL PROPERTY ORGANIZATION (2005), *available at* http://www.cptech.org/ip/wipo/futureofwipodeclaration.pdf.

A moratorium should be made on the negotiations of new treaties and the harmonization of standards that further strengthen and augment monopolies and restrict access to knowledge. The Declaration states that WIPO has, for generations, predominantly reacted "to the narrow concerns of powerful publishers, pharmaceutical manufacturers, plant breeders and other commercial interests."[19] Now it should address the fundamental needs of consumer protection and human rights: "Long-neglected concerns of the poor, the sick, the visually impaired and others must be given priority."[20]

The Argentine and Brazilian recommendation for a "development agenda" for WIPO[21] demands, among other things, that WIPO's role should not be solely limited to the promotion of intellectual property protection.[22] Treaties in this area should explicitly take into account the interest of the consumer and of the general public. It is important that the exceptions and the boundaries of the national law of member states remain protected.[23] Special attention should be paid to the idea of establishing an international regime, which would provide developing countries with access to publicly funded research results in industrialized nations. Such a regime could follow the form of the Treaty on Access to Knowledge and Technology.[24]

The recommendation further demands that the currently negotiated agreements in WIPO, such as the Substantive Patent Law Treaty ("SPLT"),[25] should include provisions on technology transfer, competition inhibiting practices, specific clauses on the principles and goals of the agreements as they are laid down in Articles 7 and 8 of TRIPs, and ensure the flexibility of public interest. However, these provisions should only be included with the concurrent clarification that the WIPO agreements "do not expressly deal with 'trade-related issues.'"[26] In other words, Argentina and Brazil do not want the agreements to contain reference to trade related aspects of intellectual property.

3.3 What has the new WTO legal system really achieved?

The given goals of the WTO legal system, within which the developing countries accepted TRIPs as an integral component, depict the liberalization of international trade and the equal distribution of its benefits throughout the developed and

19 *Id.*
20 *Id.*
21 SECRETARIAT, *supra* note 1.
22 *Id.* at 2.
23 *Id.* at 1.
24 *See* CONSUMER PROJECT ON TECHNOLOGY, TREATY ON ACCESS TO KNOWLEDGE (2005), *available at* http://www.cptech.org/a2k/consolidatedtext-may9.pdf.
25 See the report from PRINZ ZU WALDECK UND PYRMONT, WIPO, STANDING COMMITTEE ON THE LAW OF PATENTS, TENTH SESSION (2004).
26 *Id.*

developing nations.[27] This primarily demands that the markets of developed and developing countries be equally open to one another. Although it must be observed that the OECD-states are still far from fully complying with the requirements of the WTO, especially in the area of agriculture, the most recent balance between developing and industrialized nations looks positive.[28]

The national economies of these developing states are growing more quickly than those of the industrialized nations. Their growth rates are the highest in the last 30 years and three-fifths of these countries have an average rate of growth that is at least 6 percent greater than that of the industrialized states.[29] This holds true especially for the four largest national economies in the group: China, India, Brazil and Russia. The International Monetary Fund predicts the highest growth rates in the last 30 years over the next few years for even the sub-Saharan Africa region,[30] although the traditionally poor regions of Africa and the Middle East have, until now, been considered losers of globalization.[31] The development of Europe is particularly disappointing by international comparison, which lost ground not only to Asia, but also to the United States, in spite of the high-set goals of the Lisbon summit in March of 2000.[32]

India was one of the most vehement opponents of TRIPs,[33] and did not join the Paris Convention until December 7, 1998,[34] despite entering the WTO and

27 Supachai Panitchpakdi, *Balancing Competing Interests: The Future Role of the WTO*, in: THE ROLE OF THE WORLD TRADE ORGANIZATION IN GLOBAL GOVERNANCE, 29 (Gary P. Sampson ed., 2001).

28 Richard H. Steinberg & Timothy E. Josling, *Where the Peace Ends: The Vulnerability of EC and US Agricultural Subsidies to WTO Legal Challenge*, 6 J. INT'L ECON. L. 369, 371–72, 414 (2003); *see also* Joseph Straus, *Patentschutz durch TRIPs- Abkommen- Ausnahmeregelungen und- praktiken und ihre Bedeutung, insbesondere hinsichtlich pharmazeutischer Produkte*, 124, in JARBUCHER DER BITBURGER GESPRÄCHE (2003), p. 117 *et seq.* (124).

29 *See Grow Up: Developing Countries are Growing at Their Fastest Pace for Decades*, ECONOMIST, Oct. 16, 2004, at 16.

30 *Id.*

31 De Jonquières, *Dealing in Doha*, FINANCIAL TIMES, Nov. 6, 2001, at 16.

The developing countries generally have had an increasingly larger share of the industrialized world's imports, which rose from 15% in 1990 to almost 25% in 2000. Over half of Japan's manufactured imports come from developing countries, while the share for the United States was 45%. In the year 2000 alone, developing countries' exports rose by 15%—three times their GDP growth—the best rate of growth in five decades. Likewise, the exports from the 49 least developed countries rose by 28% in the same year—amounting to around US$34 billion. The developing countries' share of world trade has risen from one-fifth in the 1970s to one-third, and current trends indicate it is likely to grow to well over half of world trade in the next 25 years. Incidentally, world exports of manufactured goods have expanded by 8% annually on an average between 1948 and 2000. For the year 2000, the value of world exports of manufactured goods from these countries was more than 50 times larger than that in 1948, and while the ratio of exports in respect of goods and services to the GDP was 8% in 1948, it had increased to 29.5% in the year 2000 taken at constant 1987 prices. SHAHID ALIKHAN & RAGHUNATH MASHELKAR, INTELLECTUAL PROPERTY AND COMPETITIVE STRATEGIES IN THE 21ST CENTURY, 34 (International Law Publications 2004).

32 HIGH LEVEL GROUP, FACING THE CHALLENGE: THE LISBON STRATEGY FOR GROWTH AND EMPLOYMENT, 10 (2004), *available at* http://ec.europa.eu/growthandjobs/pdf/kok_report_en.pdf.

33 Straus, *supra* note 11, at 168.

34 *Decisions of the Enlarged Board of Appeal*, 27 ONLINE J. EPO 483, 485–86 (2004), *available at* http://www.european-patent-office.org/epo/pubs/oj004/10_04/10_4834.pdf.

TRIPs on January 1, 1995. Additionally, China was one of the states in which there was no reason to protect intellectual property because of the lack of effective competition in the domestic marketplace until the 1980s.[35] However, it is important to examine more closely the reasons for China and India's development in the light of the WTO legal system, notwithstanding the peculiarities of these developing or threshold countries.

Attention is on the development of China, not only because China is the object of much current common interest as a rising economic power, but more so because of the wealth of relevant data on its development. The Chinese State Intellectual Property Office ("SIPO") recorded 308,487 new patent applications in 2003 (this number covers all three types of patents: invention patents, design patents, and utility patents).[36] This represents a 22.1 percent increase in invention patents compared to 2002.[37] Without being able to examine the origin of these applications here,[38] some of the following figures may speak for themselves: the number of people employed in the field of research and development ("R&D") rose from 781,000 in 1986 to 1,035,000 in 2002.[39]

In this regard, China has surpassed Russia, Japan, and, by some accounts, even the United States.[40] With expenditures of US$60 billion for R&D, China was already in third place worldwide in 2001, behind only the United States (with US$282 billion) and Japan (with US$104 billion), but ahead of Germany (with US$54 billion).[41] As measured by the gross domestic product ("GDP"),

35 *See also* Zhicun Gao & Clem Tisdell, *China's Reformed Science and Technology System: An Overview and Assessment*, 22 PROMETHEUS 311, 321 (2004); William A. Fischer & Maximilian von Zedtwitz, *Chinese R&D: Naissance, Renaissance or Mirage?*, 34 R&D MGMT. 349, 354 (2004), *available at* http://www.blackwell-synergy.com/doi/abs/10.1111/j.1467-9310.2004.00346.x. Admittedly, China began preparations for a system of intellectual property protection already at the end of the 1970s, as it prepared to enter the Paris Convention. Guo, *TRIPs and Intellectual Property Protection in the People's Republic of China*, GRUR INT. 1996, 292. Advanced development of the system only took place during preparation for and adoption of TRIPs. *Id.*

36 *See* Peter Ganea, *Die Neuregelung des chinesischen Patentrechts*, GRUR INT., 686 (2002); *see also* Ai and others, in: CHINA INTELLECTUAL PROPERTY LAW GUIDE, THE HAGUE 2005, at 15, 001 *et seq.* (providing detail on the new Chinese patent system).

37 *Compare* SIPO, WHITE PAPER ON THE INTELLECTUAL PROPERTY RIGHTS PROTECTION IN CHINA IN 2003 (2004), *available at* http://english.sipo.gov.cn/laws/whitepapers/200804/t20080416_380354.html, *with* DAVID MICHAEL & KEVIN RIVETTE, FACING THE CHINA CHALLENGE: USING AN INTELLECTUAL PROPERTY STRATEGY TO CAPTURE GLOBAL ADVANTAGE 7–8 (The Boston Consulting Group 2004) (showing an increase of 100% from 1999 in Exhibit 1).

38 SIPO, *supra* note 37.

39 SIPO, *supra* note 37 (stating after China joined the Patent Cooperation Treaty ("PCT"), the foreign applications for patents of invention outnumbered domestic applications, but in 2003 the tide turned again in favor of domestic applications (57,000 domestic vs. 49,000 foreign applications)).

40 *See* Gao & Tisdell, *supra* note 35; Maximilian von Zedtwitz, *Managing Foreign R&D Laboratories in China*, 34 R&D MGMT. 439, 439 (2004), *available at* http://www.blackwell-synergy.com/doi/abs/10.1111/j.1467-9310.2004.00351.x. In 2002, Chinese Foreign Direct Investment ("FDI") amounted to US$53 billion, which surpassed the US; Oliver Gassmann & Zheng Han, *Motivations and Barriers of Foreign R&D Activities in China*, 34 R&D MGMT. 423, 423 (2004), *available at* http://www.blackwell-synergy.com/doi/abs/10.1111/j.1467-9310.2004.00350.x. This clearly shows the support China received from international investors for entering the WTO in November 2001. *Id.*

41 Gassmann & Han, *supra* note 40.

expenditures for R&D rose from 0.6 percent in 1996 to 1.3 percent in 2002, having more than doubled in only six years.[42] This is also demonstrated by the shift of R&D workers from state research institutions to industry, shown by an increase from 154,000 in 1990 to 351,000 in 1999.[43] Industry in 2001 covered 60 percent of all R&D expenditures. This significantly aided industry capabilities in optimizing the use of imported technologies, and in asserting China in international competition.[44]

Since the late 1990s, European and U.S. companies such as Siemens, Philips, Nokia, General Electric, and Motorola, as well as, Japanese, Korean, and Taiwanese companies had been moving their production facilities to China. According to some accounts, foreign companies opened 60,000 factories in China between 2000 and 2003, allowing Chinese exports to rise to over US$400 billion in 2003.[45] Von Zedtwitz identified approximately 200 R&D laboratories that had been established, or were in the process of being established in China at the beginning of 2004, which corresponds to approximately one-fourth of the foreign investment in the United States during 1998.[46]

What impressed von Zedtwitz the most was that these investments were transacted during a period of global economic instability.[47] His investigation also shows that foreign companies do not move R&D facilities to China solely in order to research according to local needs.[48] Rather, companies move with the express task of developing products and technology for the global market.[49] Nokia, for example, moved divisions crucial to the development of its third-generation software from Finland to Hangzhou.[50] One reason for the move is supposed to be cost effectiveness: Chinese engineers' salaries are about a quarter of their U.S. or European counterparts.[51] Moreover, their high level of technical competence affected Nokia's decision.[52]

China's commanding, complex, and almost scary development is doubtlessly dependent on a range of factors that cannot be explored in depth in this chapter. Without a doubt, foreign companies would not have become involved in China, at least not to this extent, had the goods produced in China not had open access

42 *See* von Zedtwitz, *supra* note 40, at 358 (according to OECD statistics in 2003, the expenditures amounted to US$69 billion); *see also* Fischer & von Zedtwitz, *supra* note 35.
43 *See* Gao & Tisdell, *supra* note 35, at 318.
44 *Id.*
45 *See also Men and Machines: Technology and Economics Have Already Revolutionized Manufacturing. White-Collar Work Will be Next*, ECONOMIST, Jan. 13, 2004, at 5–6.
46 *See* von Zedtwitz, *supra* note 40, at 440. According to the data collected by von Zedtwitz, foreign firms had established some 400 R&D Centers in China by 2002. *Id.*
47 *Id.*
48 *Id.*
49 *Id.*, at 441.
50 *Id.*
51 *Id.*, at 442.
52 *Id.* Von Zedtwitz researched 15 European, 17 U.S., and 12 Japanese companies, as well as five from other countries, including Nokia, Ericsson, Hoffmann-La Roche, Tetrapak, Volkswagen, Bayer, and Siemens. *Id.* Gassmann & Han, *supra* note 40, at 427 (providing a detailed and exhaustive analysis of the motives of transnational companies establishing R&D activities in China).

to global markets, which they did because of the new WTO legal system. Similarly, it is beyond question that China's entrance into WTO, and further development of its intellectual property rights protection played a decisive role, despite all of the still prevalent deficits to TRIPs standards.[53] Gao and Tisdell note in this context:

> Following market reforms and commercialisation, the Chinese Government started to establish a patent system. This has become the cornerstone of science and technology development in China, and has enabled China to participate in the World's Intellectual Property market. In 1983, China enacted its patent law. This was the first step in establishing a legal basis for ownership of intellectual property.[54]

Despite the many great and fundamental differences that exist between China and India, the two great economies share several notable commonalities in the context at issue. Although not widely known, it was not until the early 1990s that India liberalized its economy,[55] started a privatization process,[56] and gradually adapted its patent legislation to a large extent consistent with TRIPs standards.[57]

India now possesses a wide and well-structured scientific, technological, and industrial basis.[58] Production costs in India are also quite low.[59] Foreign direct investment in India is not quite comparable to China, but in 2001–2002 it rose to US$3.91 billion, indicating an increase of 65 percent compared to the previous year, and earning India a seventh place standing in foreign direct investment ("FDI") worldwide.[60] The value of textile and clothing exports amounted to US$ billion in 2003, and should climb to US$50 billion by 2010, according to the predictions of the Indian Government.[61]

53 *See* Can Huang and others, *Organization, Programme and Structure: An Analysis of the Chinese Innovation Policy Framework*, 34 R&D MGMT. 367, 382 (2004), *available at* http://www.blackwell-synergy.com/doi/abs/10.1111/j.1467-9310.2004.00347.x. *See generally* ANDREW C. MERTHA, THE POLITICS OF PIRACY: INTELLECTUAL PROPERTY IN CONTEMPORARY CHINA (2005).

54 Gao & Tisdell, *supra* note 35, at 324.

55 *See* Ashok K. Gupta and others, *Managing the Process of Market Orientation by Publicly Funded Laboratories: The Case of CSIR, India*, 30 R&D MGMT. 289, 289 (2000), *available at* http://www.blackwell-synergy.com/doi/abs/10.1111/1467-9310.00182.

56 See the brochure "Indien 2003–2004—Verlässicher Wirtschaftspartner—Attraktives FDI Gebiet," p. 11 *et seq.* published by the *Ministry of External Affairs* of the Indian Government [hereinafter Indien].

57 Prabuddha Ganguli, *Intellectual Property Rights in Transition*, 20 WORLD PAT. INFO. 171, 175 (1998); H. Rajeshwari & D.C. Gabriel, *An Indian Summer: Contract Research Heats Up*, 166 PAT. WORLD 19, 19 (2004). Last amendments to the Indian Patent Act were passed by the Parliament on Mar. 22, 2005. *Id.*

58 Ganguli, *supra* note 57, at 177.

59 *See* Edward Luce, *India's Investment Climate Brightens*, FINANCIAL TIMES (London), Nov. 24, 2004, at 5 (noting production costs are about 25 percent less than in China; however, the productivity of a worker in India is about 50 percent less than that of a worker in China).

60 *See* Indien, *supra* note 56, at 5–6.

61 *See id.*

These factors, paired with the especially high qualification of Indian scientists and engineers in the field of information technology,[62] attracted U.S. companies such as Texas Instruments and Motorola to Bangalore as early as the 1980s. But significant relocation of U.S. and European companies in previously unthought-of amounts first occurred in the late 1990s, *i.e.*, already under the aegis of the WTO regime, as Hewlett-Packard, American Express, Citibank, General Electric, and other companies entered India. The Indian information technology industry reached a turnover of approximately US$16 billion in 2003, three-quarters of which resulted from exports.[63] The yearly turnover is supposed to rise to about US$50 billion by 2008.[64] The turnover seen by the company Infosys, one of the largest contractors of IT services, increased eight-fold in five years, and crossed the US$1 billion boundary in the 2003 financial year.[65] Infosys maintains an annual training course capacity of 4000 students.[66]

The so-called Indian Business Process Outsourcing Industry ("BPO") makes workers in industrialized nations tremble in fear of losing their jobs. The growth in productivity in the Indian IT service industry is the highest worldwide.[67] Almost everything can be made quicker, cheaper and better in India, claims Nandan Nilekani, the managing director of Infosys.[68] His company managed to create almost 5000 new jobs in 2004.[69] But the Indian IT industry is by no means the only industry that attracts foreign capital and reasons to create R&D centers. By achieving TRIPs protection standards in the field of pharmaceutical patent protection,[70] the wave of outsourcing should also include pharmaceutical R&D, especially where clinical trials are involved. This should lead to a US$200 to US$300 million drop in development costs for every drug.

Also, German companies such as Mucos Pharma or Schering AG have become active in this domain. The Indian Central Drug Research Institute ("CDRI"), a governmental organization, is actively involved in contract negotiations and contract design for research projects of foreign companies. The already well-developed Indian pharmaceutical industry, with companies such as Dr. Reddy's,

62 *The Place to Be*, ECONOMIST, Nov. 11, 2004, at 8, 10. Every year approximately 300,000 information technology engineers graduate from Indian universities, of those about 30,000–40,000 are highly qualified and in demand from foreign companies such as IBM and Accenture. *Id.*

63 *Id.*

64 *Id.*

65 *Id.*

66 *Id.*

67 *Id.*

68 *Id.*

69 *Faster, Cheaper, Better*, ECONOMIST, Nov. 13, 2004, at 12. The Indian IT industry is projected to create 2.5 million jobs by 2008. Imam, *How Does Patent Protection Help Developing Countries?*, 37 INT'L REV. INTELL. PROP. & COMPETITION. L. 245, 256 (2006). IBM, Microsoft, Metamove, Oracle, and Sathyam computers have built corporate schools for training in India. *Id.*

70 *See* Sreenivasarao Vepachedu & Martha M. Rumore, *Patent Protection and the Pharmaceutical Industry in the Indian Union*, INTELL. PROP. TODAY, Oct. 2004, at 44; Sajeev Chandran and others, *Implications of New Patent Regime on Indian Pharmaceutical Industry: Challenges and Opportunities*, 10 J. INTELL. PROP. RTS. 269, 269 (2005).

Ranbaxy, Orchid, and Cipla, is increasing investment in its own R&D,[71] while other companies are looking for different methods of collaboration, such as joint venture, combined distribution, and, most recently, research contracts.[72] As far as India is concerned, there is no doubt that such development could not have come about without the WTO regime.[73]

3.4 What accounts for TRIPs-plus and TRIPs-minus?

When the issue of TRIPs-plus comes up, there are many different perceptions ensconced in the term that can be only briefly discussed here and only in the context of patent protection. As has already been alluded to, the endeavors to encourage greater harmonization of substantive patent law in the form of SPLT, made in the context of WIPO, were assessed by critics as an attempt to usher in TRIPs-plus standards, and, thus, to deprive developing countries the room to maneuver that TRIPs had provided them. In particular, commentators have argued that a second phase with the aim of establishing the international standard for determining the scope of protection, which would also cover equivalents, would follow the first phase of the harmonization of standards for prior art, novelty, utility, inventive step, enabling disclosure, as well as the patent claims drafting.[74]

Dutfield calls this process "immoral and 'the last insult to developing countries,'"[75] and Reichman has asked for a moratorium on the process.[76] Should these efforts for harmonization in the framework of WIPO, the supposed results of which could be subsumed under the term TRIPS-plus, eventually fail, this would harm, rather than benefit, all parties involved, especially the developing nations.[77] A failure would give the United States, which already takes part in the negotiations with rather restrained enthusiasm,[78] yet another reason for the bilateral pursuit of its aims. This pursuit, denoted as TRIPs-plus, will lead to a rather one-sided export of American protection standards to partner nations. However, the results do not coercively have to be so, since the definitions of specific patentability requirements in SPLT relate principally to purely legal/

71 *See* Khozem Merchant, *Scientists in India Develop New Cure for TB*, FINANCIAL TIMES, Sept. 7, 2004, at 9. Indian scientists have recently developed the first new medicine for the treatment of tuberculosis and have submitted patent applications for it not only in India but also in the U.S. *Id. See also* Chandran and others, *supra* note 70, at 278.

72 *See* Rajeshwari & Gabriel, *supra* note 57; *see also* Indien, *supra* note 56, at 83.

73 *See* Peter Marsh, *A New Manufacturing Mantra*, FINANCIAL TIMES, May 16, 2006, at 8 (stating the current state of Indian service-based manufacturing).

74 *See* MUSUNGU & DUTFIELD, *supra* note 6, at 12. For details of the consultation on a gradual advancement, *see Prinz zu Waldeck und Pyrmont*, GRUR INT. 2004, 840 *et seq.*

75 *See* Sangeeta Shashikant, *WIPO Has Failed In Its Development Mission*, in: NEGOTIATING A 'DEVELOPMENT AGENDA' FOR THE WORLD INTELLECTUAL PROPERTY ORGANISATION (WIPO) (Martin Khor & Sangeeta Shashikant eds., 2009).

76 *Id.*

77 *Cf. Klunker*, Informal Session des Standing Committee on the Law of Patents der WIPO in Genf von 10. bis 12. April 2006, GRUR INT. (2006).

78 *Cf. Prinz zu Waldeck und Pyrmont*, *supra* note 74, at 843.

technical aspects that are primarily disputed between the United States and the rest of the world, and whose solution would not disadvantage developing countries.[79]

As it did even before the adoption of TRIPS, the United States has been following the strategy of imposing high standards for the protection of intellectual property in bilateral free trade agreements ("FTAs"), which surpass the standards of TRIPs. This policy concerns FTA agreements with very diverse partners such as Australia, Bahrain, Chile, Jordan, Morocco, and a string of Central American countries. The core of "plus" lies primarily in the protection of pharmaceutical inventions. For instance, the possibility of granting compulsory licensing in the case of public, non-commercial use is reduced to some cases of national emergency and behavior restricting competition, which constitutes a deviation from the rules of Article 31 of TRIPS.[80]

Furthermore, the FTAs contain clauses on the exclusivity of data, which pharmaceutical companies submit to competent authorities for the purpose of gaining marketing approval for new drugs.[81] This protection clearly goes beyond that of Article 39 paragraph 2 of TRIPs against misuse of data by a third party.[82] The obligation is particularly far reaching since it does not grant marketing approval for drugs that are covered by patent claims during the patent term, as well as during the patent term extension, if any.[83] This is supposed to delay market access to generic drugs as long as possible. Other obligations touching on intellectual property relate, for instance, to the general commitment of contracting partners to reduce differences in their respective national laws. For example, the FTA with Australia obliges Australia to accept the patentability requirement of utility as fulfilled only if the latter is "specific, substantial and credible."[84]

Thus, Australia has practically adopted the standards of the Utility Examination Guidelines of the U.S. Patent and Trademark Office ("USPTO"). Critics of the FTAs, such as Drahos,[85] view this as a strategy of the United States, which wants to impose its own protection standards worldwide via the most-favored-nation

79 *Id.*

80 *See, e.g.*, U.S.-Austl. Free Trade Agreement, U.S.-Austl., art. 17.9(7), May 18, 2004, *available at* http://www.ustr.gov/Trade_Agreements/Bilateral/Australia_FTA/Final_Text/Section_Index.html [hereinafter FTA].

81 See for this problem, *e.g.* in European Law, *Gassner*, Unterlagenschutz im Europäischen Arzneimittelrecht, GRUR INT. 2004, 983 *et seq.*

82 *See* DANIEL GERVAIS, THE TRIPS AGREEMENT: DRAFTING HISTORY AND ANALYSIS 274 (Sweet & Maxwell Limited 2003) (1998).

83 *See, e.g.*, FTA, *supra* note 80, art. 17.10.

84 *See* FTA, *supra* note 80, art. 17.9(13). The free trade agreement with Bahrain seems to contain—in view of the up to now rather poor protection standards in Bahrain—an obligation to provide patent protection for plant patents and to join the International Union for the Protection of New Varieties of Plants (UPOV), and to arrange for patent protection for new uses of known products, including uses for further medical indications. *See* U.S.-Bahr. Free Trade Agreement, U.S.-Bahr., May 27, 2004, *available at* http://www.ustr.gov/Trade_Agreements/Bilateral/Bahrain_FTA/final_texts/Section_Index.html.

85 *See generally* Peter Drahos and others, *Pharmaceuticals, Intellectual Property and Free Trade: The Case of the U.S.-Australia Free Trade Agreement*, 22 PROMETHEUS 243 (2004) (discussing the U.S.-Australia free trade agreement).

clause of Article 4 of TRIPs—the contracting parties are bound to apply to all members of the WTO.

There is no room here to delve into the criticism of the U.S. TRIPS-plus strategy. However, it can basically be assumed that contracting parties apply their own cost-benefit analysis prior to signing such agreements. The analysis will without a doubt be based on actual and anticipated bilateral trade with and without the FTA. In this context, the Australian Government has calculated that the FTA will boost the Australian economy by US$6 billion in benefits annually.[86] However, other Australian institutions estimate the total costs to be US$50 billion, and that there will be a loss of up to 200,000 jobs.[87]

When trying to decide on a course of action, the choice was clear to the Australian Government, because without an FTA the country would have to fear or perhaps even suffer economic disadvantages. Drahos and his fellow authors criticize their government for the FTA encroachment on Australia's sovereign right independently to price pharmaceuticals by means of the Pharmaceutical Benefits Scheme ("PBS"), the National Health Act, and the Pharmaceuticals Benefit Pricing Authority ("PBPA"). Because future decisions of the PBPA will be reviewed by an independent organization, and because generics will be available on the market only at a later date, the FTA adds to the increasing cost of the healthcare system.[88]

In their crusading attacks, especially against the U.S. pharmaceutical industry,[89] Drahos and others misjudge something very fundamental; the philosophy of the Australian PBS is "driven by the principle of equity of access" and is based on the consideration that [A]ll Australians have a right of access to needed medicines. Need, however, has a utilitarian dimension. The PBS is not designed to provide medicines for specific individuals with specific needs. Rather, its purpose is to maximize the access of community of individuals with limited resources to essential medicines. To paraphrase Jeremy Bentham, the PBS is all about the greatest health of the greatest number.[90]

The idea that this should be part of the responsibility and the cost of the companies who effectuate the enormous investments, and the economies whose healthcare systems have rendered the highest drug prices is indeed very appealing, and could even be realized if globalization had not reached the level it is at today. However, this idea might now finally belong to the past, especially when it seems advisable in the context of the macroeconomic considerations of the state in question.

Surely the Australian Government saw this similarly. A country cannot demand access to the U.S. market for agricultural products and seek cutbacks on U.S. agricultural subsidies, while at the same time demanding access to medicines

86 *Id.*, at 244.

87 *Id.*

88 *Id.*

89 *See, e.g.*, PETER DRAHOS & JOHN BRAITHWAITE, INFORMATION FEUDALISM (The New Press 2003) (2002).

90 Drahos, *supra* note 85, at 244.

developed within the United States at a lower price than the U.S. population pays. Needless to say, the idea of the "principle of equity of access" is fundamentally correct, but Australia, as the world's 15th largest national economy, must provide access for its population with its own financial means, and not at the expense of the U.S. health care system! For countries whose own resources are insufficient, the international community of states must come to their aid.[91]

Here, it should be clearly stated that this should not be taken as a comment on the appropriateness of drug prices. Rather, no one should lose sight of, nor compromise the high level of investments that are admittedly plagued by high risks upon which the continuous flow of new medicine is dependent and upon which humans are ultimately dependent.

In summary, it can be observed that the FTAs with TRIPs-plus standards should only be accepted if they are justified in a macroeconomic context on the basis of specific provisions of the concerned agreements, and not just on vague hopes. The term "macroeconomic" can, of course, never be reduced to an isolated examination of the genuine effects of, *e.g.*, patent protection, but applies to the exact circumstances of the economies affected, both with and without the FTA. On the current level of development of globalization, every attempt to disconnect matters of intellectual property protection from matters of international trade must inevitably fail. If it ever actually came to pass, it would have negative and lasting effects on international trade.

Regarding the idea of TRIPs-minus, it should be observed that the development since the Doha WTO Ministerial Conference in November 2001 has brought about a TRIPs-minus for the least developed countries, in the respect that they are not required to start providing patent protection for pharmaceuticals until January 1, 2016.[92] Since the decision of the WTO General Council of August 30, 2003, it has been further clarified that under specific conditions deviating from Article 31(f) of TRIPs, compulsory licenses can be issued for the production of pharmaceuticals in order to satisfy the demands of third-party countries.[93]

Furthermore, developing countries were advised to exclude completely from patentability diagnostic, therapeutic, and surgical methods for the treatment of humans and animals; plants and animals, in a narrower interpretation of the term microorganism; computer programs; and business methods.[94] The countries were further advised to avoid patenting new uses of known products, the use of the patent system to protect plant species, and, when possible, genetic material.[95] The

91 *See* Straus, *supra* note 28, at 132.

92 *See Straus*, *supra* note 28, at 126 *et seq*.

93 *See* Implementation of Paragraph 6 of the DOHA Declaration on the TRIPs Agreement and Public Health, WT/L/540 and Corr. 1 (Sept. 1, 2003), *available at* http://www.wto.org/english/tratop_e/trips_e/implem_para6_e.htm; *see also* PRESS RELEASE, WTO NEWS: 2003 NEWS ITEMS, THE GENERAL COUNCIL CHAIRPERSON'S STATEMENT (Aug. 30, 2003), *available at* http://www.wto.org/english/news_ e/news03_e/trips_stat_28aug03_e.htm.

94 COMMISSION ON INTELLECTUAL PROPERTY RIGHTS, INTEGRATING INTELLECTUAL PROPERTY RIGHTS AND DEVELOPMENT POLICY 122 (2002), *available at* http://www.ipcommission.org/graphic/documents/final_report.htm.

95 *Id.*

countries of the Andean Community, and with them Argentina and Brazil, have specifically barred biological material from patent protection, even if isolated from its natural environment and commercially applicable, and have, thus, adopted standards that can be seen as TRIPs-minus standards.[96]

Disregarding that some of these measures, in part recommended and in part already introduced into law, could possibly provide grounds for a WTO dispute settlement action, they are also not in the well understood interest of the developing nations, and thus stand in clear contradiction to their own argument. For example, developing countries like Brazil and India claim, and are by all means justified in doing so, that they should be able to participate adequately in the commercial gains achieved through the use of their genetic resources, so-called "benefit sharing." Although, in view of the ability of biological material to reproduce, it cannot be questioned that such material can be effectively protected as genotypes, *i.e.*, over generations and also outside the territory of origin, and thus commercialized profitably for the country of origin only in the form of patents or other intellectual property rights.[97]

These countries exclude the material in question from patent protection and raise objections against its patent protection in industrialized countries. As Boyd, Kerr and Perdikis[98] stress, the developing nations at hand concentrate exclusively on the alleged costs of the respective exclusive rights and thus overlook the benefits of innovation, which domestic experts as well as foreign companies and research institutions could bestow upon a nation.[99] Boyd, Kerr and Perdikis accurately note:

> Thus, the real question is not how to prevent multinational biotechnology firms from exploiting developing countries, but rather, how to induce them to want to exploit developing countries. Multinationals lining up to extract monopoly rents from developing countries would be the surest sign that investments in the desired innovations are taking place. Unless developing countries or aid-givers are willing to subsidize biotechnology tailored to developing countries—and there is no evidence to suggest they will—the investment will simply not take place. The key lies in developing countries' willingness to extend and enforce IPR's biotechnology.[100]

It is beyond question that China acts according to this advice, and is therefore able to achieve convincing, even envy-inspiring success.[101]

96 *See* Joseph Straus, *Patents on Biomaterial: A New Colonialism or a Means for Technology Transfer and Benefit-Sharing?*, in: BIOETHICS IN A SMALL WORLD, 45, 59 (F. Thiele and R. Ashcroft eds., 2005).

97 *Id.* at 67.

98 Shari L. Boyd and others, *Agricultural Biotechnology Innovations Versus Intellectual Property Rights: Are Developing Countries at the Mercy of Multinationals?*, 4 J. WORLD INV. 211, 212 (2003).

99 *Id.*

100 *Id.*

101 Richard McGregor, *China's Success Inspires Envy and Awe*, FINANCIAL TIMES, May 28, 2004, at 12.

3.5 Closing remarks and further prospects

Almost 20 years after the WTO Global Economic Order was established, with GATT 1994 and TRIPs as its main pillars, everyone should realize that international trade, with open and opening markets, is tightly linked to the international system of intellectual property protection. Owing to the level of globalization already achieved, GATT 1994 and TRIPs have become practically inseparable. If the status achieved, which, as empirical data shows, has brought mostly advantages for the developing countries, and their further development are not to be endangered, every attempt to disjoin intellectual property protection from the development of international trade should cease.

In view of the effects of globalization on job markets, particularly felt in industrialized nations on account of job loss from the displacement of production and R&D to threshold and developing countries, the benefits of globalization for the national economies of the industrialized countries are not easily communicable,[102] especially as their interests are not always congruent with the interests of internationally active businesses. Attempts to overturn the laboriously achieved balance, which benefits the developing countries in every way, could produce a boomerang effect in favor of those in industrial nations who already want to betake themselves to protectionism and isolationism, no matter how incorrect the latter may be from an objective point of view.[103]

It is easy to envision what this would mean for countries such as Bangladesh, Cambodia, Macao, or Pakistan, which make 60 to 80 percent of their exports with textiles and clothing, and are already fully exposed to the overpowering competition from China and India as a result of the abolition of quota regulations on December 31, 2004.[104]

The critics of TRIPs are unwilling or unable to accept this. Just as little as critical considerations reflect the actual state of the developing economies in the pre-TRIPs era, they do not bear in mind the actual development under the influence of the WTO system. The expressed criticism rather commemorates

102 For more on this complicated problem *see* Wolfgang Streeck, *Globalisierung: Mythos und Wirklichkeit* 25, in: MAX-PLANCK-INSTITUTS FÜR GESELLSCHAFTSFORSCHUNG JAHRBUCH (2004), Munich 2004, p. 25. *Anders als im Mythosder Globalisierung unterstellt, kann dabei von einem Bedeutungsverlust staatlicher Politik keine Rede sein. Sektorale Spezialisierung erfordert im Gegenteil eine integrierte, auf den Ausbau vorhandener komparativer Vorteile hin maßgeschneiderte national Wirtschafts-, Struktur-, Sozial- und Bildungspolitik. Sie verlangt ferner angepasst institutionelle Regelwerke, etwa für den Arbeitsmarkt, die eine optimale Nutzung der nationalen Ressourcen zugunsten der jeweiligen Kernsektoren ermöglichen. Id.* at 31. *See also Into the Unknown: Where Will the Jobs of the Future Come From?*, ECONOMIST, Nov. 13, 2004, at 12; *Sink or Swim: Sourcing from Low-cost Countries Works Only in Open and Flexible Markets. Europe's are Neither*, ECONOMIST, Nov. 13, 2004, at 14.

103 *See A World of Opportunity: Why the Protectionists are Wrong*, ECONOMIST, Nov. 13, 2004, at 12. Lawrence H. Summers stated recently in this context: "The twin arguments that globalization is inevitable and protectionism is counterproductive for almost everyone have the great virtue of being correct—but they do not provide much consolation for the losers." Lawrence H. Summers, *Globalization Anxiety*, L.A. TIMES, October 30, 2006, *available at* http://articles.latimes.com/2006/oct/30/opinion/oe-summers30.

104 *See The Looming Revolution: China, the world's workshop, is poised to become its tailor. What will happen to textile industries elsewhere, especially in South Asia?*, ECONOMIST, Nov. 13, 2004, at 76.

the criticism and the suggestions made by the United Nations Conference on Trade and Development ("UNCTAD") in the 1970s,[105] which inhibited the further development of the international system for the protection of intellectual property rights, without having brought the slightest advantage for developing countries, except for dubious political victories.[106] Even if all comparisons were flawed, the numerous recommendations submitted for the alteration and amelioration of the current international system of intellectual property protection in general, in the interest of the developing countries, in particular, reminds us of Karl Popper's remark regarding the Freudian psychoanalysis: "Its logical content surely is great; but its empirical content is zero."[107]

Those who believe they can conceive the protection of intellectual property rights internationally isolated from the issues of international trade, misjudge the reality of globalization, its legal foundations, and its functional machinery. In the current state of the development of globalization, the compliance with all WTO requirements, *i.e.*, GATT and TRIPs, is decisive to avoid frictions in international trade, which inevitably would hurt the weaker and the weakest. WIPO would be well advised to take this to heart. WIPO has been beset with requests that misjudge these realities and are overwhelming, not just for WIPO, but for the entire system of intellectual property rights protection by demanding it provide solutions to all the world's problems.

Thus, for the time being, the successful functioning of the international protection of intellectual property rights in the context of the global economic order depends on the WTO members' compliance with TRIPs, GATT, TRIMs, and GATS commitments. TRIPs-minus standards based on the Doha model should remain a one-time exception, as they only distort and weaken the system without being able to provide permanent and appropriate solutions to the problems approached.[108]As far as the real TRIPs-plus deliberations are concerned, they lack the foundation as a general concept, until a balance in other areas of the WTO economic order can be achieved, *i.e.*, as long as further concessions concerning market access, possible investment, etc., are not in place. However, efforts for harmonization in the area of technical law should be a different matter. Obstruction of, for example, the work of SPLT, is counterproductive and misguided, especially as several generally acknowledged weaknesses in the system could also be remedied in this context.[109]

105 UNCTAD, THE ROLE OF THE PATENT SYSTEM IN THE TRANSFER OF TECHNOLOGY TO DEVELOPING COUNTRIES, Doc. TD/B/AC/11/19, April 21, 1974.

106 *See* on this critically *Straus*, "Patent Protection in Developing countries, an Overview," in: Equitable Patent Protection for the Developing World, Cornell Agricultural Economic Staff Paper 89–36, Ithaca, NY.

107 "Ihr logischer Gehalt ist sicher groß; aber ihr empirischer Gehalt ist Null." *Popper*, "Wissenschaftslehre in entwicklungstheoretischer und in logischer Sicht," in: *Popper*, Alles Leben ist Problemlösen—Über Erkenntnis, Geschichte und Politik, Munich and Zurich 2004, p. 15 *et seq.*

108 *See Straus*, *supra* note 28, at 129 *et seq.*; *see also* Glenn Hubbard, *Attacking Drug Makers is no Cure*, FINANCIAL TIMES, June 16, 2004, at 15.

109 *See* A PATENT SYSTEM FOR THE 21ST CENTURY, 49 (Stephen A. Merrill and others eds., National Academies Press 2004).

Part II

Venture capital

4 Financing innovation: first round of financing by venture capital

*Yochanan Shachmurove**

4.1 Introduction

This chapter examines the first round of venture capital investment in the United States from 1995Q1 to 2010Q2, taking into consideration both location and industry sector. The data concentrate only on the first sequence of financing. This point is the time when invention becomes innovation and the firm or entrepreneurs seek the cooperation of venture capitalists. In other words, it is the first time that venture capitalists become involved. Venture capitalists can invest in a firm in different stages of its development, be it seed/start-up, early stage, expansion stage, or a later stage. From the point of view of the venture capitalist, investing in a company for the first time is likely riskier than investing in a company in which it already holds equity.

The research question is whether industry and region are important factors in determining the first round of venture capital investment. Furthermore, this chapter examines the effects of a wide array of macroeconomic variables on first stage venture capital financing activity. Consequently, the venture capital data are augmented by real gross domestic product ("real GDP"), gross domestic product ("GDP"), implicit price deflator, gross private domestic investment, personal savings, producer price index ("PPI"), consumer price index ("CPI"), effective federal funds rate, bank prime rate, 3-month Treasury bill rate, 6-month Treasury bill rate, and 3-year Treasury bill rate. As detailed in the results section, only some of these variables were found to significantly impact first round venture capital investment. In addition, this chapter examines long-term trends and the effect of the current economic crisis on first round of venture capital investment.

It is worthwhile to examine the venture capital market, which relies heavily on expectations of future GDP, investment, and innovation. Confidence and uncertainty about the future economic environment are vital factors in committing to financing a new company for the first time. Furthermore, economic geography has recently risen to the frontier of research owing to the works of the 2008 Nobel laureate, Paul Krugman, who was awarded the Nobel Prize for his "analysis of trade patterns and location of economic activity." Although both international

* Professor of Economics and Business, The City College of The City University of New York.

economists and industrial organization researchers study economic geography, it has received limited consideration in the venture capital literature.

The unique data on venture capital investment activity in the United States, spanning from 1995Q1 until 2010Q2 are from the MoneyTree Survey. The survey is a quarterly study of venture capital investment activity in the United States and is considered to be a credible source of information on emerging companies that receive financing from venture capital firms. The database allows for stratifications of the data by 17 industries and 19 regions. The statistical analysis confirms that, in addition to the effects of real GDP, CPI, PPI, S&P500 and 3-month interest rate, both region and industry sector are significant factors in explaining first-round investment in the venture capital market of the U.S. economy.

The remainder of the chapter is organized as follows. Section 4.2 presents a brief review of the literature. Section 4.3 describes the data. Section 4.4 derives the empirical results, and Section 4.5 concludes.

4.2 Literature review

Davis and North (1971) offer an early overview of the importance of finance, both public and private, in generating economic growth. Economists have long held the view that innovative activities are difficult to finance in a freely competitive market place. Support for this view in the form of economic-theoretic modeling begins with the classic articles of Nelson (1959) and Arrow (1962).

The main output of innovation investment is the knowledge of how to make new goods and services. This knowledge is non-rival. Its use by one firm does not preclude its use by another (Hall 2009). To the extent that knowledge cannot be kept secret, the returns to the investment in it cannot be appropriated by the firm undertaking the investment, and therefore such firms will be reluctant to invest, leading to the under-provision of research and development ("R&D") and other innovation investments in the economy.

The topic of innovation finance has drawn a wide variety of research. Khortum and Lerner (1998, 2000) and Lerner (2001) propose an explanation for high innovation in the 1980s and 1990s through the expansion of venture capital. They note that patent trading has accelerated and that in traditional industries such as pharmaceuticals, research intensity at the firm level has contracted somewhat. Lamoreaux, Levenstein, and Sokoloff (2007) and Klepper (2007) find that start-ups were fundamental to the Second Industrial Revolution (1870–1920) and often received venture capital from small-scale sources personally affiliated with the inventors themselves. Hall (2009) explains under-investment in innovation through reasoning based on financial markets and concludes in part that venture capital is a limited solution to what he claims is under-investment.

The reemergence of economic geography theory can be attributed to the pioneering works of Krugman (1991a, 1991b, 1998), Fujita and Krugman (2004), and Venables (1996, 1998, 2003). Krugman (1991a) examines the uneven economic development of regions, emphasizing the importance of economic geography in explaining divergent regional development. Krugman (1991b) develops a simple model in which a country can endogenously become differentiated into an industrialized "core" surrounded by an agricultural "periphery." Krugman (1998) discusses the emergence of a new area of research, labeled as the "new economic geography." It differs from traditional work in economic geography by incorporating a modeling strategy that uses the same rigorous technical and mathematical tools. Furthermore, these models utilize recent developments in industrial organization that explicitly consider the notion of economies of scale, found in the "new trade" and "new growth" theories.

Lamoreaux and Sokoloff (1999a) study the geography of the market for technology in the late nineteenth and early twentieth centuries in the United States. Lamoreaux and Sokoloff (1999b) describe inventive activity and the market for technology in the United States, during 1840–1920. The same authors study the financing of U.S. innovations spanning from 1870 to the present (Lamoreaux and Sokoloff 2007).

The study of industrial location is fundamental to understanding the field of economic geography. Behrens (2005) investigates the importance of market size as a determinant for industrial location patterns. Midelfart, Overman, and Venables (2000) estimate a model of industrial locations across countries. The model combines factor endowments and geographical considerations, showing how industry and country characteristics interact to determine the location of production. Furthermore, Alonso-Villar (2005) shows that transport costs have an impact on industrial locations. He studies the location decisions of upstream and downstream industries when transport costs in each sector are analyzed separately. He concludes that the effects of cost reductions in transporting final goods are different from those in intermediate goods.

In addition to geographical location, another important consideration is industry choice. In the context of venture capital literature, the pioneering study, based on 100 start-up firms, is Murphy (1956). The importance of industry choice in achieving start-up success has also been studied by others. In a series of papers, Y. Shachmurove (2001), and A. Shachmurove and Y. Shachmurove (2004) study annual and cumulative returns of publicly traded firms which were backed by venture capital. Y. Shachmurove (2006) examines venture capital investment activity in the United States for the years 1996–2005. Y. Shachmurove (2007) relates issues in international trade to entrepreneurship, innovation, and the growth mechanism of the free-market economies. Perez (2002, 2004) proposes an explanation for the clustered nature of innovation by focusing on the nature of the financing of invention.

4.3 Data

The data on venture capital investment activity in the United States are from the MoneyTree Survey. The survey is a quarterly study of venture capital investment activity in the United States which measures cash for equity investments by the professional venture capital community in private emerging U.S. companies. The

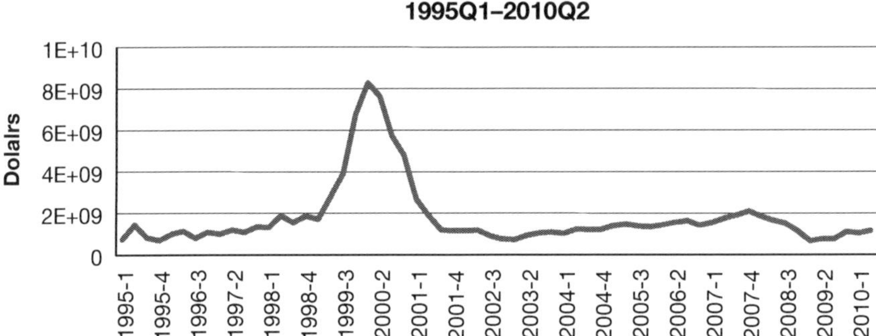

Figure 4.1 Total first round of venture capital investment in the United States 1995Q1–2010Q2

survey is a collaboration among PricewaterhouseCoopers, Thomson Venture Economics and the National Venture Capital Association, and is the only source endorsed by the venture capital industry. Table 4.1 displays summary statistics for the macroeconomic variables described in Appendix 4.4. Figure 4.1 shows the total amount of quarterly first round investment. Figure 4.2 displays the total amount of quarterly first round financing deals. Both figures clearly reach their maximum value around the year 2000. Note that there is a clear trend in both series from 1995 until the late 1990s. At this point, there is a clear disruption in both trend estimations by the dot com bubble. Since 2002, first round investment

Table 4.1 Summary statistics of macroeconomic variables, 1995Q1–2010Q2

Variable	*Mean*	*Std Dev*	*Minimum*	*Maximum*
Real GDP	11562.1	1365.58	9025.27	13363.5
GDP Deflator	94.6187	9.58319	80.969	110.488
Private Investment	1747.11	352.299	1126.2	2352.1
Personal Savings	302.744	142.152	110.2	793.5
PPI	148.01	17.0821	127.2	182.5
CPI	184.035	21.3015	150.867	218.909
Federal Fund IR	3.59365	2.11274	0.12	6.52
Prime Rate	6.61302	2.08442	3.25	9.5
IR3M	3.3027	1.96585	0.06	6.02
IR6M	3.40333	1.94469	0.16	6.04
IR3Y	4.11937	1.73122	0.83	7.27
IR5Y	4.45413	1.45542	1.55	7.39
IR10Y	4.91111	1.10128	2.74	7.48
Durable Consumer Goods	87.3661	10.0261	68.7742	101.554
S&P500	1092.6	262.008	480.47	1497.18
Change Inventories	51.0855	36.0252	3.1	179.5
Consumer Sentiment	89.7905	13.253	57.7	110.1

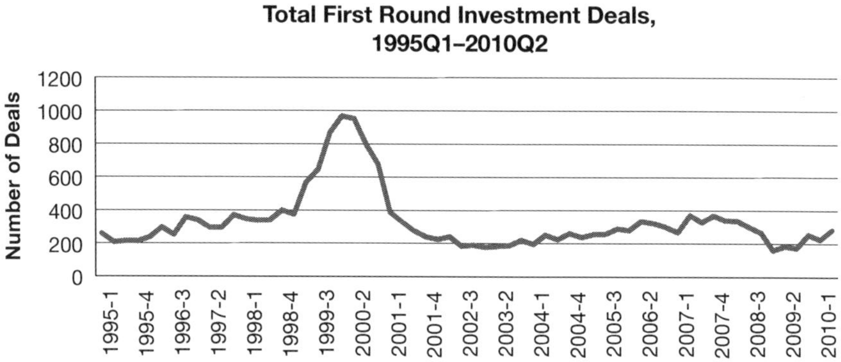

Figure 4.2 Total number of first round venture capital investment deals in the United States 1995Q1–2009Q1

has exhibited steady growth, until the recession in 2008. The slope after 2002 appears very similar to the slope of the trend before the dot com bubble. Additionally, it appears that first stage investment has already reached its lowest point during the financial crisis and is currently making a slow recovery along with the broader economy.

The MoneyTree Report records cash for equity investments as the cash is actually received by the company (also called a tranche) as opposed to when financing is committed (often referred to as a "term sheet") to a company. Accordingly, the amount reported in a given quarter may be less than the total round amount committed to the company at the time when the round of financing closed. The type of financing as it is used in the MoneyTree Report refers to the number of tranches a company has received. The number designation (1, 2, 3, etc.) does not refer to the round of financing. Rounds are usually designated alphabetically, *e.g.* Series A, Series B, and so on. The MoneyTree Report does not track rounds.

The data include the first sequence of financing by a venture capital firm in all stages of development of the firm, either at the stage of seed/start-up, early stage, expansion stage, or later stage. Appendix 4.3 provides the definitions of the various stages of development. Since the data concentrate only on the first sequence of financing, one identifies this point as the crossroad where invention becomes innovation and the firm or entrepreneurs seek the cooperation of the venture capitalists.

Figure 4.3 exhibits total first sequence financing by stage of development. It appears that venture capitalists prefer to invest during the early stage and expansion stage of development. It is probable that venture capitalists are cautious of investing in a start-up firm, which has no credit history, revenue, or track record. Although innovation and ideas are important to the venture capital industry, a firm needs to establish that it has enough financial and managerial competence to grow before a venture capital firm will invest. A firm has to demonstrate it has some degree of survivability in order to attract venture capital financing.

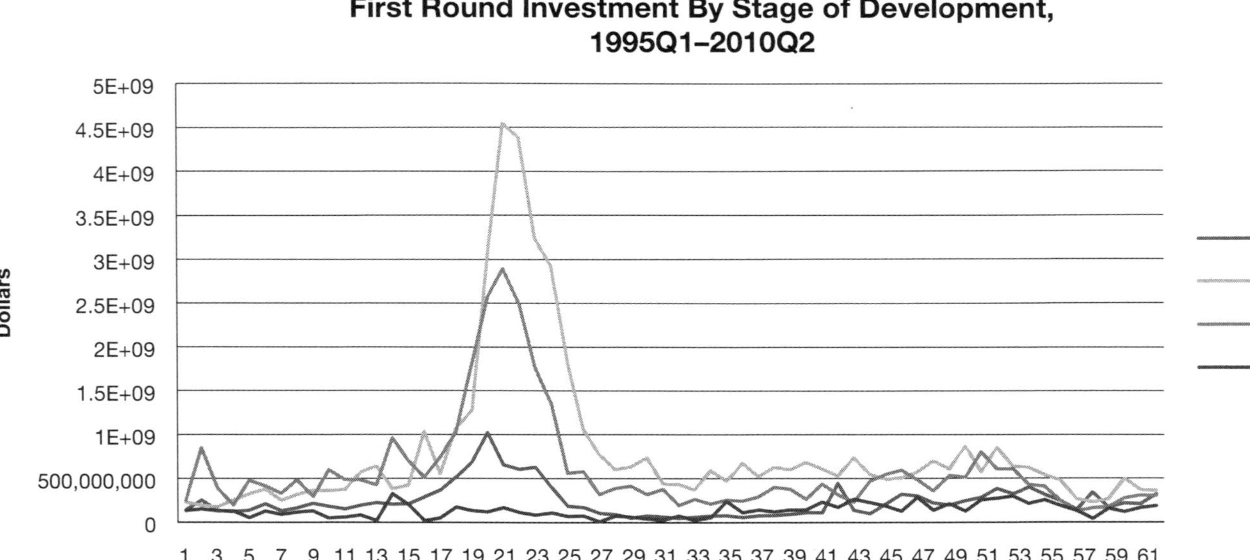

Figure 4.3 Total first round venture capital investment by stage of development 1995Q1–2010Q2

Furthermore, Figure 4.3 shows that the first sequence of financing occurs much less frequently in the later stage of development. After a firm has generated a steady revenue and profit stream, the firm is likely able to obtain financing from other creditors such as banks, and is able to access various credit markets. Venture capital firms generally do not get involved this late in the development of a company. The basis business model of a venture capital firm is to spread many high-risk, high-return investments among many promising young corporations with the hope that a few will become successful, yielding a high return for a minimal investment. Once a company has established itself, it is usually able to attain better credit terms from more traditional creditors such as banks. Figure 4.3 shows that the share of first sequence investment that goes to firms in each stage of development stays roughly constant over time. The persistence of this relationship suggests that the association between first stage financing and stage of development is important to the nature and business plan of venture capitalism.

The database stratifies the geographical areas into 18 locations. They include the following geographical areas: Alaska/Hawaii/Puerto Rico; Colorado; DC/Metroplex; LA/Orange County; Midwest; New England; New York Metro; North Central; Northwest; Philadelphia Metro; Sacramento/Northern California; San Diego; Silicon Valley; South Central; Southeast; Southwest; Texas; and Upstate New York. Appendix 4.2 provides precise definitions of all these regions. Figure 4.4 displays first stage venture capital investment stratified by region. All the regions are included except for AK/HI/PR, Sacramento/N. Cali, Unknown, and Upstate NY. The excluded regions have missing values and too many values of zero.

Figure 4.5 plots the ranking of each region relative to other regions as measured by first stage investment of venture capitalists. The figure clearly shows that different regions changed their ranking relative to their previous positions. The one exception is Silicon Valley, which except for the first year of the sample, 1995, remains the highest recipient of first stage financing throughout the 1995Q1 through 2010Q2 period. Silicon Valley is known as a hotbed for technology firm start-ups. Not surprisingly, Silicon Valley received a very large portion of first sequence financing during the dot com boom. Although there is some degree of cross-over, there are some regions, such as Silicon Valley, New York Metro, and New England which tend consistently to obtain higher first round investment than other regions over time. In addition, many regions specialize in particular industries. Hence, when a surge in demand or innovation hits a certain industry, it likely impacts the amount of first stage financing some regions receive. Thus, history is important in determining the destination of future first stage financing.

Figure 4.6 shows first stage venture capital investment stratified by industry. All the industries are included, except for "Other," which had too many missing values and values of zero. The industry classifications are: biotechnology, business products and services, computers and peripherals, consumer products and services, electronics/instrumentation, financial services, healthcare services, industrial/energy, IT services, media and entertainment, medical devices and equipment, networking and equipment, retailing/distribution, semiconductors,

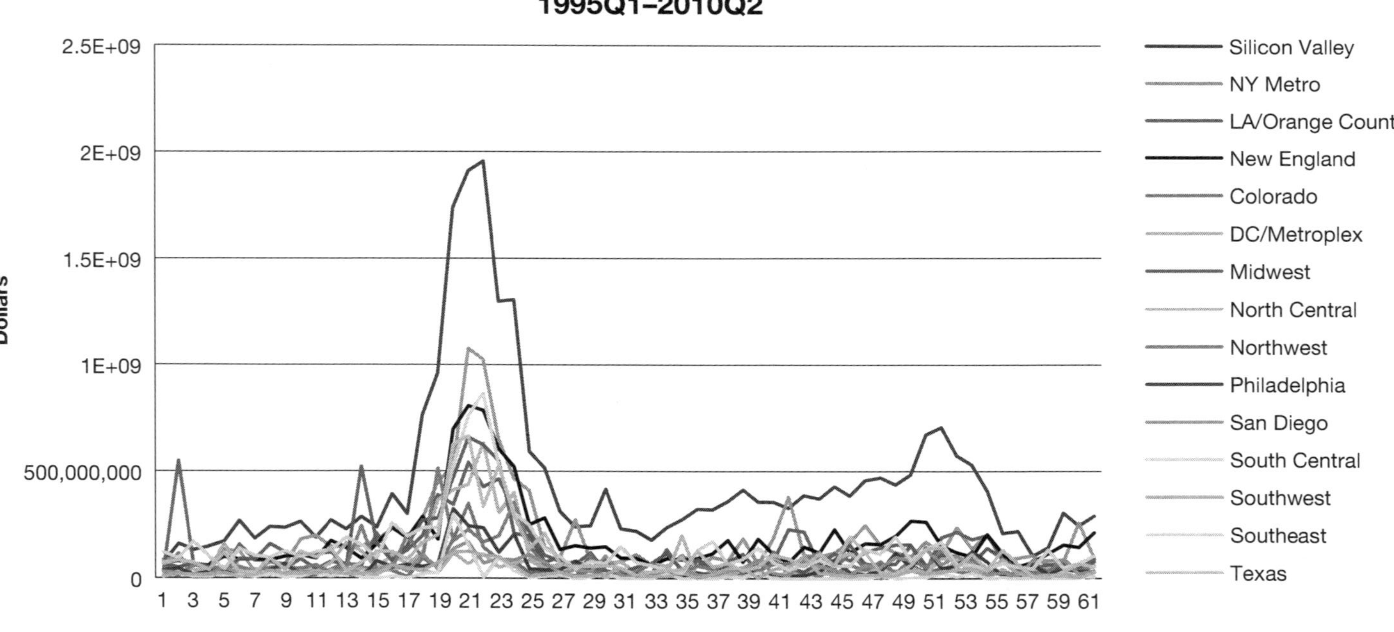

Figure 4.4 Total first round investment in venture capital by regions 1995Q1–2010Q2

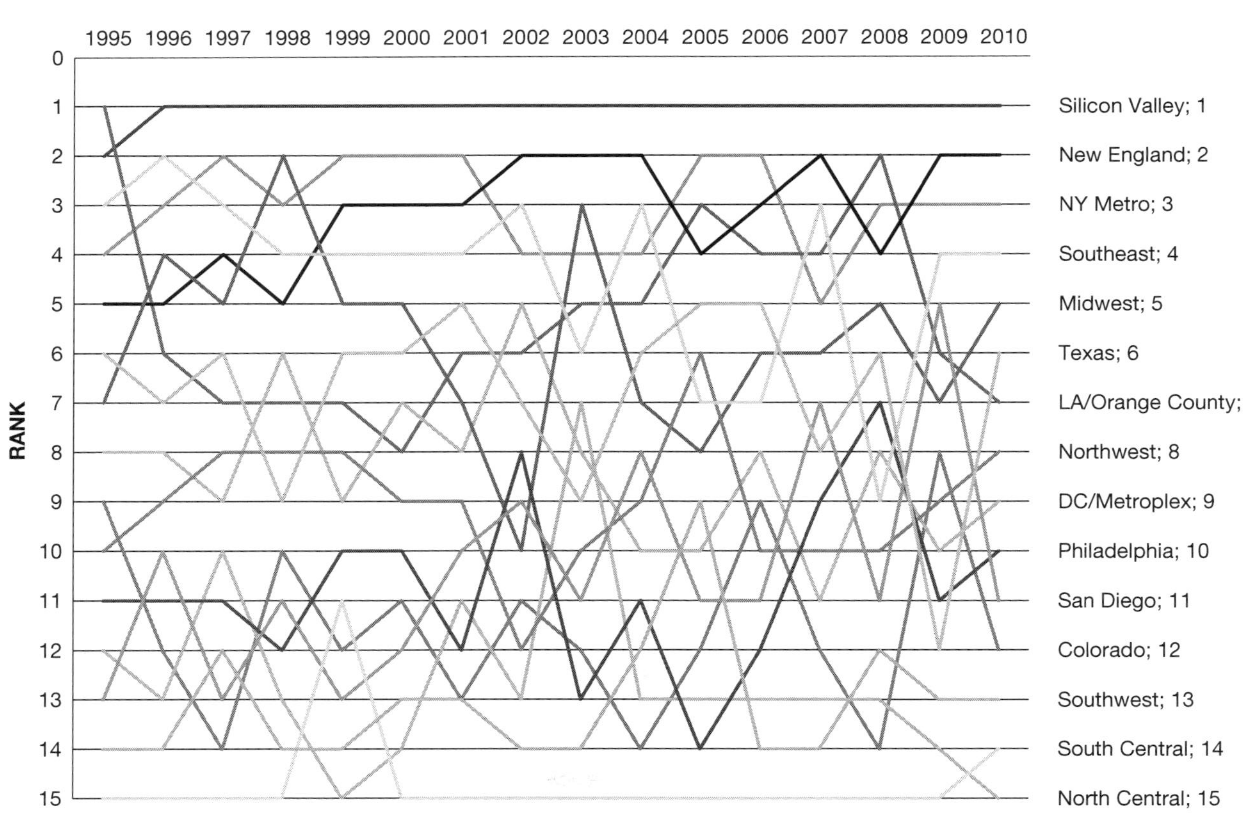

Figure 4.5 Regional ranks in venture capital investment 1995–2010

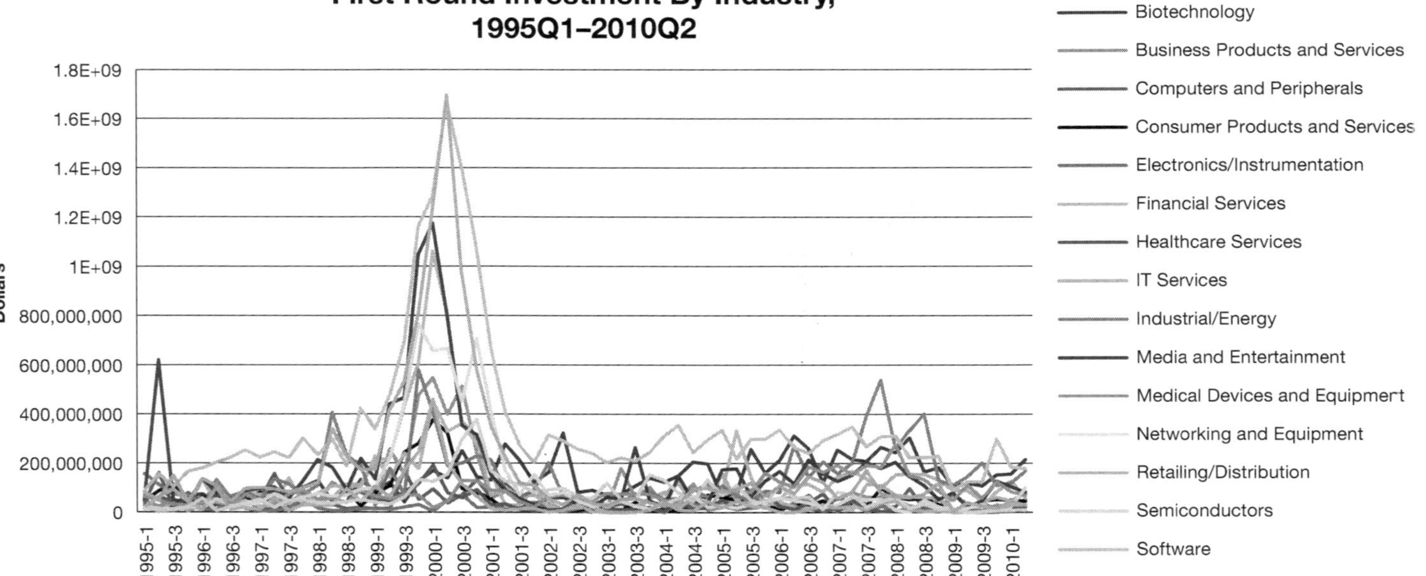

Figure 4.6 Total first round investment in venture capital by industry 1995Q1–2010Q2

software, telecommunications, and finally, Other. Appendix 4.1 contains the exact definitions of all the industries. Figure 4.7 plots the annual ranking of each industry relative to other industries from 1995 until the end of the sample. There is a good degree of cross-over in how much first round investment each industry receives. However, software appears to be the largest recipient of first stage financing over time. It can be seen that the industry and amount of first stage financing vary over time. Thus, region, industry, and time period all matter in predicting first stage investment.

There are 7872 quarterly observations of venture capital investment. The data span from the first quarter of 1995 until the second quarter of 2010. In addition to the venture capital data, the following macroeconomic variables are included in the study: real GDP, GDP: implicit price deflator, gross private domestic investment, personal savings, producer price index, consumer price index, effective federal funds rate, bank prime rate, 3-month Treasury bill rate, 6-month Treasury bill rate, 3-year Treasury rate, 5-year Treasury rate, 10-year maturity rate, industrial production: durable consumer goods, S&P500 index, change in private inventories, and the University of Michigan's consumer sentiment index.

The effect of the current recession on first stage venture capital investment has been dramatic. 2008 was the first year in which first round investment decreased since 2003, which represents a marked deviation from trend. The financial crisis negatively impacted investment in all regions and all industries. Although there are significant variations across industry and region during the current economic crisis, geography and industry remain important determinants of venture capital investment. A general recovery is observed in most industries and regions. First stage financing is up since the second quarter of 2009 in all four stages of development. Although there is currently not enough data for a statistical analysis since first stage financing hit its low point during the recession in 2009Q1, it appears that the new trend line has a less steep slope than before the financial crisis. This suggests that the recovery in first stage financing could be slow, and span a long time.

4.4 Empirical results

Table 4.2 presents the Pearson correlation coefficients for the macroeconomic variables and their corresponding significant values for the variables used in the study. Investment and real GDP deals are highly correlated, with a correlation coefficient of 0.871. Every measure of GDP is strongly negatively associated with all interest rates. The very short run overnight federal funds rate is more correlated with IR3 than IR5 and IR10 (-0.709, -0.761,-0.829 respectively). The correlation between all the interest rates is significant, as can be expected. The pairwise correlations between the interest rates are all above 0.90. The correlation between the S&P500 and real GDP is 0.638. This is of interest because both the stock market and venture capital rely heavily upon speculation between future economic prospects and returns.

Table 4.3 presents the regression results for the first round of venture capital investment as a function of the quarter of the transaction, number of deals, real

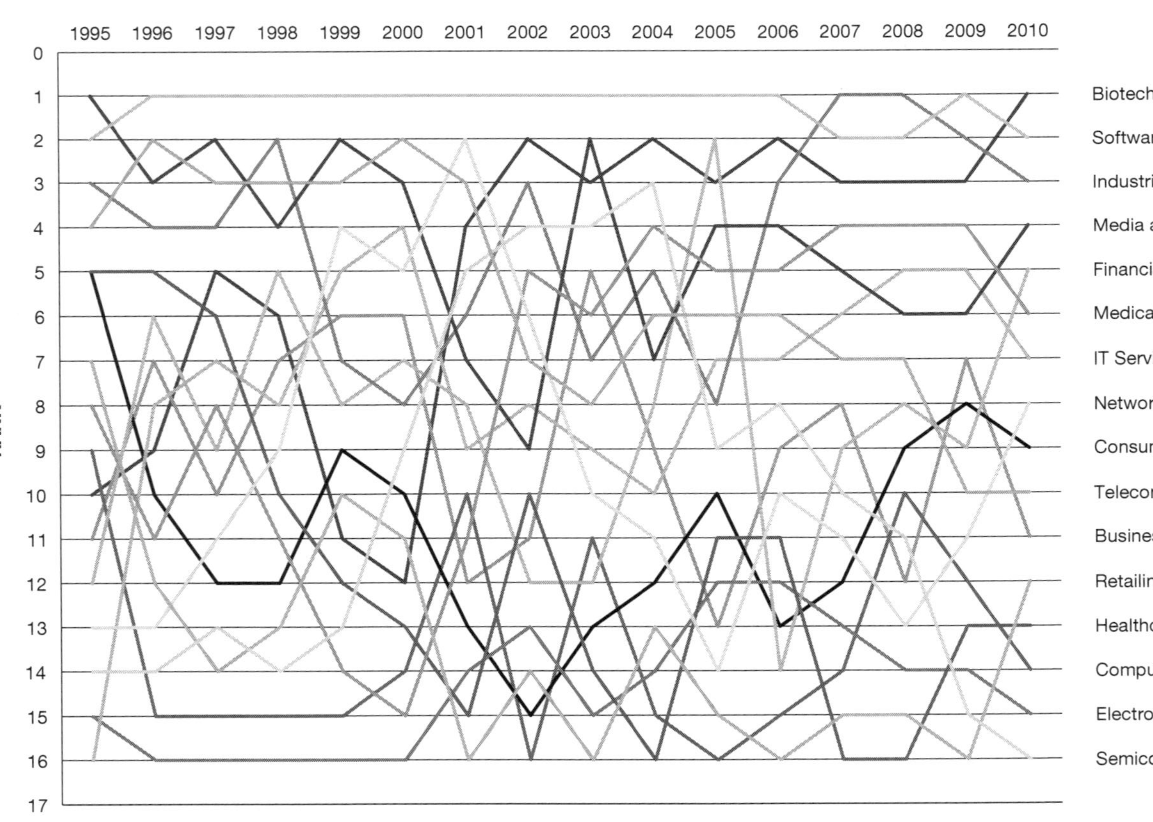

Figure 4.7 Industrial ranks in venture capital investment: 1995–2010

Table 4.2 Pearson correlation coefficients

Pearson Correlation coefficients	*Real GDP*	*GDP Deflator*	*Private Investment*	*Personal Savings*	*PPI*
Real GDP	1	0.95075	0.87119	0.24515	0.90445
		<.0001	<.0001	0.0548	<.0001
GDP Deflator	0.95075	1	0.73701	0.45729	0.98334
	<.0001		<.0001	0.0002	<.0001
Private Investment	0.87119	0.73701	1	–0.1701	0.68795
	<.0001	<.0001		0.1862	<.0001
Personal Savings	0.24515	0.45729	–0.1701	1	0.49477
	0.0548	0.0002	0.1862		<.0001
PPI	0.90445	0.98334	0.68795	0.49477	1
	<.0001	<.0001	<.0001	<.0001	
CPI	0.96425	0.99699	0.75211	0.43727	0.98006
	<.0001	<.0001	<.0001	0.0004	<.0001
Federal Fund IR	–0.57231	–0.60907	–0.19077	–0.58057	–0.58007
	<.0001	<.0001	0.1375	<.0001	<.0001
Prime Rate	–0.5682	–0.60165	–0.19023	–0.57043	–0.57212
	<.0001	<.0001	0.1386	<.0001	<.0001
IR3M	–0.59566	–0.63374	–0.21034	–0.58587	–0.60858
	<.0001	<.0001	0.1008	<.0001	<.0001
IR6M	–0.58793	–0.62468	–0.1981	–0.5839	–0.5994
	<.0001	<.0001	0.1227	<.0001	<.0001
IR3Y	–0.70931	–0.73752	–0.35173	–0.54841	–0.70614
	<.0001	<.0001	0.0051	<.0001	<.0001
IR5Y	–0.76055	–0.78397	–0.42835	–0.52534	–0.74854
	<.0001	<.0001	0.0005	<.0001	<.0001
IR10Y	–0.82882	–0.83146	–0.55005	–0.45217	–0.78562
	<.0001	<.0001	<.0001	0.0002	<.0001
Durable Consumer Goods	0.66587	0.42138	0.85655	–0.4388	0.31254
	<.0001	0.0006	<.0001	0.0004	0.0126
S&P500	0.63843	0.45085	0.78248	–0.24651	0.40338
	<.0001	0.0002	<.0001	0.0534	0.001
Change Inventories	0.13535	0.22983	–0.02177	0.47329	0.20998
	0.2942	0.0723	0.8666	0.0001	0.1014
Consumer Sentiment	–0.62546	–0.78213	–0.30417	–0.59785	–0.82206
	<.0001	<.0001	0.0162	<.0001	<.0001

(Continued)

Table 4.2 (Continued)

	CPI	*Federal Fund IR*	*Prime Rate*	*IR3M*	*IR6M*	*IR3Y*	*IR5Y*
GDP Deflator	0.99699 <.0001	–0.60907 <.0001	–0.60165 <.0001	–0.63374 <.0001	–0.62468 <.0001	–0.73752 <.0001	–0.78397 <.0001
Private Investment	0.75211 <.0001	–0.19077 0.1375	–0.19023 0.1386	–0.21034 0.1008	–0.1981 0.1227	–0.35173 0.0051	–0.42835 0.0005
Personal Savings	0.43727 0.0004	–0.58057 <.0001	–0.57043 <.0001	–0.58587 <.0001	–0.5839 <.0001	–0.54841 <.0001	–0.52534 <.0001
PPI	0.98006 <.0001	–0.58007 <.0001	–0.57212 <.0001	–0.60858 <.0001	–0.5994 <.0001	–0.70614 <.0001	–0.74854 <.0001
CPI	1	–0.64098 <.0001	–0.63442 <.0001	–0.66604 <.0001	–0.65852 <.0001	–0.76551 <.0001	–0.80725 <.0001
Federal Fund IR	–0.64098 <.0001	1	0.99939 <.0001	0.99391 <.0001	0.99112 <.0001	0.94155 <.0001	0.90524 <.0001
Prime Rate	–0.63442 <.0001	0.99939 <.0001	1	0.99243 <.0001	0.99009 <.0001	0.93883 <.0001	0.90196 <.0001
IR3M	–0.66604 <.0001	0.99391 <.0001	0.99243 <.0001	1	0.99847 <.0001	0.9618 <.0001	0.92794 <.0001
IR6M	–0.65852 <.0001	0.99112 <.0001	0.99009 <.0001	0.99847 <.0001	1	0.96704 <.0001	0.9325 <.0001
IR3Y	–0.76551 <.0001	0.94155 <.0001	0.93883 <.0001	0.9618 <.0001	0.96704 <.0001	1	0.99201 <.0001
IR5Y	–0.80725 <.0001	0.90524 <.0001	0.90196 <.0001	0.92794 <.0001	0.9325 <.0001	0.99201 <.0001	1
IR10Y	–0.85067 <.0001	0.82735 <.0001	0.82377 <.0001	0.85225 <.0001	0.85577 <.0001	0.95073 <.0001	0.98117 <.0001
Durable Consumer Goods	0.44168 0.0003	–0.15024 0.2399	–0.15662 0.2203	–0.16185 0.2051	–0.15769 0.2171	–0.25443 0.0442	–0.29593 0.0185
S&P500	0.47179 <.0001	0.06455 0.6153	0.06595 0.6076	0.03094 0.8097	0.03346 0.7946	–0.08873 0.4892	–0.15363 0.2293
Change Inventories	0.20307 0.1134	–0.19201 0.1349	–0.18422 0.1518	–0.16763 0.1928	–0.15259 0.2364	–0.13784 0.2854	–0.15766 0.221
Consumer Sentiment	–0.78351 <.0001	0.67645 <.0001	0.66636 <.0001	0.70366 <.0001	0.69887 <.0001	0.75414 <.0001	0.76198 <.0001

	IR10Y	*Durable Consumer Goods*	*SP500*	*Change Inventories*	*Consumer Sentiment*
Real GDP	–0.82882	0.66587	0.63843	0.13535	–0.62546
	<.0001	<.0001	<.0001	0.2942	<.0001
GDP Deflator	–0.83146	0.42138	0.45085	0.22983	–0.78213
	<.0001	0.0006	0.0002	0.0723	<.0001
Private	–0.55005	0.85655	0.78248	–0.02177	–0.30417
Investment	<.0001	<.0001	<.0001	0.8666	0.0162
Personal	–0.45217	–0.4388	–0.24651	0.47329	–0.59785
Savings	0.0002	0.0004	0.0534	0.0001	<.0001
PPI	–0.78562	0.31254	0.40338	0.20998	–0.82206
	<.0001	0.0126	0.001	0.1014	<.0001
CPI	–0.85067	0.44168	0.47179	0.20307	–0.78351
	<.0001	0.0003	<.0001	0.1134	<.0001
Federal Fund	0.82735	–0.15024	0.06455	–0.19201	0.67645
IR	<.0001	0.2399	0.6153	0.1349	<.0001
Prime Rate	0.82377	–0.15662	0.06595	–0.18422	0.66636
	<.0001	0.2203	0.6076	0.1518	<.0001
IR3M	0.85225	–0.16185	0.03094	–0.16763	0.70366
	<.0001	0.2051	0.8097	0.1928	<.0001
IR6M	0.85577	–0.15769	0.03346	–0.15259	0.69887
	<.0001	0.2171	0.7946	0.2364	<.0001
IR3Y	0.95073	–0.25443	–0.08873	–0.13784	0.75414
	<.0001	0.0442	0.4892	0.2854	<.0001
IR5Y	0.98117	–0.29593	–0.15363	–0.15766	0.76198
	<.0001	0.0185	0.2293	0.221	<.0001
IR10Y	1	–0.38562	–0.27948	–0.17609	0.73608
		0.0018	0.0265	0.171	<.0001
Durable	–0.38562	1	0.76883	–0.24207	0.02963
Consumer	0.0018		<.0001	0.058	0.8177
Goods					
S&P500	–0.27948	0.76883	1	–0.04578	0.06715
	0.0265	<.0001		0.7239	0.6011
Change	–0.17609	–0.24207	–0.04578	1	–0.15968
Inventories	0.171	0.058	0.7239		0.2151
Consumer	0.73608	0.02963	0.06715	–0.15968	1
Sentiment	<.0001	0.8177	0.6011	0.2151	

Table 4.3 Regression results (full model)

Dependent Variable: Investment
Number of Observations Read: 7872
Number of Observations Used: 7456
Number of Observations with Missing Values: 416

Analysis of Variance

Source	*DF*	*Sum of Squares*	*Mean Square*	*F Value*	*Pr > F*
Model	53	3.50E+18	6.60E+16	150.17	<.0001
Error	7402	3.25E+18	4.39E+14		
Corrected Total	7455	6.75E+18			
Root MSE	20958444	R–Square	0.5181		
Dependent Mean	15060360	Adj R–Sq	0.5147		
Coeff Var	139.163				

Variable	*Label*	*Parameter Estimate*	*Standard Error*	*t Value*	*Pr > |t|*
Intercept		–1.8E+08	93137068	–1.93	0.0539
Date		–654315	612198	–1.07	0.2852
Deals		5753693	82250	69.95	<.0001
Industry 2	Business Products and Services	485758	1298599	0.37	0.7084
Industry 3	Computers and Peripherals	–235572	1567065	–0.15	0.8805
Industry 4	Consumer Products and Services	–1537734	1328339	–1.16	0.247
Industry 5	Electronics/ Instrumentation	–1577111	1585420	–0.99	0.3199
Industry 6	Financial Services	3717954	1386321	2.68	0.0073
Industry 7	Healthcare Services	500314	1473881	0.34	0.7343
Industry 8	IT Services	–534143	1254704	–0.43	0.6703
Industry 9	Industrial/Energy	3123223	1183812	2.64	0.0084
Industry 10	Media and Entertainment	–1122725	1194676	–0.94	0.3474
Industry 11	Medical Devices and Equipment	–2570050	1216078	–2.11	0.0346
Industry 12	Networking and Equipment	6227662	1421708	4.38	<.0001
Industry 13	Other	–2320775	2872365	–0.81	0.4191
Industry 14	Retailing/ Distribution	–722676	1515817	–0.48	0.6335
Industry 15	Semiconductors	–78283	1429015	–0.05	0.9563
Industry 16	Software	–7738811	1149375	–6.73	<.0001
Industry 17	Telecommunications	4087630	1213290	3.37	0.0008
Region 2	Colorado	3803073	3193131	1.19	0.2337
Region 3	DC Metroplex	2381036	3118777	0.76	0.4452

Region 4	LA Orange County	6306672	3106277	2.03	0.0424
Region 5	Midwest	3492796	3096117	1.13	0.2593
Region 6	NY Metro	6692436	3097378	2.16	0.0308
Region 7	New England	2159423	3086462	0.7	0.4842
Region 8	North Central	2733909	3186790	0.86	0.391
Region 9	Northwest	3809487	3136108	1.21	0.2245
Region 10	Philadelphia Metro	2734699	3159339	0.87	0.3867
Region 11	Sacramento/N. Cali	3528804	3892599	0.91	0.3647
Region 12	San Diego	3531605	3184791	1.11	0.2675
Region 13	Silicon Valley	753486	3097643	0.24	0.8078
Region 14	South Central	4015795	3473637	1.16	0.2477
Region 15	Southwest	3098723	3210909	0.97	0.3345
Region 16	Southeast	4242227	3095777	1.37	0.1706
Region 17	Texas	5336807	3118202	1.71	0.087
Region 18	Unknown	224772	4121025	0.05	0.9565
Region 19	Upstate NY	1485302	3512374	0.42	0.6724
Real GDP		35035	6513.287	5.38	<.0001
GDP Deflator		–800356	729980	–1.1	0.2729
Private Investment		–54702	8089.057	–6.76	<.0001
Personal Savings		3930.993	4543.165	0.87	0.3869
PPI		868080	295766	2.94	0.0033
CPI		–1132673	567152	–2	0.0458
Federal Fund IR		–4562364	5307053	–0.86	0.39
Prime Rate		1634208	5491357	0.3	0.766
IR3M		–1.3E+07	4738913	–2.73	0.0063
IR6M		22921935	6873743	3.33	0.0009
IR3Y		–9727031	7725396	–1.26	0.208
IR5Y		8252948	10438702	0.79	0.4292
IR10Y		–2366016	5868269	–0.4	0.6868
Durable Consumer Goods		294653	183551	1.61	0.1085
S&P500		–4681.58	5652.01	–0.83	0.4075
Change Inventories		–3352.84	10418	–0.32	0.7476
Consumer Sentiment		60128	87929	0.68	0.4941

GDP, GDP deflator, private investment, personal savings, PPI, CPI, federal funds rate, bank prime rate, durable goods production, S&P500, change in inventories, consumer sentiment, and the interest rate on Treasury bills for maturities of 3 months, 6 months, 3 years, 5 years, and 10 years. In addition, the industry and regional indicators are included. The 16 dummy variables for the different industries were measured relative to the biotech industry, and the 18 dummies for the different regions were measured relative to the Alaska/Hawaii/Puerto Rico region.

The first regression model uses all the available variables. This regression represents the starting point from which the final model was derived. As shown in Table 4.3, the adjusted R^2 is equal to 0.5147. As expected, a rise in the number of deals increases the amount of venture capital invested. The coefficients on software, telecommunication, networking and equipment, medical devices and equipment, industrial/energy, and financial services were statistically significant. Furthermore, in terms of the regional coefficients, LA/Orange County, NY Metro, and Texas were significant. As displayed in Table 4.3, with all other variables held constant, an increase in GDP raises the amount of investment by venture capitalists. Interestingly, all the interest rates were statistically insignificant except for the 3-month and 6-month Treasury bill rates. The 3-month rate has a negative coefficient, while the 6-month rate had a positive coefficient. The high degree of collinearity between the interest rates is likely making their estimation difficult. Additionally, the coefficient on private investment is negative, which is surprising. One could explain this trend by interpreting that total private investment crowds out venture capital investment. In any case, the first model needs to be refined. Insignificant and highly correlated regressors were dropped from the regression, resulting in a reduced model.

Table 4.4 displays the results of the reduced model. The first round of venture capital investment is represented as a function of the number of deals, real GDP, private investment, PPI, CPI, federal funds rate, S&P500, and the 3-month Treasury bill rate. In addition, the industry and regional indictors are included. Many more coefficients on the regional and industrial dummies are now significant.

In terms of the industrial sector indicators, business products and services, computers and peripherals, consumer products and services, electronics/instrumentation, IT services, media and entertainment, medical devices and equipment, other, retailing/distribution, and semiconductors were all significant. All the regional dummies were highly significant with the exception of Unknown and Upstate New York. Observing the p-values, it appears that region is a more significant predictor of first round investment than industry. Furthermore, first stage investment is positively related to real GDP and the S&P500 index.

The coefficient on CPI is negative, while the coefficient on PPI is positive. It is plausible that higher prices decrease profit margins and make new investment seem less attractive. The estimated coefficient on private investment is negative again. This could be interpreted as a crowding out effect on total investment on venture capital investment. The coefficient on the federal funds rate is negative,

Table 4.4 Regression results (revised model)

Dependent Variable: Investment
Number of Observations Read: 7872
Number of Observations Used: 7454
Number of Observations with Missing Values: 418

Analysis of Variance

Source	*DF*	*Sum of Squares*	*Mean Square*	*F Value*	*Pr > F*
Model	42	6283.406	149.6049	80.38	<.0001
Error	7411	13794	1.86127		
Corrected Total	7453	20077			
Root MSE	1.36428	R-Square	0.313		
Dependent Mean	15.456	Adj R-Sq	0.3091		
Coeff Var	8.82688				

Variable	*Label*	*Parameter Estimate*	*Standard Error*	*t Value*	*Pr > |t|*
Intercept		11.24677	0.55341	20.32	<.0001
Deals		0.16374	0.00531	30.83	<.0001
Industry 2	Business Products and Services	−0.30199	0.08449	−3.57	0.0004
Industry 3	Computers and Peripherals	−0.6326	0.10211	−6.19	<.0001
Industry 4	Consumer Products and Services	−0.45641	0.08642	−5.28	<.0001
Industry 5	Electronics/ Instrumentation	−0.78895	0.10312	−7.65	<.0001
Industry 6	Financial Services	−0.07989	0.0902	−0.89	0.3758
Industry 7	Healthcare Services	−0.14644	0.0959	−1.53	0.1268
Industry 8	IT Services	−0.1442	0.08166	−1.77	0.0775
Industry 9	Industrial/Energy	−0.06757	0.07703	−0.88	0.3805
Industry 10	Media and Entertainment	−0.20648	0.07777	−2.65	0.008
Industry 11	Medical Devices and Equipment	−0.32701	0.07915	−4.13	<.0001
Industry 12	Networking and Equipment	−0.0875	0.0925	−0.95	0.3442
Industry 13	Other	−1.23497	0.18681	−6.61	<.0001
Industry 14	Retailing/ Distribution	−0.51233	0.09861	−5.2	<.0001
Industry 15	Semiconductors	−0.39192	0.09297	−4.22	<.0001
Industry 16	Software	0.02298	0.07476	0.31	0.7586
Industry 17	Telecommunications	−0.12913	0.07895	−1.64	0.1019
Region 2	Colorado	0.90829	0.20767	4.37	<.0001
Region 3	DC Metroplex	0.92022	0.20279	4.54	<.0001
Region 4	LA Orange County	1.41781	0.20195	7.02	<.0001

(Continued)

Table 4.4 (Continued)

Variable	*Label*	*Parameter Estimate*	*Standard Error*	*t Value*	*Pr >* |*t*|
Region 5	Midwest	1.13998	0.20129	5.66	<.0001
Region 6	NY Metro	1.53543	0.20141	7.62	<.0001
Region 7	New England	1.34393	0.20064	6.7	<.0001
Region 8	North Central	0.68726	0.20716	3.32	0.0009
Region 9	Northwest	1.1489	0.20388	5.64	<.0001
Region 10	Philadelphia Metro	0.57972	0.20534	2.82	0.0048
Region 11	Sacramento/N. Cali	0.76089	0.25315	3.01	0.0027
Region 12	San Diego	1.1162	0.20705	5.39	<.0001
Region 13	Silicon Valley	1.57479	0.20137	7.82	<.0001
Region 14	South Central	0.46814	0.22588	2.07	0.0383
Region 15	Southwest	0.82928	0.20873	3.97	<.0001
Region 16	Southeast	1.34291	0.20128	6.67	<.0001
Region 17	Texas	1.34743	0.20276	6.65	<.0001
Region 18	Unknown	–0.36838	0.26802	–1.37	0.1693
Region 19	Upstate NY	0.185	0.22836	0.81	0.4179
Real GDP		0.00146	0.00024961	5.85	<.0001
Private Investment		–0.00153	0.0002642	–5.8	<.0001
PPI		0.05309	0.01224	4.34	<.0001
CPI		–0.10928	0.02019	–5.41	<.0001
Federal Fund IR		–0.08796	0.07752	–1.13	0.2565
IR3M		0.19708	0.08116	2.43	0.0152
S&P500		0.00041597	0.00017839	2.33	0.0197

but insignificant. The estimate on the 3-month Treasury bill rate is positive and significant. Based on the various intermediate fits which were run to obtain this model, it does not appear that first stage investment is sensitive to interest rates.

4.5 Conclusion

This chapter investigates first round venture capital investment in the United States for the period 1995Q1 through 2010Q2, stratified by both locations and industries. The first round is the point where venture capital is invested in a company for the first time. The statistical results confirm the importance of both regions and industries in explaining the investment in venture capital. Even in light of many macroeconomic variables, industry and region are still dominant factors in determining first-sequence venture capital financing.

References

Alonso-Villar, O. "The Effects of Transport Costs Revisited." *Journal of Economic Geography*, vol. 5, no. 5, pp. 589–604. October. 2005.

Arrow, Kenneth J. 1962. "Economic Welfare and the Allocation of Resources for Invention," in: Richard Nelson (ed.), *The Rate and Direction of Inventive Activity*. Princeton, N. J.: Princeton University Press.

Behrens, K. "Market Size and Industry Location: Traded vs. Non-traded Goods." *Journal of Urban Economics*, vol. 58, no. 1, pp. 24–44, July. 2005.

Davis, Lance E., and Douglas C. North. 1971. *Institutional Change and American Economic Growth*. Cambridge: Cambridge University Press.

Fujita, M. and Paul Krugman. "The New Economic Geography: Past, Present and the Future." *Papers in Regional Science*, vol. 83, no. 1, pp. 139–64, January. 2004.

Hall, Bronwyn H. 2009. "The Financing of Innovation," in: Scott Shane (ed.), *Blackwell Handbook of Technology and Innovation Management*, Oxford: Wiley-Blackwell.

Klepper, Steven 2007. "The Organizing and Financing of Innovative Companies in the Evolution of the U.S. Automobile Industry," in: Naomi R. Lamoreaux and Kenneth L. Sokoloff (eds.) *Financing Innovation in the United States, 1870 to the Present*. Cambridge, MA: MIT Press.

Kortum, Samuel and Josh Lerner. 1998. "Stronger Protection or Technological Revolution: What is behind the Recent Surge in Patenting." Carnegie-Rochester Conference Series on Public Policy 48, 247–304.

Kortum, Samuel and Josh Lerner. "Assessing the Contribution of Venture Capital to Innovation." *RAND Journal of Economics*, vol. 31, pp. 674–92. 2000.

Krugman, Paul. "Geography and Trade." Gaston Eyskens Lecture Series Cambridge, Mass. and London: MIT Press, and Louvain, Belgium: Louvain University Press, pp. xi, 142. 1991a.

Krugman, Paul. "Increasing Returns and Economic Geography." *Journal of Political Economy*, vol. 99, no. 3, pp. 483–99, June. 1991b.

Krugman, Paul. "Innovation and Agglomeration: Two Parables Suggested by City-Size Distributions." *Japan and the World Economy*, vol. 7, no. 4, pp. 371–90, November. 1995.

Krugman, Paul. "What's New about the New Economic Geography?" *Oxford Review of Economic Policy*, vol. 14, no. 2, pp. 7–17, Summer. 1998.

Lamoreaux, Naomi R., and Kenneth L. Sokoloff. 1999a. "The Geography of the Market for Technology in the Late-Nineteenth- and Early-Twentieth Century United States." in: Gary D. Libecap (ed.) *Advances in the Study of Entrepreneurship, Innovation, and Economic Growth* (Vol. 11, 67–121). Greenwich, Conn.: JAI Press.

Lamoreaux, Naomi R., and Kenneth L. Sokoloff. 1999b. "Inventive Activity and the Market for Technology in the United States, 1840–1920," Working paper 7107, NBER, Cambridge, Mass.

Lamoreaux, Naomi R. and Kenneth L. Sokoloff 2007. *Financing Innovation in the United States, 1870 to the Present*. Edited by Naomi R. Lamoreaux and Kenneth L. Sokoloff. Cambridge, MA: MIT Press.

Lamoreaux, Naomi R., Margaret Levenstein and Kenneth L. Sokoloff 2007. "Financing Invention during the Second Industrial Revolution Cleveland, Ohio, 1870–1920," in: Naomi R. Lamoreaux and Kenneth L. Sokoloff (eds.) *Financing Innovation in the United States, 1870 to the Present*. Cambridge, MA: MIT Press.

Lerner, Josh. 2001. *Venture Capital and Private Equity: A Casebook*. 2nd edition. New York: John Wiley & Sons.

Midelfart, K.H., H. Overman and A.J. Venables. "Monetary Union and the Economic Geography of Europe." *Journal of Common Market Studies*, vol. 41, no. 5, pp. 847–68, December. 2003.

Murphy, T. 1956. *A Business of Your Own*. New York: McGraw-Hill.

Nelson, Richard R. "The Simple Economics of Basic Scientific Research," *Journal of Political Economy*, vol. 49, pp. 297–306. 1959.

Perez, Carlota. 2002. *Technological Revolutions and Financial Capital: The Dynamics of Bubbles and Golden Ages*. Cheltenham: Edward Elgar Publishing.

Perez, Carlota. 2004. "Finance and Technological Change: A Neo-Schumpeterian Perspective," Working paper no. 14, Cambridge Endowment for Research in Finance, University of Cambridge.

Shachmurove, Yochanan. 2007. "Innovation and Trade: Introduction and Comments," in: Eytan Sheshinski, Robert J. Strom and William J. Baumol (eds.), *Entrepreneurship, Innovation, and the Growth Mechanism of the Free-Enterprise Economies*, Princeton University Press, pp. 247–60.

Shachmurove, Yochanan. "An Excursion into the Venture Capital Industry Stratified by Locations and Industries 1996–2005." *Journal of Entrepreneurial Finance and Business Ventures*, vol. 11, no. 3, pp. 79–104, December. 2006.

Shachmurove, Yochanan. "Annualized Returns of Venture-Backed Public Companies Categorized by Stage of Financing." *Journal of Entrepreneurial Finance*, vol. 6, no. 1, pp. 44–58. 2001.

Shachmurove, A. and Yochanan Shachmurove. "Annualized and Cumulative Returns on Venture-Backed Public Companies Categorized by Industry." *Journal of Entrepreneurial Finance and Business Ventures*, vol. 9, no. 3, December, pp. 41–60. 2004.

Venables, A.J. "Equilibrium locations of vertically linked industries." *International Economic Review*, vol. 37, pp. 341–59. 1996.

Venables, A.J. "The Assessment: Trade and Location." *Oxford Review of Economic Policy*, vol. 14, no. 2, pp. 1–6, Summer. 1998.

Venables, A.J. "Trade, Geography, and Monopolistic Competition: Theory and an Application to Spatial Inequalities in Developing Countries." *Economics for an Imperfect World: Essays in Honor of Joseph E. Stiglitz*, pp. 501–17. 2003.

Appendix 4.1: Industry definitions

The industry classifications used in the MoneyTree Report are as follows:

Biotechnology

Developers of technology promoting drug development, disease treatment, and a deeper understanding of living organisms. Includes human, animal, and industrial biotechnology products and services. Also included are biosensors, biotechnology equipment, and pharmaceuticals.

Business products and services

Offers a product or service targeted at another business such as advertising, consulting, and engineering services. Also includes distributors, importers, and wholesalers.

Computers and peripherals

Includes manufacturers and distributors of PCs, mainframes, servers, PDAs, printers, storage devices, monitors, and memory cards. Also included are digital imaging and graphics services and equipment such as scanning hardware, graphics video cards and plotters. Integrated turnkey systems and solutions are also included in this category.

Consumer products and services

Offers products or services targeted at consumers such as restaurants, dry cleaners, automotive service centers, clothing, toiletries, and housewares.

Electronics/instrumentation

Includes electronic parts that are components of larger products and specialized instrumentation, including scientific instruments, lasers, power supplies, electronic testing products and display panels. Also included are business and consumer electronic devices such as photocopiers, calculators, and alarm systems.

Financial services

Providers of financial services to other businesses or individuals including banking, real estate, brokerage services, and financial planning.

Healthcare services

Includes both in-patient and out-patient facilities as well as health insurers. Included are hospitals, clinics, nursing facilities, managed care organizations, physician practice management companies, child care and emergency care.

Industrial/energy

Producers and suppliers of energy, chemicals, and materials, industrial automation companies and oil and gas exploration companies. Also included are environmental, agricultural, transportation, manufacturing, construction and utility-related products and services.

IT services

Providers of computer and internet-related services to businesses and consumers including computer repair, software consulting, computer training, machine leasing/rental, disaster recovery, web design, data input and processing, internet security, e-commerce services, web hosting and systems engineering.

Media and entertainment

Creators of products or providers of services designed to inform or entertain consumers including movies, music, consumer electronics such as TVs/stereos/games, sports facilities and events, recreational products or services. Online providers of consumer content are also included in this category (medical, news, education, legal).

Medical devices and equipment

Manufactures and/or sells medical instruments and devices including medical diagnostic equipment (X-ray, CAT scan, MRI), medical therapeutic devices (drug delivery, surgical instruments, pacemakers, artificial organs), and other health related products such as medical monitoring equipment, handicap aids, reading glasses and contact lenses.

Networking and equipment

Providers of data communication and fiber optics products and services. Includes WANs, LANs, switches, hubs, routers, couplers, and network management products, components and systems.

Retailing/distribution

Firms making consumer goods and services available for consumer purchase including discount stores, super centers, drug stores, clothing and accessories retailers, computer stores and book stores. Also included in this group are e-commerce companies—those selling their products or services via the Internet.

Semiconductors

Design, develop or manufacture semiconductor chips/microprocessors ore related equipment including diodes and transistors. Also includes companies that test or package integrated circuits.

Software

Producers of bundled and/or unbundled software applications for business or consumer use including software created for systems, graphics, communications and networking, security, inventory, home use, educational, or recreational. Also included is software developed for specific industries such as banking, manufacturing, transportation, or healthcare.

Telecommunications

Companies focused on the transmission of voice and data including long distance providers, local exchange carriers, and wireless communications services and components. Also included are satellite and microwave communications services and equipment.

Other

If the classification criterion in all of the other categories does not appropriately describe the product or service offered, the firm may be categorized in this group.

Appendix 4.2: Geographical definitions

The geographical classifications used in the MoneyTree Report are as follows:

Alaska/Hawaii/Puerto Rico

Alaska, Hawaii, and Puerto Rico

Colorado

The state of Colorado

DC/Metroplex

Washington, D.C., Virginia, West Virginia, and Maryland

LA/Orange County

Southern California (excluding San Diego), the Central Coast and San Joaquin Valley

Midwest

Illinois, Missouri, Indiana, Kentucky, Ohio, Michigan, and western Pennsylvania

New England

Maine, New Hampshire, Vermont, Massachusetts, Rhode Island, and parts of Connecticut (excluding Fairfield County)

New York Metro

Metropolitan NY area, northern New Jersey, and Fairfield County, Connecticut

North Central

Minnesota, Iowa, Wisconsin, North Dakota, South Dakota, and Nebraska

Northwest

Washington, Oregon, Idaho, Montana, and Wyoming

Philadelphia Metro

Eastern Pennsylvania, southern New Jersey, and Delaware

Sacramento/Northern California

Northeastern California

San Diego

San Diego area

Silicon Valley

Northern California, bay area and coastline

South Central

Kansas, Oklahoma, Arkansas, and Louisiana

Southeast

Alabama, Florida, Georgia, Mississippi, Tennessee, South Carolina, and North Carolina

Southwest

Utah, Arizona, New Mexico, and Nevada

Texas

The state of Texas

Upstate New York

Northern New York State, except Metropolitan New York City area

Appendix 4.3: Stage of development definitions

The stage of development classifications used in the MoneyTree Report are as follows:

- **Seed/start-up stage**
  The initial stage. The company has a concept or product under development, but is probably not fully operational. Usually in existence less than 18 months.
- **Early stage**
  The company has a product or service in testing or pilot production. In some cases, the product may be commercially available. May or may not be generating revenues. Usually in business less than three years.
- **Expansion stage**
  Product or service is in production and commercially available. The company demonstrates significant revenue growth, but may or may not be showing a profit. Usually in business more than three years.
- **Later stage**
  Product or service is widely available. Company is generating on-going revenue; probably positive cash flow. More likely to be, but not necessarily profitable. May include spin-offs of operating divisions of existing private companies and established private companies.

Appendix 4.4: Macroeconomic variables

Real GDP: seasonally adjusted, annualized rate, billions of chained 2005 dollars
GDP: implicit price deflator (Index 2005=100),
Gross private domestic investment, seasonally adjusted, annualized rate, billions of dollars

Personal savings, seasonally adjusted, annualized rate, billions of dollars
PPI: finished goods (Index 1982=100)
CPI for all urban consumers: all Items (Index 1982-84=100)
Effective federal funds rate
Bank prime rate
3-month Treasury bill: secondary market
6-month Treasury bill rate: secondary market
3-year Treasury rate constant maturity rate
5-year Treasury constant maturity rate
10-year Treasury constant maturity rate
Industrial production: durable consumer goods (Index 2007=100)
S&P500 Index
Change in private inventories, billions of dollars
University of Michigan: consumer sentiment (Index 1st Quarter 1966=100)

5 The political and legal determinants of venture capital investments around the world

Stefano Bonini and Senem Alkan***

5.1 Introduction

Venture Capital ("VC") is recognized as an important source of funding for countries' entrepreneurial activities (Kortum and Lerner 2000) and a major driver of economic development and innovation. Yet, there are huge differences across countries in the relative amounts raised and invested in VC.

A large body of literature has investigated the role of macroeconomic and firm level factors in explaining this surprising evidence without providing conclusive results. In this chapter we argue that the quality of the social, political and legal environment strongly influences the development of new ventures and therefore can explain the large degree of international variation.

Political risk is generally described as the likelihood of an event occurring over a given time period and is typically related to major alterations in government policies precipitated by disruptive events such as war, insurrection or political violence (Jodice 1985). Additionally, Prast and Lax (1982) define political risk from a corporate standpoint as the probability that the outcomes of a project will be affected by changes in the political environment. The changes in political environment can involve various characteristics such as the expropriation or nationalization of property or resources, the inconvertibility of currencies, actions against personnel, government intervention with contractual terms, discriminatory taxation, and politically based regulations regarding operations (Howell and Chaddick 1994).

The role of political determinants in shaping economic activity has received limited attention for at least two distinct reasons: the existence of unresolved theoretical simultaneity issues on the expected effects of political activity on growth and the lack of reliable data sources. Brunetti (1998) and Easterly (2001, 2009) among others provide a satisfactory solution to the first problem, showing how appropriate econometric treatments allow for the correct identification

* Assistant Professor, Department of Finance, Bocconi University, Milan, Italy. A version of this chapter was previously published as Stefano Bonini & Senem Alkan, *The Political and Legal Determinants of Venture Capital Investments Around the World*, 39 SMALL BUSINESS ECON. 997 (2012).

** PhD candidate, Bocconi University, Milan, Italy.

of the nexus of causality, in particular when paired with accurate variable specification. Differently, data have been available only on a limited basis, both under a cross-sectional and time-series perspective: on the one hand, acceptably long time series were available for a small number of data items. On the other hand, the large panel of variables required to allow accurate robustness testing was generally missing the necessary observations. This problem was further worsened by heterogeneity in cross-country data quality.

These issues explain to a large extent the limited number of existing studies and the relatively narrow focus they adopt. In particular, the existing literature on political risk relies on institutional economics and positive political theory to assess the outcome with regard to investors' strategies (Henisz and Williamson 1999; Henisz 2000a, 2000b). Firms tend to avoid investments with significant uncertainty and political bodies are key determinants of this uncertainty from the perspective of a foreign investor. Political risk occurs when the government's rules for doing business in the country, such as product and price regulations and relative taxation, can be quickly changed (Henisz and Williamson 1999; Henisz 2000a).

Henisz (2000a, 2000b) empirically analyzes political risk as a structural characteristic of countries that may change over time. Further empirical evidence also proves that firms tend to favor doing business in countries with low political risk (Henisz and Delios 2001). In a similar spirit Gastanaga et al., (1998) and Busse (2003) investigate the link between political stability and foreign direct investment. Finally, Brunetti and Weder (1998) demonstrate that there is a negative link between institutional uncertainty and private investment, where the latter is a well known proxy for the level of economic development and openness of a country.

The recent availability of accurate data sources, however, offers an unparalleled opportunity for deepening our level of understanding of the political effects on the strikingly uneven cross-country development of VC activity. This issue has been deemed as critical, given the well documented impact of VC on jobs creation and competitiveness and its fundamental role in smoothing economic cycles peaks and troughs (Lerner and Gurung 2008). Steven Radelet of the Center for Global Development effectively supported this view stating that: "[A reliable] data source [. . .] is of huge importance in development. Ten years ago, there was no data. Fifteen years ago, we didn't talk about this stuff."[1]

A similarly important factor in reducing investors' uncertainty is given by the characteristics and quality of the judiciary system. In a set of seminal articles, La Porta et al. (1997, 1998)[2] begin investigating the effects of legal systems on the development of financial markets and institutions. The authors cluster countries' legal origin into four main families: English, French, German or Scandinavian. LLSV argue that legal origin matters because it affects some property rights

1 NY Times, "World Bank Report on Governing Finds Level Playing Field," May 11, 2007; The Economist, "Order in the jungle," Mar. 13, 2008.

2 Henceforth LLSV.

enforcement, shareholders' protection and creditors' rights. For instance, common law systems generally experience quicker trials and shorter recovery time (Mattei 1997). The now-classical results by LLSV strongly support their hypotheses showing that the origin of the legal system captures a large fraction of the variance in the observed development.

Beck et al. (2003a, 2003b) further developed these arguments confirming the evidence but also providing a theoretical model to understand how this effect takes place. They argue that law can affect the development of the financial activity through two different channels: the political and the adaptability channel. The former mechanism posits that legal systems differ essentially for the relative priority that a political and social system assigns to individual private property rights as opposed to the state. The observed differences are then merely the outcome of different priorities which themselves shape the legal system. In this view the civil law systems show a tendency to promote and support institutions and the institutionalization of the economic activity, as opposed to common law systems which focus on the enforcement of private property rights over the state. Bodies of law are then accordingly designed resulting in the different rights observed by LLSV.

On the other hand, the adaptability channel holds that legal systems differ in the degree of flexibility to changing conditions and more rigid systems are therefore likely to hamper development. Using appropriate measures of rigidity the authors rank the LLSV four legal systems families with French origin being the most rigid system closely followed by the German, the Scandinavian with the English being the most flexible. These factors may have an effect on the previously specified measures and the level of investing in a country. In an early attempt to apply this framework to VC, Da Rin et al. (2006) have performed a set of different surveys across Europe to understand the potential impact of legal frameworks on VC structures and governance.

Cumming et al. (2008) have adopted the Legality Index introduced by Berkowitz et al. (2003) to examine the effects on different governance structures in 39 countries. Li and Resnick (2003) and Lerner and Gurung (2008) provide additional evidence of the existence of a causal link between the development of the investment activity and a stable and reliable social, political and economic environment. Surprisingly, however, no attention has been devoted yet to analyzing the impact of social and political variables on the initial development and further growth of VC investments.

Finally, Blanchflower (2000, 2001) has opened up the discussion on latent entrepreneurship as a social determinant of economic growth showing macro characteristics. Building on extensive survey and field data, they show that entrepreneurship is statistically different across countries, possibly in response to a large set of cultural variables as argued by Guiso et al. (2006). These results, however, suggest the existence of an unexplored causal link between the endogenous supply of entrepreneurs and the development of VC activity.

In this chapter, we add novel evidence of the determinants of VC activity in a cross-country setting while jointly controlling for a large set of factors separately addressed in previous literature such as gross domestic product ("GDP") growth, interest rates, initial public offering ("IPO") activity, total value of stocks traded, stock turnover, and corporate income tax rate. Our empirical results provide strong evidence that the social and political conditions in one country are prerequisites to the successful development of VC, and that this is comparatively more important for early-stage financing. Strikingly, we find mixed evidence of the effects of corruption and internal conflict/stability metrics on the dependent variables. Additionally, we support Black and Gilson (1998), Gompers and Lerner (1998) and Jeng and Wells (2000), in showing that an active IPO market and the level of interest rates are significant in determining cross-country variance in early stage VC investments.

We also show that corporate income tax rates, labor market rigidities, and GDP growth help explain the discrepancies in early-stage VC across 16 countries, while total entrepreneurial activity seem to explain the difference, at all stages, in VC intensity across these countries. These results convey important normative implications: entrepreneurship and innovation benefit significantly from an active VC industry, which also allows the ignition of virtuous cycles (Kortum and Lerner 2000). Activating this cycle, however, relies on some socioeconomic prerequisites that government and institutions should primarily address.

The remainder of this chapter is organized as follows. Section 5.2 presents the hypotheses. Section 5.3 illustrates the measures adopted for testing the hypotheses, and Section 5.4 introduces data and sampling. Section 5.5 illustrates the research methodology and empirical results. Finally, Section 5.6 summarizes and concludes the chapter.

5.2 Hypotheses

Despite the recent surge in VC investments and the large amount of research devoted to the topic, there is surprisingly limited evidence on the legal and political determinants of VC investments. Nevertheless, VC professionals include political stability among the most important determinants of growth in VC investment. For instance, Markus Ableitinger, a director of Capital Dynamics, a frontrunner of the VC industry, states that: "[. . .] Successful private equity needs macro-economic and micro-economic factors. These include political stability, sophisticated capital markets, corporate governance, strong entrepreneurial structure, and proper benchmarking [. . .]."[3]

Megginson (2004) remarks on the importance of economic, cultural and legal factors in determining VC growth. Recently, Lerner and Gurung (2008) have started to address a similar topic, looking at the global impact of private equity activity. Despite the inverse nexus of causality of their job, the underlying research agenda was similar in spirit to ours, *i.e.*, investigating the determinants of private equity activity and its fall-out on the economy.

3 EVCA (2005), "Re-awakening the bear." Country Reports, European Venture Capital Journal, http://www.ventureeconomics.com/evcj/protected/ctryreps/1107338767047.html.

Building on these issues and following previous research, we therefore define three research hypotheses investigating the role of political conditions, legal families and the entrepreneurial environment on the development of VC.

5.2.1 Political conditions

Political risk is one of the main factors affecting the level of economic development and foreign direct investment in a country (La Porta et al. 1998; Li and Resnick 2003). Capital inflows and the development of a sound financial system are quintessential prerequisites for an active VC industry that, however, are highly influenced by political conditions. In this spirit, it is reasonable to argue that the level and quality of the political conditions of a country heavily determine the development of VC activity.

This effect is apparent when dealing with high-risk countries where instability and the absence of developed financial and trading markets are detrimental to any investment activity. Yet the relationship is much less clear when restricting the analysis to more developed and stable countries. Surprisingly, there have been almost no studies addressing these issues, mainly because of the lack of a consistent set of measures of political risk and the complexity in obtaining a reliable measure of political stability (Jodice 1985).

Looking at international plant location decisions by Japanese firms, Henisz and Delios (2001) showed that firms tend to do business in countries with low political risk. Unfortunately, their approach is replicable only to a limited extent as they construct an ad hoc metric of "political hazard" that reflects a general perception of political risk by outsiders. In this chapter, we try to overcome this limitation by adopting the International Country Risk Guide ("ICRG") ratings data. which provide a consistent cross-sectional measure of political risk. We can thus test the following:

Hypothesis 1: the level of VC investment will be higher in countries with low political risk.

5.2.2 Legal systems

VC investments are characterized by a high level of risk which investors try to minimize by carefully selecting and actively monitoring ventures and by timely exiting portfolio companies. In performing these tasks an effective and efficient legal system is of utmost importance. In light of the LLSV results, academic research has started investigating the role of legal variables in shaping VC activity.

Armour and Cumming (2006, 2008) look at the effects of bankruptcy laws on the development of VC activity. Bankruptcy procedures are crucial for the development of the investment activity as an inefficient mechanism for the unwinding of insolvent ventures significantly hampers the development of financial activity. In particular, when bankruptcy laws impose overreaching consequences on entrepreneurs, it is very likely that supply of entrepreneurial venture is significantly reduced and, as a consequence the demand for venture capital declines.

Using a reduced form measure of bankruptcy law characteristics, Armour and Cumming (2006) show that this factor is significant in weakening the demand of VC and therefore the observed level of VC investments. However, bankruptcy laws are themselves a byproduct of their own legal system and as such are highly correlated with the level of efficiency of the system, which in turn provides a more or less favorable investment environment. LLSV and Beck et al. (2003a, 2003b) in particular showed that the English origin legal systems provide a generally more investor-friendly environment as opposed to the French and German ones. Accordingly, we conjecture:

Hypothesis 2: countries with English origin legal systems will have comparatively higher levels of VC investments.

5.2.3 Entrepreneurial environment

The level of entrepreneurial activity varies across countries owing to a large set of different determinants (Freytag and Thurik 2006). Furthermore, the extent of new venture origination is remarkably different owing to a degree of latent entrepreneurship that is related to levels of economic development, alongside with demographic, cultural and institutional characteristics (Blanchflower 2000; Hessels et al. 2008). These environmental conditions may reduce the supply of new ventures to VC investors, thus reducing the observed level of VC activity, as shown by Acs et al. (2009). Additionally, from a financial perspective, a venture is a risky project that should yield a positive non-linear return to compensate for the Knightian uncertainty of the project. These returns, however, are affected by several cross-sectional environmental factors, including taxes, norms and endogenous attitude towards risk-taking and risk assessment. We therefore propose that:

Hypothesis 3: An endogenously favorable entrepreneurial environment fosters higher VC investments.

5.3 Measures

To allow proper econometric testing of our hypotheses, we construct three different sets of measures capturing the characteristics of the political, legal, and entrepreneurial environment of one country. To provide robustness to our results we also identify a large set of controls, borrowed from the extant literature.

5.3.1 Political and legal factors

We adopt a set of explicit political risk metrics extracted from the Political Risk Services: International Country Risk Guide ("PRS-ICRG") ranking. While PRS-ICRG provides ranking for a much larger set of items, we restrict our analysis to four items, which allows us to investigate the demand and supply of VC investments while at the same time avoiding the multi-collinearity problem highlighted by Cumming et al. (2008). In particular, we extract the following four measures: socioeconomic conditions ("SOC"), investment profile ("INV"), internal conflict ("INT") and corruption ("CORR"). As a control metric, we also test the relationship between the level of VC activity and an aggregate measure of political conditions computed by PRS—*i.e.*, the Political Risk Index ("POL").

The first of the four metrics, socioeconomic conditions, is in fact the aggregation of three sub-rankings: unemployment, consumer confidence and poverty. Socioeconomic pressures at work can constrain government action or fuel social dissatisfaction, thus jeopardizing the profitability of VC investments. The range for this measure is 0–12, with higher values indicating a higher-quality level of the measure. We then expect a positive sign for the socioeconomic condition variable in determining VC investment intensity.

The investment profile variable is an assessment of factors affecting the risk to investment that are not covered by other political, economic and financial risk components. The investment profile measure is the sum of three sub-rankings: contract viability/expropriation, profits repatriation, and payment delays. All of these three components have a direct negative effect on the value of a company. The range for this measure is (0–12). We expect a positive sign for the investment profile variable in determining VC investment intensity.

Internal conflict is an assessment of political violence in the country and its actual and/or potential impact on governance. The internal conflict factor is constructed by totaling the ratings for three sub-components: civil war/coup threat, terrorism/political violence, and civil disorder. Also, this measure ranges from 0–12, where higher values indicate higher quality, which in this case means a lower level of conflicts. Accordingly, we expect a positive sign for internal conflict (negative relationship) in determining VC investment intensity.

The corruption measure is concerned with actual or potential corruption in the form of excessive patronage, nepotism, secret party funding, job reservations, "relationship economy", inefficient controls for the state economy, and encouragement of the development of the black market. All these factors have a direct effect on the level of risk of any investment and, *a fortiori*, on VC investments. The measure ranges from 0 to 6, with a ranking interpretation similar to that for internal conflict. We then expect a positive sign in determining VC investment intensity.

As an aggregate indicator expressing the overall level of risk represented by one country, we adopt the POL measure. This is often considered a more accurate method of "rating" of one country, given the high correlation between the POL score and standard financial ratings (Erb et al. 1996).

The score weights 12 variables, encompassing a large number of political and social items, among which are the above-specified four explicit measures. Each variable assigns risk points to a pre-set group of factors, termed political risk components. The minimum number of points that can be assigned to each component is zero, while the maximum number of points depends on the fixed weight that the component is given in the overall political risk assessment. For every

Table 5.1 PRS Political Risk Components

This table reports the constituents of the PRS-ICRG Political Risk Index and their relative score. A higher score represents a higher ranking in each specific item or in the overall index.

Component	*Points (max)*
Government Stability	12
Socioeconomic Conditions	12
Investment Profile	12
Internal Conflict	12
External Conflict	12
Corruption	6
Military in Politics	6
Religious Tensions	6
Law and Order	6
Ethnic Tensions	6
Democratic Accountability	6
Bureaucracy Quality	4
Total	100

item, the higher the overall sum of the constituents, the lower the country risk, and vice versa. The highest maximum score is 100, which corresponds to the lowest existing risk level. PRS political risk components are summarized in Table 5.1.

We predict a positive correlation between this control metric and the volume of VC investments.

5.3.2 Legal systems

As originally proposed by the seminal contribution of La Porta et al. (1998), and more recently by Cumming et al. (2008) in a VC setting, legal systems play an important role in shaping financial decisions and governance structures. In particular, contract enforcement, shareholder and creditor protection and property rights are significantly affected by the very structure of the legal system in place.

For instance, common law systems generally experience both quicker trials and shorter recovery time (Mattei 1997). These factors may have an effect on the previously specified measures and the level of investing in a country. To control for this issue, we introduce additional explanatory variables, capturing the origin of the legal system of the countries in our sample. In particular, based on La Porta et al. (1998), we introduce four dummy variables—UK origin, French origin, German origin and Scandinavian origin—identifying the characteristics of the legal systems of the 16 countries in our sample.

5.3.3 Entrepreneurial environment

We model the level of entrepreneurial activity using three instrumental variables: the corporate tax rate ("CITR), labor market rigidities ("EPL") and the level of total entrepreneurial activity ("TEA"). Gordon (1998) shows that the personal and corporate tax rates are important factors in the *ex ante* decision of starting up a new venture. Gentry and Hubbard (2000) support this evidence by showing that tax schedule convexity is negatively correlated with entrepreneurship propensity. Keuschnigg and Nielsen (2003) document that tax levels affect entrepreneurship by reducing the attractiveness of expected cash flows; this reduces cash flows to investors, thus reducing both the demand and the supply of VC. We therefore expect a negative sign for the corporate income tax variable in determining VC investment intensity.

A second factor heavily affecting entrepreneurship is labor market regulation. The rationale is that an entrepreneur has a smaller incentive to start up a company in countries with rigid labor markets than in countries with soft markets owing to the increased costs and risks associated with the move, in particular when managing downturns and financial distress. This possible *ex post* managerial rigidity is then *ex ante* factored into the decision of starting up a new venture, thus reducing the overall number of start-ups.

In this chapter, we take a novel approach to this issue by measuring labor market rigidities based on the employment protection legislation index taken from OECD. This metric is based on the aggregation of 18 basic items capturing the strength of the legal framework governing the hiring and laying off of employees. It is a measure for labor market rigidities that ranks countries from 0 to 6, with 0 being the least regulated. Yet, this is a measure available at very large time intervals[4]; accordingly, we construct an interaction variable by scaling the EPL index by the GDP growth. We expect a negative relationship between the level of labor market rigidities and VC investment intensity.

Finally, following Blanchflower (2000, 2001) we argue that the level of entrepreneurship in a country is somehow endogenous and positively affects the level of VC investment. This measure can be independent of previous variables and relates to cultural and legal issues as documented by Guiso et al. (2006). As an addition to previous literature on VC, we adopt the measure of total entrepreneurial activity index computed by Global Entrepreneurship Monitor as a proxy for the entrepreneurial propensity of one country. This index encompasses the proportion of adults involved in the creation of emerging firms and the proportion involved in the work of new firms. The value for this variable ranges from 1 to 20, with 1 indicating the lowest level of entrepreneurial activity. As with the labor market variable, TEA is also a point measure, and therefore, we developed an interaction bypass variable scaling TEA by the level of business expenditures in research and development ("R&D") ("BERD"). We expect a positive relationship between this variable and the amount of VC capital in one country.

4 The closest previous observation is a not further specified "late 1990" (OECD).

To allow for easier reference to all variables, we have summarized measures, data sources and predicted signs in Table 5.2.

5.3.4 Controls

To capture the quality and stability of an economy, we model seven different variables: GDP growth ("GDP"), inflation ("INF"), interest rates ("IR"), initial public offerings ("IPO"), amount of stocks traded ("ST"), stock turnover ("STURN") and technological opportunities ("BERD").

Gompers and Lerner (1998) and more recently Füss and Schweizer (2008) suggest that GDP growth can explain the development of VC activity in one country because it generates investment opportunities, which can attract risky capital. Accordingly, we expect the impact of GDP growth on VC investments level to be positive.

However, a common problem in high GDP-growth countries is inflation and its effect on the interest rate levels. Economies with high inflation are more likely to be associated with a weak demand for VCs, since the value of investments is by construction negatively correlated with inflation. Thus, we expect a negative sign for the inflation variable in determining VC investment intensity. Following Gompers and Lerner (1998), we also introduce the level of the interest rate: theoretically, the interest rate level should negatively affect the supply of VC, since a high level of real interest rates reduces the attractiveness of risky investment such as VC. However, both Gompers and Lerner (1998) and Füss and Schweizer (2008) find a positive sign. The explanation is that interest rates also affect bank financing costs. When bank financing becomes exceedingly costly, VC may be a better and more flexible alternative to raising funds for a new venture.

Black and Gilson (1998) and Jeng and Wells (2000) provide evidence that the level of IPO activity may affect the relative level of development of VC investments. An active IPO market is essential to providing an exit from investments. On the other hand, Gompers and Lerner (1998) do not offer statistical support for a differential level of VC investments in the US conditional on the level of IPO activity. Yet, these results are only apparently contradictory; when the IPO market is sufficiently developed, the information conveyed by changes in the absolute level of IPO activity decreases significantly, implying a decreasing informative value of this variable. Gompers and Lerner (1998) look at the US, which represents both the most active primary market and the most active VC market in the world. In such a market, an increase or decrease in the relative level of IPO issues does not significantly affect the efficiency of the exit market as a whole. A temporarily low level of issues ("closed IPO window") may have an effect in postponing exits rather than reducing the initiation of new investments.

However, when the VC industry is young and growing an active IPO market is more likely to attract more investments. Accordingly, in our tests we expect a positive sign for this variable. In a similar vein, the value of stocks traded in a country makes the stock market more attractive to investors, as the size of the market is associated with higher liquidity and better efficiency, as shown by

Table 5.2 Variables Description

This table summarizes tickers for the variables adopted in this chapter, the variable description, the source of data and the variables' predicted sign. Detailed information on the construction of the political index is reported in Table 5.1.

INDEPENDENT VARIABLE			
VC	Dollar value of the sum of venture capital investments (log)	Venture eXpert Database	
Early VC	Dollar value of the sum of early stage VC investments (log)	Venture eXpert Database	
EXPLANATORY VARIABLES			
GENERAL ECONOMY			
Variable	*Description*	*Source*	*Predicted Sign*
GDP	Annual GDP growth in percentage terms	World Bank, World Development Indicators ("WDI").	+
INF	Inflation (consumer prices annual percentage change)	WDI.	–
IR	Real interest rates (one year running yield on corporate bonds)	WDI.	–
IPO	Number of newly listed companies (IPO) in all domestic markets)	International Federation of Stock Exchanges	+
ST	Total value of stocks traded as a percentage of GDP	WDI.	+
STURN	Stock turnover rate as market value of traded shares over total average market capitalization	WDI.	+
BERD	Technological opportunities measured by business expenditures on R&D	OECD. Main Science and Technology Indicators.	+

(Continued)

Table 5.2 (Continued)

ENTREPRENEURIAL ENVIRONMENT			
CITR	Corporate Income Tax Rate: annual data in percentage terms	Michigan University, Ross School of Business, Office of Tax Policy Research	–
EPL	Employment protection legislation (EPL) is a synthetic index ranging from 0 to 6, with 0 being the least regulated and 6 the most regulated country.	OECD	–
TEA	Total entrepreneurial activity is an index computed by adding the proportion of adults involved in the creation of emerging firms and the proportion involved in new firms.	The Global Entrepreneurship Monitor	+
POLITICAL RISK			
SOC	Socio-economic conditions	PRS-ICRG	+
INV	Investment Profile	PRS-ICRG	+
INT	Internal Conflict	PRS-ICRG	+
CORR	Corruption	PRS-ICRG	+
POL	Political Risk	PRS-ICRG	+

Schertler (2003). Furthermore, a liquid stock market can provide an attractive venue for investors wishing to liquidate their positions. This should offer a favorable environment to VC investors.[5] To allow for a proper measure of stock market size in control regressions, we also introduce the stock turnover rate as a measure of stock market activity as an alternative to ST.

VC's spectacular growth in the late 1990s can be attributed to increases in technological opportunities. Gompers and Lerner (1998) and Kortum and Lerner (2000) first investigated this factor, modeling it by state-level R&D expenditures in academic and industrial activity. This is a meaningful variable for the US but may not be as informative on a cross-country basis since R&D activity outside of the US is much less based in academia and more spread-out across companies. An alternative to this measure could be the number of triadic patent families, *i.e.*, patents that are registered, in the three major economic areas: US, Europe and Japan. This measure should capture the overall output of research conducted at all levels.

At the same time, these two measures are strongly correlated, and given that patent registration occurs with a delay from the investments that generated the patents, it could be time-inconsistent with the other measures. For this reason, we choose to measure technological opportunities using BERD which is also consistent with the arguments put forth in Acs et al. (2009). We expect a positive sign for BERD in determining VC investment intensity.

5.4 Data

The data set contains annual data from 16 countries for the time period from 1995 to 2002. The selection of the time frame has been motivated by two concurrent issues. The 1995 start-date is motivated by two factors: first, data on global VC activity before 1995 are not homogeneous and largely unreliable, as documented by Boquist and Dawson (2004); second, most countries in our sample did not have VC regulation or close-end fund regulation before 1995. Although VC data seem to be available before that date, they are consistently small and not meaningful. In contrast, the 2002 cut-off is motivated by the fact that this is the last year for which the EPL measures are available.

A further requirement was the continuous availability of data over the whole research period. Finally, we required that VC investments in each country are non-zero for all years to allow meaningful inferences. According to these rules, we selected the following 16 countries: Australia, Canada, Denmark, Finland, France, Germany, Ireland, Italy, Japan, New Zealand, Norway, Poland, Spain, Sweden, the United Kingdom and the United States. This selection provides an adequate

5 This is not in contrast with what implied by the level of IPO: in fact, a stock market can be large owing to a slow-growing number of listed companies with a low level of IPO activity. In fact, a common possible bias in financial market studies is represented by the fact that markets with relatively large stocks but low turnover should be more liquid and efficient than markets with a smaller median value for stocks traded but with a higher turnover.

geographical dispersion of observation over different areas in terms of development, legal systems, and VC development.

Following the National Venture Capital Association ("NVCA") definition of VC, we adopt as a measure of VC activity the sum of the early stages and expansion investments expressed in 2002 USD. Since the countries differ considerably in size, in econometric analyses we adopt a logarithmic transformation, which also allows to capture non-linear components in the data. Variables defining the state of the general economy are collected as follows: we use annual GDP percentage growth, inflation as measured by consumer prices' annual percentage change, total value of stocks traded as a percentage of GDP, stock turnover rate as the total market value of traded shares over total average market capitalization, and real interest rates data obtained from the World Bank WDI.

Although we expect that different types of interest rates impact VC investment intensity differently, in our analysis, we opt for a measure of real interest rates because long-term and short-term nominal interest rates (taken from the International Federation of Stock Exchanges) are available only for 11 countries for the period 1996–2002, while real interest rates data are available for all of the countries included in the sample across the full period of analysis. As a measure of IPO, we use annual figures for the number of newly listed companies, obtained from the International Federation of Stock Exchanges. Our proxy for technological opportunities is BERD, with numbers obtained from OECD, Main Science and Technology Indicators.

Entrepreneurial environment data are collected as follows: as a measure of corporate taxation, we use annual corporate income tax rate data, obtained from the Office of Tax Policy Research. Total entrepreneurial activity data is available as an index computed by adding the proportion of adults involved in the creation of emerging firms and the proportion involved in new firms. This data is gathered from the Global Entrepreneurship Monitor for the year 2003. Since it is only available for one year, it varies only across countries. Consistent labor market rigidities data are available only on a limited basis, in particular for extended series. Following contributions by Nicoletti et al. (1999) and Cahuc and Koeniger (2007), we adopt OECD's employment protection legislation data. Like the TEA measure, EPL variable is time-invariant.

The independent variables capturing political risk are obtained from the PRS-ICRG. This source allows a cross-country homogeneous metric for assessing political risk and is available for 135 countries over more than 20 years. Finally, information on the origin of the legal system is obtained from La Porta's data set.[6]

6 *See* Rafael La Porta's website, *available at* http://mba.tuck.dartmouth.edu/pages/faculty/rafael.laporta/publications/LaPorta%20PDF%20Papers-ALL/Law%20and%20Finance-All/Law_Ön.xls.

5.5 Research methodology and results

Our panel data set is composed of 16 countries, and 15 explanatory variables. Data are collected annually for eight years from 1995 to 2002. Thus, our cross-sectional balanced panel data set is given by 16*8=128 observations, with no missing years or countries.[7]

In Table 5.3, we control for correlations among the variables to assess possible multi-collinearity problems.

Coefficients are generally small and insignificant, with some notable exceptions within measure classes. In particular, market variables—IPO, stock turnover, stock traded—are positively correlated with the level of BERD, which is intuitive and aligned with Gompers and Lerner (1998). The overall POL is obviously correlated with the individual measures, but since this measure is used as an alternative to explicit political determinants, this does not imply any effect on the models' specifications. Finally, GDP is positively correlated with inflation and BERD, consistent with evidence in Kortum and Lerner (2000), and negatively with the interest rate level.

Overall, the correlation structure of the explanatory variables does not indicate a significant risk of multi-collinearity in our analyses, which validates the idea of selecting variables according to the evidence presented by Cumming et al. (2008). Yet, since we are investigating a causal problem, we further control for multi-collinearity risks by performing Variance in Factors ("VIF") analyses in a parallel set of standard Ordinary Least Squares ("OLS"). We record the highest VIF value as 1.84, which allows us to rule out this risk in our econometric approach.

We then tested the three research hypotheses through a multivariate panel data regression approach, adopting as our independent variable the overall amount of VC investment and the subset of early stage investments, which may have different determinants.

For both dependent variables, we also adopt non-linear logarithmic transformations to capture the evidence that VC investment growth follows a non-linear process. The panel data regression is based on the following model:

$$Y_{it} = \beta_0 + \beta X_{it} + v_{it} + \varepsilon_{it} \qquad (1)$$

with i denoting the cross-section dimension (countries) and t denoting the time series dimension (years). We denote X_{it} as the vector of K explanatory variables. Since we may have significant country related effects, we opt for estimating the cross-sectional fixed-effects model. The choice of a fixed-effect model, as opposed to a random effects model, has been validated through a standard Hausman test, which rejected the null hypothesis that the cross-section effects are not correlated

7 In unreported tests, we have performed a robustness analysis running fixed-effects regressions on a sub-sample of 15 countries, which excludes the US, at the same time the largest VC market and also the country with the highest degree of stability for all explanatory variables. However, excluding these observations does not distort our results.

Table 5.3 Variables Correlation Matrix

This table reports the correlation matrix of the selected explanatory variables. GDP figures are annual percentage GDP change; INF, IR, CITR figures are in percentage points; IPO is the average number of IPO per year; ST is the market capitalization of stocks listed in each country's stock exchanges in billion/USD normalized on year 2002; STURN is the ratio between the dollar value of stocks traded in one year and the yearly average market cap; BERD are expressed in mil/USD normalized on year 2002; EPL is a point estimate ranging from 0 to 6 scaled by scaled by GDP; TEA is a point estimate indicating the fraction of population involved in entrepreneurial activity scaled by BERD; SOC, INV, and INT are indices ranging from 1 to 12 with 1 indicating the lowest quality of each variable and 12; CORR is an index ranging from 0 to 6 where 6 indicates the highest quality and 0 the lowest. POL is an index capturing the overall risk ranging from 1 to 100 with 1 indicating the highest risk of one country.

	GDP	*INF*	*IR*	*IPO*	*ST*	*STURN*	*BERD*	*CITR*	*EPL*GDP*	*TEA* BERD*	*SOC*	*INV*	*INT*	*CORR*	*POL*
GDP	1														
INF	0.2928*	1													
IR	–0.2541*	–0.0131	1												
IPO	–0.0907	–0.0926	0.1293	1											
ST	–0.0930	–0.1608	–0.2445*	0.3159*	1										
STURN	–0.1500	–0.0392	–0.1786*	0.2734*	0.6557*	1									
BERD	–0.4115*	–0.2888*	–0.0789	0.5781*	0.5119*	0.4024*	1								
CITR	0.0499	0.1883*	0.1231	0.0950	–0.0098	0.1392	0.1578	1							
EPL* GDP	–0.336*	–0.0595	–0.0094	–0.1958*	–0.1119	0.3318*	0.1126	–0.0597	1						

TEA *BERD	−0.0513	−0.0459	0.0610	0.5556*	0.6547*	0.4113*	0.5922*	0.1417	−0.3518*	1					
SOC	0.0064	−0.1801*	−0.3434*	0.0363	0.4459*	0.0750	0.1210	−0.2793*	−0.3413*	0.1943*	1				
INV	−0.0608	−0.0416	−0.1275	−0.0090	0.4359*	0.3073*	0.0783	−0.2178*	−0.0 671	0.1291	0.5237*	1			
INT	0.0076	−0.0196	0.1687	−0.0165	−0.4156*	−0.4443*	−0.1537	−0.1023	−0.2611*	−0.0742	−0.0352	−0.4193*	1		
CORR	0.0217	−0.0448	0.1176	−0.0175	0.0026	−0.0735	−0.2115*	0.0270	−0.2004	−0.1249	0.0527	−0.2251*	0.2666*	1	
POL	0.1055	−0.1658	−0.0886	−0.0161	0.1893*	−0.1309	−0.1406	−0.3356	−0.4184	−0.0127	0.6974*	0.4280*	0.3651*	0.4518*	1

with the explanatory variables. The standard fixed effect model assumes that all members of the panel have the same variance (homoscedastic error terms) and that there is no correlation over time, either across or within the members of the panel.

In Table 5.4, we present the results for a set of models tested on two different dependent variables, total VC investments ("Panel A") and early stage investments ("Panel B"), to control for stage-specific effects.

Models 1 and 2 directly test hypotheses 1 and 3 on the effects of the entrepreneurial environment and political risk on VC investments. Models 3 and 4 introduce and separately test controls for robustness. Models 5 and 6 jointly test the explanatory variables and further test the hypotheses.

Model 1 returns surprising results. First, consistently with our first hypothesis, socioeconomic conditions and investment environment are strongly and positively related to growth in VC activity. The evidence weakens when looking at early stage investments, where the investment environment variable becomes insignificant but is still positive. Aggregate VC investments are insignificantly related with the internal conflict variable, but there is a weak negative relationship with corruption. These results become strong and significant for early VC investments, which appear to flourish and with increasing level of instability and corruption.

Model 2 provide support for the third hypothesis. Consistent with Gentry and Hubbard (2000) and Keuschnigg and Nielsen (2003), the corporate tax rate has a significant negative impact on the development of VC activity at all stages; similarly investment activity is reduced through increasing rigidity in labor market regulations. As expected, higher levels of entrepreneurial activity attract venture investors, generating growth in both early- and later-stage VC commitments.

Models 3 and 4 adopt two different measures of stock market activity that we have shown to be slightly different in interpretation but highly correlated. Stock turnover provides less convincing results when testing both Total VC investments and early stage investments only. For this reason, we exclude it from joint analysis in models 5–6. The results offer support for hypothesis 1: GDP growth shows an opposite sign but is insignificant. However, all other variables are significant, and signs are concordant with our predictions. In particular, the level of R&D is an important, positive factor in explaining the development of VC activity for both early stage and overall investments; similarly, inflation negatively and significantly affects investment activity.

Models 5 and 6 hierarchically test the explanatory variables to extract joint effects and provide a robustness check of previous results. In these specifications, we drop the entrepreneurial activity and labor protection variables, as they are point measures that we had to scale by continuous factors (namely, GDP and BERD), which are accounted for as independent variables. Including them in the models would therefore generate collinearity problems.

The first result worth noting is that the aggregate political variable seems to be too coarse a measure to convey appropriate information. The coefficient is positive as expected but insignificant in both the overall and reduced models. In contrast,

Table 5.4 Fixed effects regression

This table present results for the cross-section fixed (within) effects regressions for the 6 models hierarchically tested on Total VC investments and Early VC investments. Explanatory variables are defined as follows: GDP figures are annual percentage GDP change; inflation ("INF"), interest rate ("IR"), Corporate Tax rate ("CITR") figures are in percentage points; IPO is the average number of IPO per year; Stock Traded ("ST") is the market capitalization of stocks listed in each country's stock exchanges in billion/USD normalized on year 2002; Stock turnover ("STURN") is the ratio between the dollar value of stocks traded in one year and the yearly average market cap; Business expenditures in R&D ("BERD") are the natural logarithm of constant 2002 mil/USD expenditures; Employment Protection ("EPL") is a point estimate ranging from 0 to 6 scaled by scaled by GDP; TEA is a point estimate indicating the fraction of population involved in entrepreneurial activity scaled by BERD; socioeconomic conditions ("SOC"), investment environment ("INV"), and internal conflicts ("INT") are indices ranging from 1 to 12 with 1 indicating the lowest quality of each variable and 12; Corruption ("CORR") is an index ranging from 0 to 6 where 6 indicates the highest quality and 0 the lowest. Political index is an index capturing the overall risk ranging from 1 to 100 with 1 indicating the highest risk of one country. t-statistics for coefficients are in parentheses. Significance at the 1%; 5% and 10% level is denoted by ***,**,* respectively.

	PANEL A					
	Total VC investments					
	1	*2*	*3*	*4*	*5*	*6*
Intercept	2.305	16.13	–28.15**	–35.50***	–28.83***	–10.43*
	(1.21)	(0.73)	(–5.63)	(–7.70)	(–5.70)	(–1.79)
GDP			–0.0289	–0.0519	–0.0255	0.0311
			(–0.34)	(–0.18)	(–0.30)	(0.38)
INF			–0.133**	–0.163***	–0.137**	–0.0794
			(–2.41)	(–2.86)	(–2.46)	(–1.37)
IR			–0.108*	–0.149**	–0.110**	–0.0560
			(–1.96)	(–2.55)	(–2.01)	(–1.11)
IPO			0.000915	0.000490	0.000838	0.00142
			(0.91)	(0.48)	(0.83)	(1.56)

(Continued)

Table 5.4 (Continued)

	PANEL A					
	Total VC investments					
	1	*2*	*3*	*4*	*5*	*6*
ST			0.00993***		0.00914**	0.00450
			(2.74)		(2.46)	(1.30)
STURN				−0.00213		
				(−0.49)		
BERD			3.893***	4.870***	3.639***	1.688**
			(6.63)	(9.07)	(5.63)	(2.29)
CITR		−0.107***				
		(−2.77)				
EPL*GDP		−1.079				
		(−1.27)				
TEA*BERD		0.335***				
		(5.32)				
SOC	0.448***					0.349***
	(4.88)					(3.24)
INV	0.269***					0.131
	(3.90)					(1.49)
INT	−0.183					−0.160
	(−1.48)					(−1.27)
CORR	−0.264*					−0.266
	(−1.68)					(−1.62)
POL					0.0346	
					(0.95)	
Country F.E.	YES	YES	YES	YES	YES	YES
R^2	0.605	0.279	0.550	0.520	0.554	0.650
F	41.31	14.07	21.63	19.11	18.65	18.98
N	128	128	128	128	128	128

	PANEL B					
	Total VC investments					
	1	*2*	*3*	*4*	*5*	*6*
Intercept	3.659**	44.68**	–22.13***	–30.76***	–22.99***	–0.590
	(2.12)	(2.24)	(–4.38)	(–6.75)	(–4.51)	(–0.11)
GDP			0.0732	0.0903	0.0774	0.103
			(0.86)	(1.06)	(0.92)	(1.42)
INF			–0.0738	–0.112**	–0.0781	–0.0239
			(–1.32)	(–2.00)	(–1.40)	(–0.46)
IR			–0.00907	–0.0770	–0.0127	0.0513
			(–0.16)	(–1.33)	(–0.23)	(1.14)
IPO			0.00197*	0.00145	0.00187*	0.00267***
			(1.94)	(1.43)	(1.84)	(3.30)
ST			0.00937**		0.00837**	0.00183
			(2.56)		(2.23)	(0.59)
STURN				–0.00877**		
				(–2.04)		
BERD			2.744***	3.944***	2.421***	0.364
			(4.62)	(7.43)	(3.72)	(0.56)
CITR		–0.0919***				
		(–2.66)				
EPL*GDP		–2.071***				
		(–2.72)				

(Continued)

Table 5.4 (Continued)

	PANEL B					
	Total VC investments					
	1	*2*	*3*	*4*	*5*	*6*
TEA*BERD		0.220***				
		(3.90)				
SOC	0.504***					0.523***
	(6.07)					(5.46)
INV	0.0459					0.0360
	(0.74)					(0.46)
INT	–0.425***					–0.384***
	(–3.81)					(–3.41)
CORR	–0.239*					–0.307**
	(–1.69)					(–2.10)
POL					0.0439	
					(1.19)	
Country F.E.	YES	YES	YES	YES	YES	YES
R^2	0563	0.218	0.380	0.366	0.388	0.627
F	34.77	10.12	10.83	10.22	9.519	17.15
N	128	128	128	128	128	128

the results from Model 6 offer further support to the role of social and political determinants in spurring VC investments and adding additional insights; the political components retain their explanatory power when compared to the results from Model 1 and mitigate to some extent the role of investments in R&D in particular for early-stage VC.

This result can be interpreted in the spirit of the evidence in Dimov and Murray (2008) and Elango et al. (1995) on the development pattern of the VC industry. In these contributions, the authors conclusively show that once the VC industry grows in scale, the amount of capital devoted to early-stage investment decreases, as investors have to trade off the superior returns of seed investments with the higher costs of managing a large number of ventures when their assets under management grow. In such a case, it is more rational to devote capital to larger and more consolidated investments in more capital-intensive industries.

Our results support this interpretation: when an industry is absent, initial investments are devoted to filling gaps in the supply side of the economy. The decision to enter an investment market therefore is motivated more by the stability of the country, which allows medium- to long-term planning of returns on investment. Once an investment industry is established, the focus shifts to higher value-added investments of larger size, which require greater innovation content, which is typically associated with R&D expenditures. This investment shift is further supported by the findings in Kortum and Lerner (2000), which show that a well established VC industry can activate a virtuous cycle of growth in innovation.

It is worrisome that in these models we find increased evidence of the negative impact of internal conflict and corruption on VC investments. While estimates are not significant for total VC investments, they are negative and strongly significant for early VC. This result is in part coherent with the conflicting theoretical arguments and puzzling empirical evidence on the effects of corruption and instability on growth, as first highlighted by Mauro (1995) and surveyed by Abed and Gupta (2002). Yet we cannot safely infer that a weaker system (as measured by these variables) provides an incentive for investments. The interpretation for these results may be three-fold.

First, there may be an issue of simultaneity, *i.e.*, the corruption and internal conflict measures may not be causal priors to VC investment data. Yet, adopting common techniques such as using lagged variables and two-stage least-squared regressions, does not provide any meaningful improvement and excludes endogeneity problems. Second, there may be an issue of data aggregation: corruption and internal conflicts may be endogenously different conditional on the characteristics of the legal system. We test this effect in the following paragraph. Third, these two variables are known to be potentially inconsistent conditional on the measurement methodology.

To test for this effect, we need a substitute instrumental variable. Two measures are available. The first one is the corruption perception index ("CPI") compiled by Transparency International. This is a weighted index of several metrics produced by ten independent sources.[8] However, this measure has been heavily criticized for its lack of consistency (Galtung 2006). A better metric is provided by the Worldwide Governance Indicators ("WGI-Kaufmann") compiled for the World Bank by Kaufmann et al. (2008) This project measures six dimensions of governance, among which control of corruption and absence of violence/terrorism provide suitable alternatives to the PRS-ICRG corruption and internal conflict measures. We perform this control in Section 5.5.2.

5.5.1 The effect of legal origin

Following the intuitions in the law and finance literature we modeled hypothesis 2 arguing that the level of VC investments is affected by the legal system in place. To test this intuition, we estimate a standard multivariate OLS model controlling for the type of legal system in place. To avoid perfect multi-collinearity, we assume countries whose legal systems show a UK origin as the baseline group.[9] We therefore estimate the following regression:

$$Y_i = \beta_0 + \beta_{it} X_{it} + \gamma_k LEG_k + \varepsilon_{it} \tag{2}$$

where LEG_k is a vector of dummy variables indicating whether the country's legal system is of French, German or Scandinavian origin.

The results presented in Table 5.5 add interesting evidence showing that legal origin plays a role in determining the level of VC activity, both disconnected from and connected to the stage at play.

First we notice that VC activity in UK-based legal systems is significantly larger at all levels. Second, French-related legal systems seem to offer a more favorable environment for new entrepreneurs, as the level of VC activity, controlling for all other factors, is marginally and insignificantly smaller than that of the baseline UK-origin group.

Yet, countries where the legal system is of French origin are significantly less effective in supporting the development of these firms (–1.144 as a parameter sign, significant at the 1 percent level). Third, German-related—and more strongly Scandinavian-related—systems provide a consistent environment for established companies that are then more easily targeted by later-stage VC investors. On the other hand, early-stage financing and new ventures are comparatively lower than in both UK-related systems and French-related systems.

Socioeconomic conditions and investment environment parameters are robustly significant and aligned in sign with previous results, thus validating hypothesis 1 and confirming that a prerequisite of the inception and growth of an

8 CPI constituents are provided by: Columbia University, Economist Intelligence Unit, Freedom House, Information International, International Institute for Management Development, Merchant International Group, Political and Economic Risk Consultancy, United Nations Economic Commission for Africa, World Economic Forum and World Markets Research Centre.

9 To further control for multi-collinearity issues we rerun VIF tests, obtaining a value of 2.29.

Table 5.5 Legal origin

This table presents results for OLS regression controlling for legal systems' origin. The dependent variables are VC (all stages) investments and Early VC (only early-stage) investments. The independent variables are defined as follows: GDP figures are annual percentage GDP change; inflation ("INF"), interest rate ("IR"), Corporate Tax rate ("CITR") figures are in percentage points; IPO is the average number of IPO per year; Stock Traded ("ST") is the market capitalization of stocks listed in each country's stock exchanges in billion/USD normalized on year 2002; Stock turnover ("STURN") is the ratio between the dollar value of stocks traded in one year and the yearly average market cap; Business expenditures in R&D ("BERD") are the natural logarithm of constant 2002 mil/USD expenditures; Employment Protection ("EPL") is a point estimate ranging from 0 to 6 scaled by scaled by GDP; TEA is a point estimate indicating the fraction of population involved in entrepreneurial activity scaled by BERD; socioeconomic conditions ("SOC"), investment environment ("INV"), and internal conflicts ("INT") are indices ranging from 1 to 12 with 1 indicating the lowest quality of each variable and 12; Corruption ("CORR") is an index ranging from 0 to 6 where 6 indicates the highest quality and 0 the lowest. Political index is and index capturing the overall risk ranging from 1 to 100 with 1 indicating the highest risk of one country. The dummy variables indicate the origin of the legal system assuming UK origin as the baseline case. t-statistics for coefficients are in parentheses. Significance at the 1%; 5% and 10% level is denoted by ***,**,* respectively.

	Total VC investments	*Early Stage VC investments*
Intercept	–3.920*	–1.880
	(1.82)	(0.93)
GDP	0.0647	0.154***
	(1.03)	(2.89)
INF	0.102***	0.0988***
	(2.87)	(3.28)
IR	0.0877**	0.171***
	(2.25)	(5.09)
IPO	0.00134	0.00307***
	(1.59)	(4.30)
ST	0.00672**	0.00138
	(2.35)	(0.55)
BERD	0.787***	0.640***
	(6.94)	(6.62)
SOC	0.219**	0.447***
	(2.37)	(5.00)
INV	0.302***	0.106
	(4.22)	(1.64)
INT	–0.170	–0.456***
	(–1.49)	(–4.14)
CORR	–0.260**	–0.456***
	(–2.06)	(–4.13)
French Origin	–1.144***	–0.311
	(–2.68)	(–1.13)
German Origin	–1.291***	–1.685***
	(–3.07)	(–3.62)
Scandinavian Origin	–0.816**	–1.744***
	(–2.53)	(–3.87)

(Continued)

Table 5.5 (Continued)

	Total VC investments	*Early Stage VC investments*
R^2	0.808	0.817
F	36.89	89.24
N	128	128

active VC investment industry is a stable social environment where investors and entrepreneurs can deploy long-term commitments. Unfortunately, controlling for the origin of the legal system extends and strengthens the surprising effects of corruption and, to a lesser extent internal conflict measures on the level of investments. Signs are negative and, in particular, a lower level of corruption appears to be negatively related to investments, as in previous analyses. This counterintuitive result is further addressed in Section 5.5.2.

5.5.2 Alternative measures

An alternative explanation for the surprising negative impact of lower levels of corruption and stability on the development of VC activity may be measurement inconsistency. Corruption and stability are highly qualitative variables that are difficult to measure for two distinct reasons: first, they can be only indirectly measured, which makes for higher noise in the data, particularly when based on questionnaire surveys, which are highly questions-dependent; and second, several methodologies proxy corruption with the "perception" of corruption, thus introducing a potential variable mis-specification.

To overcome these issues, a commonly accepted procedure (UNDP 2008) is the aggregation of several sources to develop a single and consistent metric. In this capacity, a weakness of the PRS-ICRG guide is that, although extremely rigorous in its compilation, it is a single source. In contrast, WGI-Kaufmann measures address exactly this issue: they aggregate several sources in an econometrically consistent way, generating a measure that is comparable across countries and over time. Additionally, WGI-Kaufmann estimates are provided with a companion measurement error that allows for better treatment of the data.

The WGI-Kaufmann methodology develops measures for each of the six governance indicators, which are essentially values of a normal function distributed as $N \sim (0; 1)$. Three properties are associated with this methodology: first is ordinality, which implies that each measure is increasing in quality from $-\infty$ to $+\infty$; the second implies that as values are drawn from such a normal distribution, observations fall between a tractable range (–2.5; +2.5) with 99 percent confidence; and the third property is that as estimate means from a density function, they come with companion standard deviations that can be used to assess the quality of each estimate. As such, these measures offer a suitable alternative to the PRS-ICRG estimates. Unfortunately, data have been compiled biannually from 1996 to 2000 and annually henceforth. To deal with this problem, we fill each missing year by interpolating the two closest estimates. Although this is a rough adjustment, as we have limited data variation, we believe that it should allow for an acceptable cross-check of the PRS-ICRG metrics.

We then run fixed-effect and OLS regressions, substituting the original corruption and internal conflict measures with the WGI-Kaufmann measures. Results are reported in Table 5.6.

Results for standard macro and social variables are aligned with previous analyses. The substitution of the conflict and corruption variables has not altered the explanatory structure. The new measures are largely insignificant, but when they are significant, the sign is positive as expected. In particular, the conflict measure is positive and significant in model 1 for both early stage and aggregate VC investments, and the corruption variable is positive and significant, albeit only at the 10% level, for aggregate investments in Model 2. Following the Kaufmann methodological approach, we have also run control regressions by scaling the estimates by the standard errors, but the results were not affected.

These results support our original hypothesis and hint at a possible problem in the methodology followed by PRS to collect data for these measures. The WGI-Kaufmann methodology seems robustly to deliver the expected outcome of more reliable comparability across countries and time. Nevertheless, our outcome relies on a raw adjustment of available data and should be reconsidered in the future when more observation points will be available.

5.6 Summary and conclusions

The worldwide level of investments in VC has grown spectacularly in the last two decades, but the observed rates of growth have been extremely different across countries. Given its well documented positive impact on economic development and entrepreneurship, understanding the determinants of the VC industry has been a primary goal of both academics and regulators. Surprisingly, however, the sociopolitical and legal determinants of VC intensity around the world have received little or no attention. A possible explanation for this lack of empirical research is the absence, up until a few years ago, of reliable data on social and political variables. In this chapter, we try to fill this gap by investigating the determinants of VC activity around the world through a comprehensive set of political, legal, and macroeconomic factors.

Using panel data from 16 countries from 1995 to 2002, we confirm previous studies in showing that active IPO markets, interest rates, corporate income tax rates and, most importantly, R&D spending, are meaningful factors in explaining the cross-country variation in levels of investment. In addition to the existing evidence, we also show that VC investments are strongly facilitated by a more favorable entrepreneurial environment. For the first time, we introduce a homogeneous set of social and political variables, developed by PRS, investigating the impact of sociopolitical risk factors on the development and growth of VC activity.

Table 5.6 Robustness regressions with WGI-Kaufmann measures

This table present results for two sets of control regressions run by substituting the PRS-ICRG measures for Corruption and Internal Conflict with the World Bank Kaufmann-WGI indicators. Explanatory variables are defined as follows: GDP figures are annual percentage GDP change; inflation ("INF"), interest rate ("IR"), Corporate Tax rate ("CITR") figures are in percentage points; IPO is the average number of IPO per year; Stock Traded ("ST") is the market capitalization of stocks listed in each country's stock exchanges in billion/USD normalized on year 2002; Stock turnover ("STURN") is the ratio between the dollar value of stocks traded in one year and the yearly average market cap; Business expenditures in R&D ("BERD") are the natural logarithm of constant 2002 mil/USD expenditures; Socioeconomic conditions ("SOC") and investment environment ("INV") are indices ranging from 1 to 12 with 1 indicating the lowest quality of each variable and 12 the highest; Corruption Control ("CorruptionK") and Absence of Conflicts ("ConflictK") are aggregate measures ranging between ± infinite, with higher, positive values indicating better quality and vice versa. t-statistics for coefficients are in parentheses. Significance at the 1%; 5% and 10% level is denoted by ***,**,* respectively.

	Total VC investments				*Early stage VC investments*			
	1	*2*	*3*	*4*	*1*	*2*	*3*	*4*
Intercept	1.931	–5.407**	–15.47**	–6.572***	–0.125	–6.101***	–6.686	–8.915***
	(0.65)	(–2.61)	(–2.55)	(–3.91)	(–0.05)	(–3.08)	(–1.17)	(–5.83)
GDP			0.0371	0.0943			0.144*	0.211***
			(0.47)	(1.46)			(1.95)	(3.60)
INF			–0.121**	0.0577			–0.0825	0.0342
			(–2.18)	(1.34)			(–1.57)	(0.87)
IR			–0.0748	0.0742*			0.0333	0.147***
			(–1.46)	(1.88)			(0.69)	(4.09)
IPO			0.000910	0.00149*			0.00229**	0.00324***
			(0.87)	(1.67)			(2.32)	(4.00)
ST			0.00334	0.00663**			0.00180	0.00299
			(0.86)	(2.20)			(0.49)	(1.09)
BERD			1.593**	0.761***			0.167	0.594***
			(2.14)	(6.46)			(0.24)	(5.55)

SOC		0.476***	0.406***	0.280***		0.502***	0.585***	0.492***
		(5.00)	(3.49)	(2.71)		(5.53)	(5.34)	(5.24)
INV		0.326***	0.174**	0.346***		0.146**	0.126	0.197***
		(5.14)	(2.04)	(5.05)		(2.41)	(1.57)	(3.16)
ConflictK	3.062**	0.619	0.426	–0.685	3.189***	1.225	0.0513	–0.895
	(2.49)	(0.74)	(0.44)	(–1.01)	(3.06)	(1.54)	(0.06)	(–1.45)
CorruptionK	–0.144	1.762*	1.061	–0.182	–0.647	0.982	0.514	–0.226
	(0.10)	(1.75)	(0.98)	(–0.47)	(–0.51)	(1.02)	(0.50)	(–0.64)
French Origin				–0.887*				–0.523
				(–1.96)				(–1.27)
German Origin				–1.127**				–1.128***
				(–2.50)				(–2.75)
Scandinavian Origin				–0.954***				–0.0433
				(–2.89)				(–0.14)
Country F.E.	YES	YES	YES	NO	YES	YES	YES	NO
R^2	0.0538	0.599	0.640	0.801	0.082	0.508	0.568	0.783
F	3.130	40.40	18.12	35.39	4.921	27.83	13.43	31.66
N	128	128	128	128	128	128	128	128

Our results show strong and positive effects of favorable socioeconomic and investment environment on the inception and development of VC investment activity. Surprisingly, we find mixed evidence of the effects of corruption and internal conflict/stability metrics on the independent variables. However, these puzzling results are likely driven by noise in data collection. To overcome this issue, we have adopted WGI-Kaufmann as instrumental control variables in an additional set of robustness and control tests, finding a better fit for our hypotheses. We also test for the effects of the rigidity of the legal system that prevails in each country finding strong evidence that this factor plays an important role in explaining cross-sectional variance.

Although this is a first step in the development of what will likely be a growing interest in investigations incorporating social, political and environmental variables in explanatory models of economic and financial phenomena, our results convey interesting normative implications for the development and growth of entrepreneurship and innovation. These activities benefit significantly from an effective VC industry, which also allows the ignition of virtuous cycles. Activating this cycle, however, relies on some socioeconomic prerequisites that government and institutions should primarily address in their development agendas.

References

Abed, G. T. and Gupta, S. (2002), *Governance, Corruption, and Economic Performance*, George T. Abed and Sanjeev Gupta Eds., International Monetary Fund.

Acs, Z., Audretsch, D., Braunerhhjem, P. and Carlsson, B. (2009), "The Knowledge Spillover Theory of Entrepreneurship," *Small Business Economic*, 32, 15–30.

Armour, J., and Cumming, D.J. (2006), "The Legislative Road to Silicon Valley," *Oxford Economic Papers* 58, 596–635.

Armour, J. and Cumming, D.J. (2008), "Bankruptcy Law and Entrepreneurship," *American Law and Economics Review* 10(2), 303–50.

Beck, T., Demirguc-Kunt, A. and Levine, R. (2003a), "Law and finance: why does legal origin matter?" *Journal of Comparative Economics*, 4, 653–75.

Beck, T., Demirguc-Kunt, A. and Levine, R. (2003b), "Law, endowments, and finance," *Journal of Financial Economics*, 2, 137–81.

Berkowitz, D., Pistor, K. and Richard, J.F. (2003), "Economic Development, Legality and the Transplant Effect," *European Economic Review*, 47(1), 165–95.

Black, B.S. and Gilson, R.J. (1998), "Venture capital and the structure of capital markets: banks versus stock markets," *Journal of Financial Economics*, 47, 243–77.

Blanchflower, D.G. (2000), "Self-employment in OECD countries." *Labour Economics* 7(5), 471–505.

Blanchflower, D.G., Oswald A. and Stutzer, A. (2001), "Latent entrepreneurship across nations," *European Economic Review*, 45(4–6), 680–91.

Boquist, A. and Dawson, J. (2004), "US Venture Capital in Europe in the 1980s and the 1990s," *Journal of Private Equity*, 8(1), 39–54.

Brunetti, A. (1998), "Political variables in cross-country growth analysis," *Journal of Economic Surveys*, 11(2), 163–90.

Brunetti, A. and Weder, B. (1998), "Investment and Institutional Uncertainty: A Comparative Study of Different Uncertainty Measures," *Weltwirtschaftliches Archiv*, 134(3), 513–33.

Busse, M. (2003), "Democracy and FDI." HWWA Discussion Paper No. 220.

Cahuc, P. and Koeniger, W. (2007), "Employment Protection Legislation," *The Economic Journal*, 117(521), F185–F188, June 2007.

Cumming, D., Schmidt, D. and Waltz, U. (2008), "Legality and Venture Capital Governance around the world," *Journal of Business Venturing*, 7(1), 54–72.

Da Rin, M., Hege U., Liobet G. and Walz U. (2006), "The Law And Finance of Venture Capital Financing in Europe," *European Business Organization Law Review*, 7, 525–47.

Dimov, D. and Murray, G. (2008), "Determinants of the Incidence and Scale of Seed Capital Investments by Venture Capital Firms," *Small Business Economics*, 30(127), 127–52.

Easterly, W. (2001), "The Lost Decades: Explaining Developing Countries' Stagnation in Spite of Policy Reform 1980–1998," *Journal of Economic Growth*, 6(2), June 2001, 135–57.

Easterly, W. (2009), "Can the West save Africa?" *Journal of Economic Literature*, June, 47(2), 373–447.

Elango, B., Fried, V.H., Hisrich, R.D. and Polonchek, A. (1995), "How Venture Capital Firms Differ," *Journal of Business Venturing*, 10, 157–79.

Erb, C., Harvey, C., and Viskanta, T. (1996), "Expected Returns and Volatility in 135 Countries", Journal of Portfolio Management, Vol. 22, Issue 3, pp. 46–58, Spring 1996.

Freytag, A. and Thurik, R. (2006), "Entrepreneurship and its determinants in a cross-country setting," *Journal of Evolutionary Economics*, 17, 117–31.

Fuss, R. and Schweizer, D. (2008), "Dynamic Interactions between Venture Capital Returns and the Macroeconomy: Theoretical and Empirical Evidence from the United States," unpublished Working Paper, European Business School (EBS) and WHU.

Galtung, F. (2006), "Measuring the Immeasurable: Boundaries and Functions of (Macro) Corruption Indices," in: *Measuring Corruption*, Charles Sampford, Arthur Shacklock, Carmel Connors, and Fredrik Galtung, Eds. (Ashgate): 101–30.

Gastanaga, V.M., Nugent, J. B. and Pashamova, B. (1998), "Host Country Reforms and FDI Inflows: How Much Difference Do They Make?" *World Development*, 26(7), 1299–314.

Gentry, W.M. and Hubbard, R.G. (2000), "Tax Policy and Entrepreneurial Entry," The American Economic Review, 90(2), Papers and Proceedings of the One Hundred Twelfth Annual Meeting of the American Economic Association, 283–87.

Gompers, P. and Lerner, J. (1998), "What Drives Venture Fundraising?" Brookings Papers on Economic Activity," Microeconomics, 149–92.

Gordon, R. (1998), "Can High Personal Tax Rates Encourage Entrepreneurial Activity?," *IMF Staff Papers*, 45, 49–80.

Guiso, L., Sapienza, P. and Zingales, L. (2006), "Does Culture Affect Economic Outcomes?" *Journal of Economic Perspectives*, 20(2), 23–48.

Henisz, W. J. (2000a), "The institutional environment for economic growth," *Economics and Politics*, 12, 1–31.

Henisz, W.J. (2000b), "The institutional environment for multinational investment," *Journal of Law, Economics and Organization*, 16, 334–64.

Henisz, W.J. and Delios, A. (2001), "Uncertainty, imitation, and plant location: Japanese multinational corporations, 1990–1996," *Administrative Science Quarterly*, 46, 443–75.

Henisz, W.J. and Williamson, O. (1999), "Comparative economic organization—within and between countries," *Business and Politics*, 1, 261–77.

Hessels, J., van Gelderen, M. and Thurik, R. (2008), "Entrepreneurial aspirations, motivations, and their drivers," *Small Business Economics*, 31, 3.

Howell, L.D. and Chaddick, B. (1994), "Models of Political Risk for Foreign Investment and Trade," *Columbia Journal of World Business*, Fall, 70–91.

Jeng, L.A. and Wells, Ph.C. (2000), "The determinants of venture capital funding: evidence across countries," *Journal of Corporate Finance*, 6(3), 241–89.

Jodice, D. (1985), *Political Risk Assessment: An Annotated Biography*, Westport: Greenwood Press.

Kaufmann, D., Kraay, A. and Mastruzzi, M. (2008). "Governance Matters VIII: Aggregate and Individual Governance Indicators, 1996–2008," World Bank Policy Research Working Paper No. 4978.

Keuschnigg, C. and Nielsen, S. (2003), "Tax Policy, Venture Capital and entrepreneurship," *Journal of Public Economics*, 87, 1, 175–203.

Kortum, S. and Lerner, J. (2000), "Assessing the Contribution of Venture Capital to Innovation," *RAND Journal of Economics*, 31(4), 674–92.

La Porta, R., López-de-Silanes, F., Shleifer, A. and Vishny, R. (1997), "Legal Determinants of External Finance," *Journal of Finance*, July, 1131–1150.

La Porta, R., López-de-Silanes, F., Shleifer, A. and Vishny, R. (1998), "Law and Finance," *Journal of Political Economy*, December, 1113–1155.

Lerner, J. and Gurung, A. (eds) (2008), "The Global Economic Impact of Private Equity Report 2008," World Economic Forum, Geneva.

Li, Q. and Resnick, A. (2003), "Reversal of Fortunes: Democratic Institutions and Foreign Direct Investment Inflows to Developing Countries," *International Organization*, 57(1), 175–211.

Mattei, U. (1997), *Comparative Law and Economics*, Michigan University Press.

Mauro, P. (1995), "Corruption and Growth," *The Quarterly Journal of Economics*, 110(3), 681–712.

Megginson, W.L. (2004), "Towards a Global Model of Venture Capital?" *Journal of Applied Corporate Finance*, 89–107.

Nicoletti, G., Scarpetta, S. and Boylaud, O. (1999), "Summary Indicators of Product Market Regulation with an Extension to Employment Protection Legislation OECD," ECO Working Paper No. 226.

OECD (2004), "Employment Protection Regulation and Labour Market Performance", OECD Employment Outlook 2, pp. 61–125, Organization for Economic Co-operation and Development, 2004.

Prast, W.G. and Lax, H.L. (1982), "Political risk as a variable in the TNC decision-making," *Natural Resources Forum*, 6, 183–91.

Schertler, A. (2003), "Driving Forces of Venture Capital Investments in Europe: a Dynamic Panel Data Analysis," European Integration, Financial Systems and Corporate Performance (EIFC), working paper n°03-27, United Nations University.

UNDP (2008), "A user's guide to measuring corruption," United Nations Development Programme, Oslo, Norway, First Edition, *available at* http://www.undp.org/content/dam/aplaws/publication/en/publications/democratic-governance/dg-publications-for-website/a-users-guide-to-measuring-corruption/users_guide_measuring_corruption.pdf.

6 The impact of venture capital on innovation behavior and firm growth

*Michael Peneder**

6.1 Introduction

Ample anecdotal evidence illustrates the importance of venture capital (VC) in enabling firms to carry out ambitious business plans and to sustain and grow during particularly critical phases of their development. Based on this track record, venture capital has earned permanent mention in international scoreboards and strategy papers on innovation and enterprise policies. Owing to its complex mode of operation, however, there is also a danger of creating uncontested myths, where exaggerated expectations and consequent disappointments stand opposed to a more realistic understanding of the actual effects of venture capital on firm performance.

The aim of this study is to test the presumed impact of venture capital financing on the innovation behavior and growth of firms based on a unique micro-data set of Austrian companies. Two questions are of special significance here. First, are there systematic differences in performance between firms that use venture capital financing and firms that do not? Second, if they exist, are these differences due to the fact that venture capital involves diligent screening for firms with a given high performance potential, or does venture capital have an additional direct impact on firm performance owing to the particular mode of financing through informed and active investors? In other words, are any differences in performance caused by selection effects or genuine causal impacts?

This chapter contributes to advancing our knowledge about the economic impacts of venture capital financing on several levels. From a theoretical perspective, the analysis demonstrates that a proper application and interpretation of the econometric matching method must take account of the specific context of entrepreneurial finance. This is important, because in previous studies the methodology has often been transposed too literally from applications in labor economics, which typically focus only on the separation of direct causal effects from so-called "selection errors." In this chapter, therefore, I take particular care

* Austrian Institute of Economic Research. A version of this chapter was previously published as Michael Peneder, *The Impact of Venture Capital on Innovation Behaviour and Firm Growth*, 12 VENTURE CAPITAL 83 (2010).

to distinguish the different transmission channels of how venture capital can have an impact on firm behavior and performance. On the one hand, this brings back into the picture the particular financing function of venture capital, which tends to be ignored in the purely econometric studies. On the other hand, I argue that selection effects may be "errors" in econometric terms, but in the context of financial markets also have an important economic meaning. They reflect how successfully the markets channel scarce resources into their most profitable uses.[1]

From a methodological perspective, I propose a novel research design which extends the conventional propensity score matching procedure by a two-stage approach. The first matching originates in a large micro-database of about 250,000 Austrian firms, controlling for differences in the legal status, size, age, geographical location, sector, and financial rating of the companies. While most studies stop at this point and make their inferences, in this study the first matching is used to select the control group for an additional enterprise survey of 166 firms with and 663 firms without venture capital financing.

In the second step, firms are asked to provide additional information about their motives for either using venture financing or choosing alternative sources of finance, and collect additional firm characteristics, such as their export orientation and innovation behavior. These provide additional control variables that allow for a more comprehensive identification of selection effects. The final matching is then based on data from the enterprise survey. The two-stage approach thus offers a powerful tool to lift restrictions on the available control variables and allows for a more accurate separation of selection and direct causal effects.[2]

Finally, from an empirical perspective, the chapter adds new evidence to the available literature on the economic impacts of venture capital financing. It is the first study of this kind for Austria. More generally, it presents the case of a small country with an as yet little developed venture capital market. While large countries with mature and well developed markets offer better data and larger firm samples, countries with young and less developed venture capital markets tend to be under-reported in the literature. However, there are many such countries, and for many entrepreneurs and VC investors the Austrian experience may better reflect their situation than studies from the better known and more developed markets.

To summarize, the empirical findings for Austria confirm that most recipients had little access to satisfactory alternative financing sources. Furthermore, the data reveal that firms with venture capital financing grew significantly faster than other firms. After controlling for positive selection effects, the analysis identifies an additional causal impact, which amounts to a faster annual growth of at least 70 percent as a robust lower boundary across a wide range of alternative

1 Note that this is quite the opposite interpretation of a selection effect in most applications by labor economists, who study, for instance, the impact of public training programs to get unemployed people back into work. In their specific context, positive selection effects usually imply that a public program does not reach those who are most in need of it.

2 The second matching also has the advantage of eliminating any bias from different response rates by VC-financed and non-VC financed companies.

specifications of the model. Firms with venture capital financing also performed significantly better in terms of their innovation output. However, the second stage of the matching process reveals these differences as pure selection effects, demonstrating that venture capital made firms grow faster but did not make them more innovative.

Overall, the results demonstrate the improved discriminatory power of the two-stage matching procedure. However, the study also shows that, even for this extended procedure, it is impossible fully to control for all selection effects, and thus precisely quantify their importance. As a consequence, we restrict our interpretation to what can be considered robust lower boundaries of the impacts across a range of alternative model specifications.

The chapter is organized as follows. Section 6.2 provides a brief review of the literature. Section 6.3 illustrates the specific financing function of venture capital. Section 6.4 explains the data and the particular research strategy. Section 6.5 reports the empirical findings from the enterprise survey on the financing function. Section 6.6 presents the econometric impact analysis, identifying the scope of pure selection effects versus additional causal impacts of venture capital financing. Section 6.7 briefly summarizes and concludes.

6.2 Literature review

There is a small but swiftly growing body of literature analyzing the economic impact of venture capital (for a recent review, see *e.g.*, Wright, Gilligan, and Amess 2009). These studies range from macroeconomic panel estimations (*e.g.* Romain and van Pottelsberghe 2004), to estimations mainly based on sectoral data (*e.g.*, Kortum and Lerner 2000; Tykvová 2000; Hirukawa and Ueda 2008a, 2008b) as well as microeconometric analyses and paired sample tests (*e.g.* Hellmann and Puri 2000, 2002; Belden, Keeley, and Knapp 2001; Bottazzi and Da Rin 2002; Engel 2003; Engel and Keilbach 2007; Sorensen 2007; Lerner, Sorensen, and Stromberg 2008; Bloom, Sadun, and van Reenen 2009). This chapter is part of the latter strand, which contrasts the development of individual firms backed by venture capital with a hypothetical "counterfactual" observation based on the careful selection of a comparable control group.

The expectation of a positive impact of venture capital on firm performance originates in the idea that venture capitalists are active investors who provide not only finance, but additional services of value to entrepreneurs who "are often technologically competent but commercially inexperienced" (Keuschnigg 2004: 285). Generally, venture capitalists specialize in the skills of screening, contracting, and advising (Kaplan and Strömberg 2001). Depending on the particular market context and firm characteristics, the latter can vary considerably in type and intensity. For example, venture capitalists often consult their portfolio firms with respect to their financial management, or help to establish contacts with key customers, suppliers, and additional investors (Hochberg, Lu, and Ljungqvist 2007). They may push entrepreneurs to expand more aggressively into the market (Hellman and Puri 2000), support the professionalization of the organization

(Hellman and Puri 2002; Bottazzi, Da Rin, and Hellmann 2008), or facilitate strategic alliances among firms in their own portfolio (Lindsey 2008). Reviewing numerous empirical studies, Large and Muegge (2008) categorize these and other value-adding inputs into the eight salient types of legitimation, outreach, strategic planning, consulting, recruiting, mandating, mentoring, and operating.

Owing to the better availability of data, most micro-econometric studies focus on companies listed on the stock markets. For example, Megginson and Weiss (1991) report a positive impact of venture capital on the initial public offering (IPO) process in the USA. More recently, Bottazzi and Da Rin (2002) have found that European venture capital financed firms are able to come up with significantly more capital in the IPO process, but have not detected any statistically significant impact of venture capital financing on firm growth. Similarly, Wang, Wang, and Lu (2003) confirm that venture capital backed-companies in Singapore enjoy lower underpricing and higher quality underwriters in the IPO process, while reporting inferior returns on assets after the IPO.

In contrast, impact studies that include companies not (yet) listed on the stock market are still rare. One of the earliest examples is Manigart and Van Hyfte (1999), who study venture capital-financed firms in Belgium and find a significant impact relative to the control group in terms of greater growth of assets and cash flow, but not growth of sales revenue and employment. Extending the analysis to firm duration, Manigart, Baeyens, and Van Hyfte (2002) find no significant difference in the survival rates of VC-backed companies. Another example is Engel (2003), who reports significant positive growth effects using a broad sample of German firms provided by the country's leading credit rating agency. Using a propensity score matching, he finds that VC-financed firms achieve more than double the annual employment growth of firms in the control group.

In another application of statistical matching procedures, Engel and Keilbach (2007) use firm data to examine the influence of venture capital financing on innovation behavior, specifically on the number of patent registrations at the German patent office. The study above all confirms a positive selection effect. Innovative firms have a higher chance of getting venture capital investment and VC-financed firms subsequently grow faster than their "twin firms" in the control group. However, innovation performance after the receipt of venture capital financing is no longer significantly different from that of other firms when one controls for the level of patent registrations at the time of firm founding. The authors therefore conclude that venture capitalists tend to finance innovative firms, and then foster the commercialization and marketing of new products, thereby accelerating firm growth.

Among the studies available, Hellmann and Puri (2000, 2002) stand out by adding focus on particular channels of transmission of VC impacts. Using micro-data from the Stanford Project on Emerging Companies in the Silicon Valley area, they demonstrate, for instance, that venture capitalists help companies to bring their products earlier to the market, or to professionalize the internal organization by recruiting experienced managers, or even replacing CEOs. Overall, they find that venture capital provides significant value in addition to mere financial resources. Since the added value comes at a considerable cost, firms are likely to self-select, with innovative companies in need of lead time and first mover advantages being more inclined to accept this source of financing.

Because of the heterogeneous data sources, consequent choice of methods and control variables, and varying contexts of different national venture capital markets, one must be cautious about drawing general conclusions. However, the careful examination of these studies reveals at least three different transmission mechanisms by which venture capital may exert an influence on overall economic performance:

- To begin with, the specific financing function applies when venture capital markets generate new business cases that have not had access to (adequate) financing through traditional sources of capital.
- Second, the specific selection function involves the allocation of financial resources to the most profitable uses when uncertainty and problems of asymmetric information are particularly high.
- Finally, venture capital firms often claim to fulfill a genuine value adding function, since they contribute not only capital but also managerial experience, access to informal networks and professional business models.[3]

6.3 The specific financing function

With respect to the financing function, a first step towards a comprehensive assessment is to acknowledge that venture capital comes at a considerable cost. In addition to excess returns expected by the investors,[4] venture capital demands wealth-constrained entrepreneurs to relinquish control rights to outside investors. Potential causes for conflicting interest, opportunistic behavior, and agency problems (see *e.g.* Bergemann and Hege 1998; Trester 1998; Tirole 2006; Winton and Yerramilli 2008; Bergemann, Hege, and Peng 2009) are abundant and costly to contain. Therefore, as a rule, entrepreneurs who can meet their capital needs using other sources will generally do so (Berger and Udell 1998; Bozkaya and van Pottelsberghe 2008). We consequently expect venture capital to go to companies at the margins, *i.e.*, to firms whose particular opportunity-risk profile does not allow them to access alternative forms of finance. However, in order to perform a conclusive econometric test, one would need to obtain the full life histories of the target and control groups and estimate their hazard or duration functions. For the time being, such data are not available.

3 See, for instance, Cumming, Fleming, and Suchard (2005), Jeng and Wells (2000), or Riyanto and Schwienbacher (2006).

4 See *e.g.*, Jovanovic and Szentes (2007), who explain the "sizeable excess return" to venture capital with the high VC-discount rates. The reason is that VC investors can more easily move their funds from non-performing firms to new companies, which raises their opportunity cost of forgone earnings above that for ventures financed by their founders.

Figures 6.1A to 6.1C summarize the theoretical argument for the specific financing function of venture capital. The diagrams are plotted on two independent axes: the expected profits E(π) and the degree of uncertainty Var(π). The figures describe the expected profits and accompanying uncertainty of the project's success in the form of its variance. By means of bisecting all angles, the independent dimension Var(π) is drawn along a 45° degree diagonal line (and not, as is more commonly done, orthogonally at a 90° angle). Consequently, E(p) is folded at E(π) = 0, so that the vertical axis depicts financing projects with a positive value of expected profits (*i.e.*, when E(π) > 0), and the horizontal axis analogously depicts projects with expected losses (*i.e.*, when E(π) < 0). It is important to note that both axes nevertheless represent the same single dimension E(π); they are only mirrored along the 45° diagonal originating at E(π) = 0. Each project is uniquely located in either the upper triangle (if it is expected to be profitable), the lower triangle (if not profitable), or on the diagonal (if it just breaks even). The area below and on the diagonal line shows all projects that are not in a position to receive financing because they have an expected profit value equal to or less than zero.

In the ideal case of perfect markets without information problems, the number of financially feasible projects for risk-neutral capital investors is exclusively determined through the expected profits and therefore independent of the extent of uncertainty Var(π). In imperfect markets with asymmetric information, additional costs m are generated through the need for more elaborate selection and monitoring processes in order to mitigate problems of adverse selection and moral hazard (Carpenter and Petersen 2002; Tirole 2006). In Figure 6.1B the boundary of financially feasible projects with a given Var(π) therefore moves upward and away from the diagonal by the distance m. In this situation a *financing gap* arises, as certain projects are no longer considered financially feasible because of increased monitoring, advising, and control costs. We also assume that m grows progressively with uncertainty, so that $\delta^2 m/\delta^2$ Var(π) > 0 and $\delta^2 m/\delta^2$ Var(π) > 0 for all Var(π).

Given such a situation, venture capital management funds take advantage of their role as specialized finance intermediaries (Gompers and Lerner 1999, 2001; Kanniainen and Keuschnigg 2004; Keuschnigg and Nielsen 2004). As a result of their diligent project screening and monitoring, as well as their accompanying advisory services, they shift the boundary of financially feasible projects outward, thereby creating a new segment in the corporate finance market (Figure 6.1C).

This argument rests on the assumption that, owing to specialization advantages, the marginal costs of overcoming problems of asymmetric information are lower for projects financed by venture capital (m_{VC}) than for those using traditional financing instruments (m_{tr}). Under the plausible additional assumption that specialization incurs significant fixed costs (*e.g.*, through the founding of a new organization or the development of know-how) which must be covered by the VC companies, we find that only wealth-constrained entrepreneurs without sufficient access to traditional financing will accept the higher price they have to pay for venture capital.

The upshot is that the additional cost for screening, monitoring, and advising m_{VC} is the price to be paid for overcoming information problems and thus securing

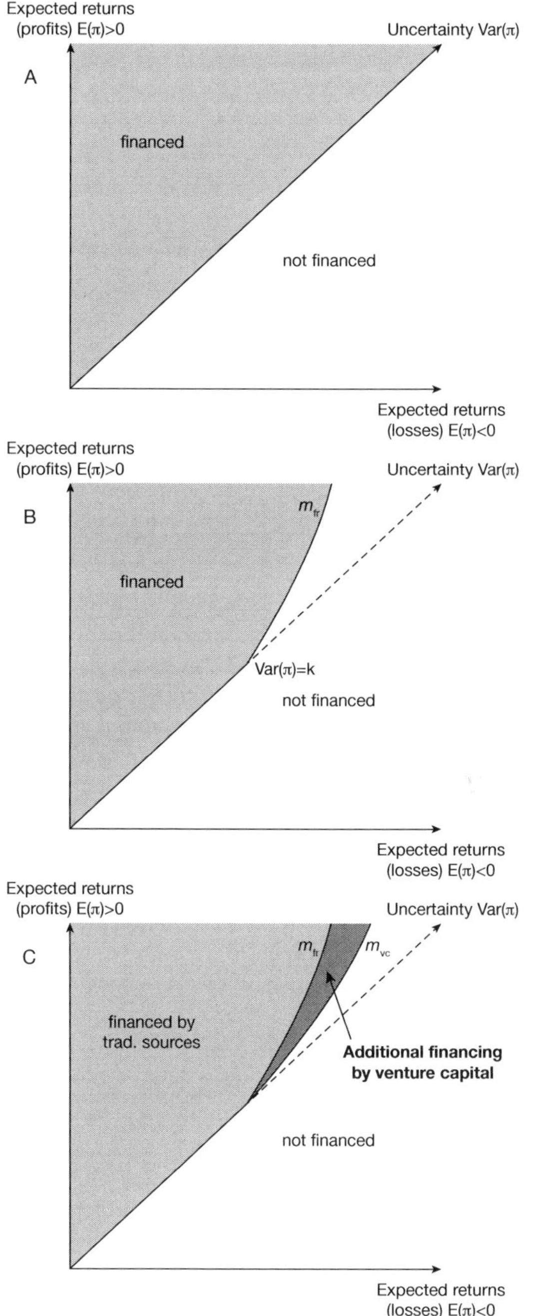

Figure 6.1 The specific financing function of venture capital.

Note: A. Perfect capital markets without asymmetric information. B. Imperfect capital markets with asymmetric information. C. Imperfect capital markets with asymmetric information and venture capital.

financing for projects with a high degree of uncertainty and informational asymmetries. If these assumptions hold true and venture capital investments do generally develop new financing opportunities, then the supply of venture capital will increase the number of feasible projects and thereby reduce the financing gap resulting from market failures.

From the perspective of individual entrepreneurs, the ability to receive financing in the first place is an important impact and desirable for the economy at large, as long as it results in the establishment of viable businesses with at least average profitability. This impact does not depend on whether and why VC-backed firms perform differently from others, which is why we treat it separately from the other functions. While I present some tentative empirical evidence for the financing function in Section 6.4, the separation of the selection and direct causal effects lies at the heart of the following econometric assessment.

6.4 Data, research plan, and general firm characteristics

The data for the empirical analysis are drawn from three different sources. First, the test group consisted of a collection of 166 VC-financed companies in Austria. This test group was initially compiled by the Austrian Private Equity & Venture Capital Organization (AVCO) and subsequently aligned with a list of additional firms from independent enquiries available to the author. Statistical tests rejected any significant difference in performance between the VC firms collected from AVCO and those independently compiled. This confirmed that there was no bias as a result of pre-selection and that the two samples of VC-financed firms could be merged.[5] Second, a comparison group was selected based on a wide range of control variables using the firm database of the leading Austrian credit rating agency, the Kreditschutzverband von 1870 (KSV). Finally, a comprehensive enterprise survey of both the VC-financed firms and the control group was conducted in order to gather additional information on firm performance, their motives for the choice of financing instruments, and missing structural variables that may have had an impact on the selection process.

The causal impact that constitutes the difference in performance of the same firm *with* or *without* venture capital financing under otherwise identical initial conditions cannot be directly identified. It can only be estimated as a hypothetical amount by relying on assumptions derived from theory and by using statistical and econometric methods. Using the notation of Heckman, LaLonde, and Smith (1999), the evaluation problem in this study can be represented as follows (see also Blundell and Costa Dias 2002). All firms i find themselves in one of two alternative states: $D = 1$ in the case of venture capital financing or $D = 0$ if venture capital

5 The latter accounted for more than one-third of the total sample and displayed a somewhat higher growth rate of employment and sales revenues. The differences, however, were not statistically significant.

financing is absent. The outcome variable Y^i corresponds to the performance indicators used (*e.g.*, the average annual growth of the firm) and is a function of structural variables X^i (such as company size and sector) as well as idiosyncratic deviations U^i as to which we assume that they are independent and identically distributed. For each firm, we are interested in the two possible alternative results Y_0 without and Y_1 with venture capital financing:

$$Y_0 = \mu_0(X) + U_0 = E(Y_0/X) + U_0 \tag{1}$$

and

$$Y_1 = \mu_1(X) + U_1 = E(Y_1/X) + U_1 \tag{2}$$

If the observable structural variants X comprise all systematic influences on the realization of a venture capital investment project D, then the *assumption of conditional independence* holds, which states that after controlling for the influence of X on Y, the value of the targeted performance variable and the receipt of VC financing are independent of one another: $(Y_0 \perp D)X$ (Rubin 1977). The *impact* of VC financing is then measured as the difference of the two alternative states:

$$Impact = \Delta = Y_1 - Y_0 \tag{3}$$

Under the assumption $U_1 - U_0 = 0$, for the standard regression model with a constant average impact α of VC financing on the outcome variable Y, it holds that:

$$Y_i = \beta X_i + \alpha D_i + U_i \tag{4}$$

If the assumption of conditional independence is not fulfilled, then, because of the correlation of D with U, the observed difference in performance $Y_1 - Y_0$ is biased by an additional selection effect s:

$$\alpha = \delta Y/\delta D - s \tag{5}$$

The following steps aimed to identify a comprehensive vector of observable structural variables X, with whose help the impact of VC financing would be limited as narrowly as possible to the direct causal impact $\delta Y/\delta D$.

Even before the matching was carried out, the large number of over 250,000 firms in the KSV database made it possible to limit the control group to firms having an identical legal structure and being active in identical sectors (*i.e.*, keeping only firms in those Nomenclature generale des Activites economiques dans Les Communautes Européenes (NACE) three-digit industries, in which at least one firm of the test group operates). The remaining 54,772 observations are used for a probit estimation, which explains the probability of the alternative states $D_i = 1$

(firms with VC financing) or $D_i = 0$ (firms without VC financing), based on the vector of observable structural variables X_i with the functional form of the standard normal distribution Φ:

$$E[D/X_i] = \Pr(D_i = 1/X_i) = \Phi(\beta'^{X_i}) \text{ for all i} = 1, \ldots \text{N}$$

For the probit estimation the following observable structural variables were considered: (i) *sector* (measured at the level of the NACE three-digit classification); (ii) *region* (applying the Nomenclature des unités territoriales statistiques (NUTS) two-digit nomenclature); (iii) *legal form* of the organization (all being limited liability companies, including only very few stock corporations); (iv) *age* (measured as the number of years in operation since foundation); and (v) *size* (measured in average sales revenue, employment, and capitalization, *i.e.*, stockholders' equity). Finally, information on (vi) the firm's *credit rating* by the KSV was added. Since we aim to identify pure value added effects, the credit rating variable refers to the situation after the VC financing decision. This allows us to control for "trivial" financing effects, in the sense that firms grow faster simply because they receive more financing to grow, while others remain constrained. Finally, to control for nonlinear influences, with the exception of dummy variables, all variables were also employed in quadratic form for the estimation. The outcome of the procedure is a control group of firms for which the estimated probability to have received VC financing is the highest.

Table 6.1 summarizes the parameters b from the probit model. For 33,729 firms, 132 of them VC-backed, the structural variables were available. These were considered as observations. The first column presented in Table 6.1 shows the results for this large sample of firms. We find that age has a significant negative impact on a firm's probability to be venture financed, even though at a diminishing rate (as revealed by the negative coefficient for the quadratic term). As this sample includes a large number of very small firms, firm size as measured by employment and capitalization has a positive influence on the probability of venture financing. With respect to employment, the quadratic term is also significant and positive.

Table 6.1 Probit estimation (venture capital financing = dependent variable)

Structural variables	*I.*	*II.*	*III.*	*IV.*
Legal dummies	yes	yes	yes	yes
Regional dummies	yes	yes	yes	yes
Industry dummies	yes	yes	yes	yes
Age	–0.00680**	–0.0083**		–0.01665
Age[b]	0.00003***	–0.00005**		0.00009
Sales revenue	0.00000	–0.00000		0.00000
Sales revenue[b]	0.00000	–0.00000		0.00000
Employment	0.00464***	–0.00185		–0.00005
Employment[b]	0.00005***	–0.00002*		–0.00001
Capitalization	0.00003*	0.00003		0.00000
Capitalization[b]	0.00000	0.00000		0.00000

Credit rating	0.95715***	–0.68450**		–1.25726
Credit rating[b]	–0.10276***	–0.08067**		0.23383
Equity ratio		–0.00090		
Equity ratio[b]		–0.00004		
Cash flow ratio		–0.00481*		
Cash flow ratio[b]		–0.00008*		
Debt repayment duration		–0.00134		
Debt repayment duration[b]		–0.00002		
ROI		–0.01001*		
ROI[b]		–0.00003**		
Export orientation				
Local			c.g.	c.g.
National			0.39243	0.46270
European Union			0.49119	0.41855
Global (outside EU)			0.86982**	0.61176
Innovation:				
Products, new to market			0.27286	0.41117
Products, new to firm			–0.54817	–0.19432
Process innovation			0.24149	0.61224
Other			c.g.	c.g.
Appropriation of IPRs				
Formal (*e.g.* patents)			0.65951***	0.07772***
Secrecy			–0.03581	–0.07115
Lead time			–0.18618	–0.04159
Other			c.g.	c.g.
Number of observations	33,729[a]	4061[a]	228[b]	209[b]
R^2	0.269	0.320	0.264	0.309

Notes:

[a] Data from KSV firm database, ca.1996–2004.

[b] Data from enterprise survey, 2002–05.

The variables are defined as follows: *Legal*: legal form of the organization; *Region*: NUTS two-digit classification; *Industry*: NACE three-digit classification; *Age*: number of years in operation since firm foundation; *Capitalization*: stockholders' equity; *Credit rating*: degree of creditworthiness (interval scaled) assessed by the Kreditschutzverband von 1870 (KSV); *Equity ratio*: share of own capital contribution to total assets; *Cash flow ratio*: share of cash flow in sales revenues; *Debt repayment ratio*: time needed to repay debt by own cash flow; *Return on investment* (ROI): return on capital employed; *Export orientation*: Question from the enterprise survey: What is the major sales territory of your company? Reply categories: (i) local; (ii) national; (iii) European Union; (iv) outside the European Union; *Product innovation*: Question from the enterprise survey: Has your company introduced any new products or services since 2002? Reply categories: Yes/No; *Intellectual property rights* (IPRs): Question from the enterprise survey: Has your company made use of patents or other formal measures to protect IPRs since 2002? Reply categories: Yes/No.

Finally, higher credit ratings increase the probability of a firm drawn from this large sample to be venture financed. Again, the significant quadratic term reveals that this positive influence diminishes for higher levels of creditworthiness. A large share of the overall variation is of course explained by the dummy variables for industry, region, and legal form.

For a sub-sample of 4061 firms, of which 81 were known to be venture capital financed, the KSV database also contained select indicators from the balance sheets. For these firms we were able to add the equity ratio, cash flow ratio, debt repayment duration, and return on investment as structural variables for the estimation. The main purpose of the above probit estimations is to select an accurate control group for the later matching procedure, and not to find a generally valid explanation of venture financing. Desiring a comprehensive set of controls, I therefore included many variables with a potential impact, even if these were not significant.

The descriptive statistics in Tables 6.2 and 6.3 show the mean values for the structural variables for the test group of VC-financed firms and the control group of non-VC financed firms, both before and after matching. They also display the selection bias as measured by the difference in the sample means between the test and the control group, the reduction of bias achieved by the matching in percentage, and tests of significance. The second column in Table 6.1 summarizes the parameters from this model specification. Here, age has a negative influence, in both its linear and quadratic forms, while firm size has a positive impact if measured by capitalization, and a negative coefficient on the quadratic employment term. Now the coefficient on credit rating is negative. The switch in sign indicates problems of endogeneity with the other added financial indicators, but not a bias due to the smaller sample. Using the same variables as in model I on the smaller sample of model II produces a negative coefficient on credit rating, just as it did in the initial estimation. The coefficient is significant at the 5 percent level and somewhat smaller. Also, the other coefficients are robust in the smaller sample size.

We further find that with a lower cash flow ratio and a lower return on investment, the probability of drawing a VC-backed firm from the sample increases (again in both the linear and quadratic terms).

In the next step, the vector of parameters β from the probit model was used to calculate the propensity score of venture capital financing for each firm i. For each VC-financed firm $I = vc$, four firms $j \neq vc$ were selected as the control group by using the smallest measure of distance $d_{ij} = (\beta X_{i=vc}) - (\beta X_{j \neq vc})$. Tables 6.2 and 6.3 combine the descriptive statistics of the initial values for the test and control groups, together with the counterfactual information about how much of the selection bias has been eliminated through the matching. A comparison of the structural variables X confirmed the success of the procedure, as no significant deviations from the means between the test and the control groups remained after the matching.

This also applies to the industry and regional dummy variables (not displayed in the tables) and thus allows us to exclude any systematic selection errors stemming from differences in sector, age, number of employees, sales revenue, capitalization, or the credit rating of the firms. For the firms with balance sheet data, the

Table 6.2 Descriptive and test statistics for the structural variables used in the matching procedure: model I

Variable	*Sample*	*Test group*[a]	*Control group*[b]	*Bias in %*[c]	*Bias reduction*[d]	t	$p > t$
Age	Unmatched	18.356	21.508	–10.7		–1.43	0.154
	Matched	*18.356*	*18.434*	*–0.3*	*97.5*	*–0.04*	*0.968*
Age[b]	Unmatched	1418.8	1102.4	5		0.93	0.351
	Matched	*1418.8*	*1124.3*	*4.6*	*6.9*	*0.61*	*0.540*
Sales revenue	Unmatched	1.40E+07	5.80E+06	18.3		1.72	0.085
	Matched	*1.40E+07*	*1.70E+07*	*–6*	*67.5*	*–1.28*	*0.200*
Sales revenue[b]	Unmatched	1.20E+15	3.00E+15	–1.5		–0.12	0.901
	Matched	*1.20E+15*	*1.50E+15*	*–0.2*	*86.8*	*–0.57*	*0.568*
Employment	Unmatched	74.18	30.605	8		0.66	0.511
	Matched	*74.18*	*85.007*	*–2*	*75.2*	*–1.22*	*0.223*
Employment[b]	Unmatched	23712	5.80E+05	–0.8		–0.07	0.947
	Matched	*23712*	*28645*	*0*	*99.1*	*–0.74*	*0.460*
Capitalization	Unmatched	2.80E+06	3.50E+05	31.1		4.9	0
	Matched	*2.80E+06*	*2.60E+06*	*2.4*	*92.3*	*0.31*	*0.757*
Capitalization[b]	Unmatched	9.90E+13	3.30E+13	4.4		0.38	0.702
	Matched	*9.90E+13*	*1.00E+14*	*–0.4*	*91.7*	*–0.11*	*0.910*
Credit rating	Unmatched	3.4486	3.3353	12		1.34	0.182
	Matched	*3.4486*	*3.4021*	*4.9*	*59*	*0.82*	*0.415*
Credit rating[b]	Unmatched	12.709	12.071	8.4		0.88	0.381
	Matched	*12.709*	*12.388*	*4.2*	*49.7*	*0.73*	*0.467*

Notes:
[a] Mean of the test group of VC-financed firms.
[b] Mean of the control group of non-VC-financed firms.
[c] Difference in the sample means between the test and the control group.
[d] Reduction of selection bias in %.

Table 6.3 Descriptive and test statistics for the structural variables used in the matching procedure: model II

Variable	*Sample*	*Test group*[a]	*Control group*[b]	*Bias in %*[c]	*Bias reduction*[d]	*t*	*p > t*
Age	Unmatched	22.716	28.414	–16.3		–1.69	0.091
	Matched	*22.716*	*26.145*	*–9.8*	*39.8*	*–1*	*0.320*
Age[b]	Unmatched	2040.4	1698.3	4.3		0.65	0.518
	Matched	*2040.4*	*2429*	*–4.9*	*–13.6*	*–0.43*	*0.667*
Sales revenue	Unmatched	2.10E+07	2.60E+07	–5.9		–0.41	0.682
	Matched	*2.10E+07*	*2.40E+07*	*–3.6*	*39.2*	*–0.8*	*0.422*
Sales revenue[b]	Unmatched	2.00E+15	9.20E+15	–3.7		–0.23	0.816
	Matched	*2.00E+15*	*1.90E+15*	*0*	*98.9*	*0.12*	*0.903*
Employment	Unmatched	106.93	96.607	4.4		0.32	0.751
	Matched	*106.93*	*120.6*	*–5.8*	*–32.4*	*–1*	*0.319*
Employment[b]	Unmatched	37641	94572	–5.3		–0.34	0.735
	Matched	*37641*	*40147*	*–0.2*	*95.6*	*–0.22*	*0.825*
Capitalization	Unmatched	4.50E+06	1.90+06	19.8		1.67	0.095
	Matched	*4.50E+06*	*4.80E+06*	*–2.9*	*85.2*	*–0.34*	*0.733*
Capitalization[b]	Unmatched	1.60E+14	1.90E+14	–0.9		–0.06	0.954
	Matched	*1.60E+14*	*2.10E+14*	*–1.8*	*–106.3*	*–0.56*	*0.575*
Credit rating	Unmatched	3.3295	3.0203	32.5		2.87	0.004
	Matched	*3.3295*	*3.2548*	*7.9*	*75.8*	*0.94*	*0.349*
Credit rating[b]	Unmatched	11.962	10.045	25.3		2.18	0.029
	Matched	*11.962*	*11.468*	*6.5*	*74.3*	*0.8*	*0.425*
Equity ratio	Unmatched	19.13	22.42	–9.3		–0.86	0.391
	Matched	*19.13*	*19.569*	*–1.2*	*86.6*	*–0.14*	*0.885*
Equity ratio[b]	Unmatched	1712	1665.9	2		0.17	0.863
	Matched	*1712*	*1577.3*	*6*	*–192.3*	*0.73*	*0.464*

Debt repayment duration	Unmatched	2.1516	9.2915	−16.1		−1.27	0.203
	Matched	*2.1516*	*0.93129*	*2.8*	*82.9*	*0.37*	*0.714*
Debt repayment duration[b]	Unmatched	1398.2	2603.2	−9.5		−0.66	0.507
	Matched	*1398.2*	*1670.6*	*−2.2*	*77.4*	*−0.35*	*0.729*
Cash flow ratio	Unmatched	−55.918	2.1933	−60.4		−7.11	0.000
	Matched	*−55.918*	*−48.877*	*−7.3*	*87.9*	*−0.73*	*0.463*
Cash flow ratio[b]	Unmatched	16319	5148.5	29.2		3.31	0.001
	Matched	*16319*	*14589*	*4.5*	*84.5*	*0.47*	*0.639*
ROI	Unmatched	−27.839	2.9274	−62.1		−7.43	0.000
	Matched	*−27.839*	*−26.892*	*−1.9*	*96.9*	*−0.19*	*0.852*
ROI[b]	Unmatched	4326.2	1325	22.2		2.14	0.032
	Matched	*4326.2*	*4282.2*	*0.3*	*98.5*	*0.04*	*0.971*

Notes:

[a] Mean of the test group of VC-financed firms.

[b] Mean of the control group of nonVC financed firms.

[c] Difference in the sample means between the test and the control group.

[d] Reduction of selection bias in %.

procedure also eliminated potential distortions arising from differences in equity ratio, duration of debt repayment, cash flow ratio, and return on investment.

The following enterprise survey was based on this matching and served two purposes. The first was to acquire comparable performance measures on, for example, growth of sales revenue, employment, and exports or the share of "new or significantly improved products or services" in sales revenues. The second aim was to make available additional structural characteristics and use them in the final matching procedure. This allowed us to separate more narrowly further selection effects from the causal impacts of venture capital financing.

In total, 829 questionnaires were sent out. Reflecting a response rate of 29 percent, a net sample of 84 replies among VC-backed companies and 154 responses in the control group of firms without venture capital financing was obtained. Based on a gross sample of 166 firms, the response rate thus amounted to 51 percent for the test group. In the control group, a response rate of 23 percent was achieved for a gross sample of 663 firms.

The median firm in the gross sample was seven years old with 20 employees. For the firms which responded to the survey, the medians were six years and 20 employees. The sector distribution of venture capital financing was mainly concentrated in knowledge-intensive business-related services (*e.g.*, software and IT services; legal, tax or consulting services; research and development). Within the manufacturing sector, machinery and equipment constituted the largest group. The remaining firms were scattered among various sectors in manufacturing, trade, and other services.

In the test group, 53 percent of the respondents said they required venture capital in order to finance growth, 39 percent said it was necessary for the firm's start-up phase, and 11 percent said it was used for seed financing. Preparation for stock market flotation played a role for 4 percent of firms, while 21 percent named change of ownership as their specific reason for opting for venture capital financing.

Nearly 68 percent of all the firms in the survey considered the European Union their *main market*. However, the data also revealed a significantly higher orientation towards international markets among VC-financed firms than among firms in the control group. Tables 6.4 and 6.5 summarize the information for the samples used in models III and IV. If we look, for example, at the descriptive information for the "unmatched" samples in Table 6.5, we find that only 14 percent of the VC-financed firms considered Austria their main market, compared to 18 percent of the firms without venture capital. Conversely, 35 percent of the VC-backed firms regard the world "outside EU" as their main market, compared to 21 percent of the non-VC backed firms.

Innovation behavior proved to be another dimension where the survey results revealed pronounced differences between the two groups despite the first matching. If we take another look at the mean values for the "unmatched" test and control groups in Table 6.5, venture capital financed firms reported more product innovations that are new to the market (89 percent) than the control group without VC financing (68 percent), and they were more inclined to protect against imitation by securing intellectual property rights through formal methods,

Table 6.4 Descriptive and test statistics for the structural variables used in the matching procedure: model III

Variable	*Sample*	*Test group*[a]	*Control group*[b]	*Bias in %*[c]	*Bias reduction*[d]	*T*	*p > t*
National	Unmatched	0.13333	0.17647	–11.9		–0.83	0.409
	Matched	*0.13333*	*0.09333*	*11*	*7.3*	*0.67*	*0.505*
European Union	Unmatched	0.42667	0.45098	–4.9		–0.35	0.730
	Matched	*0.42667*	*0.46667*	*–8*	*–64.5*	*–0.43*	*0.671*
Outside EU	Unmatched	0.38667	0.21569	37.7		2.76	0.006
	Matched	*0.38667*	*0.41333*	*–5.9*	*84.4*	*–0.29*	*0.774*
Product new	Unmatched	0.86667	0.68627	44.2		2.98	0.003
to market	*Matched*	*0.86667*	*0.90667*	*–9.8*	*77.8*	*–0.67*	*0.505*
Product new	Unmatched	0.01333	0.05229	–21.9		–1.42	0.157
to firm	*Matched*	*0.01333*	*0*	*7.5*	*65.8*	*0.87*	*0.386*
Process	Unmatched	0.01333	0.01961	–4.9		–0.34	0.736
	Matched	*0.01333*	*0*	*10.4*	*–112.5*	*0.87*	*0.386*
Formal	Unmatched	0.6	0.30719	61.2		4.39	0.000
(*e.g.* patents)	*Matched*	*0.6*	*0.6*	*0*	*100*	*0*	*1.000*
Secrecy	Unmatched	0.32	0.15686	38.8		2.88	0.004
	Matched	*0.32*	*0.29333*	*6.3*	*83.7*	*0.31*	*0.760*
Lead time	Unmatched	0.29333	0.23529	13.1		0.94	0.347
	Matched	*0.29333*	*0.16*	*30.1*	*–129.7*	*1.71*	*0.091*

Notes:

[a] Mean of the test group of VC-financed firms.

[b] Mean of the control group of non-VC financed firms.

[c] Difference in the sample means between the test and the control group.

[d] Reduction of selection bias in %.

Table 6.5 Descriptive and test statistics for the structural variables used in the matching procedure: model IV

Variable	*Sample*	*Test group*[a]	*Control group*[b]	*Bias in %*[c]	*Bias reduction*[d]	t	$p > t$
Age	Unmatched	15.778	28.329	–42.2		–2.61	0.010
	Matched	*15.778*	*14.603*	*4*	*90.6*	*0.29*	*0.771*
Age[b]	Unmatched	798.03	2004.7	–25.1		–1.48	0.140
	Matched	*798.03*	*433.37*	*7.6*	*69.8*	*0.84*	*0.405*
Sales revenue	Unmatched	1.10E+07	2.00E+07	–31.4		–1.93	0.055
	Matched	*1.10E+07*	*1.20E+07*	*–3.8*	*87.7*	*–0.27*	*0.786*
Sales revenue[b]	Unmatched	5.90E+14	1.50E+07	–17.3		–0.99	0.321
	Matched	*5.90E+14*	*4.40E+14*	*2.6*	*85.1*	*0.42*	*0.678*
Employment	Unmatched	63.464	97.387	–29.7		–1.94	0.054
	Matched	*63.464*	*70.456*	*–6.1*	*79.4*	*–0.32*	*0.750*
Employment[b]	Unmatched	15736	23574	–12.3		–0.85	0.394
	Matched	*15736*	*15995*	*–0.4*	*96.7*	*–0.02*	*0.983*
Capitalization	Unmatched	2.10E+06	1.60E+06	11		0.79	0.431
	Matched	*2.10E+06*	*9.80E+05*	*22.8*	*–106.6*	*1.17*	*0.244*
Capitalization[b]	Unmatched	3.60E+13	1.80E+13	13.9		1.06	0.290
	Matched	*3.60E+13*	*1.20E+13*	*18.2*	*–31.3*	*0.94*	*0.349*
Credit rating	Unmatched	3.5225	3.0029	61.1		4.41	0.000
	Matched	*3.5225*	*3.3479*	*20.5*	*66.4*	*0.9*	*0.370*
Credit rating[b]	Unmatched	13.397	9.4569	61.7		4.65	0.000
	Matched	*13.397*	*12.007*	*21.8*	*64.7*	*0.96*	*0.340*
National	Unmatched	0.14286	0.17808	–9.6		–0.62	0.534
	Matched	*0.14286*	*0.14286*	*0*	*100*	*0*	*1.000*
European Union	Unmatched	0.44444	0.44521	–0.2		–0.01	0.992
	Matched	*0.44444*	*0.4127*	*6.4*	*–4071.4*	*0.31*	*0.755*
Outside EU	Unmatched	0.34921	0.21233	30.6		2.1	0.037
	Matched	*0.34921*	*0.39683*	*–10.7*	*65.2*	*–0.48*	*0.632*

Product new to market	Unmatched	0.88889	0.68493	51.2		3.17	0.002
	Matched	*0.88889*	*0.87302*	*4*	*92.2*	*0.24*	*0.812*
Product new to firm	Unmatched	0.01587	0.05479	–21.1		–1.27	0.205
	Matched	*0.01587*	*0*	*8.6*	*59.2*	*0.88*	*0.384*
Process	Unmatched	0.01587	0.02055	–3.5		–0.23	0.822
	Matched	*0.01587*	*0*	*11.8*	*–239.5*	*0.88*	*0.384*
Formal (*e.g.* patents)	Unmatched	0.60317	0.30822	61.6		4.14	0.000
	Matched	*0.60317*	*0.72429*	*–23.2*	*62.3*	*–1.15*	*0.253*
Secrecy	Unmatched	0.31746	0.15753	38		2.66	0.009
	Matched	*0.31746*	*0.30159*	*3.8*	*90.1*	*0.17*	*0.867*
Lead time	Unmatched	0.33333	0.23288	22.3		1.51	0.131
	Matched	*0.33333*	*0.38095*	*–10.6*	*52.6*	*–0.48*	*0.629*

Notes:

[a] Mean of the test group of VC-financed firms.

[b] Mean of the control group of non-VC financed firms.

[illegible]fference in the sample means between the test and the control group.

[illegible]f selection bias in %.

such as patents (60 percent vs. 31 percent), or by other measures such as secrecy (32 percent vs. 16 percent) and lead time (33 percent vs. 23 percent).

To conclude, the two groups of firms differ significantly with respect to both their export orientation and their innovation behavior. While, as a result of the matching, there were no significant differences between the two groups with respect to age, size, sector, equity ratio, etc., the additional information gathered in the survey concerning export orientation and innovation behavior indicated further potential sources of selection effects. These have been taken into consideration in the second stage of the matching procedure.

6.5 Motives for the choice of venture capital financing

This section briefly summarizes the empirical evidence on the specific financing function of venture capital from the enterprise survey, whereas the subsequent section will then turn to the task of separating selection and causal impacts by means of the two-stage matching procedure. To begin with, the survey asked the firms in the control group why they did not opt for VC financing. From the 138 firms that replied to this question, over 52 percent explained that this was because they had sufficient self-financing resources, 27 percent said they received enough financing through loans and 26 percent indicated that they were adequately financed by their stockholders. A surprisingly modest 17 percent replied that they were not interested in VC financing because they did not wish to relinquish any control rights. Fewer than 6 percent expressed a fundamental rejection of VC equity. The different categories for response were not mutually exclusive.

Conversely, the survey asked the VC-financed firms why they preferred venture capital to other forms of finance. Among the 31 to 45 replies we received for each category, initial public offering as well as corporate bonds or securities were considered inappropriate by almost all the firms questioned. Financing through loans was not available to 47 percent of the firms and not sufficient in 40 percent of cases. Over 90 percent of the VC-backed firms said that further financing through their owners had been either impossible or insufficient. About half of the firms were generally opposed to any types of strategic investors. Finally, public support programs were considered attractive and accessible, but insufficient in eeting the firms' current capital needs.

Furthermore, when managers were asked what impact VC financing had had he development of their firms, we received 71 responses, of which a total of percent replied that the (continued) existence of the firm would not have ossible without venture capital, while 46.5 percent believed the firm's nent improved as a result of VC equity. Only 8.5 percent said their firm e experienced the same development with or without VC financing. At ne, 5.6 percent of managers said they were convinced their firms had ore poorly as a result of VC financing. The rest refrained from a ion and chose to reply in the open answer category. Some firms ple, that development had been positive in the beginning, but that l become an increasing burden over time.

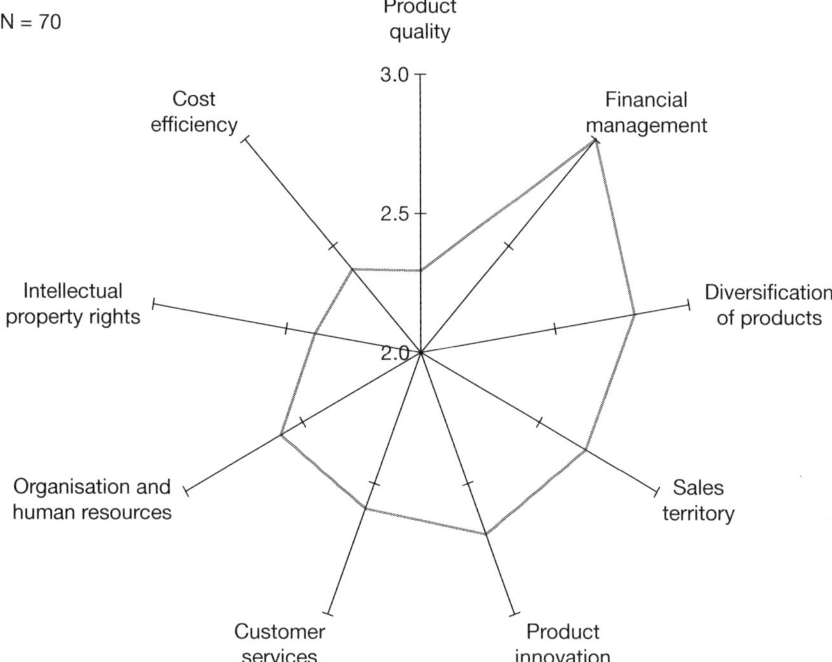

Figure 6.2 Subjective assessment of how venture capital has had an impact on the company.

Note: 0 = much deteriorated, 1 = deteriorated, 2 = no impact, 3 = improved, 4 = much improved.

The survey also asked managers specifically what kinds of firm activities changed as a result of VC financing (Figure 6.2). Not surprisingly, among the 70 responses financial management was named as the most important area of change, followed by the development of three typically growth-oriented strategies: (i) expanding the variety ("diversification"); or (ii) geographical sales area ("internationalization") of existing products; and (iii) introducing new goods and services ("product innovation"). Conversely, the managers thought VC financing had had comparatively little impact on cost efficiency, product quality, and measures to protect the firm's intellectual property.

To summarize, the data confirm that (in contrast to the respondents from the control group) the VC-backed firms were generally constrained in their ability to obtain financing from traditional sources. Consistent with the specific financing function of venture capital as postulated in Section 6.2, the majority of firms said they would no longer exist or have been able to finance their projects without it. The specific financing function thus points towards an essential impact of venture capital, which does not depend on the presumed differences in performance which we explore in Section 6.6.

6.6 Innovation and growth performance – causal impacts vs. selection

We finally turn to the core question of the empirical analysis: do firms with and without venture equity exhibit significant differences in growth and innovation performance? And, if so, to what extent can these differences be causally attributed to the choice of venture capital as a financing instrument?

An analysis of the survey data reveals marked differences with respect to the firms' export orientation and the variables on innovation behavior. Venture capital backed firms generally appear to have a stronger orientation towards international markets, a more frequent introduction of new products, and a greater inclination to protect their innovations by means of explicit appropriation measures (*i.e.*, intellectual property rights). These observed differences in export and innovation behavior indicate potential sources of a selection bias that has not been eliminated in the first matching. To correct for these, we must carry out a second matching using the additional information as control variables.

In the second matching, the vector of observable structural variables X is consequently expanded to include answers from the enterprise survey on: (i) geographical scope of operations; (ii) innovation performance; and (iii) measures taken to protect innovations. In the selected specifications of the probit estimation, the balance sheet data are no longer taken into consideration. This is because their limited availability would considerably reduce the number of observations. Tests for robustness based on the balance sheet data show them to have either little effect or a positive effect on the measured impact, while at the same time rendering many of them insignificant owing to the smaller sample.

The third and fourth columns of Table 6.1 report the coefficients from the new probit estimations. The matching in the final and preferred model was limited to a sample of 209 firms. With an R^2 of 0.31, it is above all the regional dummies and applications for intellectual property rights which show significant coefficients in the probit estimate. Tables 6.4 and 6.5 present the summary statistics for the test and control groups. The success of the matching procedure is again confirmed by the elimination of any significant bias for the matched pairs in the latter test statistics, even though the orientation towards international markets, the introduction of product innovations, and the use of formal methods to protect IPRs proved to be significant sources of selection before matching.

Table 6.6 summarizes the results of the final statistical tests on the mean of the chosen performance variables for all the four model specifications. The comparison of means is the method consistent with evaluation theory, which is based on expected values and assumes a normal distribution of the outcome variable. At the same time, the influence of individual outliers, which are typically found among small, rapidly growing firms, can violate the assumption of a normal distribution and lead to an upward bias in the observed differences of performance. To test the robustness of the results even further, Table 6.7 reports the results when using medians instead of means and applying the nonparametric Mann-Whitney rank sum test to determine the significance of observed deviations.

Table 6.6 Estimated impacts of VC financing—mean values in percent

	VC-backed firms	*Control group . . . before*		*. . . after matching*		*Impact factor*[c]
MATCHING 1st stage						
Model I (n = 33,729; R^2 = 0.27)	Mean	Mean	t-value	Mean	t-value	
Sales revenue growth[a]	20.1	6.5	*7.48***	8.8	*2.41***	*1.292*
Employment growth[a]	11.8	2.9	*5.80***	2.9	*7.07***	*3.008*
Model II (n = 4,061; R^2 = 0.32)						
Sales revenue growth[a]	20.2	5.5	*6.22***	9.7	*4.17***	*1.088*
Employment growth[a]	10.9	1.6	*5.10***	1.5	*6.94***	*6.431*
MATCHING 2nd stage						
Model III (n = 228; R^2 = 0.264)	Mean	Mean	t-value	Mean	t-value	
Sales revenue growth[a]	24.9	9.2	*4.23***	11.0	*3.83***	*1.272*
Employment growth[a]	14.4	2.9	*5.47***	4.6	*3.4***	*2.127*
Sales revenue growth[b]	26.3	6.1	*5.56***	6.9	*3.80***	*2.838*
Employment growth[b]	10.6	3.0	*1.83**	0.6	*1.59*	*18.092*
Sales from innovation/total sales revenue[b]	45.6	28.2	*3.71***	35.3	*1.66*	*0.291*
Model IV (n = 209; R^2 = 0.31)						
Sales revenue growth[a]	24.9	9.4	*4.13***	14.4	*2.38**	*0.725*
Employment growth[a]	13.3	3.3	*4.90***	3.1	*3.47*	*3.357*
Sales revenue growth[b]	24.7	6.0	*4.96***	6.6	*3.32***	*2.718*
Employment growth[b]	8.5	3.2	*1.26*	–1.3	*1.49*	*–7.604*
Sales from innovation/total sales revenue[b]	43.6	27.4	*3.40***	38.4	*0.78*	*0.136*

Notes:
***significant at 1%, **significant at 5%, *significant at 10%.
[a] Data from KSV firm database, ca.1996–2004.
[b] Data from enterprise survey, 2002–05.
[c] The impact factor is the ratio of the difference between the mean of the test group of VC-financed firms and the mean of the control group to the mean of the control group.

Data on sales revenue and employment are available from two sources – the KSV firm database and the enterprise survey. The KSV data consist of collected balance sheets and targeted inquiries carried out by the credit rating agency itself. The database covers the period from 1996 to 2004, but there are many gaps, especially for the earlier years. As a consequence, it does not provide panel data, which for a sub-sample of firms might allow comparison of performance before and after VC financing. Instead, firm growth is measured as average geometrical growth between the first and last year of available data, and calculated for both sales revenue and employment figures. To calculate

Table 6.7 Estimated impacts of VC-financing—mean values in percent

	VC-backed firms	*Control group . . . before . . . after matching*				*Impact factor*[c]
MATCHING 1st stage						
Model I (n = 33,729; R^2 = 0.27)	Median	Median	z-value	Median	z-value	
Sales revenue growth[a]	19.4	2.8	*5.06****	4.4	*4.17****	*3.464*
Employment growth[a]	13.6	2.4	*4.69****	4.2	*3.57****	*2.219*
Model II (n = 4,061; R^2 = 0.32)						
Sales revenue growth[a]	11.1	2.8	*5.52****	4.4	*4.26****	*1.539*
Employment growth[a]	7.5	2.5	*4.18****	0.8	*5.00***	*8.456*
MATCHING 2nd stage						
Model III (n = 228; R^2 = 0.264)	Median	Median	z-value	Median	z-value	
Sales revenue growth[a]	20.3	3.6	*5.00****	4.9	*4.63****	*3.116*
Employment growth[a]	11.7	2.2	*4.11****	2.9	*2.94****	*3.079*
Sales revenue growth[b]	14.5	5.7	*3.65****	4.1	*3.43****	*2.490*
Employment growth[b]	3.7	2.3	*0.85*	1.4	*1.3*	*1.565*
Sales from innovation/total sales revenue[b]	35.0	20.0	*2.76****	20.0	*1.86**	*0.750*
Model IV (n = 209; R^2 = 0.31)						
Sales revenue growth[a]	19.9	3.6	*6.10****	5.1	*2.91****	*2.905*
Employment growth[a]	9.8	2.0	*4.18****	4.2	*1.69**	*1.321*
Sales revenue growth[b]	15.2	5.6	*3.61****	4.4	*2.84****	*2.424*
Employment growth[b]	3.7	1.9	*1.15*	2.5	*0.17*	*0.454*
Sales from innovation/total sales revenue[b]	30.0	20.0	*1.85**	25.0	*0.78*	*0.200*

Notes:
***significant at 1%, **significant at 5%, *significant at 10%.
[a] Data from KSV firm database, ca.1996–2004.
[b] Data from enterprise survey, 2002–05.
[c] The impact factor is the ratio of the difference between the mean of the test group of VC-financed firms and the mean of the control group to the mean of the control group.

growth rates from the enterprise survey, I have only taken into consideration those firms that provided information on sales revenue and employment for both 2002 and 2005.

To recapitulate briefly, the first specification uses a sample of firms from the KSV database that has been restricted to identical legal status and industry codes (NACE three-digit) as the test group of VC-backed companies. This sample consists of over 33,000 firms. The mean annual growth rate of sales revenues of 20.1 percent among VC-financed firms stands in contrast with a growth rate in the control group of 6.5 percent before and 8.8 percent after the matching. The second specification also considers balance sheet data from the KSV database. This reduces the sample of firms with compatible records to about 4000. The inclusion of balance sheet data somewhat increases the selection bias we have accounted for, but does not significantly change the outcome.

In the control group, we now find a growth rate of 5.5 percent before the matching and 9.7 percent after the matching, compared to the original 20.2 percent annual growth of sales revenue among VC-financed firms. This result means that 4.2 percentage points of the original growth difference can be explained as selection effects, while the direct VC impact amounts to 10.5 percentage points. With an impact factor of 1, VC investment results in a doubling of the growth of sales revenues. The impact is much greater in terms of employment growth, where both models fail to identify substantial distortions from selection effects.

While models I and II offer the advantage of a larger sample, both are restricted to the structural variables accounted for in the KSV database. In contrast, the third and fourth specifications show the results before and after the second matching, that is, after controlling for additional structural variables in the subsequently smaller sample of firms from the survey.

The third and fourth specifications show very similar results. Based on the more comprehensive set of structural variables, I prefer to consider model IV the main result. In this estimation, an average annual growth in sales revenue among VC-financed firms of 25 percent contrasts with an average growth of just over 9 percent after the first matching in the control group. By again taking into consideration age, size, equity ratio, etc., as well as additionally controlling for differences in product innovation, applications for intellectual property rights, and its export orientation, the second matching procedure identifies another 5 percentage points as a bias resulting from selection, while the average growth of the control group increases to 14.5 percent. In this model, the specific impact factor amounts to 0.7. In other words, VC financing increased the growth of sales revenues of the firms in question by 70 percent, compared to the reference value of the control group.

The impact factor of 0.7 percent is the lowest value of all the specifications and can be considered a robust lower boundary. If, instead of considering the KSV data, we were to consider the sales revenue figures presented by the companies in the questionnaire for the period from 2002 to 2005, the VC impact on the growth of sales revenues would increase to a value of 2.7. We also find similar values when comparing the medians instead of the means. In this case, the impact factor for the sales revenue figures from the KSV is 2.9 and the impact factor for those in the questionnaire is 2.4. With values ranging from 0.7 to 3.1, the impact factors for the growth of sales revenues are not only all positive and surprisingly high, but also significant in all conceivable specifications (for both the mean and the median). While the exact amount varies greatly depending on the specification selected, the general finding of a positive impact of VC financing on sales revenue growth is extremely robust.

This statement does not apply to the same extent to growth in employment. While we also find a high positive impact of VC financing in each of the specifications, the variation is much greater and the differences are no longer significant in the smaller sample from the enterprise survey. Among the significant results, the impact factor ranges from 1.3 to 3.4. The lower boundary (among absolute values)[6] consists of the (non-significant) factor of 0.5 in the comparison of the medians in model IV. Even though the precise impact is very sensitive to the selected specifications and available sample, in general we can also expect a positive impact of VC financing on employment growth.[7]

Next, we consider the share of sales revenues of "new or significantly improved products and services in the total sales revenue for the year 2005" to be a measure of the actual success of innovation and therefore a performance indicator.[8] This question was only answered by those firms which previously said they had been active in product innovation since 2002. The difference in the mean values of 43.6 percent among the VC-financed firms and 27.4 percent among the firms in the control group was the result of the one-stage matching procedure. In the second matching, which contained the additional structural variables from the survey, a large part of this difference is captured by the selection effect, so that the deviation of the new control group is no longer significant. We consequently must reject a direct impact of VC financing on the share of sales revenues resulting from the firms' own product innovations.

Given the prominence accrued to venture capital in debates about radical technological change, innovation policy and economic growth (*e.g.*, Antonelli and Teubal 2009; Avnimelech and Teubal 2008), the lack of a direct causal impact on the firms' innovation output may come as a surprise for several reasons. First, the many examples of successful VC-backed firms in high-tech industries (such as software or biotech) tend to suggest otherwise. Second, some of the theoretical literature also nourishes expectations about a causal impact of venture capital on innovation. For example, in a model of vertical product differentiation by Schwienbacher (2008), VC-backed entrepreneurs may even innovate more than what is optimal relative to the profit maximizing equilibrium in order to preserve better control of the company through an exit by IPO instead of a trade sale. Finally, there is considerable empirical evidence of a positive link between VC financing and innovation at the sector and macro-economic levels (*e.g.*, Kortum and Lerner 2000; Tykvová 2000; Romain and van Pottelsberghe 2004).

Most of the literature, however, stresses the financing function of venture capital or its impact on firm growth. In particular, the results presented in this chapter are consistent with the findings of Engel and Keilbach (2007), who proved

6 Note that in contrast to its negative sign, the (non-significant) factor of –7.6 for average employment growth in model IV of Table 6.6 implies a very high and positive impact. The sign is negative because the matched group exhibits a decline in employment, whereas among VC-financed firms employment had grown.

7 In a final test of the robustness of the findings, I expanded model IV by the balance sheet data used in model II. This reduced the number of observations.

8 Recall that the innovation-related structural variables in the second matching only indicated whether a company carried out innovations, and if so, took measures to protect these.

similar impacts in their sample of German companies (despite a different research design). Furthermore, combining the findings on firm growth and innovation resolves the seeming contradiction between the evidence at the micro-level versus more aggregate levels of observation. Apparently, providing financing to credit-constrained innovative firms, helping them to professionalize their management and to bring their products more rapidly to the market (Hellmann and Puri 2000, 2002) not only increases their growth, but also raises the share of innovative activity in the firm population. What is generally referred to as a selection "error" turns out to be an important driver of structural change in the context of corporate finance and industrial development.[9]

6.7 Summary and conclusions

This chapter tests the impact of venture capital financing on corporate performance by applying a two-stage propensity score matching on Austrian micro-data. The presumed impact mechanisms are threefold. First, venture capital enables the pursuit of business operations that would otherwise lack the necessary resources owing to particularly high uncertainty and asymmetric information (financing function). Second, under the same circumstances, venture capital attempts to allocate scarce financial resources to the most profitable uses (selection function). Finally, venture equity involves the contribution not only of capital, but also of managerial experience, professional monitoring and advising (value adding function).

To summarize, the results lend support to the following three general conclusions. First, the empirical findings on the sample of Austrian companies confirm that VC-backed firms are constrained in their ability to obtain financing through traditional channels. Consistent with the specific financing function, venture capital is shown to provide financial resources to firms operating at the margins.

Second, the data show that, on average, VC-financed firms are more innovative and grow faster in terms of employment and sales revenue than other firms. However, the differences analyzed above in innovation performance (measured as the share in sales revenue of new products and services) prove to be the result of pure selection effects and not the direct causal impact of VC financing on innovation. In other words, VC equity tends to finance firms with above average levels of innovation, rather than of itself making the firms more innovative. From the standpoint of the individual firms, this observation does not constitute a separate impact beyond that already captured by the specific financing function. However, from the perspective of the economy at large, it offers evidence of the selection function, telling us that venture capital succeeds

9 Note that this conclusion only holds in combination with the specific financing function of venture capital. If firms with high growth potential could equally finance their expansion from other sources, we face simple substitution effects with no or little impact on the composition of the firm population (*i.e.*, on structural change).

in allocating resources to innovative firms, thereby fostering structural change and development.

Third, the data show that, on average, VC-financed firms grow faster than firms in comparable control groups. The two-stage statistical matching procedure controlled for the influence of selection (as indicated, for example, by the legal structure, industry, regional distribution, age, size, equity ratio, innovation behavior, and export orientation of the firms). Under the assumption that the matching procedure captures the relevant structural variables, the various estimated models obtained the robust observation of a positive VC-specific impact on growth of sales revenue and employment. The difference in growth performance encompasses both causal effects, as in the value adding function of informed and active investors, and selection effects, as in the targeting of firms with particularly high growth potential.

Finally, when comparing alternative model specifications, the closer look at the range of impact factors shows them to lie between 0.5 and 3.4. Knowing that the specific figures can vary greatly depending on the available sample and the selected control variables and that the result for a certain sample of firms in the past does not mean that the same impact will apply to other firms in the future, the individual coefficients must be interpreted cautiously.

Overall, the study demonstrates the need for a comprehensive approach in the elimination of potential selection biases. Suggesting a deliberate two-stage design, this chapter combines the benefits of selecting an initial control group from a large firm database with the opportunity to control for additional behavioral characteristics through an independent enterprise survey. However, even with this extended approach, one can never be sure to have controlled for all selection effects but only attempt to minimize the impact of missing variables. A preferable "difference-in-difference" matching was not feasible because of the lack of sufficient data for periods before the VC financing. Also, one must be cautious about endogeneity problems in the initial probit estimations. Finally, quantitative impact studies always produce a retrospective picture. What had been valid control variables or impacts in the past need not necessarily be the same for present or future VC-backed firms. However, the proposed two-stage design has the advantage of facilitating the addition of further controls in future studies. Alleviating the restrictions from administrative firm databases, complementary enterprise surveys in particular add much flexibility to the choice of control variables.

Despite these caveats, the empirical findings bear considerable significance for practitioners and the public debate on venture capital. For example, entrepreneurs seeking external finance should be wary of venture capitalists who suggest that they can improve innovation, but rather expect them to boost the capacity to commercialize innovations and grow. The results also demonstrate that a developed venture capital market is no substitute for, but a complement to, public research and development policies. Despite the lack of a direct causal impact on innovation, access to venture capital therefore remains an important pillar of effective innovation systems.

References

Antonelli, C., and M. Teubal. 2009. "Venture capitalism, new-markets and innovation-led economic growth." ICER Working Paper 03/2009.

Avnimelech, G., and M. Teubal. 2008. "From direct support of business sector R&D/ innovation to targeting venture capital/private equity: A catching-up innovation and technology policy life cycle perspective." *Economics of Innovation and New Technology* 17, nos. 1–2: 153–72.

Belden, S., R. Keeley, and R. Knapp. 2001. "Can venture capital-backed IPOs compete with seasoned public companies?" *Venture Capital 3*, no. 4: 327–36.

Bergemann, D., and U. Hege. 1998. "Venture capital financing, moral hazard, and learning." *Journal of Banking and Finance* 22: 703–35.

Bergemann, D., U. Hege, and L. Peng. 2009. "Venture capital and sequential investments." Cowles Foundation Discussion Paper No. 1682R, Yale University.

Berger, A.N., and G.F. Udell. 1998. "The economics of small business finance: The roles of private equity and debt markets in the financial growth cycle." *Journal of Banking and Finance* 22: 613–73.

Bloom, N., R. Sadun, and J. van Reenen. 2009. "Do private equity-owned firms have better management practices?" in: Globalization of alternative investments: The global economic impact of private equity report 2009, 3–24. Cologne/Geneva: World Economic Forum.

Blundell, R., and M. Costa Dias. 2002. "Alternative approaches to evaluation in empirical microeconomics." CeMMAP Working Paper CWP 10/02.

Bottazzi, L., and M. Da Rin. 2002. "Venture capital in Europe and the financing of innovative companies." *Economic Policy* 17: 229–70.

Bottazzi, L., M. Da Rin, and T. Hellmann. 2008. "Who are the active investors? Evidence from venture capital." *Journal of Financial Economics* 89: 488–512.

Bozkaya, A., and B. van Pottelsberghe. 2008. "Who funds technology-based small firms? Evidence from Belgium." *Economics of Innovation and New Technology* 17, nos. 1–2: 97–112.

Carpenter, R.E., and B.C. Petersen. 2002. "Capital market imperfections, high-tech investment, and new equity financing." *The Economic Journal* 112: 54–72.

Cumming, D., G. Fleming, and J.-A. Suchard. 2005. "Venture capitalist value-added activities, fundraising and drawdowns." Journal of Banking and Finance 29: 295–331.

Engel, D. 2003. "Höheres Beschäftigungswachstum durch Venture Capital?" *Jahrbücher für Nationalökonomie und Statistik* 223, no. 1: 1–22.

Engel, D., and M. Keilbach. 2007. "Firm level implications of early stage venture capital investment – an empirical investigation." *Journal of Empirical Finance* 14: 150–67.

Gompers, P., and J. Lerner. 1999. *The venture capital cycle*. Cambridge, MA: MIT Press.

Gompers, P., and J. Lerner. 2001. "The venture capital revolution." *Journal of Economic Perspectives* 15, no. 2: 145–68.

Heckman, J.J., R.J. LaLonde, and J.A. Smith. 1999. "The economics and econometrics of active labor market programs." in: *Handbook of labor economics*, Vol. 3, ed. A. Ashenfelter, and D. Card, 1865–2097. Amsterdam: North Holland.

Hellman, T., and M. Puri. 2000. "The interaction between product market and financing strategy: The role of venture capital." *Review of Financial Studies* 13: 959–84.

Hellman, T., and M. Puri. 2002. "Venture capital and the professionalization of start-up firms: Empirical evidence." *Journal of Finance* 57: 169–97.

Hirukawa, M., and M. Ueda. 2008a. "Venture capital and industrial 'innovation'." CEPR Discussion Paper No. 7089.

Hirukawa, M., and M. Ueda. 2008b. "Venture capital and innovation: Which is first?" CEPR Discussion Paper No. 7090.

Hochberg, Y., Y. Lu, and A. Ljungqvist. 2007. "Whom you know matters: Venture capital networks and investment performance." *Journal of Finance* 62: 251–301.

Jeng, L.A., and P.C. Wells. 2000. "The determinants of venture capital funding: Evidence across countries." *Journal of Corporate Finance* 6: 241–89.

Jovanovic, B., and B. Szentes. 2007. "On the return to venture capital." NBER Working Paper 12874, Cambridge, MA.

Kanniainen, V., and C. Keuschnigg. 2004. "Start-up investment with scarce venture capital support." *Journal of Banking and Finance* 28: 1935–59.

Kaplan, S.N., and P. Strömberg. 2001. "Venture capitalists as principals: Contracting, screening, and monitoring." *American Economic Review* 91: 426–30.

Keuschnigg, C. 2004. "Taxation of a venture capitalist with a portfolio of firms." *Oxford Economic Papers* 56: 285–306.

Keuschnigg, C., and S.B. Nielsen. 2004. "Start-ups, venture capitalists, and the capital gains tax." *Journal of Public Economics* 88: 1011–42.

Kortum, S., and J. Lerner. 2000. "Assessing the contribution of venture capital to innovation." *The Rand Journal of Economics* 31, no. 4: 674–92.

Large, D., and S. Muegge. 2008. "Charting how venture capitalists add nonfinancial value to a venture." *Venture Capital* 10, no. 1: 21–53.

Lerner, J., M. Sorenson, and P. Stromberg. 2008. "Private equity and long-run investment: The case of innovation." in: Globalization of alternative investments: The global economic impact of private equity report 2008, 45–60. Cologne/Geneva: World Economic Forum.

Lindsay, L. 2008. "Blurring firm boundaries: The role of venture capital in strategic alliances." *Kyklos* 63, no. 3: 1137–68.

Manigart, S., K. Baeyens, and W. Van Hyfte. 2002. "The survival of venture capital backed companies." *Venture Capital* 4, no. 2: 103–24.

Manigart, S., and W. Van Hyfte. 1999. "Post-investment evolution of Belgian venture capital backed companies: An empirical study." in: *Frontiers of entrepreneurship research*, ed P.D. Reynolds, W.D. Bygrave, N.M. Carter, et al. Babson Park, MA: Babson College. http://www.babson.edu/entrep/fer/papers99/XVIII/XVIII_B/XVIII_B.html.

Megginson, W., and K. Weiss. 1991. "Venture capitalist certification in initial public offerings." *Journal of Finance* 46: 879–903.

Riyanto, Y.E., and A. Schwienbacher. 2006. "The strategic use of corporate venture financing for securing demand." *Journal of Banking and Finance* 30: 2809–33.

Romain, A., and B. van Pottelsberghe. 2004. "The economic impact of venture capital." Discussion Paper No. 18/2004, Deutsche Bundesbank, Frankfurt am Main.

Rubin, D.B. 1977. "Assignment to treatment group on the basis of a covariate." *Journal of Educational Statistics* 2, no. 1: 1–26.

Schwienbacher, A. 2008. "Innovation and venture capital exits." *The Economic Journal* 118, no. 533: 1888–916.

Sorensen, M. 2007. "How smart is smart money? An empirical two-sided matching model of venture capital." *Journal of Finance* 62: 2725–62.

Tirole, J. 2006. *The theory of corporate finance.* Princeton, NJ: Princeton University Press.

Trester, J.J. 1998. "Venture capital contracting under asymmetric information." *Journal of Banking and Finance* 22: 675–99.

Tykvová, T. 2000. "Venture capital in Germany and its impact on innovation." Paper presented at the 2000 EFMA Conference in Athens, June.

Wang, C.K., K. Wang, and Q. Lu. 2003. "Effects of venture capitalists' participation in listed companies." *Journal of Banking and Finance* 27: 2015–34.

Winton, A., and V. Yerramilli. 2008. "Entrepreneurial finance: Banks versus venture capital." *Journal of Financial Economics* 88: 51–79.

Wright, M., J. Gilligan, and K. Amess. 2009. "The economic impact of private equity: What we know and what we would like to know." *Venture Capital* 11, no. 1: 1–21.

7 Savings and innovation in the United States capital market: defined benefit plans and venture capital funds

*Tamir Agmon, Shubhashis Gangopadhyay and Stefan Sjogren**

7.1 Introduction

An important role of the capital market is to make it possible for investors who have ideas (investment projects) but no money to raise the necessary capital and for consumers who would like to secure their future consumption to transfer their current income in an efficient way for future consumption. Venture capital funds provide an organized solution to this need. As discussed by Merton and Bodie (2005) financial intermediaries are often developed in a response to a real need in the market. The rise and the development of the venture capital industries and venture capital funds as special purpose intermediaries can be associated with the development of new technologies after World War II.

The modern venture capital industry dates back to the establishment of the American Research and Development Corporation ("ARDC") by Doriot in 1946. Their legendary investment of US$70,000 in the Digital Equipment Corporation ("DEC") in 1959 generated an annual rate of return of more than 100 percent in the next year until DEC went public in 1968 with a market capitalization of US$37 million. Another famous investment by early venture capital funds was in the investment in Fairchild Semiconductors, the first venture capital backed start-up.

At the early stage, venture capital investment was funded by wealthy individuals and families and the total investments were small. In 1980 US legislation made it possible for pension funds to invest in venture capital funds. Since then there have been two major trends in the venture capital industry; the size of the investment

* Tamir Agmon is a Professor of Financial Economics at the School of Business, Economics and Law at Goteborg University, Sweden; he is also Associate Dean for Research and Development at the School of Management and Economics at the Academic College of Tel Aviv – Yaffo, Israel. Shubhashis Gangopadhyay is a Professor of Financial Economics at the School of Business, Economics and Business, Goteborg University, Sweden; he is also the founder of India Development Foundation and the Dean of Social Sciences and Humanities at S N University in India. Stefan Sjogren is an Associate Professor at the School of Business, Economics and Law at Goteborg University, Sweden.

is growing over time, although with substantial volatility and institutional investors in general and of defined benefit plans in particular are becoming the main source of capital for venture capital funds.

In the 15 years following the change in the legislation that allowed pension funds to invest in venture capital funds the total global investment in venture capital funds amounted to about US$10 billion (in 2007 US$). The big jump in IT and other technologies such as microelectronics, telecommunications and the Internet brought about a more than tenfold increase with global investment in venture capital funds of about US$140 billion. Overoptimism and overinvestment brought about a sharp decline to about US$12 billion in 2002, but renewed optimism in the years 2004–2007 was expressed in higher investment in venture capital funds. Global investment in venture capital funds peaked at US$90 billion in 2007. The financial crisis that began in 2008 brought down the rate of investment to about US$30 billion in the years 2008 to 2010.

Investment in venture capital funds is long term, about 10 years, and is not liquid. As has been demonstrated in many studies it is hard to measure. Yet, in a recent survey paper Kaiser and Westarp (2010) estimated the average pooled return ("IRR") for about 1200 US venture capital funds with inception up to 2006 (the estimate is based on VentureXpert database). The average IRR over all the funds and all the years was 15.9 percent (very close to another pooled estimate by Driessen, Lin, and Phalippou (2010) that used a different methodology). The average return on the lowest 25 percent of the funds for the period was (3.2). (The negative return is due to management fees paid by the limited partners.) The public market equivalent ("PME") of the average return of venture capital funds reported by them is negative. (Driessen, Lin and Phalippou (2010) reported insufficient return relative to the estimated beta and negative alpha.) However, investment of pension funds and other institutional investors in venture capital funds has increased since 2000. Although some venture capital funds were very successful, the top 5 percent of the funds realized more than 100 percent average IRR; what matters to large pension funds who invest in a large number of venture capital funds is the industry average IRR.

In this chapter we discuss two related issues:

- Why do institutional investors invest in venture capital funds in the face of "too low" risk adjusted return?
- Why does most of the capital invested in venture capital funds in the US by institutional investors come from defined benefit plans?

In a recent presentation by Warburg Pincus (2010) the authors claim that institutional investors were lured into investment in venture capital funds by past high returns. In this chapter we provide another explanation. We see the investment by institutional investors in venture capital funds, and in particular on whose behalf the investments were made (*i.e.*, the savers). US legislation and practices by the federal government encourage defined benefit plans to invest in venture capital funds, which they did in the past and continue to do now.

In Section 7.2, we present some well known basic relationships in economics. The purpose of the presentation is to demonstrate that the source for all investment is in income not consumed by the household sector. In principle, there are two sources for investment in innovative technology; savings or taxes. In this Section we present data and discuss the connection between institutional investors and investment in venture capital funds. A discussion of what are intellectual assets and how ideas are sold in the capital market through venture capital funds is presented in this section.

Venture capital funds are special purpose financial intermediaries. Their role in the financial intermediation system is presented and analyzed in Section 7.4. The savers are the principal stakeholders of institutional investors. Their main concern is protecting their future consumption. The contribution of venture capital funds to future consumption is discussed in Section 7.5. Although defined benefit plans are not government organizations the US Government takes partial responsibility for their operation. This is expressed in special legislation, the Employee Retirement Income Security Act of 1974 ("ERISA"), and in the government insurance company, the Public Benefit Guarantee Company ("PBGC"). The involvement of the federal government makes defined benefit plans particularly appropriate vehicles to invest in venture capital funds. This issue is presented and discussed in Section 7.6. The chapter is concluded in Section 7.7.

7.2 The sources for investment in innovative technology

A basic way to present the relationship between income, current consumption, savings, and taxes is by the well known equation that states that the total income of the household sector, all the people in the economy, is allocated to three uses: current consumption, savings, and taxes. We assume that taxes are allocated between current consumption of the public sector and public investment. In a close economy the savings of the household sector equals private investment. Investment in innovation in general and in innovative technology in particular is a part of total investment. It follows that there are only two primary sources for investment in innovative technology: savings and taxes. Obviously this is true for the household sector as a whole. It is an interesting question how the investment in innovative technology is distributed among different sectors of the household. This question is discussed below, but the general statement that innovation is financed by savings and taxes of the household sector is correct.

Another important and relevant relation is between current and future consumption. Modern economics is based on the assumption that the objective function of the individual is to maximize the utility of the consumption over her lifetime, (including intergenerational transfer). Two implications follow this basic statement: (1) The purpose of savings is to protect and facilitate future consumption; and (2) the right way to measure the return on savings is in terms of future consumption. Financial measures like the rate of return on the investment are an approximation. We discuss later in the chapter the importance and the relevance of these two implications to the investment decisions of specific institutional investors in innovative technology.

In this chapter we focus on the first source of investment in innovative technology; savings by households. The role of taxes as a source of investment in innovative technology primarily in basic research, but also in other stages of the investment is substantial. In some countries taxes are the major source for investment in innovative technology. However, in this chapter the focus is on the US where the role of institutional investors is paramount.

Institutional investors play an important role in the capital market in the US. In the period 1980–2009 institutional investors managed on the average slightly more than 19 percent of all outstanding assets in the US. The proportion of assets managed by institutional investors in this period varies between a high of 21.5 percent in 1999 to a low of 15.9 percent in 2008. Total outstanding assets and the assets managed by institutional investors grew about 10 times between 1980 and 2009. Institutional investors manage the capital that they raise through asset allocation with the aim of mimicking the real market. In Table 7.1 data on the asset allocation of different types of institutional investors for the year 2009 is presented.

Institutional investors invest in liabilities (securities) issued by corporations, agencies and other business organizations. The liabilities finance assets of firms, agencies and business organizations. Assets are the risk adjusted discounted cash flows of different activities managed and owned by the issuers of the liabilities (firms, agencies, and business organizations). It follows that the outcomes of the investments made by institutional investors can be measured in financial and in real terms. The rate of return on the different assets in the portfolios of the institutional investors represents the financial dimension, the actual future cash flows and the streams of future goods and services that generate the cash flows are the real dimension. Savings managed by institutional investors represent claims on future consumption (goods and services), which are normally measured in financial terms.

In this study the focus is on liabilities issued by venture capital funds. These are liabilities that the fund issued to its limited partners. The rights of the limited partners are specified in a contract between the fund, most often a limited liability partnership ("LLP"), and its investors, the limited partners. In general, the limited

Table 7.1 Asset allocation by US institutional investors in year 2009 (%)

Type of Institution	*Equity*	*Bonds*	*Cash Items*	*Other*
Private Trustees	33.5	18.1	4.8	43.6
Private Insured	41.4	43.7	4.3	10.5
State and Local	57.1	29.8	3.5	9.6
Open Investment	59.4	38.2	2.2	–
Closed Investment	39.5	60.5	–	–
Life Insurance	28.0	63.4	4.7	5.8
Property and Casualty	16.1	64.8	8.0	11.1
Savings Institutions	1.8	35.6	50.5	12.1
Foundations	56.0	26.0	13.0	5.0

Source: Tonello and Rabimov 2010.

Table 7.2 Fundraising and investment by US venture capital funds 2000–2010 (US$ billion)

Year	*Fund raising*	*Investment*
2000	106.1	99.2
2001	37.1	38.1
2002	3.8	20.8
2003	10.7	18.8
2004	18.6	21.8
2005	27.0	22.7
2006	31.7	26.2
2007	31.1	30.2
2008	26.1	28.7
2009	16.3	19.4
2010	12.5	23.2

Source: Pricewaterhouse Coopers/National Venture Capital Association Money Tree™ Report.

partners commit themselves to provide capital up to an agreed upon amount, their commitment. The amounts and the timing of the investment of the committed capital are decided by the investment committee of the fund. The investments are illiquid in the long term, usually 5–7 years, and involve substantial risk.

In the period 1995–2010 about US$450 billion was invested by venture capital funds. In Table 7.2 we present data on fundraising and actual investment by venture capital funds in the US in the period 2000–2010. Owing to the nature of the contract between the investors, the limited partners, and the fund money is raised (committed) first and thereafter invested over a number of years. That means that if the fundraising declines it does not mean that the investment declines in the same year at the same rate, as occurred in the period 2001–2003.

Investment in venture capital funds by institutional investors is classified as “Other Assets” or “Alternative Investments.” This asset class includes hedge funds, private equity and venture capital funds. Although most of the institutional investors invest in this class of assets (see Table 7.1) most of the investment in venture capital funds comes from defined benefit plans, often managed by large state owned and other pension funds. For example, in 2009, total outstanding assets managed by institutional investors according to the Conference Board were US$25,351 billion. The largest 200 defined benefit plans managed in 2009 was US$4,540 billion, 17.8 percent of the total. Yet, they invest US$23.8 billion in venture capital funds. In practice they finance all of the venture capital funds in the US. (Owing to the different definition of physical years and different populations of venture capital funds the data presented in Table 7.2 is not fully consistent with the above statement.)

The investment of the largest 200 defined benefit plans in venture capital funds is presented in Table 7.3.

Two interesting implications arise from the data presented in Table 7.3. First, the total annual investment in venture capital funds by institutional investors is

Table 7.3 Investment in venture capital funds by the 200 largest defined benefit ("DB") plans in the US 2007–2009 (billions of US$)

Year	*Total assets managed by institutional investors*	*Assets managed by DB plans*	*Percentage of assets managed by DB plans*	*Investment in Venture Capital*
2007	28 265.3	5 597.5	19.7	28.5
2008	22 237.6	4 706.8	21.1	26.8
2009	25 351.1	4 540.2	17.8	23.8

Source: Tonello and Rabimov 2010.

very small relative to the total assets managed by them, being approximately one-tenth of one per cent, yet it almost the only source for the capital investment by venture capital funds, particularly after 2005. However, owing to different sources of data, different definitions of funds and different fiscal years the data presented in Tables 7.1, 7.2, and 7.3 is not completely congruent.

The second implication is that the 200 largest defined benefit plans which manage about 20 percent of the total assets managed by institutional investors invest almost 100 percent of the investment by institutional investors in venture capital funds. That means that middle income workers who comprise most of the beneficiaries of the 200 largest defined benefit plans invest almost all the money in revolutionary technology innovation. Most of these beneficiaries work in the public sector or their defined benefit plans are insured by the federal government. Public sector defined benefit plans are governed by the US Tax Code and by federal law; state plans are governed by the Tax Code and by state law.

7.3 The unique nature of the assets of venture capital funds – intellectual assets and revolutionary ideas

Venture capital funds are special purpose financial intermediaries organized as limited partnerships (Chan 1983; Gompers and Lerner 1998). The liabilities of the venture capital funds are equity commitments raised from investors, the limited partners of the fund, and the assets are shares of companies. In most cases the companies are small innovative technology companies known in the venture capital industry as "start-ups."

In the following the focus is on what is called "early stage" investments. A simple way to understand the function of venture capital funds is as follows: entrepreneurs come up with ideas about new products, services, or production services. If the idea is an improvement on current (incumbent) technology the entrepreneurs can seek the required resources to develop and commercialize their ideas in the research and development divisions of existing corporations or in corporate venture capital funds (CVCs).

If the entrepreneurs have revolutionary ideas that can change the currently incumbent technology they have a better chance to raise the necessary capital through the capital market. This is so as revolutionary ideas in technology create risk to the rent of the incumbent technology. (This argument was developed in the industrial organization literature many years ago. For example see Fudenberg and Tirole 1984. A recent application of this concept to the venture capital industry is provided by Agmon, Gangopadhyay, and Sjogren 2011.) The preference for revolutionary ideas by venture capital funds is expressed in the industry by looking for the upside. It is common to aim at a cash on cash return of ten times in successful cases. The other side of the coin is that most investment projects by venture capital funds end with a loss to the investors (the limited partners).

Although almost all of the assets held by venture capital funds are preferred shares they differ from regular equity. In the reporting of institutional investors investment in venture capital funds (as well as investment in private equity funds) is classified under "other assets" and not under equity.

To see the unique nature of the assets held by venture capital funds consider the following example. The example is based on an "early stage" investment by a venture capital fund in a new start-up firm. A team of entrepreneurs approach a venture capital fund with an idea to generate a new service, product, or a production service. If it proves to be successful the new idea will change the current incumbent technology and replace it. It will transfer the rent from the incumbents to the new developers and producers of the new technology. In order to do so the entrepreneurs need to develop and test the technology and to begin the commercialization process. The venture capital fund agrees to invest the necessary capital to finance the process of development, testing and commercialization of the new technology over the next three years.

We assume for simplicity that at the end of this period one of two things will happen: either the process will not succeed and the investors will lose the investment, or the process will be successful. In this case more money is invested for one or more rounds. At the end of this process if the company is successful one of two things will happen: either the company is sold to a bigger company, or it is developed into a full scale independent company. In terms of the industry the first case is an mergers and acquistions (M&A) exit and the second is an initial public offering (IPO) exit. In both cases the special preferred shares are replaced by regular liabilities such as equity and bonds. The venture capital fund sells its preferred shares and the limited partners get the money minus the fees and the success fee for the general partners. At the same time, the idea of the entrepreneurs turns into future cash flow in the forms of sales of services, products, or production processes.

Although the assets held by venture capital funds are defined as shares they are really options where the underlying asset is the future value of the idea developed by the entrepreneurs. In the case of options, the higher the volatility the higher the value. This is the reason for the emphasis on "scalabilty" in the venture capital industry. Options are a part of a well diversified portfolio. Holdings in venture capital funds consist of about 0.5 percent of the portfolio of defined benefit plans.

Investment in innovative technology with a potential for revolutionary change makes sense from a macroeconomic point of view as well. Breeden and Litzenberger (1978) developed an equilibrium model where they show that in a world where consumers are concerned about lifetime consumption it does make sense for the consumers (who are also the savers) to invest in options on future consumption. (Technically, Breeden and Litzenberger (1978) show that if individuals have a time-additive and state-independent lifetime utility function for consumption expenditures, then it can be shown that optimal investment can be expressed in terms of European call options on future consumption.) Revolutionary innovative technology affects future consumption and one would expect that savers (consumers) will invest in options of that part of the future consumption as they do through the investment of defined benefit plans.

7.4 Venture capital funds as special purpose financial intermediaries

Venture capital funds have two unique features: first, the general partners who manage the funds have a compensation agreement that makes them focus on the upside rather than on the expected value in their investments. The second feature is that they have a fixed and relatively short horizon for their investment (about 10–12 years). The compensation and the legal structure of private equity funds and venture capital funds are functional for their purpose in two different but related aspects. The two aspects relate to the fact that both private equity funds and venture capital funds generate value from innovative ideas. Therefore the general partners of venture capital funds need to bridge the informational gap between ambiguous and unambiguous information and they need to focus on investments that are not made as a part of the ongoing investment of the corporate sector. These two aspects are discussed below in the context of financial intermediation.

Coval and Thakor (2005) discuss the major role of financial intermediation in the period of the IT revolution as building a bridge between optimistic entrepreneurs and pessimistic investors. Financial intermediaries do that by participating in the investment projects that they select for their investors and in this way they make themselves credible. General partners of private equity funds and of venture capital funds face a similar problem. They invest money for savers in projects based on innovative technology ideas and on innovative changes in existing companies. If successful these investments will yield a high return, but statistically most innovative ideas do not succeed. The savers and their agents (that is, the institutional investors) rely on the credibility of the general partners of the venture capital funds to select those ideas that have a better chance of success. The general partners gain their credibility through the compensation contract that they have with the limited partners and through them with the savers. The compensation contract is composed of two components: a management fee and carried over interest. The management fee covers the cost of the operation of the funds and it does not generate profits for the general partners. The interest element is normally 20 percent of the accrued profit for the limited partners provided that the profit over the total investment in the fund over the life of the fund exceeds an agreed upon hurdle rate.

The carried over interest is similar to an investment by the general partners of the fund. Following the analysis presented by Coval and Thakor (2005) such an investment is a necessary condition to establish the credibility of the financial intermediary as a rational agent in the eyes of those who provide the money for the investment.

To see how the carried interest compensation contract acts as an investment, consider the following example. Assume that a general partner raised a venture capital fund of US$100 million (the analysis would be the same if the general partner raised a private equity fund). Assume further that the general partner plans to make 10 equal investments of US$10 million and that the general partner expects to receive and examine 1000 business plans from entrepreneurs (innovators) who have innovative ideas in the relevant technology in which the fund plans to invest. The life of the fund is 10 years. The general partner knows that he has to make all the investments in the first three years of the fund to allow time for development and commercialization that may lead to an exit within the ten year life of the fund. The expectation of the general partner is that a "star" project will yield a ten times cash on cash return (X10), that a good project will yield six times cash on cash (X6), a reasonable project will yield three times the money (X3), a bad project will return the investment (X1) and a losing project will end up with zero cash (X0).

Assume further that the general partner expects one star project, two good projects, two reasonable projects, two bad projects and three losing projects. The portfolio in this example will yield an expected return of 2.7 times cash on cash in ten years. In other words, at the end of the life of the fund the limited partners will get US$270 million. Assume a management fee over the life of the fund of US$10 million after fee return to the limited investors is US$160 million on their investment (the actual investment depends on when the committed US$100 million funds were called by the general partner). Assume also for simplicity that the return on the investment was above the hurdle rate and therefore the general partner's expected carried interest from the fund is US$32 million to be received 10 years from now. The expected value of each investment projects in terms of the carried interest for the general partner is US$3.2 million. This cost is similar to the required investment by the financial intermediary, the rational agent, in the Coval and Thakor model. Making a bad selection in a probabilistic sense costs money to the general partner. Making a better selection, again in a probabilistic sense, increases the value of the general partner both in terms of the current fund, but also in the future as success in one fund increases the probability of raising a consecutive fund.

Venture capital funds are secondary financial intermediaries. They raise funds from institutional investors that manage the savings of the households sector through defined benefit plans. The need for having specific secondary financial intermediaries comes from the different nature of the role that they fulfill for the savers compared to most institutional investors (Merton and Bodie 2005). This specific role is reflected in their legal structure and in the compensation scheme of the general partner. Their specific role is also reflected in their investment policy.

For the savers (the households) the investment made by the general partners of the private equity and venture capital funds answers the need for "betting" on probable changes in the future that, if successful, will yield a very high return both in financial terms and in terms of future consumption.

There is a distinction between two parts in the portfolio of savers (households): one is the bulk of the savings where savers behave in a risk averse way, and one much smaller where savers behave as risk takers. This distinction was introduced and analyzed by Friedman and Savage (1948). In a seminal study Friedman and Savage introduced and discussed a model whereby consumers (savers) are willing to pay a premium to buy risk reducing insurance and risk increasing lotteries at the same time. (The premium is measured by the cost over the actuarial value.) The idea presented and discussed by Friedman and Savage can be applied to the allocation of savings by institutional investors to high risk investment in alternative investment (private equity, including venture capital). Friedman and Savage summarize their proposition by the following: "On this interpretation (a convex, concave, convex utility function), increases in income that raise the relative position of the consumer unit in its own class but do not shift the unit out of its class yield diminishing marginal utility, while increases that shift it to a new class, that give it a new social and economic status yield increasing marginal utility" (Friedman and Savage 1948: 298).

Following the Friedman Savage proposition it can be said that savers (households) are willing to take risk in allocating some of their savings to innovative technology projects that can extend their future consumption space in a significant way, "shifting them to a new class" in the terms of Friedman and Savage. The institutional investors, like pension funds, life insurance companies, savings institutions and other institutions, manage most of the money saved and contributed by the savers in a way that followed risk aversion. They allocate their investment to equity, debt, and cash items. The risk-return structure on fixed income securities and equity that together form most of the investment portfolio is congruent with the normal investment behavior where investors are willing to assume higher risk (volatility) for a higher expected return. This part of the portfolio of the savers (households) is similar to the "insurance" part in the Friedman and Savage analysis. Investments in venture capital funds and in private equity funds are much smaller.

More importantly, venture capital investments are similar to options. The investment manager, the general partner, is looking for the upside. There is a need for specific financial intermediaries to manage this type of investment with congruent compensation and length of life. Venture capital funds manage part of the "betting" investment in the terms of Friedman and Savage. As there is separation between those firms that sell insurance and those that sell betting services, this is true also in the case of financial intermediation. Primary financial intermediaries such as pension funds sell management services for the bulk of the portfolio ("insurance" services); special purpose intermediaries such as private equity funds and venture capital funds sell betting services.

The length of life and the compensation contract of the general partner make venture capital funds particularly appropriate to manage the high risk upside looking part of the portfolio for the savers. Venture capital funds are organized as limited partnerships with a contractually given length of time, in most cases 10–12 years. The finite and short length of life means that they do not have a long time to build up value. Therefore, they look for investment projects that have the potential to generate value in a short time, normally 5–7 years. The compensation contract of the general partners means that they receive payments only if the return on the total committed capital in the fund exceeds the agreed upon hurdle rate. The combined effect of the length of life and the required high rate of return is that general partners of venture capital funds look for investments that have a potential to introduce a meaningful change in relatively short time. In venture capital funds this means investing in potential revolutionary technology ideas.

7.5 Innovation and future consumption

Investment in innovation like all investment can be discussed in the context of the flow of funds. In general, savings are the source of all investments. In a closed economy with no government savings domestic households are the only source of investment. Consumers give up a portion of their current income (and current consumption) in order to be able to consume more in the future. The investors take this part of the income, the investment, and generate value by different types of investment. The financial intermediation system is the mechanism that transfers savings to different types of investment.

Like many other economic activities savings have a real dimension and a financial dimension. The real dimension is the transfer of consumption of goods and services by consumers from the present to the future. The financial dimension is the return that the savers (consumers) will receive on their investment (savings). The two dimensions describe the ability of the savers of today to consume later in life when they will retire. The first dimension is discussed in the economic literature under what is known as the Life Cycle Theory of Saving. The second dimension is discussed in capital market theories like the Capital Asset Pricing Model (CAPM) or the Arbitrage Pricing Theory (APT).

The main motivation for savings is to provide for future consumption. The life cycle theory of consumption provides insights into asset allocation and savings. Bodie, Treussard, and Willen (2007) present the three principles of savings according to the life-cycle theory. These are:

- focus on future consumption and not on the financial plan;
- financial assets are vehicles from moving consumption from the preset to a future period;
- the value of a dollar for investor depends on the consumption context.

By investing in the market at large the institutional investors who manage the savings provide the savers the protection that they seek in terms of their future consumption. This is so as financial assets are the rights to future cash flows. The cash flows are generated by the production of goods and services by different organizations including corporations, financial institutions, professional service providers and government agencies. Buying the securities issued by these organizations is like buying rights to their future production streams.

The transformation of current savings by households to actual flows of goods and services in the future through the process of financial intermediation by institutional investors is demonstrated in Figure 7.1.

Households transfer savings to institutional investors. The institutional investors allocate the money to different classes of assets such as fixed income, equity, real estate, private equity funds and venture capital funds. The investment is expressed by buying securities, liabilities of corporations and other business organizations by the institutional investors. The securities held by the institutional investors are claims against assets of the organizations that issue the securities (their liabilities).

It is possible to arrange the securities held by the institutional investor as liabilities in a balance sheet and put all the assets that they "command" on the other side of the balance sheet. By definition the assets are identically equal in value to the liabilities. In other words, the assets are the current value of the liabilities held by the institutional investors for the savers (the households). The assets in this case represent expected future cash flows. The expected future cash flows will be realized in the future as a stream of sales from selling goods and services in the future. (It is likely that the actual streams of sales, cash flows, will differ from the expected cash flows represented by the assets at the time of the investment by the institutional investors. As shown in Figure 7.1 it is possible to map expected future consumption from the current assets' allocation (investment) of institutional investors.)

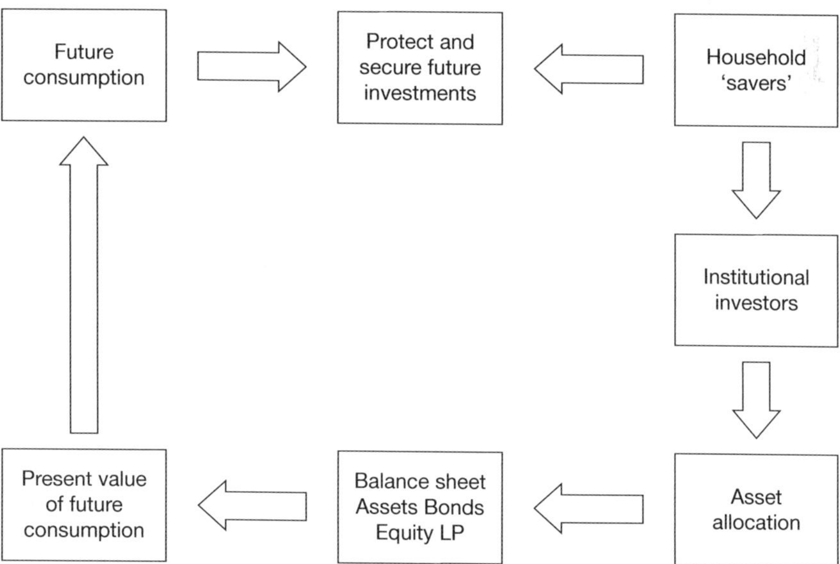

Figure 7.1 The transfer of savings to venture capital industries to secure future investments

A part of future consumption is comprised of products and services that do not exist today, for example a cellular phone did not exist 30 years ago, and did not become an important part of the consumption basket until about 10 years ago. In a study on the use of cellular phones at the "Base of the Pyramid" (very low income families) Agüero and de Silva (2011) found that cellular phones, which were unknown until recently, became a necessity in the consumption baskets of poor people in Asia. The same is true for a number of products, services and production processes. In general, consumers who maximize their lifetime consumption allocate a portion of their investment (savings) to goods, services and production processes that do not exist today. They do so by investing in real options on innovation. Venture capital funds provide this class of assets for savers.

There is a strong positive relationship between changes in the demand for innovation based on past performance and the allocation of capital to venture capital funds by institutional investors. When looking back at the changes in their consumption baskets consumers can see that the percentage of new goods and services relative to earlier periods increases over time. That explains why consumers are investing a higher percentage of their savings today in financing innovation. This is evident from the data on fund raising by venture capital funds. The highest years of raising capital by venture capital funds were in 1999–2001 period, when consumers were very optimistic about the rate at which new products, services and production processes will be added to their consumption baskets or will replace incumbent technologies and products. Where it turns out that the actual rate of innovation was much slower, the allocation by savers to venture capital funds went down.

The real dimension in investment by institutional investors in venture capital funds and the realization that the preferred shares held by venture capital funds, and through them by the savers, are real options on future consumption of innovative goods and services explain the less than expected financial result. In a recent paper Driessen, Lin and Phalippou (2010) report what may appear as substantial underperformance by venture capital funds in terms of risk adjusted average rate of return measured over a long time and a large number of funds using the concept of the CAPM.

7.6 What makes venture capital attractive to defined benefit plans?

The argument developed above is appropriate for every institutional investor. Yet, almost all the investment in venture capital funds is coming from defined benefit plans. This goes against the grain of the popular view of venture capital funds as representing investment by high net worth risk taking capitalists. In reality venture capital funds in the US are funded by risk averse middle income consumers, many of whom are employed in the public sector (about 80 percent of the employees in the public sector are members (beneficiaries) in defined benefit plans).

Defined benefit plans have three main stakeholders: the employers who use them as a part of the benefits package to their employees; the employees who are the beneficiaries of the plan; and the government, particularly the federal government, which regards future consumption of retirees as an important social and political issue. The most relevant legislation pertaining to defined benefit plans is the ERISA of 1974. The other body of regulations and laws is the Federal Tax Code, as well as the bankruptcy law and relevant state laws. The most important federal agency in the field of defined benefit plans is the PBGC. All this structure is aimed at securing the payments to the beneficiaries, (the employees) once they retire according to the contract between them and their employers. In general, it can be said that the federal government and to a lesser extent states and other public sector employers guarantee the contracts between the employees and the employers.

The concern for the retirees of defined benefit plans by the federal government is expressed in the web page of PBGC, where it is stated that the mission of the agency (company) is to protect the retirement income of more than 44 million Americans (PBGC insures beneficiaries in private sector defined benefit plans). A report issued by the GAO ("General Accountability Office") of the US Government and submitted to the US Congress in August 2008 is another expression of the concern and to some extent the responsibility that the US Government feels toward the beneficiaries of the defined benefit plans.

Investment in innovation is regarded as a public responsibility in the European Union. In a report entitled "Financing Innovation and SME" (2009) that represents the official and professional view of the European Union the authors claim that it is the responsibility of the government to arrange and support financing for early stage innovation. In a publication of the National Institute on Retirement Security, Boivie and Almeida (2008) argue that the managers of defined benefit plans provide what the authors call "patience capital" to long-term investments and by doing so they contribute both to the community as a whole and to their beneficiaries. At the same time Boivie and Almeida say that most if not all the managers of defined benefit plans invest in private equity (including venture capital) as a way to achieve higher returns. The decision made by CalPERS, one of the largest managers of defined benefit plans, to allocate almost 15 percent per cent of its portfolio in 2011 in "Alternative Investment," an asset class that includes venture capital, is evidence that the trend reported by Boivie and Almeida in 2008 is still alive.

The tendency for high risk investment by the managers of defined benefit plans is supported by the insurance and other risk reduction official and unofficial programs by the US Government. These programs were developed in an effort to protect the beneficiary, but at the same time they help the financing of early stage revolutionary innovation by making it attractive to the managers of defined benefit plans to invest in venture capital funds. (Defined contribution funds hardly invest in venture capital funds.)

7.7 Conclusion

The public sector in the US in general and the federal government in particular have not intentionally used defined benefit plans as a way to finance innovation.

Yet, the explicit and the implicit "safety net" provided to defined benefit plans induce them to invest a small part of their assets in venture capital funds. What was and is a small asset class for the defined benefit plans is almost all the investment in venture funds in the US. A change in the structure of institutional savings in the US, like the ongoing change from defined benefit plans to defined contribution plans, and even more so a reduction in the protection against the downside in existing defined benefit plans, will have a substantial impact on the financing of venture capital funds and on the market for revolutionary innovative ideas.

References

Agmon, T., S. Gangopadhyay, and S. Sjogren, 2011, "Why are Venture Capital Funds Necessary for Promoting Innovation in Monopolistic Markets?," Center for Finance, School of Business, Economics and Law, Goteborg University.

Agüero, A. and H. de Silva, 2011, "Bottom of the Pyramid Expenditure Patterns on Mobile Phone Services in Selected Emerging Asia Countries," *Information Technologies and International Development*, 7–3, 19–32.

Bodie, Z., J. Treussard, and P. Willen, 2007, "The Theory of Life Cycle Savings and Investment," FRB, Boston.

Boivie, I. and B. Almeida, 2008, "Patience is a Virtue," Issue Brief, National Institute on Retirement Security, July.

Breeden, D. and R. Litzenberger, 1978, "Prices of State Contingent Claims Implicit in Option Prices," *Journal of Business*, 51, 621–51.

Chan, Y., 1983, "On the positive role of financial intermediation in allocation of venture capital in a market with imperfect information", *Journal of Finance*, Vol. 38, Issue 5, pp. 1543–1568.

Coval, J. and A. Thakor, 2005, "Financial Intermediation as a Belief Bridge Between Optimists and Pessimists," *Journal of Financial Economics*, 75–3, 535–69, March.

Driessen, J., T.S. Lin and L. Phalippou, 2010, "A New Method to Estimate Risk and Return of Non-Traded Assets from cash Flows: The Case of Private Equity Funds," NBER WP #W14144.

European Commission, 2009, "Financing Innovation and SMEs", pp. 1–24 http://ec.europa.eu/enterprise/policies/innovation/files/swd_financing_innovation.pdf.

Financing Innovation and SME, Staff Commission Report, The European Union, Brussels, 2009.

Friedman, M. and L. Savage, 1948, "The Utility Analysis of Choice Involving Risk," *Journal of Political Economy*, LVI 4, 279–304.

Fudenberg, D. and J. Tirole, 1984, "The Fat Cat Effect, the Puppy Dog Ploy and the Lean and Hungry Look," *American Economic Review*, 74–2, 361–66.

GAO Report, 2008, "Defined Benefit Pension Plans."

Gompers, P. and Lerner, J., 1998, "An analysis of compensation in the U.S. venture capital partnership", *Journal of Financial Economics*, Vol. 51, Issue 1, 3–44.

Kaiser, K. and C. Westarp, 2010, "Value Creation in the Private Equity and Venture Capital Industry" Faculty and Research Working Paper, INSEAD.

Merton, R.C., and Z. Bodie, 2005, "Design of Financial Systems: Towards a Synthesis of Function and Form," *Journal of Investment Management*, 3–1, 1–23.

Tonello, M. and S. Rabimov, 2010, "The 2010 Institutional Investment Report: Trends in Asset Allocation and Portfolio Composition," The Conference Board.

Warburg Pincus, 2010, "Perspectives on the Venture Capital 'Industry'".

8 Capital gains and entrepreneurial entry

*Victor Fleischer**

8.1 Introduction

Founders of a start-up usually receive common stock as a large portion of their compensation for current and future labor efforts. When structured correctly, founders' stock allows entrepreneurs to defer paying tax until they sell the stock and—more importantly—allows them to pay tax at the lower long-term capital gains rate.[1] While founders' stock[2] has some attributes of a long-term, risky investment, the founders' income nonetheless represents (mostly) a return on human capital rather than financial capital. As such, gain from the appreciation of founders' stock can also be thought of as labor income that would normally be treated as compensation for services rendered and taxed at ordinary income rates, just like other forms of compensation.[3] The tax treatment of founders' stock as investment income rather than labor income is what allows entrepreneurs to pay tax at a lower rate than ordinary employees or corporate executives.[4]

* Professor, University of San Diego Law School. This chapter is an abbreviated version of Victor Fleischer, *Taxing Founder's Stock*, 59 UCLA L. REV. 60 (2011).

1 The long-term capital gains rate is currently 15%. *See* I.R.C. § 1(h)(1)(C). Founders' stock sometimes qualifies for the special rate that applies to qualified small business stock under § 1202, which historically has allowed for exclusion of a percentage of gains measured from the ordinary income tax baseline, not taking deferral or inflation into account. The exclusion is available to both investors and founders. Recent legislation temporarily excludes up to US$10 million of gains from qualified small business stock. *See* American Taxpayer Relief Act of 2012, Pub. L. No. 112–240, § 324, 126 Stat. 2313 (extending temporary 100% exclusion under I.R.C. § 1202 to January 1, 2014). For simplicity, I assume in this chapter that the Qualified Small Business Stock (QSBS) rules will remain in place, but reference the long-term capital gains rate in the discussion. For analytic clarity, it helpful to assume that any policy change would exempt the first US$1 million (or US$10 million) of gains from tax; the more controversial question is whether additional gains should be taxed, and if so, at what rate.

2 The term "founders' stock" is not a technical term found in the tax code or legal documents. Rather, the term is widely used in the industry to distinguish between the stock issued to founders when they start a company and stock issued to investors in exchange for capital.

3 Executives who receive stock or stock options are typically taxed at ordinary rates on the value of the equity received at the time of grant or when the options are exercised. *See generally* §§ 61, 83. Employees who receive Incentive Stock Options (ISOs), are taxed at capital gains rates in limited circumstances.

4 The deferral and conversion of labor income into low-taxed capital gain is conceptually similar to the tax treatment of carried interest. See Victor Fleischer, *Two and Twenty: Taxing Partnership Profits in Private Equity Funds*, 83 NYU L. REV. 1 (2008) (critiquing ability of investment fund managers to

This tax break for founders results from a *valuation wedge* created when a start-up receives outside financing. By capitalizing the company with two classes of stock, common and preferred, founders take the low-value common stock in exchange for their performance of future services and report only a nominal amount of ordinary income. In many cases, this planning strategy relies on a timing gambit offered as an unintended consequence of a 1969 amendment to the tax code. The amendment, codified as Section 83, curbed the abusive deferral of income from restricted stock awards to corporate executives.[5] Under this regime, executives of most companies now pay tax at ordinary income rates when they receive stock awards; they pay capital gains tax (or recognize capital losses) only on later changes in the stock price. By treating the receipt of stock as a taxable event when the stock is vested,[6] Section 83 normally makes it impossible to both defer service income and convert that service income into capital gain. But Section 83 also contains an election—the Section 83(b) election—which allows executives to accelerate their recognition of ordinary income on restricted stock to the time of the award, even if their ownership of the stock is subject to vesting or other restrictions.[7]

The Section 83(b) election allows founders to take advantage of the valuation wedge created when investors buy stock to finance the company's operations.[8] If advised by competent counsel, founders routinely make the Section 83(b) election, accelerating the ordinary income portion of the tax hit to the point in time where

convert labor income into capital gains). The economic subsidy argument is plausible for founders; it is implausible to think that an economic subsidy is necessary to produce an adequate supply of private equity fund managers. Fund managers appear to be adequately compensated by the private labor market.

5 See Senate Report 91–552, 1969–3 Cum. Bull. 500 ("The present law treatment of restricted stock plans is significantly more generous than the treatment specifically provided in the law for other types of similarly funded deferred compensation arrangements."). See also *id.* at 500–01 ("To the extent that a restricted stock plan can be considered a means of giving employees a stake in the business, the committee believes the present tax treatment of these plans is inconsistent with the specific rules provided by Congress in the case of qualified stock options, which were considered by Congress as the appropriate means by which an employee could be given a shareholder's interest in the business.").

6 Section 83(a) imposes tax when the stock is vested ("not subject to a substantial risk of forfeiture") or transferable, whichever occurs earlier. For ease of exposition, I assume that stock which is vested is not subject to other continuing conditions or restrictions that might allow further deferral under § 83.

Founders' stock usually vests over a period of three to five years. In the language of § 83, stock which is "not subject to a substantial risk of forfeiture" is treated as property that was transferred to the employee in exchange for services, and thus subject to tax at ordinary rates like other forms of compensation.

7 The § 83(b) election was intended to provide flexibility, allowing employees to treat the stock award as compensation in the year it was received. See Senate Report 91–552, 1969–3 Cum. Bull. 502 ("To add flexibility, the committee adopted a provision allowing recipients of restricted property the option of treating it as compensation in the year it is received, even though it is nontransferable and subject to a substantial risk of forfeiture."). To guard against gamesmanship, the stock must be valued as if it were unrestricted, and the employer's deduction is limited to the amount included by the employee as income. Furthermore, the employee receives no basis in the stock for purposes of measuring loss on forfeiture; if the property is forfeited, no deduction is allowed.

8 The valuation wedge is created by issuing convertible preferred stock to the investors while the founders retain common stock. *See infra* Section 8.2.

the value of the company is speculative and arguably worthless—the proverbial founding moment when two engineers with an idea start working out of a Silicon Valley garage.[9] By making the election, the founders transform their compensation for future services into capital gain on the appreciation of the stock. Founders are taxed at ordinary income rates only on the liquidation value of the stock, which happens to be zero. The appreciation potential or "option value" of the common stock (its only real value at that point) is not taxed until the "option" is eventually exercised and the stock sold, and even then it is only taxed at capital gains rates.[10] By contrast, an actual stock option would give rise to ordinary income.[11]

Founders' stock—not high executive salaries and bonuses—accounts for a significant part of the growing inequality of wealth in the United States. But policymakers from both sides of the aisle rationalize the tax subsidy as a critical feature of the legal infrastructure of entrepreneurship. President Obama's new initiative on entrepreneurship, for example, would permanently exempt the first US$10 million of gains from founders' stock and would tax additional gains at a 15 percent rate, as under current law.[12] Many academics agree with this approach. In a recent *Harvard Law Review* article, Professors Ron Gilson and David Schizer argued that the favorable tax treatment of founders' stock is a well designed subsidy for entrepreneurship.[13] Their article was descriptive, not normative: they argued that the founders' stock subsidy explains the venture capitalists' (VCs') use of convertible preferred stock. Given this analytic focus, they chose not consider whether the tax break for founders was normatively justified in the first place.[14] This chapter takes a step back analytically and answers the question that Gilson and Schizer set aside: *Should* founders be taxed at a low rate?

9 For the history of the garage where Bill Hewlett and Dave Packard started their company, *see HP Garage*, available at http://www8.hp.com/us/en/hp-information/about-hp/history/hp-garage/hp-garage.html

10 Common stock of a firm with a large amount of debt or senior equity performs economically like a call option. Fisher Black & Myron S. Scholes, *The Pricing of Options and Corporate Liabilities*, 81 J. POL. ECON. 637, 649 (1973).

11 Nonqualified stock options give rise to ordinary income when exercised. ISOs can achieve tax results similar to founders' stock, subject to limitations. See § 422.

12 See Fiscal Year 2012 Budget of the U.S. Government 161, available at http://www.whitehouse.gov/files/documents/budget_2012.pdf ("the Administration proposes to permanently extend the Acts provision eliminating all capital gains taxes on investments in small business stock in order to enhance the flow of capital to small businesses"); Fact Sheet: White House Launches "Startup America" Initiative, *available at* http://www.whitehouse.gov/startup-america-fact-sheet.

13 Ronald J. Gilson & David M. Schizer, *Understanding Venture Capital Structure: A Tax Explanation for Convertible Preferred Stock*, 116 HARV. L. REV. 874, 909–15 (2003) (highlighting valuation rules as subsidy); *id.* at 910 ("Specifically, the government's tolerance of aggressively low valuations might be understood as a form of tax subsidy for high-tech startups, targeted at a critical feature of the venture capital contracting process: the high-intensity performance incentives provided to managers of early-stage companies. The IRS allows a substantial portion of a high-tech startup manager's compensation—in effect, wages for services—to be taxed as capital gain, instead of as ordinary income.").

14 *Id.* at 910 ("We take no position here about the wisdom of this goal . . ."); *id.* at 915 ("Ultimately, though, our point here is not to advocate particular forms of venture capital subsidies; indeed, we have not addressed the substantive case for a subsidy at all. Rather, we want only to highlight the unusual characteristics of the indirect subsidy that has developed.").

While this chapter focuses on the possible efficiency justification for taxing founders at a low rate, principles of distributive justice explain why we should care about the issue. The tax treatment of founders' stock is a conspicuous loophole in the fabric of the progressive income tax, allowing the very wealthiest Americans to pay tax at a low rate. Most of the Forbes 400[15] accumulated their wealth in the form of lightly-taxed founders' stock, or through founders' stock inherited with a stepped-up tax basis. The top ten on the most recent list, for example, includes no athletes, movie stars, lawyers, doctors, investment bankers, or fund managers—only founders and their heirs.[16]

The recurring fights about raising marginal ordinary income tax rates on the rich have little relevance for this privileged group of founders and heirs, as the income they enjoy comes from the sale of stock taxed at lower long-term capital gains rates. Increasing the tax rate on gains from founders' stock would raise significant revenue and induce larger amounts of charitable giving. As it stands, this entrepreneurial wealth is taxed at a low rate or not at all, allowing founders to leave behind a legacy of dynastic wealth subject only to the rather dodgy application of the estate tax.

It is clear that founders are taxed differently than most other providers of human capital. This chapter thus focuses on whether founders *should* be taxed differently than ordinary employees and executives. Founders and VCs argue that entrepreneurial wealth is different from all other forms of wealth.[17] Concerns about distributive justice and inequality should be set aside, they argue, in light of the new jobs created by entrepreneurship. Successful new companies do not merely make founders rich; these new firms ignite the dynamic capitalism that enriches all of us.[18] This narrative appeals to our collective aspiration to a society marked by resourcefulness, creativity, imagination, ambition, and class mobility. The problem is that the story does not logically lead

15 The Forbes 400 is a popular business magazine's annual list of the richest Americans. While hardly a perfect dataset, it is often used in academic research as a useful proxy for the very top of the wealth scale. *See, e.g.*, Wojciech Kopczuk & Emmanuel Saez, *Top Wealth Shares in the United States, 1916–2000: Evidence from Estate Tax Returns*, 57 NAT'L TAX J. 445, 482 (2004).

16 The top 10 are Bill Gates (Microsoft), Warren Buffett (Berkshire Hathaway), Larry Ellison (Oracle), Michael Bloomberg (Bloomberg), two Koches (Koch Industries), and four Waltons (Walmart). See *The 400 Richest Americans 2009*, FORBES.COM, *available at* http://www.forbes.com/lists/2009/10/billionaires-2009-richest-people_The-Worlds-Billionaires_Rank/.html (site last visited Sept. 13, 2010).

17 For a similar argument, *see* David A. Weisbach, *The Taxation of Carried Interests in Private Equity*, 94 VA. L. REV. 715, n.70 ("[T]he more entrepreneurial the activity, the more likely the treatment will be capital. . . . [s]elf-created assets, including, significantly, patents under §1235, get capital gains treatment. An inventor who puts in many hours of labor gets capital gains treatment when the invention is sold. A proprietor who raises capital to start a business and uses his expertise and labor to build the business receives capital gains when he sells the business. Similarly, founders of companies get capital gains treatment when they sell their shares, even if the gains are attributable to labor income. For example, most, if not all, of Bill Gates's fortune comes from his performing services for Microsoft, but the overwhelming majority of his earnings from Microsoft will be taxed as capital gains.").

18 William J. Baumol and others, GOOD CAPITALISM, BAD CAPITALISM, AND THE ECONOMICS OF GROWTH AND PROSPERITY (Yale University Press 2007).

to the conclusion that founders should pay tax at a lower rate than other employees.[19]

In places like Silicon Valley, Austin, Seattle, and Boulder, it is a matter of faith that a low tax rate on founders' stock increases the number of venture-backed entrepreneurs. Despite years of searching and multiple studies, however, economists offer little empirical support for the claim.[20] The evidence instead suggests that tax policy has only a small marginal effect on entrepreneurial entry.[21] The effect, rather, is mostly inframarginal: the tax benefit goes mainly to entrepreneurs who would have started businesses anyway. Nor is there empirical evidence suggesting that those who might be influenced, on the margins, are the "right" kind of entrepreneurs who create growth businesses with positive externalities.[22] Tax policy did not lead Zuckerberg, Gates, Jobs or Ellison to start companies. Economic theory and empirical studies show that tax policy is less important than geographic,[23] cultural, and environmental factors.[24] Moreover, tax policy is less important than other elements of the legal infrastructure, such as intellectual property law,[25] immigration law, bankruptcy law,[26] securities law,[27] the Employee Retirement Income Security Act of 1974 (ERISA),[28] and employment law.[29]

The best normative justification for the status quo is what conservatives might call a *tax version of the precautionary principle*: in the absence of academic consensus or conclusive data proving that eliminating a tax subsidy would not harm the valuable activity in question, the burden of proof is on those who would eliminate

19 I am not making a claim about whether entrepreneurship should or should not be subsidized. If the government wants to subsidize entrepreneurship, however, tax policy may not be the optimal instrument.

20 *See, e.g.,* James M. Poterba, *Capital Gains Tax Policy and Entrepreneurship*, 42 NAT'L TAX J. 375, 379 (finding "very little support" for the claim that entrepreneurial activity declined following the steep rise in the capital gains tax rate in 1986). For further discussion of the empirical evidence, *see infra* Section 8.3.2.

21 *See infra* Section 8.3.2.

22 *Id.*

23 AnnaLee Saxenian, REGIONAL ADVANTAGE: CULTURE AND COMPETITION IN SILICON VALLEY AND ROUTE 128 (Harvard University Press 1994).

24 *See* Baumol, *supra* note 18.

25 *See, e.g.,* Brett M. Frischmann & Mark A. Lemley, *Spillovers*, 107 COLUM. L. REV. 257, 258 (2007) ("Spillovers do not always interfere with incentives to invest; in some cases, spillovers actually drive further innovation.").

26 *See, e.g.,* Kenneth Ayotte, *Bankruptcy and Entrepreneurship: The Value of a Fresh Start*, 23 J. L. ECON. ORG. 161, 179 (2007) ("In particular, social gains can be made from bankruptcy law that offers entrepreneurs an opportunity for a fresh start—a second chance to succeed that would otherwise be encumbered by debt obligations carried over from its previous failure.").

27 *See, e.g.,* Ehud Kamar, Pinar Karaca-Mandic & Eric Talley, *Going-Private Decisions and the Sarbanes-Oxley Act of* 2002, 25 J. L. ECON. ORG. 107, 108 (using evidence of going private decisions to show that Sarbanes Oxley Act of 2002 puts small firms at a disadvantage).

28 Paul Gompers & Josh Lerner, *The Venture Capital Revolution*, 15 J. ECON. PERSP. 145, 148 (2001) (noting importance of Department of Labor's 1979 clarification of "prudent man" rule to allow pension fund managers to invest in high-risk assets as part of a diversified portfolio).

29 Ronald J. Gilson, *The Legal Infrastructure of High Technology Industrial Districts: Silicon Valley, Route 128, and Covenants Not to Compete*, 74 N.Y.U. L. REV. 575, 578 ("I suggest here an alternative explanation for the two districts' differing efficiency at transferring knowledge between firms: differences in the districts' legal infrastructures, particularly the rules governing the enforceability of postemployment covenants not to compete.").

the subsidy. This rationale for a lower tax rate is at odds, however, with the usual tax policy baseline that the most efficient tax system is one with a broad base and lower rates. Still, if one takes the view that entrepreneurship is both fragile and valuable, and more easily fractured by taxation than other desirable economic activities, a tax version of the precautionary principle is a plausible normative justification.

While I conclude that it would be normatively desirable to eliminate the tax subsidy and instead tax gains from founders' stock as labor income, I concede that fixing the problem is not administratively feasible within our current tax system.[30] I conclude that because of the administrative challenges associated with implementing reform under the current system, the structural distortion created by taxing founders at a low rate would be best addressed as part of a broader fundamental tax reform effort.

8.2 The tax treatment of founders' stock

Suppose two entrepreneurs, Mark and Eduardo,[31] form a new start-up, NewCo. Mark and Eduardo locate outside equity investors—VCs—to finance the new venture.[32] The founders contribute no tangible assets and only US$25,000 of financial capital. Their primary contribution is human capital: their experience, their technical expertise and knowhow, and an implicit promise of future services to the company. They also contribute what might be called intellectual capital—the idea for the new business and related intellectual property.

The VCs contribute US$5 million to NewCo in exchange for stock. The VCs' primary contribution is money, but they also provide nonmonetary contributions: they take seats on the board of directors, obtain various control rights and negative covenants to ensure themselves a seat at the table, and in doing so they make an implicit promise to provide management advice and mentorship to Mark and Eduardo. Finally, the VCs make an implicit promise to participate in later rounds of financing if the company meets certain milestones.

With this venture capital investment in mind, Mark and Eduardo organize NewCo as a corporation rather than a partnership or limited liability company (LLC).[33] While similar economic arrangements can be made using an LLC, some

30 For a discussion of reform options, *see* Victor Fleischer, *Taxing Founders' Stock*, 59 UCLA L. REV. 60, 68–9 (2011).

31 THE SOCIAL NETWORK (Columbia Pictures 2010).

32 Start-ups often take on debt as well; the introduction of debt into the capital structure does not normally affect the tax issues discussed herein. For more on the debt financing of venture-backed companies, *see* Darian M. Ibrahim, *Debt as Venture Capital*, 2010 U. ILL. L. REV. 1169, 1176–80 (describing venture lenders).

33 Victor Fleischer, *The Rational Exuberance of Structuring Venture Capital Start-ups*, 57 TAX L. REV. 137, 137 (2004) ("A typical start-up is organized as a corporation under state law, which means that it is treated as a separate entity from its owners for tax purposes. If a start-up instead were organized as a partnership or limited liability company (LLC), it could elect pass-through treatment for tax purposes."). Joseph Bankman, *The Structure of Silicon Valley Start-Ups*, 41 UCLA L. REV. 1737, 1738 (1994).

practical drawbacks associated with LLCs keep the C Corporation entrenched as the industry-standard form.[34] The equity investment of both the founders and the VCs therefore takes the form of stock rather than partnership interests.

Mark and Eduardo take common stock—subject to new vesting requirements imposed by the VCs—while the VCs receive newly-issued convertible preferred stock. Both tax and nontax motivations determine the structure of the deal. From a business standpoint, the VCs need a structure that addresses the critical transaction costs that pose a barrier to contracting—chiefly, the information asymmetry between the founders and the investors and the strategic behavior risk that results from letting the founders build a company with someone else's money.[35] The liquidation preference of the preferred stock performs this role, protecting the VCs' investment in the start-up if things go badly. The liquidation preference also ensures that only founders who expect a start-up to generate an extraordinary return on investment will accept VC money on these terms. Founders of a slow-growth business, by contrast, will seek financing from banks, or friends and family, or they will bootstrap using cash generated by the business itself. The conversion feature of the convertible preferred stock allows the VCs to convert into common stock and participate in residual profits if things go well.[36]

The use of convertible preferred stock also facilitates tax planning. Specifically, using a separate class of stock allows the founders to create a valuation wedge and to report a low (or nil) valuation on their common stock.[37] To illustrate, imagine a simpler structure in which both the founders and the VCs take common stock. Suppose the VCs invest US$5 million into NewCo in exchange for 1 million shares of NewCo common stock, which comprises one-third of the common stock outstanding after the investment. Mark and Eduardo retain one million shares each, or two-thirds of the total common stock. On these facts, NewCo would have an implied pre-money valuation of US$10 million, and a post-money valuation of US$15 million. If the VCs' shares are worth US$5 million, or US$5 per share—a price negotiated at arm's length—each founder's common shares, if unrestricted, would arguably also be worth the same amount. Because each founder received this stock in exchange for the performance of current and future services, each would face a huge tax bill for services they have yet to perform.[38] If, as is typical, the stock is restricted and vests over a four-year period, the valuation of the founders' common would be lower at the outset, and

34 Fleischer, *supra* note 33, at 139 ("Partnerships are, on paper, more tax-efficient than corporations. But various "frictions"—nontax business costs such as transaction costs, information problems, reputational concerns, and adverse accounting treatment—currently prevent deal planners from using the theoretically tax-favorable form."); *id.*

35 Ronald J. Gilson, *Engineering a Venture Capital Market: Lessons from the American Experience*, 55 STAN. L. REV. 1067 (2003).

36 Sometimes early stage investors use convertible debt, which performs economically much like convertible preferred stock.

37 *See* Ronald J. Gilson & David M. Schizer, *Understanding Venture Capital Structure: A Tax Explanation for Convertible Preferred Stock*, 116 HARV. L. REV. 874 (2003).

38 Section 83(a) requires the service provider to recognize the value of property received without regard to restrictions on transferability.

realization of the income would be deferred until the restrictions lapse. But the character of the income would be ordinary and would be recognized as it vests, even if there is no cash available to pay the tax.

The use of convertible preferred stock avoids this punitive result. Section 83 governs the timing of the taxation of property exchanged for services. The section was enacted in 1969 to address gamesmanship with restricted stock; companies were paying executives in stock and putting restrictions on the stock so executives could defer recognition of tax until they sold the stock, at which point they reported capital gains on the appreciation of the stock. Section 83 counters this gambit by giving executives a choice. Either:

(1) the executives treat the exchange as an *open transaction* under Section 83(a) until the stock is unrestricted, at which point they report the then current market value of the stock as ordinary income (less any amount originally paid for the stock), or
(2) they elect under Section 83(b) to treat the exchange as a *closed transaction*, recognizing ordinary income immediately on the value of the stock (without regard to restrictions, and less any amount paid for the stock), in which case any appreciation in the stock is capital gain, and any loss is a capital loss.

The idea behind Section 83 is that executives can defer tax until they own the stock free and clear, or they can pay capital gain on the appreciation in the value of the stock in the interim, but they cannot do both.

So how do founders, unlike other corporate executives, get *both* deferral and conversion? The VCs' use of convertible preferred stock allows the founders to make a Section 83(b) election and artificially accelerate the recognition of income to the very beginning of the company—a point in time when the Internal Revenue Service (IRS) is in no position to challenge the low valuation of the founders' common stock. In our example, Mark contributes US$25,000 worth of software code and Eduardo contributes US$25,000 cash. Each makes the Section 83(b) election and reports that amount as the fair value of the common stock received. Mark and Eduardo therefore recognize no ordinary income at all. At the same time, they secure venture financing. In exchange for the US$5 million investment, the VCs take convertible preferred stock in NewCo. From that point forward, the founders are treated like other investors in the company, with gains and losses treated as capital, not ordinary income.[39]

39 If the § 83(b) property is sold at a loss, and the property is a capital asset in the hands of the taxpayer, the loss is a capital loss. If the property is forfeited while substantially nonvested, however, the loss is limited to the amount paid for the property over any amount realized through the forfeiture. See Treas. Reg. § 1.83–2(a). In the founders' stock scenario, the § 83(b) election is always made unless omitted by oversight. See Matt Galligan, *To 83(b) or Not to 83(b), There Is No Question*, *in* David Cohen & Brad Feld, DO MORE FASTER (2010) (reporting his costly oversight of the 83(b) election as a first-time entrepreneur). The founders hold their shares of NewCo as they vest and appreciate in value, but recognize no income until there is a sale or other disposition of the stock.

The loophole arises because the common stock has no current liquidation value. In economic terms, each founder holds the equivalent of an at-the-money or out-of-the-money call option on one-third of the assets of the firm.[40] Unlike an actual stock option, however, which would generate ordinary income to the service providers once exercised,[41] the founders convert the character of the income into capital gain by taking common stock with nominal liquidation value and then making the Section 83(b) election.[42] The use of convertible preferred stock thus creates a regulatory arbitrage opportunity by exploiting the difference between the liquidation value and option value of the common stock.[43] For tax purposes, founders report the liquidation value of the stock, adding only a nominal amount for the option value. Because NewCo stock is privately-held, valuation is more art than science, and one practitioner has noted that the IRS has never successfully challenged a founder's valuation of common stock under these circumstances.[44]

40 If the value of the firm (which currently holds US$5 million in cash) were to increase to US$8 million, Mark and Eduardo would each receive US$1 million in liquidation. The preferred stock would receive the first US$5 million, and it would then participate in further distributions on an as-converted basis, which would give the VCs, Mark and Eduardo a one-third each claim on the US$3 million of assets remaining in the firm. The payout to each founder is equivalent to buying one-third of the assets of the firm (US$2.66 million) for the strike price of US$1.66 million, netting US$1 million.

41 Section 83(e)(3); Treas. Reg. § 1.83–7. The amount of ordinary income would be the value of the stock less any amount paid (*i.e.*, the strike price of the option).

42 The irony is that § 83 was intended to reduce tax-motivated structuring of executive compensation. The 83(b) election, which permits founders to elect to value the stock within 30 days of issuance and treat the stock grant as a closed transaction, was designed for operating companies, not start-ups. With seasoned companies, the fact that the § 83(b) election accelerates the recognition of ordinary income acts as a check against gamesmanship.

43 One might wonder why this common-preferred structure is so prevalent in venture capital start-ups but not elsewhere. The reason is that the arbitrage opportunity is only valuable under specific conditions: (1) the company must be organized as a corporation; (2) the option value of the common stock must be significantly greater than the liquidation value of the stock; (3) the employer's tax rate is lower than the employee's tax rate; and (4) the company cannot be publicly-traded or otherwise have a readily ascertainable fair market value. It is worth noting, then, that the founders' stock "loophole" is also available to other executives, including the executives or privately-held portfolio companies of private equity funds.

44 See Joseph W. Bartlett, EQUITY FINANCE: VENTURE CAPITAL, BUYOUTS, RESTRUCTURINGS AND REORGANIZATIONs, Vol 1., at 82 (2d ed. 1995). It is not self-evident to me that this tax strategy—known as the "cheap stock" or "thin common" strategy—actually works under current law. Treasury Regulation § 1.83–3(a)(1) states that a transfer of property for § 83 purposes takes place "when a person acquires a beneficial ownership interest in such property." While the founders have several indicia of ownership, such as voting rights and claims on residual cash flows, the regulations go on to explain that the grant of an option does not constitute a transfer of property, and in certain circumstances where the stock grant "may be in substance the same as the grant of an option," § 83 will not apply. See Treas. Reg. § 1.83–3(a)(2); (a)(4) ("An indication that no transfer has occurred is the extent to which the conditions relating to a transfer are similar to an option."); (a)(6) (risk of loss); (a)(7), Example (5) (stock grant equivalent to an at-the-money call option recharacterized as an option). If § 83 does not apply, the stock grant would instead be treated as an open transaction, and founders would recognize ordinary income when the stock is later sold. A substance over form challenge under the § 83 regulations would not require the IRS to prove a specific valuation; rather, all the government would have to show is that, under the facts and circumstances, the stock grant resembles an at-the-money or out-of-the-money call option. The IRS' practice of not challenging this structure, however, is consistent with its administrative

8.3 The efficiency case

What happens if we consider the optimal tax rate on founders' stock from an efficiency perspective? Ideal income tax analysis starts from the baseline that all income should be taxed equally regardless of source, thus allowing the broadest base of income and the lowest possible overall rates. Policymakers may wish to depart from the ideal, however, for administrative reasons or to promote social policy goals. If an activity generates positive externalities, for example, a lower tax rate on that activity could make everyone better off.

8.3.1 Entrepreneurial entry

The economic literature supports the view that entrepreneurship creates positive externalities. In *Good Capitalism, Bad Capitalism*, Baumol, Litan & Schramm make a persuasive case that entrepreneurship is a key component to a dynamic, growth-friendly economy.[45] They identify the key attributes of the "entrepreneurial capitalism" of the United States, with its combination of bold innovation by small firms and incremental innovation by large firms.[46] They argue that entrepreneurial capitalism creates more long-term economic growth, prosperity, and advancement of democratic values than the state-guided capitalism of Southeast Asia, the oligarchic capitalism of Latin America, Russia and the Gulf states, or the big firm capitalism of Continental Europe and Japan.[47] In the same vein, other economic research suggests that most new, lasting jobs are created by start-ups and rapidly growing firms, not by large, established firms.[48]

The need to subsidize entrepreneurship and encourage entrepreneurial entry is often cited as a reason for taxing capital gains at a lower rate.[49] The theoretical case is straightforward. If founders' stock is taxed at a lower rate than wages, then the tax system encourages workers, on the margins, to become entrepreneurs. Moreover, because the tax benefits accrue only to successful entrepreneurs, the tax system provides this subsidy only to workers who gauge that they have a reasonable likelihood of success if they go out and start a company.

The problem is that the empirical support for the tax subsidy argument is weak. Anecdotal evidence makes one skeptical that tax is of first-order importance; most entrepreneurs keep a steely focus on questions of technology,

practice in other similar situations, and the IRS practice of nonenforcement presumably gives sufficient comfort to practitioners who advise founders to report a zero value on the stock. Common stock can always be bifurcated into liquidation and option value, thus giving all stock grants some degree of option resemblance. A significant risk of loss, however, is sufficient to make the stock grant qualify as a "transfer" for purposes of § 83. See Treas. Reg. § 1.83–3(a)(6).

45 Baumol, *supra* note 18, at 85–92.

46 *Id.*

47 *Id.* at 60–85.

48 Scott A. Shane, ACADEMIC ENTREPRENEURSHIP: UNIVERSITY SPINOFFS AND WEALTH CREATION 21–22 (Edward Elgar 2004); Bruce A. Kirchhoff & Bruce D. Phillips, *The Effect of Firm Formation and Growth on Job Creation in the United States*, 3 J. BUS. VENTURING 261, 268 (1988).

49 William M. Gentry & R. Glenn Hubbard, *Tax Policy and Entrepreneurial Entry*, 90 AER PAPERS & PROCEEDINGS 283 (2000).

customers, and business models, not tax. The effect of the tax subsidy is mostly inframarginal, rewarding entrepreneurs for activity they would have conducted anyway.[50] However, one cannot dismiss the likelihood that tax has some effect at the margins, as it undoubtedly would if the tax rate on founders' stock were increased to 100 percent.[51]

8.3.1.1 Defining entrepreneurship

Several factors make it difficult to draw firm conclusions about the relationship between tax and entrepreneurial entry. First, because of the way that tax data is reported, it is difficult to distinguish between: (1) entrepreneurs, and (2) the self-employed who work for themselves because no one else will hire them. The recent recession has created a boom in "entrepreneurship" as the unemployed and underemployed do what they can to eke out a living. But there is little evidence that this sort of accidental entrepreneurship leads to the same sort of bold innovation and positive knowledge spillovers that venture-backed start-ups are said to promote.[52] Defining entrepreneurship is a vexing problem in the economic literature, which typically counts as an entrepreneur anyone who is self-employed. Ironically, this definition *excludes* founders, the very group that we presumably ought to care about the most from a capital gains tax policy perspective. (Founders usually work for an externally-financed start-up corporation, not for themselves.)

In a recent article, for example, Professors Gentry and Hubbard provide a theoretical model and empirical support for the proposition that increasing the progressivity of the income tax discourages entrepreneurial entry.[53] But by relying on self-employment as the relevant measure of entrepreneurial entry, their study tells us little about the optimal tax rate on founders' stock. All it tells us is that the behavior of people *other than* founders is sometimes responsive to tax rates. Moreover, as they concede, "whether such encouragement [of entrepreneurial entry] is efficient (that is, stimulating the most talented entrepreneurs)" is not yet known.[54]

8.3.1.2 A blunt device

Second, as economist James Poterba has emphasized, cutting the capital gains rate is a relatively blunt device for subsidizing entrepreneurship.[55] Poterba notes that the capital gains rate, while relevant to founders, is not relevant to tax-exempt

50 *Cf.* Norway, *available at* http://www.inc.com/magazine/20110201/in-norway-start-ups-say-ja-to-socialism.html.

51 A higher tax rate does not necessarily dampen economic activity, as investors may scale up investment to offset the expected tax implications of gains and losses. Importantly, however, the U.S. tax system imposes substantial restrictions on tax losses, and this asymmetric treatment of gains and losses means that tax tends to discourage investment in risky activities.

52 Scott A. Shane, ILLUSIONS OF ENTREPRENEURSHIP (Yale University Press 2008).

53 Gentry & Hubbard, *supra* note 49.

54 *Id.*

55 James M. Poterba, *Capital Gains Tax Policy Toward Entrepreneurship*, 42 NAT'L TAX J. 375 (1989).

investors who provide most of the investment capital to the sector. And he notes that less than one-third of reported capital gains are the result of corporate equity, and only a small fraction of the gains on equity are related to venture capital investments.[56] The strongest evidence of tax-sensitivity among entrepreneurs is based on interview data from the 1960s, when top marginal ordinary income rates ranged from 70 to 91 percent. In 1986, by contrast, when the capital gains preference was briefly eliminated, the various data series "provide very little support for the view that the supply of entrepreneurial activity declined" in the two years following the elimination of the tax subsidy.[57]

8.3.1.3 Knowledge of institutional detail and tax law

Third, the tax code is complicated, and economists may not always fully grasp how it applies in practice. The problem is even more acute in the field of entrepreneurship, where knowledge of the practices of venture capital contracting is relevant to the tax issues. One recent article, for example, investigates the relationship between taxes and entrepreneurial risk-taking, concluding that tax is of first-order importance.[58] But the model and empirical data in that paper are based on the assumption that unsuccessful firms retain pass-through tax status (so as to pass through losses to taxable individual investors) and successful firms incorporate only once they have profits, using the lower corporate tax rate as a tax shelter. The authors exploit this "option to incorporate" to draw their conclusions about the effect of tax on entrepreneurial activity. They claim that "start-up firms almost invariably are noncorporate,"[59] and they use, as their measure of entrepreneurial firms, firms with noncorporate business losses.[60] But the devil is in the institutional detail. The study tells us nothing about venture capital backed start-ups, which are almost always organized as corporations, not partnerships or LLCs.[61] Their measure of entrepreneurial firms perfectly *excludes* the group of entrepreneurs that, from a tax policy standpoint, we might want to subsidize. In sum, the design of empirical research in this area is hampered by data sets that cannot distinguish between the founder of a start-up and the self-employed, and research questions are often muddied by the institutional detail of venture capital contracting against the backdrop of a complicated tax code.

56 *Id.*

57 *Id.*

58 Julie Berry Cullen & Roger H. Gordon, *Taxes and entrepreneurial risk-taking: Theory and evidence for the U.S.*, 91 J. PUB. ECON. 1479 (2007).

59 *Id.* at 1487.

60 *Id.* at 1487 ("Only the high-risk firms are likely to generate ex post losses, so these entrepreneurial firms should dominate the sample of firms with tax losses. . . . Second, by the theory, business losses should (mostly) show up on the tax return as noncorporate business losses.").

61 *See* Bankman, *supra* note 33, Fleischer, *supra* note 33.

8.3.1.4 Deferral

Finally, deferral provides another reason to think that the nominal tax rate on founders' stock may not be of first-order importance to entrepreneurs. Gains from founders' stock are usually deferred for several years, and this deferral benefit lowers the effective tax rate substantially. Changing the nominal capital gains rate thus has a muted effect on ex ante incentives.[62] Indeed, it is hard to imagine that an entrepreneur, trying to figure out how to find money and form a team to commercialize a new technology for a customer market that does not exist yet, spends a lot of time thinking about whether their tax rate will be 20 percent or 40 percent when they sell their stock five or 10 or 20 years down the road in the unlikely event they achieve a "home run" return.[63]

8.3.1.5 First-order effects

Many other factors, meanwhile, are of first-order importance to the rate of entrepreneurial entry. Perhaps the most important is geography. Entrepreneurship flourishes where tacit knowledge can flow freely—thus the prevalence of concentrated entrepreneurship hubs in places like Silicon Valley, Boston, the Research Triangle in North Carolina, and Austin.[64] Geographic concentration of entrepreneurship is often industry-specific, as with biotechnology start-ups in San Diego, or natural foods and social networking start-ups in Boulder.

Cultural factors are important. The Silicon Valley entrepreneur is a revered figure in the United States. The number of undergraduates majoring in business has climbed in the last generation from 14 to 22 percent; at the same time, the numbers of those majoring in the humanities dropped from a total of 30 percent to less than 16 percent.[65] While the decline of Great Books from the curricula of U.S. universities may not be an altogether positive development, it does reflect a broad aspiration towards entrepreneurship and business success that exceeds most other countries. An open attitude towards change is important even among those who work for large firms. Amar Bhide has emphasized the role of innovative users in the infrastructure of entrepreneurship—the number of hours that U.S. employees have spent figuring out how to use Microsoft Outlook, for example, represents a significantly larger investment in the innovation than the underlying technological advance.[66]

62 *See* Poterba, *supra* note 20.

63 If one assumes that the first US$1 million, or US$10 million, of capital gains is exempt, it becomes even less likely that the entrepreneur makes this calculation.

64 *See* Saxenian, *supra* note 23; Gilson, *supra* note 29.

65 William M. Chase, *The Decline of the English Department*, THE AMERICAN SCHOLAR, Autumn 2009, *available at* http://www.theamericanscholar.org/the-decline-of-the-english-department/.

66 Amar Bhide, THE VENTURESOME ECONOMY (2008). See also Edward Glaeser, TRIUMPH OF THE CITY: HOW OUR GREATEST INVENTION MAKES US RICHER, SMARTER, GREENER, HEALTHIER AND HAPPIER (Penguin Press 2011); Edward L. Glaeser, *Entrepreneurship and the City* (Harvard University Working Paper 2007).

8.3.1.6 Legal infrastructure

Other elements of the legal infrastructure appear to be more important than tax. Having strong intellectual property rights may be critical to entrepreneurship.[67] Bankruptcy law is important to entrepreneurship; the ability to get a fresh start if things do not turn out well may give founders the confidence to borrow money on their credit cards to get the company going.[68] Employment law may be important; Ron Gilson has attributed Silicon Valley's success in part to the nonenforceability of noncompete clauses in California—thereby allowing the transfer of tacit knowledge from one firm to another.[69] Finally, securities law is often cited as a hindrance to entrepreneurship.[70]

Of all of the elements of the legal infrastructure, a change in ERISA has proven to be the most important change of all. In 1978, the Department of Labor (which oversees pension plans subject to ERISA) modified the prudent investor doctrine to allow trustees to invest in alternative asset classes like private equity and venture capital.[71] The flood of investment capital into the sector in the 1980s created the venture capital industry we have today.

Against this backdrop, it is difficult to see how the nominal rate of tax on capital gains would greatly affect the rate of entrepreneurial entry. The strongest argument to the contrary, I think, is that because the empirical record is so thin, there is much we do not know about the relationship between taxes and entrepreneurship. Perhaps, one could argue, if the costs of setting the tax rate too high (a reduction in entrepreneurship) are so much worse than the costs of setting the tax rate too low (increased inequality) then we should apply the tax precautionary principle[72] and err on the side of lower taxes. There might also be some merit in an approach that exempts the first US$1 million (or US$10 million) of gains from tax.

8.3.2 Lock-in effect

The capital gains preference is most often understood among academics as an imperfect mechanism to reduce the lock-in effect caused by the realization

67 *See* Harold Demsetz, *Toward a Theory of Property Rights*, 57 AM. ECON. REV. (PAPERS & PROC.) 347, 348 (1967); Edmund W. Kitch, *The Nature and Function of the Patent System*, 20 J.L. & ECON. 265, 276 (1977); F. Scott Kieff, *Property Rights and Property Rules for Commercializing Inventions*, 85 MINN. L. REV. 697, 717 (2001); Mark A. Lemley, *Property, Intellectual Property, and Free Riding*, 83 TEX. L. REV. 1031, 1033–46 (2005) (discussing rise of IP rights discussion in real property terms).

68 *See* Ayotte, *supra* note 26; John Armour & Douglas Cumming, *Bankruptcy Law and Entrepreneurship*, 10 AM. L. ECON. REV. 303, 337 (2008) ("Controlling for a range of other legal, economic and social factors that may affect national levels of entrepreneurship, we show that bankruptcy law has a pronounced effect on levels of entrepreneurship.").

69 *See* Gilson, *supra* note 29.

70 *See* Kamar and others, *supra* note 27; Robert P. Bartlett III, *Going Private but Staying Public: Reexamining the Effect of Sarbanes-Oxley on Firms' Going-private Decisions*, 76 U. CHI. L. REV. 7, 33–38 (2009) (examining impact of SOX on small-cap and medium-cap companies). Roberta Romano, *Does the Sarbanes-Oxley Act Have a Future*, 26 YALE J. REG. 229, 274–75 (2009) (discussing complaints from small business).

71 *See* Gompers & Lerner, *supra* note 28.

72 *See supra* text accompanying notes 28–29.

doctrine.[73] The usual arguments that politicians make—that capital gains are not really income, that the capital gains preference mitigates the double taxation of corporate earnings, incentivizes risk-taking, or avoids taxing inflationary gains—do not hold up well to analysis.[74]

The lock-in effect may be less problematic in the context of founders' stock than in the context of portfolio investors. Because founders have both their human capital and much of their financial capital tied up in a single business, they should rationally seek to sell their stock and diversify their investment portfolio as soon as they are able.[75] This urgent need for diversification allows the optimal tax rate to reduce lock-in to be higher for founders than for portfolio investors.

A recent paper by economist Bill Gentry raises the possibility that, for many entrepreneurs, the tax advantage of deferral outweighs the nontax advantage of diversification.[76] Using household-level data, Gentry finds strikingly high levels of unrealized gains on entrepreneurial assets.[77] Gentry's data set includes partnership and LLC interests in addition to founders' stock, but the data shows that entrepreneurs of all stripes tend to hold onto equity in their company for a long time.[78] If this behavior is attributable to the lock-in effect of the realization doctrine, the economic consequences of the lock-in effect in the founder context could be particularly bad. As small businesses grow, founders might maintain control in ways that may not be economically efficient. In the context of venture-capital backed start-ups, the VCs often find ways to ensure a smooth transition to professional management prior to or in conjunction with an initial public offering (IPO) or acquisition of the company. Post-IPO, however, founders may retain large blocks of stock and interfere with managerial decisions in ways that are unhelpful.

But there are also reasons to think that the lock-in effect identified by Gentry is not tax-driven, at least to the extent his dataset includes founders of venture-backed companies.[79] Most successful exits of venture-backed companies are acquisitions.[80] In many of these acquisitions, founders receive shares of the publicly-traded stock of the acquirer in a tax-free reorganization, allowing further deferral of unrealized gains. Sometimes these acquisitions are structured as taxable deals to allow the buyer a step-up in basis; in such deals the founders' tax penalty for selling is partially or completely offset by the acquirer's tax benefit for buying. In such circumstances, the founders are typically compensated for being forced to realize tax gains. For many successful start-up founders, in other

73 *See* Noel B. Cunningham & Deborah H. Schenk, *The Case for a Capital Gains Preference*, 48 TAX L. REV. 319 (1993).

74 *See id.*

75 *See* Sanjai Bhagat & Brian Bolton, *Bank Executive Compensation and Capital Requirements Reform*, Working Paper (on file with the author).

76 *See* William Gentry, *Capital Gains Taxation and Entrepreneurship*, Working Paper (on file with the author).

77 *See id.*

78 *See id.*

79 Gentry does not draw any conclusions with respect to founders' stock as such.

80 *See* Mark Heesen, NVCA, 2010 Exit Mark Sets Stage for 2011, *available at* http://nvcaccess.nvca.org/index.php/topics/research-and-trends/165-2010-exit-mark-sets-stage-for-2011.html (noting 72 IPOs, only 45 from U.S.-based companies, compared to 420 acquisitions).

words, there is no lock-in effect; they continue deferral upon a successful exit or receive substantial economic benefits specifically to help offset the realization of built-in gains.

Moreover, for founders of successful companies that go public, or wish to remain private, the ready availability of monetization techniques suggests that tax may not be what is causing the deadweight loss when founders hold onto stock in cases where it would be economically efficient for them to sell.[81] Founders can (and often do) enter into a variable prepaid forward (VPF) contract to monetize their interest in the firm. A VPF is a derivative contract with a counterparty (an investment bank or institutional investor) that pays the founder some cash upfront in exchange for a variable number of shares in the future, the number of which depends on the valuation of the shares at that later point in the future. Founders can monetize a large portion of their interest without immediately realizing gains for tax purposes.[82]

There are tax-motivated reasons to hold on to founders' stock. The transaction fees associated with monetization techniques are costly. And holding equity in a closely-held firm is useful for estate tax planning purposes. By contributing founders' stock to a Grantor Retained Annuity Trust (GRAT) prior to IPO or exit, future estate tax obligations can be cut by half or even more.[83]

In sum, the efficiency argument for taxing founders' stock at a low rate is weak. Existing empirical studies fail to establish a link between tax rates and entrepreneurial entry, and there are theoretical and practical reasons to believe that the effect is small. If the government must be in the business of subsidizing

81 Specifically, successful founders are not trapped by the problem of realizing gains; they can and often do exit through a tax-free reorganization, exchanging founders' stock for the publicly-traded stock of a company like Google, Yahoo, Microsoft, Cisco, or Intel, thereby further deferring their unrealized gains, possibly forever. If the start-up itself goes public, the founders often enter into a variable prepaid forward or other self-help monetization techniques to reduce economic exposure without triggering a realization event. Even in taxable deals, the lock-in effect is muted. Founders often negotiate to share the tax benefit from the step up in basis the acquiring company receives, thereby shielding themselves from the capital gains realized on the sale of their founders' stock. Successful founders can (and do) monetize their holdings without paying income tax by entering into derivative contracts or by selling the stock in a tax-free reorganization. While there is a great deal of wealth locked up in the equity of closely-held businesses, it is not clear that tax policy has much of a causal effect. Founders often have idiosyncratic, even irrational reasons for holding on to the equity in their company long after economic theory would suggest diversification as their optimal wealth management strategy. For founders of successful businesses who do want to cash out, the relatively fixed transaction costs associated with entering into a monetization strategy make tax planning a more appealing option as the value of the firm increases. Founders in this position usually part with voting control of the firm as they hedge their economic exposure to the firm, holding on only to nominal ownership of the stock to prevent a realization event for tax purposes. Because the efficiency gains associated with lower capital gains rates occur from the shifting of control and economic ownership, not legal ownership, and because this shifting already occurs when it should under current law, it is doubtful that raising the tax rate would produce substantial efficiency losses. Much of the lock-in that occurs is driven by the estate tax, not the income tax; holding or transferring stock of an illiquid closely-held firm can be advantageous for estate tax planning purposes.

82 David M. Schizer, *Frictions as a Constraint on Tax Planning*, 101 COLUM. L. REV. 1312 (2001) (discussing weak frictions associated with constructive sale rule).

83 Leo L. Schmolka, *FLPs and GRATs: What to Do?*, 86 TAX NOTES 1473 (2000).

entrepreneurship, investment in math, science, and engineering education is more likely to have a positive effect.

8.4 Conclusion

This chapter has argued that the favorable tax treatment of founders' stock unjustly contributes to the increasing inequality in the United States, and that the efficiency case for subsidizing founders is weak. Addressing the problem within our existing income tax system would be administratively difficult, however. The goal of this chapter is to draw attention to the tax treatment of founders' stock and to ensure that policymakers consider the issue as part of future fundamental tax reform efforts. In my view, the most promising solutions are a shift to a post-paid consumption tax or a dual income tax. While adoption of a consumption tax or dual income tax would obviously be driven primarily by broader concerns of efficiency and distributive justice, the tax treatment of founders will provide a useful focal point for the debate.

Part III

Financial engineering in capital markets

9 Tweaking governance for small companies after Dodd-Frank

*James D. Cox**

Small public companies scored a number of victories with the enactment of the Dodd-Frank Financial Reform Act of 2010 (Dodd-Frank). The most notable victory is their exemption from the now infamous Section 404 requirement enacted by the Sarbanes-Oxley Act of 2002 (SOX) that management's assessment of the reporting company's internal controls be annually attested to by the firm's independent auditor. Although so-called non-accelerated filers had not been subject to this requirement, the stream of delays in imposing Section 404 appeared unlikely to be continued. Congress stepped in and provided the exemption from the requirement in Section 989(G) of Dodd-Frank.[1] This exemption, therefore, removed nearly 6000 reporting companies, representing about 6 percent of U.S. equity capital, from the internal control attestation requirement.[2] Moreover, the legislation also called on the Securities and Exchange Commission (SEC) to study whether firms with a market capitalization of US$75–200 million should also be exempted.[3]

9.1 Dodd-Frank's dispensations

Small issuers received favorable mention in other areas as well. Section 951(e) of Dodd-Frank authorizes the SEC to provide exemptions when it believes regulation would disproportionately burden small issuers. Listing requirements may also relax or eliminate independence requirements for compensation committees.[4] More broadly, Dodd-Frank authorizes exchanges and the Financial Industry Regulatary Authority to exempt categories of issuers, and mandates that they

* Brainerd Currie Professor of Law, Duke University School of Law.

1 Amending 15 U.S.C. §7201 *et seq.* containing SOX Section 404(c); the other provisions related to internal controls remain including the Section 404(a)'s requirement that the issuer's annual report include a report of management on the issuer's internal control over financial reporting and management's assessment of the effectiveness of such internal controls. These changes were implemented by the SEC in Internal Control Over Financial Reporting In Exchange Act Periodic Reports Of Non-Accelerated Filers, Securities Act Rel. No. 9142 (Sept. 15, 2010).

2 *Cf.* GAO, Sarbanes-Oxley Act, "Consideration of Key Principles Needed in Addressing Implementation for Smaller Public Companies," 6 (April 2006) (reporting on the findings and recommendations of the SEC's Advisory Committee on Smaller Public Companies).

3 Dodd-Frank Section 989(b).

4 Dodd-Frank Section 952(a).

shall take into consideration the impact of their regulations on small issuers.[5] Section 971, in providing a means for shareholders to nominate directors, not only delays for three years that provision's application to small issuers, but also requires the SEC to consider whether its application to small issuers will have a disproportionate impact on small issuers.

As a generalization, non-accelerated filers and more broadly yet, small cap companies (most market professionals consider a market capitalization of less than US$1 billion to be small), have more limited product lines, possess fewer financial resources, trade in thin markets (frequently on the non-regulated Over-The-Counter Bulletin Board (OTCBB) market), are followed by few, if any analysts, and enjoy a limited following among institutional investors. It is not surprising that the shares for this group of firms are widely believed to be valued inefficiently. This is an inefficiency that breeds opportunity both for investors, but also insiders. More positively, returns for small cap firms historically are higher, reflecting their need to yield greater financial rewards to investors to compensate for their greater risk.[6]

It is hard to say that Section 404 was without material social benefits.[7] For example, studies of accounting restatements consistently track significant increases in the number of accounting restatements following partial implementation of Section 404. The restatements peaked in 2006 with 1564 [888] reporting issuers recording material restatements and have declined each year since that time to reach 630 [374] restatements in 2009.[8] The numbers in brackets report the number of non-accelerated filers reporting restatements. The data reflect the well documented phenomenon that the number of restatements are inversely related to market capitalization.[9] Moreover, nearly 70 percent of firms reporting material weaknesses in their internal controls that have not been remediated were firms with market capitalizations less than US$75 million.[10] Moreover, in the years 2004–2007, the vast percentage of firms receiving a qualified audit opinion on their internal controls were firms with a market capitalization below US$75 million and this group also experiences the highest percentage of auditor changes among all reporting companies.[11]

5 *Id.*

6 *See, e.g.*, "Fidelity Supplement to Small Cap Stock Fund, Fidelity Mid Cap Stock Fund and Fidelity Large Cap Stock Fund," June 29, 2005 (reviewing risks and returns of three major categories of indexed funds).

7 The SEC's Chief Accountant during the early implementation period of the internal controls requirement observed, "I believe that, of all the recent reforms, the internal controls requirements have the greatest potential to improve the reliability of financial reporting. Our capital markets run on faith and trust that the vast majority of companies present reliable and complete financial data for investment and policy decision-making." Donald T. Nicolaisen, Keynote Speech, 11th Annual Midwestern Financial Reporting Symposium (Oct. 7, 2004).

8 Audit Analytics, "2009 Financial Restatements: A Nine Year Comparison," 18 (Feb. 2010). See also the study commissioned by the U.S. Treasury, Susan Scholz, "The Changing Nature And Consequences Of Public Company Financial Restatements 1997–2006" (April 2008) (reflecting that greatest percentage of restatements are for firms that do not trade on a major stock exchange and that restatements began to accelerate prior to the enactment of SOX).

9 *See, e.g.*, Glass Lewis & Co., "The Tide is Turning," 3 Charts 3 & 9 (Jan. 15, 2008).

10 *Id.*, 8 Tbl. 2 (Jan. 15, 2008).

11 *See id.*, Tbl. 4 at 9 and Tbl. 13 at 11.

Since there seems little basis to contest the notion that greater accuracy in financial reporting leads to improved pricing of the company's securities, reduction in the number of restatements should be viewed positively. Moreover, there is evidence that SOX introduced reporting requirements also reduced "financial slack" among complying firms, where post-SOX implementation studies report that mandatory filers cut total CEO compensation (most through reductions in stock-based compensation), increased payouts to shareholders, and reduced investment and employment) relative to what occurred with comparable non-404 filers.[12] Also, mandatory filers' post compliance with Section 404 experienced longer maturities for their debt than was the experience for non-filers.

9.2 Some data points on the profile of non-accelerated issuers

While the earlier report that significant numbers of restatements occur with non-accelerated filers may suggest that restatements will be detected even though there is no mandated compliance with Section 404, there has long been a good deal of concern that absent formal independent assessment of a firm's internal controls that weak financial reporting systems will exist and substantial numbers of reporting problems are going undetected.[13] To be sure, not all reports of material weakness in internal controls elicit strong market adjustments; markets more likely adjust, and negatively, for matters that are less auditable, when the accompanying disclosures are vague, and when the reporting company is not audited by a Big 4 auditor.[14] But the benefits of improving the quality and trustworthiness of financial reporting come at a significant cost.[15] These costs were greater in the

12 *See* Jun Qian, Philip E. Strahan & Julie Zhu, "The Economic Benefits of the Sarbanes-Oxley Act? Evidence from a Natural Experiment," Working Paper (Dec. 2009).

13 Glass Lewis & Co., "The Tide is Turning" (Jan. 15, 2008) ("If microcap companies disclosed this many material weaknesses on their own – without having to comply with SOX 404 – how many more material weaknesses would be discovered if independent auditing firms were required to conduct internal-control audits at these companies?"); Melissa Klein Aguilar, "404 Disclosures Show Dramatic Improvement," 2 (Nov. 27, 2007) (quoting Mr. Robert Benoit, partner at Lord & Benoit, an auditing firm which focuses on small issuers: "Almost none of the smaller public companies have done any SOX work."), *available at* http://www.complianceweek.com/index.cfm?printable=1&fuseaction=article.viewAritcle&article_ID=3804.

14 *See* Jacqueline S. Hammersley, Linda A. Myers & Catherine Shakespeare, "Market Reactions to the Disclosure of Internal Control Weaknesses and the Characteristics of those Weaknesses under Section 302 of the Sarbanes Oxley Act of 2002," Working Paper (Jan. 2007), *available at* http://ssrn.com/abstract=951085. Moreover, the strongest reaction appears to accompany disclosures of internal control weaknesses by smaller firms rather than larger firms. *See* Messod Daniel Beneish, Mary Brooke Billings & Leslie D. Hodder, "Internal Control Weaknesses and Information Uncertainty," 83 Accounting Review 665–703 (2008) (material weakness disclosures by non-accelerate filers were accompanied by significant negative price reductions whereas 404 disclosures for larger filers did not suggesting that the latter group operate in as richer information environment than do the non-accelerated filers).

15 *See, e.g.*, Charles River Associates, "Sarbanes-Oxley Section 404 Costs and Remediation of Deficiencies: Estimates From A Sample of Fortune 1000 Companies" (April 2005) (reporting firms average cost to comply with the internal control requirement was US$5.9 million). Of interest here is the now much discredited SEC estimate of compliance cost averaging US$91,000 per

early years of Section 404, reflecting not just the "deferred maintenance" that had to be addressed with the SOX-imposed requirements, but also the poor implementation of Section 404 by the regulators and the auditors. There were plenty of problems in the early years of implementing Section 404 for accelerated filers. Indeed, it is likely that the now permanent exemption for small issuers, as well as the broader recognition that financial reporting regulation disproportionately impacts small issuers, would not have occurred had there been a less troubled experience in the early years of Section 404. In any case, concern for regulation and particularly that reporting requirements have a disproportionate impact on smaller companies is well documented. For example, median audit fees in 2003 and 2004 that implemented internal control reports were 1.14 percent of reported revenues for non-accelerated filers but 0.13 percent for firms with a market capitalization greater than US$1 billion.[16] Interestingly, non-accelerated filers not providing a report on internal controls had audit fees that were 0.35 *less* than their reporting cohort, whereas this difference was 0.06 for filers with a market capitalization greater than US$1 billion. Thus, it was no surprise that while the cost of being a reporting company was identified prior to Sarbanes-Oxley by 12 percent of the companies as a reason for deregistering, that percentage jumped to 62 percent in 2005.[17] Interestingly, less than 20 percent of the companies deregistering were listed on either the NYSE or NASDAQ; the largest percentage traded on the OTCBB (36.9 percent) or had no formal market (24.8 percent).[18]

Of special concern for reporting in small companies is that among public companies with a market capitalization of US$125 million or less, the SEC Office of Economic Analysis reports that insiders own an average of 30 percent of the company's shares. To the extent one of the goals of financial reporting is to diminish opportunities for opportunistic behavior by managers versus outside owners, the smaller firm may well be seen as posing greater risks because of the significant

issuer. SEC, Final Rule: Management's Report on Internal Controls Over Financial Reporting and Certification of Disclosure in Exchange Act Periodic Reports, Securities Act Rel. No. 8238 (Aug. 14, 2003). Internal controls attestation contributes substantially to the audit fees during the first years of compliance, but on a declining basis. *See* R. Mithu Dey & Mary W. Sullivan, "What Will Non-Accelerated Filers Have to Pay for the Section 404 Internal Control Audit," Working Paper (April 16, 2009) (median cost of internal control assessment for previously non-accelerated filers represented 42% of total audit fees in 2006 and declined modestly to 37% in 2007 with the introduction of Auditing Standard No. 5).

16 GAO, "Sarbanes-Oxley Act, Consideration of Key Principles Needed in Addressing Implementation for Smaller Public Companies," 16, Fig. 1 (GAO-06-361, April 2006). The study reflects ever diminishing median costs as a percentage of revenues as company size increases. *See also Id.* Tbl. 4 (reflecting the same relationship between size of revenues and direct IPO expenses). *See also* Finance Executives International Annual Survey, "The 404 Cost Study" (Sept. 2009) (U.S. companies with revenues exceeding US$5 billion spent 0.06% of revenue on SOX compliance while companies with less than US$100 million in revenue spent 2.55% (in 2004. This cost represented about 40% of total audit fees and had declined to approximately 32.5% in 2007).

17 *Id.* at 22. There is, however, a good deal of evidence that SOX was a rationalization of other reasons for companies going dark.

18 *Id.* at 25, Fig. 3.

interest held by managers. There has long been concern in small companies that their large block holders can reap rewards at the expense of outside owners through a variety of strategies. One such strategy is going private. Many have reported that the number of going private transactions increased following the passage of SOX. Share prices of firms announcing in their Section 13(e) filing that they would be going private increased. This prompted some to reason that the observed increase reflected, at least in part, the cost of being a public firm.[19] Another interpretation is part of the price change is the cost of so-called unresolved agency problems between the minority and controlling insiders. The going private transaction in effect reverses the valuation discounts that were caused by unresolved agency problems.[20] There is a small but growing body of evidence that heightened reporting post-SOX has improved the quality of disclosure and reduced the negative effects of unresolved agency costs. Examples of this work include studies reflecting declines in earnings management[21] and reductions in the firms' costs of capital.[22]

Because of the substantial insider ownership that frequently exists among non-accelerated filers, there are greater challenges confronting activist investors seeking to alter prior practices that are believed adversely to impact shareholder value. This occurs not solely because the insider's holdings pose a serious obstacle to wresting control but also because the smallness of the firm combined with the insiders' holdings tend to attract friends and associates of the insiders to the board, rather than more independent representatives of the shareholders at large.[23]

There is also evidence that firms not only exited SOX by going dark, but that many public firms have pursued strategies to remain non-accelerated filers. That is, firms below the US$75 million market capitalization level have

19 *See* Ellen Engel, Rachel M. Hayes & Xue Wang, "The Sarbanes-Oxley Act and Firms' Going Private Decisions," 27 J. Law and Econ. (2006). There are other explanations, namely the increase in the number of private equity firms and the availability of low interest loans for such transactions. Moreover, the pattern observed in the U.S. began before SOX was passed and paralleled the trend in Europe. *See* Christian Leuz, "Was the Sarbanes-Oxley Act of 2002 Really This Costly? A Discussion of Evidence from Event Returns and Going-Private Decisions," J. Accounting Research pp.1–27 (2007). Professor Leuz makes the point that we need to distinguish going dark from going private transactions such that the former are really more a response to heightened reporting costs, does appear to be related to the passage of SOX, and this group of firms were smaller, more distressed, and had weaker performance and governance than firms going private. *Id.* Indeed, the increase in deregistrations post-SOX was primarily driven by going dark rather than going private transactions.

20 *See* Christian Leuz, Alexander Triantis & Tracy Wang, "Why Do Firms Go Dark? Causes and Economic Consequences of Voluntary SEC Deregistrations," J. Accounting and Economics pp. 1–62 (2007).

21 *See, e.g.*, Daniel Cohen, A. Dey & T. Lys, "Trends in Earnings Management and Informativeness of Earnings Announcements in the Pre- and Post-Sarbanes Oxley Periods," Working Paper (2006).

22 *See, e.g.*, H. Ashbaugh, D. Collins, W. Kinney & R. Lafond, "The Effect of Internal Control Deficiencies on Firm Risk and the Cost of Capital," Working Paper University of Iowa (2006).

23 *See, e.g.*, Stephen Davis & Jon Lukomnik, "How to Improve Governance at Small Companies," Compliance Week (Aug. 10, 2010), *available at* http://complianceweek.com/article/6104/how-to-improve-governance-at-small-companies (discussing efforts of two shareholders to introduce change to a company whose yearly compensation was twice the cumulative profits of each of the preceding two years).

remained small by undertaking less investment, increasing their cash payouts to shareholders, reducing the number of shares held by non-affiliates, making more bad news announcements, and reporting lower earnings than a matched sample (control group) of firms.[24] It also appears that firms more likely to pursue strategies to be a non-accelerated filer were more complex with more international operations so that they likely would incur greater internal control auditing costs than firms that crossed to become a mandatory filer. Interestingly, firms that "crossed" from being a non-accelerated filer to a mandatory filer and firms that remained a non-accelerated filer each increased their percentage of independent directors after the passage of SOX and also decreased the size of their boards.

A further reflection of the risk posed by small companies is the migration of non-accelerated filers away from Big 4 accounting firms to other auditors. This migration picked up pace after SOX and is in part identified as being a reflection of the Big 4 firms' decision to manage their risks by ridding themselves of smaller companies that were believed to pose serious audit risks.[25] This is not to suggest that second- or third-tier auditing firms are less professional, skillful or diligent than their Big 4 counterparts; the migration supports the view that firms discarded by the Big 4 are believed *ex ante* to pose risks that do not justify from the accounting firm's perspective sufficient rewards to justify continuing the relationship.

9.3 Gap fillings through governance

As discussed above, non-accelerated filers operate in an environment that is quite different from that of mandatory filers. Because of their small market capitalizations, they do not attract institutional owners and similarly are not closely followed by analysts. Thus, they do not operate in an environment that is as information rich as that of the larger mandatory filers. They trade largely in the more unregulated market of the OTCBB and overall there is reason to believe their securities are not priced efficiently. To be sure, such OTCBB traded companies are reporting companies, but those reports do not have the reassurance of the CPA's attestation of internal controls. Moreover, for three years the nonaccelerated filers are immune from the proxy access proposals, which make them less attractive to the disciplining forces of activist stockholders. We might wonder whether the proxy access provision will, like Section 404, meet a series of delays beyond the three-year introductory period. We have yet to see what other dispensations will be accorded small issuers.

The lacunae in external forces to strengthen the trustworthiness of financial reporting for non-accelerated filers invites us to consider what internal steps

24 *See* GAO "Unintended Consequences of Granting Small Firms Exemptions from Securities Regulation: Evidence from the Sarbanes-Oxley Act," 47 J. Accounting Research pp. 1–9 (May 2009).

25 GAO, "Sarbanes-Oxley Act, Consideration of Key Principles Needed in Addressing Implementation for Smaller Public Companies," 7 (GAO-06-361 April 2006).

a company might pursue to address these gaps? As the pre-Dodd-Frank history reflects, many non-accelerated filers voluntarily subjected themselves to Section 404 and we also are aware that many companies have voluntarily embraced "say on pay" procedures and even adopted procedures for shareholders to nominate directors. The following reviews other steps that should be considered by non-accelerated filers to address concerns that the regulatory dispensations came at a price of posing greater risks for their investors.

The first line of defense in assuring the reliability of financial reports is the annual audit. After SOX, the audit committee is the linchpin that joins the outside auditor to the financial reports released to investors. Each audit committee of an accelerated filer should measure its value by assuring itself annually that the firm obtains a first-rate audit. Efforts should be focused first on the risks posed by the firm and not on whether this year's audit costs more or less than last year's. Unfortunately, during the economic maelstrom of the last few years, stories abound that firms are "squeezing" their auditors to reduce their charges. This is not money well saved. In seeking a high quality audit, the audit committee must bear in mind that the sine qua non for the auditor to attest to any item in the financial reports is by assuring herself there are adequate internal controls, that is, internal controls have been a core requirement of auditing for as long as the task of auditing has existed. To be sure, extra steps were introduced into the assessment of internal controls by Section 404's mandate that auditors formally attest to management's assessment of the adequacy of internal controls. Nonetheless, significant steps in evaluating internal controls are a core feature of auditing, present long before the introduction of a formal attestation function.

Thus, just as the audit committee is required to discuss with the auditor the critical estimates, assumptions, choices and judgments that underlie management's financial statements, the audit committee needs similarly to engage the auditors on their assessment of the firm's control environment. More particularly, the auditors should identify the risks that surround the reporting environment and provide assurance to the audit committee how the audit was able to move forward in light of these risks. Good corporate governance requires nothing less than the members of the audit committee satisfying themselves that the base on which audit procedures are carried out, namely the presence of adequate internal controls, does in fact exist.

A second step in this process is for the audit committee to render a report on the steps it has taken to assure that the audit secured was a good audit. Thus, the annual report by the audit committee should be included in the annual report. This report would include a general affirmation that the audit committee has fulfilled its duties and had an active dialogue with the auditors on the critical accounting estimates, assumptions, choices and judgments, and in addition to that has probed the auditor on the steps taken to assure there was an adequate control environment.

A necessary third step for non-accelerated filers is to make an inventory of their corporate governance practices. There are ample review sheets for the board and board committees annually to assess themselves against. The most critical aspect of this self-assessment will be a judgment whether the board is sufficiently independent of management. This is a much greater challenge for small companies. Minimally, this requires a strong subgroup of the board with a clear mandate to assure board independence. There may well be a place here for "term limits" on board members. But the overarching point is that with fewer external forces to police and even discipline managers, the effort must come from within the firm.

A fourth step is for the management and board to maintain good communications with shareholders. Increased transparency, particularly with respect to the directors' efforts to monitor the firm's financial performance and position naturally invites input from significant holders. The board should pursue steps to receive the input from such holders regarding their concerns about the board's oversight and generally the direction of the company. Minimally, such input should be an important consideration in the directors' self-assessment and decisions related to the future composition of the board of directors.

Fifth, the financial compensation of senior executives must be right-sized and hewn to sustainable profits. History continues to document the wisdom that individuals manage what gets measured. And there is no measurement that captures the attention like the metrics for executive compensation. A very deliberate, thoughtful, and transparent incentive plan is worth thousands of votes on "say on pay". This proposal complements the preceding step; there is likely no better barometer for whether the board has announced the right incentives than how it is received among those who have maintained a substantial stake in the company. Thus, executive pay, and more particularly, incentives for management should be the point for conversation with substantial shareholders on a regular, not episodic, basis.

Afterword

A Stuntzian approach to scholarship

*Peter Conti-Brown**

1 Introduction

The scholars who contributed to this volume are leaders in their field, and taken as individual contributions or the volume as a whole, it makes an important contribution to the way we think not only about venture capital, intellectual property, and financial engineering, but the process of innovation in general.

Importantly for academics, the term "innovation" in this context refers not simply to the creation of new ideas and artifacts of commercial value, but also the creation of new ideas valuable for their own sake. Ultimately, of course, the pursuit of this intellectual innovation, the effort to bring to light facts or analysis not previously discovered, motivates the academic enterprise wherever it is engaged, irrespective of discipline or subject of inquiry.

So much is essentially a truism. Scholars want to produce new ideas, new knowledge, new approaches. In light thereof, it is worth pausing to contemplate exactly what it means to produce innovative scholarship. And the invitation to contemplate this question is particularly appropriate these days: the legal academy is mourning the loss of an extraordinary example of an innovator, the inimitable Harvard Law School professor William J. Stuntz, perhaps the leading scholar in criminal procedure of his generation. His substantive work may not be familiar to the business law scholars most interested in the chapters of this book, but his approach to scholarship is one that all academics might consider as they navigate their own efforts to pursue the creation of knowledge. For that reason, this Afterword presents what I take to be the Stuntzian approach to scholarship, an approach that yielded for Stuntz—and those who benefited from Stuntz's many insights—extraordinary innovations in every field he touched. In doing so, I will also illustrate how a Stuntzian approach might be profitably deployed in the context of business law scholarship in particular.

* Academic Fellow, Rock Center for Corporate Governance, Stanford Law School and Stanford Graduate School of Business. I thank Nikki Conti-Brown, Larry Mitchell, David Skeel, Art Wilmarth, and the participants at the Financing Innovation conference at the George Washington University Law School for helpful comments and discussion. One disclosure: all written here is based on Stuntz's written work, published interviews, and some published eulogies after his death. To my detriment, I never had the opportunity to meet or learn from Professor Stuntz in person.

Briefly, a Stuntzian approach to scholarship contains three elements: (1) deep challenges to conventional wisdom; (2) the defiance of traditional ideological labels; and (3) scholarly humility. I will address each in turn.

2 Challenging conventional wisdom

Stuntz is famous for turning long-held narratives about the criminal justice system on their heads. One of Stuntz's preferred stylistic approaches to describing a problem he sought to resolve was to identify the problem in a way both familiar and persuasive to readers, and then show why that familiar and persuasive narrative was, "of course, wrong."[1] For example, Stuntz wrote in 2000 about the assumption that tougher social norms should, descriptively and prescriptively, produce tougher criminal laws. "That assumption," he wrote, "seems both natural and convenient. It is also probably wrong."[2]

Stuntz's preferred structure was not simply cute rhetorical quip. He really did identify plausible, widely accepted narratives, and show how they actually were wrong, popular acceptance notwithstanding. For example, one of Stuntz's most creative arguments, presented over several articles, placed liberal appellate judges, conservative legislators, overeager prosecutors, and upper-middle class suburbanites in an unholy alliance to incarcerate an egregious number of the disadvantaged poor, particularly racial minorities.[3] The narrative of the Warren Court revolution representing the last best hope for criminal defendants received a serious blow at Stuntz's hands.

In a similar tradition, but in a different vein, despite the fact that *Roe v. Wade*[4] has been the scourge of conservatives for two generations, Stuntz argued that the case actually did much more for the anti-abortion movement than either side has admitted. It created more force, not less, for the anti-abortion norm that it sought to remove.[5]

This is the Stuntzian way—to look deeply at the prevailing scholarly, legal, and policy narratives of our time, and put pressure on their most foundational assumptions. Once identified, the flaws in the conventional logic seemed perhaps

1 William J. Stuntz, *The Uneasy Relationship Between Criminal Procedure and Criminal Justice*, 107 YALE L. J. 1, 3 (1997).

2 William J. Stuntz, *Self-Defeating Crimes*, 86 VA. L. REV. 1871, 1872 (2000). Stuntz does the same thing.

3 Stuntz, *supra* note 1 (1997) (arguing that the apportionment of power, funding and obligations of prosecutors, judges, and legislators, together with institutional incentives of each, creates perverse results for criminal defendants); William J. Stuntz, *Unequal Justice*, 121 HARV. L. REV. 1969, 1969 (2007) (arguing that the decline of local democratic participation in the criminal justice process accounted for the sharp rise in a less just, less equal system that discriminated against racial minorities).

4 *See* 410 U.S. 113 (1973).

5 See Stuntz, *supra* note 2, at 1886–89. The entire article situates *Roe* and abortion in the context of the law resolving hotly contested social norms only to give the loser of those legal contests greater social normative strength than would have been the case without the legal resolution. Other examples Stuntz includes are alcohol consumption following Prohibition, slavery following the Fugitive Slave Act, and homosexuality following *Bowers v. Hardwick* (478 U.S. 186 (1986)).

obvious in retrospect. But such discoveries were not obvious, nor were they inevitable: they took a scholar of Stuntz's talent and imagination to bring them to light.

Of course, Stuntz cannot and would not claim as his own the concept that conventional wisdom should be challenged. John Kenneth Galbraith introduced the term to describe the tempting heuristic people use to reduce aspects of life that are "incoherent, inchoate, and intellectually frustrating" to something more agreeable to one's social or intellectual tastes.[6] That is, in the "persistent and never-ending competition between what is right and what is merely acceptable," the conventional wisdom sways always toward the "merely acceptable," and is thus the frequently preferred—although intellectually dubious—alternative.[7] Stuntz's scholarship shows a profound impatience with "the merely acceptable," and in doing so teaches us as much about humility and courage as about genius. The humility to admit that the way things are at present may not be the way things should be, and the courage to declare as much—with exhaustive research and rigorous methodologies—are at the core of the Stuntzian approach.

Stuntz credited his religious faith for this two-part perspective, which gave him the ability to understand "that the world is not what it should be, and that our own capacities to understand it are severely limited."[8] I return to the humility prong of this test below—for now, the fact that Stuntz's work peered quizzically at the prevailing narratives of his field and refused to accept those narratives at face value illustrates the first facet of his unique approach.

3 Defy easy labels

The second aspect of a Stuntzian approach—to defy easy ideological labels—flows from the first. Stuntz self-identified as a conservative Republican[9] and evangelical Christian.[10] At the same time, as mentioned, he lambasted Republican legislators for under-funding public defenders, had hard words for the legal advocacy of intelligent design,[11] and called originalism a form of idolatry.[12] Labeling

6 JOHN KENNETH GALBRAITH, THE AFFLUENT SOCIETY, 6 (1958, 1998).

7 *Id.*

8 Timothy Darymple, *You Will Call, I Will Answer: An Interview with William Stuntz*, PATHEOS, *available at* http://www.patheos.com/Resources/Additional-Resources/You-Will-Call-I-Will-Answer.html.

9 At least, so asserts Lincoln Caplan in an editorial eulogy in the *New York Times*. See Lincoln Caplan, *William Stuntz*, N.Y. TIMES, Editorial (Mar. 23, 2011).

10 See the biographical heading in *Less than the Least*, the blog Stuntz co-wrote with friend and co-author David Skeel, *available at* http://www.law.upenn.edu/blogs/dskeel/.

11 *Ask the Professor: William Stuntz*, HARVARD LAW BULLETIN. In response to the question of whether intelligent design advocates would prevail in presenting their theories as legitimate science, Stuntz said, unequivocally, no. "Nonbelievers think that believers are strategic, that we will embrace any argument that works to our benefit. To a large degree, they're right. Unless and until that changes, religious believers won't have any credibility with the secular academic world. We don't deserve to have credibility if we're not honestly engaged in truth-seeking."

12 See Caplan, *supra* note 9.

him a liberal is no better. His article on the *Miranda v. Arizona*[13] case illustrates another perfect example of the Stuntzian move to present the conventional story, only to show why that conventional story is, this time, "backward[s]."[14] He argues that the Warren Court icon has the "perverse" effect of putting *suspects* into the role of adjudicators of police misconduct, rather than the judges that had formerly occupied that position.[15] If one aspect of being a liberal is a full-throated defense of *Miranda*, then Stuntz is obviously no liberal. One simply cannot label Stuntz; trying to do so is an exercise in frustration.

Business scholars might learn something from this approach. Among the most basic ideological divides in business law scholarship is left vs. right, government vs. markets. Many scholars line up nicely behind one set of assumptions or another. In some cases, a reader with sufficient experience with the ideological backdrop of the author need not always pay close attention to the arguments presented: the author can reliably expound on why the markets, left to their own devices, will always produce results that will leave the rest of us better (worse) off.

There is much to be gained from the scholarship of these ideologically convinced thinkers. It is hard to argue, for example, that the contributions of Friedman or Galbraith did not amount to much simply because one knows where each stood on the basic premises of free vs. regulated markets. But to be Stuntzian is not to be Friedmanite[16] or Galbraithian. The Stuntzian approach rejects those easy categorizations, and requires instead that interlocutors pay close attention: the approach is not particularly interested in the ideological identity behind the assumptions it challenges, only in the question of whether the assumptions are defensible. Thus, while knowing the answers to questions before they have been completely asked can sometimes lead to important insights, it can also lead to sclerotic dogma of the worst sort. And whatever the Stuntzian approach is, it is emphatically not dogmatic.

4 Scholarly humility

The third aspect of a Stuntzian approach is humility, the most personal of the three. Stuntz was famous for it, both professionally and personally. And while his personal humility is something for which a great deal can be said, it is the scholarly humility, or rather, epistemological modesty,[17] that is the third element of the Stuntzian approach.

13 384 U.S. 436 (1966).

14 William J. Stuntz, "Miranda's *Mistake*," 99 MICH. L. REV. 975, 976 (2000).

15 *Id.*

16 With apologies to Milton Friedman. For better or worse, some proper names are rendered adjectives more elegantly than others. But here I follow Lawrence Summers, an eminent example who applies to Friedman followers the same sobriquet. Lawrence Summers, *The Great Liberator*, N.Y. TIMES (Nov. 19, 2006).

17 The term is probably indistinct enough to avoid the need for a footnote. But it is not original: David Brooks used the term in a column, and attributes the concept to Burke. See David Brooks, *The Big Test*, N.Y. TIMES (Feb. 23, 2009) (citing EDMUND BURKE, REFLECTIONS ON THE REVOLUTION IN FRANCE (1790)).

Epistemological modesty, as I mean the term here, is not Burkean conservatism, whatever its virtues, but something different. It is the idea that one's insights may be stunning, may be rigorous, and may be elegant. They may also be wrong. So too with one's methods for reaching those conclusions, and the philosophical tradition from which those ideas have sprung. It is, to invoke the probably over-quoted Learned Hand, the basic spirit that "is not too sure that it is right."[18]

Earlier, I said that Stuntz enjoyed setting up the attractive conventional wisdom as the foil for the solutions that he presented for a particular problem in law or policy. But that is actually not very accurate. Stuntz was not seeking to push an agenda of solutions, or to present "The Answer." In one of his most famous articles, published in 1997, regarding the perverse consequences of the current apportionment of roles and obligations of judges, prosecutors, legislators, and public defenders in the criminal justice system, the concluding paragraph of his introduction is indicative of the epistemological modesty that is essential to the Stuntzian approach:

> These discussions are sketchy and speculative; the goal is to begin an argument, not to end one. They are also one-sided: My aim is to suggest that constitutional criminal procedure has substantial unappreciated costs; I do not discuss its (better appreciated) benefits, which may also be substantial. The argument thus does not lead to any confident bottom line. It does, however, undermine what seems to be the confident bottom line of most judges and most academics in the field—that the current approach to constitutional law and criminal justice is unambiguously sound.[19]

This epistemological modesty was a hallmark of Stuntz's personal scholarly life in another important respect. David Skeel, his friend and co-author, wrote that Stuntz believed that our enterprise as legal scholars of trying better to understand and perhaps improve the world is a collective one. This commitment to our common mission was perhaps most evident in something Bill, unlike most scholars of his stature, did not have: disciples. The work of some scholars would be hard to imagine without Bill's inspiration. And countless scholars have borrowed from Stuntz—"stealing" his insights, as David Sklansky has written. But Bill encouraged new thinking, not devotion to his own ideas.[20]

This preference for "new thinking," the emphasis on the "collective" improvement that legal scholars might contribute, is at the core of the Stuntzian approach to scholarship.

As business law scholars making sense of sometimes crushingly complex innovations in finance and markets, the humility to insist—of ourselves and others—on clarity about what we know and modesty about what we do not, will

18 Learned Hand, *The Spirit of Liberty*, in THE SPIRIT OF LIBERTY: PAPERS AND ADDRESSES OF LEARNED HAND, 190 (ed. Irving Dillard, 1959)

19 Stuntz, *supra* note 1, at 7.

20 David Skeel, *Tribute: William J. Stuntz*, 124 HARV. L. REV. 1, 2 (2011).

go a long way to making sure ours is an enterprise that is more than mere navel-gazing and the angry recitation of hackneyed banalities. Epistemological modesty about our methods, analysis, and conclusions, without detracting from the rigor of any of these, will make us more honest and, ultimately, more effective. That may be the naïveté of one at the beginning of a scholarly career, but one thing that made Stuntz great was that he was comfortable with changing his mind, being persuaded, and saying some of the most powerful words in the scholarly vernacular: "That's a good question. I'd like to learn more." Or "My intuition may be off-target here." Or best of all: "I didn't know that."

I mentioned earlier that Stuntz credited his faith "that our own capacities to understand [the world] are severely limited." Whatever its source, the sentiment is the last prong, and perhaps the most important, of the Stuntzian approach to scholarly inquiry.

5 Conclusion

That is, then, the Stuntzian approach to scholarship, applicable to those who study business law generally or innovation specifically: deep challenges to conventional wisdom; an inability easily to pigeon-hole these challenges into pre-existing ideologies; and general humility in our methods, analysis, and conclusions. It is certainly not the only approach—the academy is a big tent, with room for plenty of proper names to become adjectives alongside "Stuntzian." But the Stuntzian approach is an admirable one; one with which many others have already engaged, and one that will, in the hands of business law scholars, make powerful contributions to the pursuit of ideas that would otherwise not be possible.

Index

Note: Page numbers in **bold** type refer to **figures**
Page numbers in *italic* type refer to *tables*
Page numbers followed by 'n' refer to notes